The Reluctant Revolutionary

The Reluctant Revolutionary

Dietrich Bonhoeffer's Collision with Prusso-German History

John A. Moses

First published in 2009 by

Berghahn Books

www.berghahnbooks.com

©2009, 2014 John A. Moses
First paperback edition published in 2014

All rights reserved. Except for the quotation of short passages
for the purposes of criticism and review, no part of this book
may be reproduced in any form or by any means, electronic or
mechanical, including photocopying, recording, or any information
storage and retrieval system now known or to be invented,
without written permission of the publisher.

Library of Congress Cataloging-in-Publication Data
Moses, John Anthony, 1930-
  The reluctant revolutionary : Dietrich Bonhoeffer's collision with Prusso-German history / John A. Moses.
    p. cm.
  Includes bibliographical references and index.
  ISBN 978-1-84545-531-6 (hardback) -- ISBN 978-1-84545-910-9 (institutional ebook) -- ISBN 978-1-78238-340-6 (paperback) -- ISBN 978-1-78238-341-3 (retail ebook)
  1. Bonhoeffer, Dietrich, 1906–1945. 2. Church and state—Germany—History—1933–1945. I. Title.
  BX4827.B57M68 2009
  230'.044092—dc22

British Library Cataloguing in Publication Data
A catalogue record for this book is available from the British Library

Printed on acid-free paper

ISBN: 978-1-78238-340-6 paperback
ISBN: 978-1-78238-341-3 retail ebook

Christianity stands or falls with its revolutionary protest against violence, arbitrariness and pride of power and with its apologia for the weak.—I feel that Christianity is rather doing too little in showing these points than too much. Christianity has adjusted itself to the worship of power. It should give much more offence, more shock to the world, than it is doing. Christianity should take a much more definite stand for the weak than to consider the potential moral right of the strong.

—Dietrich Bonhoeffer,
Sermon on II Corinthians 12:9,
London, 1934.

Contents

Foreword *Michael Lattke*	ix
Preface	xi
Abbreviations	xv
Introduction	xvii
1. The "Peculiarity" of German Political Culture	1
2. Bonhoeffer's Formation	27
3. The Problem of Anti-Semitism in Germany from Luther to Hitler	46
4. Bonhoeffer's Opening to the West and the Involvement in Ecumenism	74
5. The Church Struggle to 1937	103
6. The Ethics of Conspiracy	130
7. Bonhoeffer and the Jewish Question	148
8. Bonhoeffer as Critic of His Class in Retrospect	173
9. The Postwar Confrontation with the Nazi Past	204
Epilogue Bonhoeffer Reception in Postwar Germany	233

APPENDIX I The Barmen Declaration of Faith	**255**
APPENDIX II The Stuttgart Declaration of Guilt	**259**
APPENDIX III The Darmstadt Statement	**261**
APPENDIX IV Ecumenical Assembly: More Justice in the GDR	**263**
BIBLIOGRAPHY	**273**
INDEX	**291**

Foreword

At least in Australia, Professor John Moses is one of the few secular historians who consider church history, religion, and theology to be essential factors in the Rankean reconstruction and critical evaluation of what happened in the past, and why it happened as it happened.

When I met John Moses, an Alexander von Humboldt Fellow, and his German wife Ingrid, for the first time in 1981, I had already studied the most influential books of Dietrich Bonhoeffer and, also as an integral part of German theological curricula, Eberhard Bethge's monumental biography of 1967, which has been kept in print to this day. Over the past twenty-five years John's learned papers and publications have opened my eyes to new dimensions of modern German history, East and West. I witnessed how Professor Moses developed into one of the leading Dietrich Bonhoeffer specialists. His voice—never boring—has been heard at quite a few international Bonhoeffer conferences. His insatiable scholarship has been rewarded by many prestigious grants and commissioned publications, such as his contribution to *The Cambridge Companion to Dietrich Bonhoeffer* (1999).

What John Moses has to say on the "reluctant revolutionary" Dietrich Bonhoeffer is summed up in his own Preface. Instead of summarizing his summary, I would rather point out that his study, matured like an exquisite Australian Shiraz, is published at a time of renewed interest in Dietrich Bonhoeffer's life and work—neither of which was allowed by Hitler's murderous Nazis to ripen and come into full flower. Clear evidence of this strong interest is given by both international Bonhoeffer publications and the thriving of the English Language Section of the International Bonhoeffer Society. Even in Australia, the name of Dietrich Bonhoeffer has entered the public domain since Australian Prime Minister and leader of the Labor Party Kevin Rudd has referred to the German theologian and resistance fighter as one of his formative forces. Historians, politicians and theologians of the English-speaking world will greatly benefit from the book that Professor Moses has given us.

Professor Michael Lattke
The University of Queensland
Brisbane, Australia
November 2007

🎵 Preface

German history attracts many and varied investigators, each driven by his or her particular concern to determine precisely what distinctive elements in the German past made it "peculiar." It is fair to say that Anglo-Saxon scholars, especially, have pondered the "extremes" that German history manifests, and tried to explain them to their readers and students. One thing, however, is central, and that is the religious dimension to German history. If a historian of modern Germany fails to understand the crucial function of religion in forming German political culture, then his or her work will be fatally flawed. A balance must be striven for. Consequently, the present contribution by one who is both an Anglican priest and a modern historian tries to evaluate the career of Dietrich Bonhoeffer within the broader context of German history, and concludes that Bonhoeffer is best explained as a peculiarly German Lutheran kind of revolutionary.

Naturally, these ideas have been discussed with a number of scholars in the course of the preparation of the present study, and these I wish here to acknowledge. First, there is Professor John S. Conway of the University of British Columbia, the pioneer expert on the history of the German Church Struggle. His critical comments and advice over many years have been greatly valued. Secondly, I am deeply indebted to Dr. Ilse Tödt, who encouraged me to persist with my Bonhoeffer studies. She is a coeditor of the *Dietrich Bonhoeffer Werke* (DBW) in seventeen volumes, and as such, her knowledge of Bonhoeffer's writings is encyclopedic. Her donation of these volumes from the Dietrich Bonhoeffer Society in Germany was a gesture of encouragement that would have to be exceedingly rare in academic circles, and it has been greatly appreciated. As well, her counsel has been most helpful. Similarly, that of Professor Dr. Wolf Krötke, also a coeditor of DBW, has helped me understand some of the complexities of Bonhoeffer's peculiarly Lutheran theological method. Also among the leading Bonhoeffer scholars is my former countryman, now a U.S. citizen, Professor Clifford Green, whose pioneering work on Bonhoeffer has been an inspiration. His advice has helped to clarify not a few misconceptions.

The attendance at several Bonhoeffer Congresses in Germany and elsewhere, such as South Africa and Italy, served to bring me into contact with the leading Bonhoeffer scholars from several countries, and these have all been forthcoming with their friendly advice and encouragement. Among these has been Professor John de Gruchy of Capetown and Pastor Dr. Ralph Wüstenberg of Berlin, both of whom have been and still are prolific Bonhoeffer scholars. As well, in Berlin I have been privileged to enjoy the hospitality of the Institut für vergleichende Staats-Kirche Forschung through the kindness and helpfulness of its deputy director, Dr. Hans-Joachim Heise, who has followed my Bonhoeffer research with great personal interest.

In Australia, there are a number of outstanding theological scholars and specialists in Bonhoeffer studies who have been helpful with both their insights and their knowledge of sources. My former colleague at the University of Queensland, Professor Michael Lattke in the Department of Studies in Religion, is German-trained and has over many years been the most generous friend and interlocutor on the religious dimension of modern German history and has graciously granted me access to his magnificent personal library. The reverend Dr. Maurice Schild, a long-serving member of the staff of Luther Seminary in Adelaide, has been a responsive sounding board over many years. As well, Dr. Christine Winter of Canberra, a scholar also trained in German Protestant theology (finally at the University of Hamburg) was able to explain Bonhoeffer from an insider's standpoint. She was also most generous in allowing me unrestricted access to her considerable personal theological library. Also in Canberra, Professor Dr. Thorwald Lorenzen of St Mark's National Theological Centre has been a most rewarding colleague in dialogue, as have been his colleagues Professor John Painter, Dr. Graeme Garrett, Dr. Scott Cowdell, and the director himself, the Most Reverend Dr. Tom Frame.

In the field of German anti-Semitism, I have benefited from the expert advice of Professor Konrad Kwiet and Dr. Dirk Moses, both of whom teach at the University of Sydney and who are at the cutting edge of this aspect of the discipline. In acknowledging scholars who have helped me along the way, I am most indebted to the expertise of Professor Dr. Georg Iggers, whose knowledge of German intellectual and political history is unsurpassed and who has been an inspiration from my earliest years as a teacher of modern German history. Inevitably, too, over a long teaching career one attracts doctoral students who have themselves become independent scholars in the field of modern German church history, and here I am proud to name Dr. Julian Jenkins and Dr. Gregory Munro, both of whom have produced pioneering studies in the area of German Church Struggle history.

Very importantly, I wish to record my gratitude to the School of Classics, History and Religion of the University of New England, Armidale,

New South Wales, Australia. On my arrival in Armidale I was immediately offered the status of Adjunct Professor and thereby I was afforded access to the university's library facilities, without which no scholar can function, and a study within the school. Above all, the opportunity for friendly dialogue with fellow historians as well as the invitation to present seminars and public lectures on occasions provided an encouraging atmosphere in which I could pursue all my interests to advantage. My warmest thanks are due to Natasha Wheatley and Dirk Moses who painstakingly formatted my complicated manuscript to conform to the house style of Berghahn Books. In the preparation of this revised and corrected paperback edition, I am greatly indebted to the professionalism of Marianne Erhardt.

JM
Canberra, November 2007

Abbreviations

CSCE	Conference on Security and Cooperation in Europe
DBW	*Dietrich Bonhoeffer Werke* (Complete Works of Dietrich Bonhoeffer)
EKD	Evangelische Kirche Deutschlands
FDJ	Free German Youth (the East German Communist Party's youth organization)
GDR	German Democratic Republic, i.e., the former communist East Germany
Gestapo	Geheime Staatspolizei, i.e., Nazi secret state police
LPP	Letters and Papers from Prison
NCO	Non-Commissioned Officer
RES	Real-Existierende-Sozialismus, i.e., real or actually existing socialism
SA	Sturmabteilung, i.e., the Nazi "Brown Shirts"
SED	Sozialistische Einheitspartei Deutschlands, i.e., Socialist Unity Party of the GDR, the communist party
SPD	Sozialdemokratische Partei Deutschlands, i.e., Social Democratic Party of Germany
SS	Schutzstaffel, i.e., the Nazi "Blackshirts"
Stasi	Staats- Sicherheitsdienst, i.e., State Secret Service of the German Democratic Republic

INTRODUCTION

As indicated in the Preface, this book is the work of a historian of modern Germany, and was written in the conviction that many interested people, particularly clergy in the Anglo-Saxon world, who may or may not have a background in German history, could benefit from having a straightforward text that explained in broad outline the peculiarities of German history, especially where it differs from British and American history. And here, of course, Reformation history is of crucial importance. Without this background knowledge, it is argued, a full appreciation of Bonhoeffer's historic achievement would not be possible. It would not be unfair to comment that Anglo-Saxon students of German history, in the experience of the present writer, are usually very surprised to realize to what extent the Reformation in the sixteenth century, a movement of Europe-wide impact, had influenced both the development of modern German as well as English and consequently Anglo-Saxon political culture. Students found it remarkable to realize, for example, that it was the different courses that the Reformation took in Germany and England that led, in the former instance (and paradoxically so, given the influence of Martin Luther) to the consolidation of princely absolutism, while in the latter instance it was the precondition for the rise of political parties and a parliamentary political culture. This certainly illustrates the importance of bearing in mind the "peculiarities" of differing national political cultures.

As well, Australian students had little or no understanding of the phenomenon of anti-Semitism, something a teacher of modern German history cannot avoid in light of the Holocaust and the lead up to it under the Third Reich. And, here again, the strong religious undercurrent of European history had to be acknowledged. Indeed, all these pedagogic experiences coalesced when teaching the history of the Third Reich, especially when the focus was on the resistance movement in which Dietrich Bonhoeffer was involved so significantly. It was always a challenge to explain why Bonhoeffer, or indeed any of the personalities who conspired to overthrow the Nazi regime, could not be understood like the other famous revolutionaries in modern history, whether we were dealing with the English revolution of the seventeenth century, or the American and French revolutions of the eighteenth century.

Bonhoeffer could not be compared to a Cromwell or a Milton in England, a George Washington or a Benjamin Franklin in America, or a Danton or Robespierre in France. Rather, Bonhoeffer was a distinctively German *Lutheran* revolutionary, and it is this that distinguishes him as quintessentially *sui generis*.

The idea that Bonhoeffer was a reluctant revolutionary was planted in my mind back in 1971 when I saw a television program presented by the Australian Broadcasting Commission in which none other than Professor Hermann Sasse, a former collaborator of Bonhoeffer in the founding of the Confessing Church at the beginning of the Third Reich was being interviewed. The program was entitled "I Knew Dietrich Bonhoeffer." Hermann Sasse had left Germany after the war to take up a teaching post at Adelaide's famous Luther Seminary.[1] In the interview Sasse experienced difficulty in explaining to his Australian interviewer (a former minister of the Uniting Church) that Lutheranism did not endorse revolution because of the doctrine of the two kingdoms, that is, *die Zwei-Reiche-Lehre*. Bonhoeffer, through his actions, had broken with that tradition. He became a revolutionary against the very tradition that had formed him.

What brought Bonhoeffer to the barricades, as it were, was in the first instance the conditional pacifism that he acquired from his exposure to Western liberal Christian ideas during his sojourn in Union Theological Seminary in New York during 1930–31. From the encounter with both his American professors and other students—such as the Frenchman Jean Lasserre, the Swiss Erwin Sutz, and, in a particular way, the black American Frank Fisher—Bonhoeffer radically revised the traditional Lutheran-Hegelian understanding of war as part of God's ordering of Creation. This led him to become highly critical of the Nazi party even before it came to power in Germany in January 1933.

Secondly, when Bonhoeffer comprehended the implications of Nazi policy toward citizens of Jewish origin, he became a convinced advocate of the need to have Hitler removed from office because he saw him as a grotesque caricature of what a genuine German head of state should be. Indeed, for Bonhoeffer, Hitler was the agent of the Antichrist. In these two respects only was Bonhoeffer motivated to become a revolutionary. Clearly, his principles for ultimately endorsing tyrannicide were strictly circumscribed and, as such, very different from any of the past English, American, or French revolutionaries in their situation. It would not be accurate to see Bonhoeffer, say, as a German Cromwell since the latter's religious principles were fundamentally different from the Lutheran beliefs about the state in which Bonhoeffer had been formed. He had more admiration for Mahatma Ghandi in India than he would have had for the fiery English commander of the Roundheads in the seventeenth century.

Consequently, the present study begins with an explanation of how, in the development of Prusso-German history, the use of military force became sanctioned as an expression of divine will for the life of the state. Indeed, through the influence of Lutheran and then Hegelian thought on the German intellectual world in general, not simply on Protestant theologians, violence—the resort to force in the life of states, or, in other words, *Realpolitik*—was a given. This was anchored in German intellectual history by the so-called Prussian Solution to the German Question under Otto von Bismarck in 1871.

Chapter 2 focuses on Bonhoeffer's formation as a child of his times, born into an upper-class, highly academic German family and emerging as an outstanding product of the so-called *Bildungsbürgertum*, that is, the uniquely German manifestation of educated bourgeoisie for whom learning and *Kultur* were concepts of central significance. This chapter surveys Bonhoeffer's upbringing, family influences, his formal university education, the values of his ultrapatriotic professors, and refers finally to the theological position that Bonhoeffer adopted as a consequence of his introduction to the thought of the Swiss theologian Karl Barth.

As Bonhoeffer's major distinguishing contribution to revising the "German Paradigm" was the repudiation of anti-Semitism, chapter 3 outlines the role that this stream in German theological thinking played, especially from Luther to Hitler. This is a key section in the book because by demonstrating how deeply rooted both in theology and popular prejudice anti-Judaism, and then anti-Semitism, was, one can gauge the revolutionary significance of Bonhoeffer's eventual radical repudiation of it.

In chapter 4, the crucial influence of Western (read Anglo-Saxon) theological ideas with regard to peace and interchurch collaboration is evaluated. Here, Bonhoeffer was highly critical of the lack of intellectual rigor in Western thought in this regard but became, through his constructive criticism, an ardent advocate of ecumenism as an instrument that could be employed to advocate peace among nations. As will become evident, Bonhoeffer developed into a champion of international peace, though not a pacifist, in the sense as usually understood in Western circles.

With the advent of Hitler to power in 1933 and his initial support of the pro-Nazi so-called German Christians with the aim of co-opting the churches to the Nazi movement, the Church Struggle is joined. Consequently, chapter 5 is devoted to tracing Bonhoeffer's crucial role, to 1937, in trying to purify the German church of anti-Semitism and in opposing the doctrine that Hitler must be regarded, despite his obvious criminality, as a legal head of state. It is in this phase that Bonhoeffer assumes responsibility for the training of theological students who were called to ordination in the Confessing Church, which sought to uphold the purity of the gospel against the heresies of the German Christians—a period in which Bonhoeffer's thinking certainly was developing from passive to active opposition to the criminal regime.

Chapter 6 traces the evolution of Bonhoeffer's thought that led him from passive to conspiratorial opposition. In this phase, Bonhoeffer abandoned his initial hope of the ecumenical movement being able to help the Church Struggle in Germany, and so, after a very brief period of reflection in New York prior to the outbreak of war in 1939, he returns to Germany to become a courier for German military counterintelligence, the *Abwehr*, a decision that made him effectively into a double agent. It is in this phase that Bonhoeffer begins to evolve his *ethics of responsibility*. This becomes Bonhoeffer's major contribution to revising the established Lutheran doctrine of the state, an unquestionably revolutionary idea.

The subject matter of chapter 7 follows on by focusing on the changed role and nature of the Jewish Question. Here Bonhoeffer radically revised the traditional anti-Jewish theology of Christian-Jewish relations, work that becomes for him not a study in the repudiation by Christianity of Judaism but, on the contrary, the advocacy of the *interdependence* of Christianity and Judaism. Consequently, Bonhoeffer, through his role as an active conspirator against the regime, has become a political revolutionary in the sense usually understood by the word (i.e., one seeking to overthrow the "legal" government), but he has also become simultaneously a *theological* revolutionary. This is expressed most rigorously in his manuscript *Ethics*.

Chapter 8 looks back over Bonhoeffer's pilgrimage from an archetypical *Bildungsbürger* to an opponent of the Nazi regime to the point of endorsing tyrannicide. This chapter investigates Bonhoeffer's ideas for the possible relationship between church and state after the Third Reich has been overthrown. It is here, in particular, that his ideas appear to be unexpectedly reactionary. And this is what stamps Bonhoeffer as a uniquely *German Lutheran* revolutionary. His hopes for the future of Germany were not inspired by liberal Anglo-Saxon concepts of parliamentary democracy but by a purified Lutheranism that still regards the state authorities (*Obrigkeit*) as "ordained by God," as St. Paul expresses it in his Epistle to the Romans (Rom. 13). To this extent, Bonhoeffer was not anticipating a restoration of a revised version of the Weimar constitution (which he regarded as allowing far too much freedom for undisciplined elements to jostle for power) but rather he envisaged a German state that resembled in its structure and administration a modified Bismarckian model. Consequently, this chapter is an essential exercise in defining precisely what kind of revolutionary Bonhoeffer was.

Chapter 9 sums up Bonhoeffer's achievement and investigates to what extent his influence through such personalities as Martin Niemöller and Hans-Joachim Iwand survived into the post-war Bonn republic. Finally, an Epilogue traces the impact of Bonhoeffer's career on the Protestant Church in the divided Germany over the period 1945 to 1989.

As indicated in the Preface, the essential source for this introductory study to Bonhoeffer's revolution has been the seventeen volumes of his collected works. In addition, the most recent analyses of Bonhoeffer's thought have been consulted, and the works concerned are identified in footnotes where relevant. Beyond these studies, I have also made extensive use of recent monographic literature on aspects of Bonhoeffer's theology that numerous scholars both within and outside Germany have produced. As well, the key works on modern German social and political history have been consulted with the aim of placing Bonhoeffer's revolutionary achievement within the overall context of that complex story in a way that is made comprehensible to both the interested lay reader and the student of German history.

Notes

1. See Maurice Schild, "Sasse and Bonhoeffer: Churchmen on the Brink," *Lutheran Theological Journal* 29, no. 1 May (1995): 3–6. This edition published several articles by other authors remembering both German theologians. Efforts to recover the 1971 interview on ABC TV have disappointingly proved unsuccessful, so I am relying here entirely on my memory of the interview. I have discussed this with Dr. Schild and he agrees that my report is essentially correct.

1

THE "PECULIARITY" OF GERMAN POLITICAL CULTURE

> Denk ich an Deutschland in der Nacht
> Dann bin ich um den Schlaf gebracht
> [If I think about Germany in bed at night, I cannot get to sleep]
>
> Heinrich Heine, *Nachtgedanken* 1843

The word *peculiarity* in the German context takes its meaning from a work by two British historians, David Blackbourn and Geoff Eley, entitled *The Peculiarities of German History: Bourgeois Society and Politics in Nineteenth Century Germany*.[1] The work challenged current German historiographical explanations based on the so-called *Sonderweg* thesis, which argued that the Nazi regime was the endpoint of a historical *Fehlgang*, or "wrong way," constituted by the failure of the middle class in nineteenth-century Germany to progress to a level of parliamentarianism similar to that achieved in Western Europe and North America. In fact, Blackbourn and Eley argued, Imperial Germany was very bourgeois in a number of important ways, such as in economic power and the rule of law. Its authoritarianism was less a "permanent falling away from the western norm" than "a heightened version of what occurred elsewhere."[2]

This thesis did not go uncontested, but by and large, *Sonderweg* arguments now have little currency. The new research did identify a German particularity, however—namely, the relationship of the educated middle class (*Bildungsbürgertum*) with the state. More than their French and British counterparts, German professionals, civil servants, and even businessmen looked to the state as the guarantor of order and progress, trusting more in the tradition of "reform from above" than in initiatives from below. The extraordinary prestige of the state and its officials came at the expense of civic activism, and thus led to the attenuation of political opposition; deference to authority was the norm. As shall be seen, this political culture contained an anti-Semitic dimension, one, moreover, that was theologically underpinned. In a real sense, and for very good reasons, Bonhoeffer's protest against the Third Reich was also a protest against this "peculiar" religious culture of nineteenth-century Germany, the roots of which went back to the Reformation of Martin Luther.

Most of the writing about Dietrich Bonhoeffer has been by theologians, doubtless because Bonhoeffer was a highly creative and inspirational systematic theologian. In fact, he is arguably the most historically significant Protestant German theologian since Martin Luther. Indeed, the number of studies that have appeared on Bonhoeffer over recent decades and which continue to appear is eloquent testimony to the stimulus that his thought has generated in scholars from many countries. As well, there exists an International Dietrich Bonhoeffer Society based in Germany with an English-language section in the United States that has, since its inception in the 1970s, organized biennial conferences focused on aspects of Bonhoeffer's theology. In addition to these international conferences, there occur so-called *Regionaltreffen*, that is, Bonhoeffer conferences organized within individual countries. These events are taking place in more and more countries with the involvement of scholars from a variety of humanistic disciplines including history, and literature as well as theology.

As a general rule, the crossing of disciplinary boundaries is comparatively rare. Scholars tend to avoid launching into regions remote from their own particular field of expertise. Consequently, it would be unusual for a non-theologian to embark, say, on a biography of a theologian or even a study of an aspect of the theologian's life work. Such ventures seldom occur unless the subject displays so many interrelated facets as to justify it. This would seem to be the case with such a complex figure as Dietrich Bonhoeffer (1906–45), whose theology was so dramatically shaped by the momentous historical events through which he lived. His biography, therefore, presents a challenge both to theologians and historians alike such that a departure from the general rule is certainly warranted. What follows here, though, is not a new biography but rather an attempt to explain the revolutionary component as it developed in Bonhoeffer's thought. He was a product of his historical environment but someone who became, as a result of intellectual/spiritual experiences, an agent determined to change that environment. By virtue of his theological acumen, stimulated by his encounter with the world outside the Germany that had molded him, Bonhoeffer became the most radical critic of both Prusso-German history and key aspects of its formidable Protestant theological tradition.

Indeed, so penetrating was Bonhoeffer's analysis and subsequent indictment of Protestant theology and the politics of his fatherland that he must be considered a revolutionary. In order, then, to account for

Bonhoeffer's path to that position, a professional training in modern German history together with a working knowledge of the post-Reformation theological traditions in Germany would be a prerequisite. In short, a satisfactory appreciation of Bonhoeffer's achievements cannot be provided by focusing exclusively on his theology. However crucial that discipline is, it needs to be augmented by reference to the political and ecclesiastical history of Germany since the Reformation. To this extent, the present task constitutes, indeed, an interdisciplinary challenge. A strictly compartmentalized approach would not deliver the overall understanding that is urgently needed; and so in what follows, Prusso-German history will be portrayed in broad strokes, even while one must remain aware that reduction to ideal types (Max Weber) can obscure the often significant details. The important thing is that in this way the distinguishing "peculiarities" can be highlighted.

Religion and Political Values

It should not be difficult, even in this post-Christian age, for the average citizen who takes notice of world events to appreciate that religious belief, or adherence or loyalty to a particular culture that has been shaped by religion, plays a key role in political events. Wherever one looks to regions of conflict, be it in Ireland, the Middle East, the Darfur region of Sudan, the Indian subcontinent, or the former Yugoslavia, religious rivalry is an ever-present factor. It is striking that regardless of which side we are discussing, there are claims that the cause is holy and just, and that the violence perpetrated against one's neighbor, often a traditional tribal rival, is somehow sanctioned by almighty God. Indeed, various international conflicts, not to mention examples of terrorism, that have been raging in many countries throughout the twentieth and early twenty-first centuries on an unprecedented scale (and including violence perpetrated by Islamic extremists), may accurately be designated "sacred violence." Above all, violence is justified in the overcoming of real or imagined threats to doctrinal purity, tribal or national unity or security.[3] Such violence has a long pedigree. The prophets of the Old Testament frequently incited their people to exterminate disruptive elements within their own tribe as well as to declare "holy war" on rival peoples in order to cement their own ethnic cohesiveness. This occurred even in the case of Moses himself, who, immediately after receiving the commandments on Sinai, ordered the tribe of Levi to carry out a massive punitive decimation of Israelites because of their disobedience in having participated in acts of orgiastic worship.[4]

That Moses, the lawgiver, believed he had to resort to this measure in order to restore tribal discipline and unity based on cultic conformity, indicates a certain ambivalence regarding the true nature of almighty God. Was he a caring, loving father of all humankind or a vengeful warrior God, the champion of one chosen people, always ready to strike down rival nations with ruthless ferocity? This ambiguity remained unresolved until the crucifixion of Jesus of Nazareth. The fact is that Jesus was the victim of institutional violence demanded by the leaders of the synagogue in order to promote the inner cohesiveness and solidarity of the Jewish people, especially as they were living at that time under Roman occupation. As the high priest Ciaphas said, it was expedient that one man should die for the people.[5] But the crucifixion, seen against the background of Jesus' previous preaching, is really to be understood as an indictment of institutional violence and the tradition of killing victims, whether an individual, a putatively disruptive group, or a neighboring tribe, in order to promote national unity. Jesus radically opposed all of this. He had consistently preached justice, peace, universal love, and, in the Sermon on the Mount, even love of enemies. God did not require scapegoats to be sacrificed to satisfy nationalistic passions. Rather, the image of God that Jesus projected was unequivocally that of a father who cares for and nurtures all his children.[6] That was the point of the crucifixion of Jesus of Nazareth, not the appeasement of an angry God, as falsely but passionately maintained by fundamentalist advocates of the theory of "penal substitutionary atonement," but rather to illustrate the grotesqueness of institutional violence.[7]

What is puzzling is that for subsequent world history it was the warrior God of the Old Testament who was apparently in control, even for Christian countries. The doctrine of "holy war" was embraced by the church, as illustrated, for example, by the Crusades under Pope Urban II (c.1035–99). And Machiavellism,[8] the doctrine that the prince may—indeed, must—employ the utmost force if deemed necessary for the preservation of national security, recognized that the existence of states was predicated on the right of the prince to employ all means at his disposal to guarantee the continued existence of his realm. This meant that the history of Christendom was characterized by the spectacle of Christian rulers periodically making war on each other and on non-Christian states alike, however regretfully, in the name of a higher necessity, that is, national security. Violence was built into the system of international relations from the beginning, but in the Christian era it had to be somehow explained away because it was a contradiction of the unequivocal ethics of the gospel. Strictly speaking, if a Christian prince waged war he would be expected to have a guilty conscience before God, whose commandment he had broken.

Indeed, since the Christian era, heads of government have lived with an unresolved dualism: on the one hand they paid lip service to the gospel of peace while on the other they pursued the extension of their power by all means, foul and fair. Certainly, the great lesson that history taught, as Niccolò Machiavelli (1469–1527) observed, was that states acted always in their own interest, regardless of the moral law. But, while having noted that, Machiavelli confirmed that statesmen did not deny the existence of a moral law; they simply lived with a permanent guilty conscience because of it. One could say that statesmen existed in a mental condition of permanent "cognitive dissonance"; in theory, they should have known that they were committing crimes against humanity, yet they were powerless to overthrow the habits acquired over centuries of ruthless practice.

Enter Martin Luther (1483–1546)

There was no serious attempt to overcome this dualism until the Reformation, and it was significantly the figure of Martin Luther in Germany who was forced to confront it because he had to answer the question, What was a Christian man to do if his prince required him to perform an act that conflicted with his conscience, that is, which was against the ethics of the gospel?

The medieval church had attempted to solve this by postulating the existence of two realms, the spiritual and the secular, sometimes called the "regiment of the two swords." In the realm of the spirit, the Christian person obeyed the church represented by the pope and his deputies, the bishops. Kings ruled over the secular world and the subjects were required to obey the laws made by them. Obviously, there were many opportunities for conflict between the two realms, but in Christendom, specifically pre-Reformation Europe, the authority of the pope was assumed to be final. After all, it was assumed that he, as the "Vicar of Christ" on earth, was the source of all authority, including, ultimately, that of sovereigns. The pope's authority had been, of course, quite often challenged by ambitious princes resulting in endless disputes between popes and emperors, bishops and kings, over the issue of whose authority was to prevail in a given contested situation. These conflicts made up the warp and woof of European medieval history. What seemed so clear-cut in theory was more often than not a source of friction in practice. There had always been rivalry between church and state. Indeed, since the Emperor Constantine in the fourth century had made Christianity the official religion of the Roman Empire, the structures were set in place for recurrent debate between the two as to which had the primacy of authority.

The Reformation initiated by Martin Luther in 1517, however, placed the issue of authority in a completely new context. For Luther, the pope had not only disqualified himself from his historic role as Christ's representative on earth, he was the Antichrist. Thus, the bishop of Rome's position was not only theologically untenable because of his anti-Scriptural stance in the controversy over justification, and the related issue of the sale of indulgences, he was also the epitome of evil, and obedience to him would guarantee the individual Christian eternal damnation.

With the papacy and the episcopate no longer the channels of God's authority on earth, the question arose, Who now was? For Luther it was the anti-papist prince, God's anointed, the "powers-that-be" ordained by God, as St. Paul had affirmed in chapter 13 of his Epistle to the Romans. So that now the prince had authority over both state and church. He had become for Luther a *Notbischof*, that is, an emergency or substitute bishop with responsibility for maintaining oversight over the church. Under the Lutheran solution, the state, previously a rival of the church, assumes a status that appears to be on a plane higher than the church, virtually absorbing the church. Seen in a radical light, the state is the agent of God's will for the secular realm, as it certainly was before the Reformation, but now it had also uncontested responsibility for the church. Indeed, the Protestant prince of the Holy Roman Empire of the German Nation became the *summus episcopus* in his realm.

Thus, the German Reformation blurred the borderline between church and state. Luther sought to resolve the question by restating the doctrine of the two realms or the "doctrine of the two kingdoms" (a matter that will be dealt with in greater detail in a later chapter). Briefly, the doctrine taught that there were two realms of responsibility. The spiritual realm was the domain of the church, whose task was to preach the gospel for the cure of souls. The state, on the other hand, was responsible for the secular world, to ensure that law and order and national security were maintained. The colorful way in which Luther expressed it was that the world without the gospel was *ein Stall voller böser Buben* (literally, "a stall full of wicked characters").[9] It was certainly a fallen world inhabited by thieves, murderers, and prostitutes. Sin abounded. However, in the world were Christian people who sought to live according to the gospel. In order that they might have a chance of doing so, there had to be wielded the strong sword of justice for the punishment of crime. This was the realm of the state. It existed first and foremost to enable the church to survive. And, as St. Paul had spelled out in Romans 13, the "powers-that-be" were "not a terror to good works." In other words, if a Christian person obeyed the law and fulfilled his or her daily duties there was nothing to fear from the state.

Church and State in Lutheranism

The post-Reformation practice of church-state relations resulted in the church becoming a virtual department of state, and, indeed, in country parishes in Prussia, for example, the pastor often fulfilled the duties of a state official.[10] It was as though in his person, the pastor was bureaucratically schizophrenic. Certainly, he had the autonomy to preach the gospel, but at the same time he functioned as a secular official. A serious consequence of this development was that the church was never in a position to criticize the state in any of its policies, foreign or domestic. It was relegated strictly to attending to the cultic/spiritual enhancement of everyday life. The Protestant Church became, in short, a bulwark of conservatism, committed to obey the prince who exercised final jurisdiction over it. Thus did the secular order of things have the appearance of being a reflection of the divine will. The state and its organs, the judiciary, the bureaucracy, and in a unique way the army, were regarded virtually as the executive arms of God's will on earth. All this flowed from the doctrine that absolutist monarchy was empowered by the grace of God, *Königtum durch Gottes Gnaden*, the German equivalent of the divine right of kings.[11]

The Church-State Problem in England

A sideways glance at the course of events in England at the time of the Reformation will help our understanding of the consequences of this same historical phenomenon in the Holy Roman Empire. This is because the Protestant German way of regarding the state stood in sharp contrast to the development of church-state relations in Britain, where after the revolution of 1649, when the forces of Parliament (Oliver Cromwell's Roundheads) overthrew the king's forces, the Cavaliers, and Charles I was sentenced to be beheaded by decision of parliament. This was the essential precondition for the triumph of the doctrine of the sovereignty of the "King-in-Parliament" and the development of political parties, a unique consequence of the English Reformation. The Reformation in Germany, on the other hand, had the very opposite effect, namely, that of strengthening the executive powers of the monarchs, insisting still that, as a divinely ordained institution, the monarchy should be respected accordingly. In this way, the religious history of both Britain and Germany in the sixteenth and seventeenth centuries had laid the foundations for the divergent political cultures of both countries. In Britain, the struggle between the Whigs and the Tories that was carried out in Parliament ultimately led to the evolution of parliamentary democracy and the marginalization of the church with respect to the process of political decision making, despite the establishment of the Church of England as the official state church. In the German principalities "benevolent despotism" was the only sanctioned political system, and that held, despite the imposition in 1871 of a constitution by the Prussian minister-president, Otto von Bismarck (1815–98), for a united Prussia-Germany, until the abdication of the Kaiser and the other German princes in 1918. Bismarck's constitution was a not-so-subtle instrument for the suppression of modern liberal parliamentary institutions and practices. Its intention was to freeze the social structures of Prusso-Germany in their preindustrial state, largely out of fear of the rising social democratic movement. Indeed, Bismarck had in 1878 taken the radical step to outlaw the social democratic party and trade unions, a move that more than anything accelerated the polarization of German society by victimizing the political organs of the rising working class.[12]

This distinction between the English and German experiences in the evolution of church-state relations is crucial, and a detailed comparative study of the subject would be instructive.[13] However, for present purpose it is essential to note how in German political philosophy the church became subordinated to the state precisely because in the circumstances of Luther's time, the prince acquired the role of *summus episcopus* and the clergy henceforth became quasi public servants. What we see developing is a concept that the state is virtually the church working in the world.[14]

The Importance of the Philosophy of G.W.F. Hegel

Certainly, the distinction between church and state in post-Reformation Germany is not very clear. And it is against this background that the state philosophy of Georg Friedrich Wilhelm Hegel (1770–1831) was developed and later virtually adopted as the official philosophy of what became the largest Germanic state, Prussia.[15]

Hegel's highly influential work can be summed up roughly as the systematization of what he took to be the Lutheran theology of state power. A broad understanding of it is essential for any meaningful explanation of the course of modern German history. What it comes down to is the elevation of the state to being the agency of almighty God on earth. The state becomes, in fact, an entity above and separate from the society out of which it emerged. This is, indeed, the point. The state is not a man-made agency like a dairy cooperative, designed to facilitate commercial activity, for human purposes,[16] but essentially a spiritual entity intended to implement the will of God on earth to which humanity must submit, a process described by Hegel as constituting real freedom. It is a concept of freedom, however, that scarcely equates with the Anglo-Saxon idea of individual freedom. In the Hegelian system, an individual became free to the extent that he submitted to the authority of a state that, it was understood, guaranteed his protection.[17]

The Hegelian concept of the state was, despite its apparent rigor, somewhat abstracted from reality. It left out of account the fact that the state officials were obviously fallible, and hence corruptible, human beings, including the monarch, but this did not seem to matter. A sort of fiction was maintained that the state was above the sordid machinations of pressure groups and the not infrequent scandalous private lives of monarchs. The bureaucracy, public servants, in this scheme of things was a distinct "estate" that ensured the continuation of good government regardless of the agendas of individual sections of society, such as the aristocracy or the Junker class (landowners) or the merchant class. Above all, the state was not there to be manipulated according to anybody's sectional interest, but rather was to serve the long-term good of the whole community. And the professional public servants, *das Beamtentum*, were there precisely to ensure that.

That was one key aspect of Hegel's systematization of Prussian political practice. The other crucial element was what the philosopher had to say about the role of the state in world history. As we have seen, the state was the agent of God on earth. But, as history illustrates, there were many states competing with each other for domination of the world, or at least regions of it. History was for Hegel, a record of power struggles. But each state was part of the divine plan for the universe. And the remarkable thing is that states were locked in what appeared to be an endless cycle of violence engendered by their rivalry for control of the earth's resources. It is indeed an essential characteristic of a state that it should be able, by means of its armed forces, not only to defend itself but to expand at the expense of lesser powers. The latter have by the very fact that they were weaker, no justification to continue to exist, in Hegel's view, and therefore rightly ought to be absorbed into the greater, more upwardly mobile state/power.

Clearly, with such a philosophy of the state the concept of basic human rights evaporates. Under the Hegelian state, such values are absurd. The state as a moral entity has far greater concerns than the rights of individual subjects. Above all, it must be ever vigilant regarding the possible dangers to its integrity from the outside. Indeed, the state must seek to read the intentions of those neighboring countries capable of posing a security threat and be ready to take action to prevent them from violating national sovereignty. Consequently, already in Hegel we find the endorsement of preventive war. And, although there were defenders of the Hegelian position in Germany such as the renowned Freiburg historian and ardent Lutheran, Professor Gerhard Ritter (1888–1967), who claimed that Hegel was not advocating or endorsing a policy of unrestrained violence, nevertheless Ritter affirmed that war preserved the moral health of nations, "as the motion of the winds keeps the sea from stagnation, to which it would succumb by constant stillness, just as would nations by an enduring peace, let alone peace everlasting."[18] It is of some significance that the figure of Professor Gerhard Ritter reappears in chapter 8 of the present book as a *Bildungsbürger* involved in the resistance movement against Hitler, and as a personality well known to Dietrich Bonhoeffer.

What is noteworthy about the all-pervasiveness of Hegelian thought in Prusso-Germany is that it ruled out the possibility, and even the desirability, of the attainment of enduring peace in the world. It thereby committed the human race to intermittent but certain mayhem, and all that was by a theological sleight of hand in which God was made to appear as the author and perpetrator of a never-ending cycle of death and destruction within his creation. This is extremely puzzling when one reads in the Genesis account that Creation was meant to be "very good" and sustaining of human life. Curiously German Protestant theology from Schleiermacher (1768–1834) to von Harnack (1851–1930) and on through the Third Reich emphatically and increasingly endorsed the notion of a warrior God. The only challenges, apart from a minority of subdued pacifists,[19] came from the Swiss theologian Karl Barth and, subsequently and more emphatically, as we shall see, from von Harnack's most brilliant pupil, Dietrich Bonhoeffer.

Hegel and the German Reich

When one is confronted with Hegel's doctrine of the power state (*Machtstaat*), one is struck by its strong family resemblance to what Machiavelli observed three centuries previously about how princes behaved. Yet there is one crucial difference. Whereas Machiavelli was describing the behavior of principalities in pre-Reformation Europe, when even monarchs were subject to the moral law, Hegel in early nineteenth-century Protestant Prussia, located states/principalities in an autonomous realm, beyond the moral law. With that, Hegel resolved the tension-loaded dualism that characterized the life of states previously by postulating that the divine will was manifest on earth by monarchical states, and most clearly through the most powerful state. This is the one that had survived in the struggle for domination over the others by virtue of its superior culture and had thereby demonstrated its intrinsic worthiness to impose itself upon its lesser neighbors, thus advancing the progress of world history. Such a state was bearer of the "world Spirit," in Hegel's language.[20]

At this point, it will suffice to note that Bonhoeffer, already in 1932 at an ecumenical meeting in Czechoslovakia, quite emphatically rejected this concept of the state.[21] He was, however, a voice crying in the wilderness. The Hegelian concept of the state, which Bismarck had so brilliantly demonstrated was efficacious, still claimed the allegiance of most educated Germans in the first half of the twentieth century. This was because many Germans under Bismarck's chancellorship of the Reich, which he founded under Prussian leadership in 1871 and led effectively until 1890, came to believe that Germany was, in fact, the "World Historical Nation," effectively chosen by almighty God to dominate the world. And these ideas became paradigmatic for most German scholars and the *Bildungsbürgertum* generally during the reign of Kaiser Wilhelm II (1888–1918). Indeed, not even the defeat of 1918 and the imposition of the Treaty of Versailles in June 1919 could eliminate the idea that Germany had a prior right from God to impose its *Kultur* upon the world for the benefit of all humankind. The then leading Hegelian scholar in Germany, Georg Lasson (1862–1932), also a Lutheran pastor, writing in 1920, referred to the situation after the lost war, the infamous peace settlement of Versailles and the founding of the League of Nations, in these words:

> It [i.e., war] will not come to an end until the nation [i.e., Germany] to which Providence has allotted the task of establishing the principle of the true cultivation of the state throughout the world, has been so physically strengthened and spiritually matured that those Powers which today fancy themselves justified in subjecting the planet to their inferior principles can no longer resist it.[22]

This means that educated Germans at the time of the Peace Settlement and the creation of the League of Nations were still unequivocally and emphatically committed to the Hegelian view of world history. They consciously despised and rejected Western ideas of peace and justice, preferring to believe still in what they took to be a Lutheran and Hegelian God who would, after the setback of the lost war in 1918, eventually bestow victory upon the German nation by allowing it to fulfil its rightful destiny. Democratic political principles and parliamentary democracy were largely alien to this class. For this reason many regarded the new Weimar Republic as a foreign imposition. This mentality played right into the hands of what would become the Nazi movement. When Hitler and his supporters finally succeeded in overthrowing the Republic, he having been appointed Chancellor on 30 January 1933, these Germans hailed him as a virtual savior.

What this teaches us about the dominant German political culture as it had crystallized by the mid-nineteenth century is that any idea that international relations could ever be made peaceful was regarded as utopian nonsense. The contrary view of Hegel's Königsberg rival, Immanuel Kant (1724–1804), who had tried to advance the doctrine of eternal peace, lost any meaningful support in German universities in the nineteenth century. At that time, the struggle for unification under Prussian military leadership was the chief political priority. Hegelianism, in contrast to Kant's system of thought, sanctified the use of force to attain political goals. Indeed, the attraction of Hegel's philosophy was precisely that its author had removed the moral opprobrium from power politics. More than that, Hegelianism affirmed that the power state actively implemented the will of God for humanity at large. Hegel's achievement was to make it appear incontestable in German eyes that political force, even warfare, exerted in the interests of the state was divinely sanctioned. Consequently, statesmen need have no qualms about declaring war, even against a weaker power, as it was always for the purpose of strengthening the state and hence advancing the cause of freedom. True freedom in the world would come about when the most powerful state had imposed its superior will over all the others. That would mean the end of all conflicts and so universal peace and tranquillity would prevail.

The fundamental importance of Hegel's philosophy for German history becomes even clearer when it is appreciated that it underlay not only the discipline of history but also that of Protestant theology in German universities. It exercised a veritable intellectual hegemony.[23] The state was, in essence, sanctified power. It operated above the moral law in an autonomous sphere, pursuing goals that would always lead to its increased growth. Indeed, the power state was the motor of world history. Finally, with regard to this summary of Hegel's philosophy of the power state, Hegel made the point that when two states opposed each other in the eternal struggle for hegemony, it was not ever a case in which one was right and the other was wrong; rather, it was always a case of right versus right. The power that emerged victorious, however, was the one that represented the will of God. Indeed, such power struggles were endemic to the human condition and essential for God's plan of salvation.

It can only be reiterated here that this kind of thinking about the state and church-state relations permeated German political culture until after World War II, when the then prevailing conditions allowed some questioning as to the appropriateness of this way of understanding history for producing harmonious international relations, and as to whether it was valid as "historical theology" (*Geschichtstheologie*). Since that time, a more liberal political philosophy and a more ecumenical theology have characterized German civic discourse. Within that context, the lifework of Dietrich Bonhoeffer played a central, if not decisive role, seen in retrospect. Admittedly, the vast majority of Bonhoeffer's contemporaries in the immediate postwar era were still steeped in the neo-Lutheran-Hegelian understanding of the role of the state in world history, and took a considerable time to revise their views in the changed political context. An appreciation of Bonhoeffer's significance in the readjustment of German political culture only gradually gained ground within the pastorate, as will be shown. However, the publications of Eberhard Bethge and Hans-Joachim Iwand, among others, accompanied by the efforts of the International Dietrich Bonhoeffer Society, have ensured that the pioneering, indeed, revolutionary, contribution of the Protestant martyr has been kept in the foreground of the public discourse about German political culture.

The significance of Dietrich Bonhoeffer for German history, and indeed, world history, is that he managed, with relatively little support from a handful of like-minded colleagues, to break the dominant Hegelian paradigm within which most educated Germans, the *Bildungsbürgertum*, used to think. The latter class was derived from those Germans who had experienced the privilege of a formal secondary school education at the *humanistisches Gymnasium*, a special kind of educational institution between public primary school and university. What distinguished the humanistic from other kinds of secondary school was the fact that the core disciplines were the classical languages of Greek and Latin, and sometimes also Hebrew. When a student had completed the *Abitur*, the equivalent of the leaving certificate or diploma, usually around the age of eighteen, he or she would have acquired a very high proficiency in these subjects. Naturally, the other major disciplines consisting of German, mathematics, physics, and chemistry as well as history and modern languages were on the curriculum, but pride of place was given to the Classics.

Germans were inordinately proud of their education system at all levels, and it was much admired by outsiders for the excellence it produced. Indeed, there was a tradition of Anglo-Saxon students traveling to Wilhelmine Germany to complete their studies in various disciplines, particularly in Classics, theology, philosophy, and history, but also in the natural sciences. It was a source of great satisfaction to the German professoriate that they were so highly regarded abroad, and they understandably felt their claim to be at the cutting edge of their respective areas of expertise to be amply justified.

It was in this tradition that Dietrich Bonhoeffer was educated, and he was without doubt a brilliant example of it. He had acquired an encompassing competence in the Classics as well as the necessary biblical languages, and would, in addition, by the time he had completed his doctorate, have been able to communicate in Italian, Spanish, English and French. But languages were simply the tools of the theologian's trade. Bonhoeffer, having trained under such internationally reputed scholars as Adolf von Harnack (1851–1930), Reinhold Seeberg (1859–1935), Karl Holl (1866–1926), and Adolf Deissmann (1866–1937), became a formidable systematic theologian at an extraordinarily early age. And it was by virtue of his incisive mind and immense erudition that Bonhoeffer was equipped to critique and eventually to overthrow the theological and political paradigm by which most educated Germans comprehended the world and lived their lives. Bonhoeffer's achievement was both an intellectual and ideological revolution for it invalidated most of the assumptions on which the illusions of German cultural superiority and divine sense of mission to the world rested.

The German Paradigm

From what has been said above about the all-pervading influence of Hegel, we can now enquire in what the "German paradigm" consisted. We may do this by simply posing the question about the assumptions of Bonhoeffer's class concerning God, the church, the state, and history, politics, and culture. Although later chapters will deal with aspects of these categories in greater detail, they need to be flagged here. Obviously, these assumptions were not completely uniform throughout the *Bildungsbürgertum*, and we have to make allowances for individual variations. For example, there were well-known freethinkers among this class who were agnostic or atheist, but such persons would have shared many of the other assumptions of the "German paradigm." First and foremost, the God of German liberal as well as orthodox theology of the nineteenth and twentieth centuries was undoubtedly a warrior God, a "God of battles." This becomes evident when a study is made of German war sermons from the time of the War of Liberation (1813) against Napoleonic France and the wars of unification (1864, against Denmark; 1866, against Austria; and 1870/71, against France). The victorious outcomes of these conflicts indicated to most German preachers that God must have been guiding the Prusso-German sword. This was attributed to Prussia's assumed moral superiority, on the one hand, and the fact, especially in the war against France, that Germany, homeland of the Reformation, represented the purified catholic faith against the immoral and heretical papists. By the time of World War I, the great majority of German theologians had assumed the validity of the Hegelian schema of world history and were convinced that Prusso-Germany not only was favored by God but was really God's agent on earth—indeed, God's hammer—chosen to lead the nations to true *Kultur*, and to punish those who sought to frustrate the fulfilment of the Prusso-German mission. The public expression of this belief was formulated in the motto embossed on the buckles of German soldiers' belts: *Gott mit uns* ("God with us" or "God is on our side"). As well, the German war insignia was the Iron Cross, an emphatically Christian symbol. The First World War was, indeed, a holy war. And because Britain misguidedly opposed Germany by placing itself at the side of the barbarous Orthodox Russians and the immoral and effete papist French, deserting her true putatively Protestant faith and, as well, betraying her Teutonic blood, there was a separate motto formulated for Britain: *Gott strafe England*, literally, "May God punish England."[24]

With regard to the church, it was well embedded in the German Protestant mind that the church's role was to assist the Reich to victory by preaching the righteousness of Germany's cause.[25] The Great War was most certainly one that had been forced upon Germany by the Triple Entente led by an envious Britain, which through her sinister diplomacy had "encircled" the German Reich to prevent its justifiable expansion. Significantly, the Roman Catholic Church in Germany aligned itself with the Protestant-led Reich by proclaiming that the Great War was a "just war" from Germany's point of view.[26] Of course, the Allied side also believed that their cause was just and that Germany was a rogue empire that had blatantly violated international law through the invasion of Belgium, thus behaving in a most un-Christian way. For the Allies, Prusso-Germany had become an apostate Power, and, indeed, the Kaiser was even denounced as the Antichrist. But these accusations from the enemy only served to convince German intellectual leaders, including many Protestant theologians, that the German nation really was the agent of God on earth and that its enemies lacked the perception and, of course, the *Kultur*, to comprehend the truth.

The state in Prussia-Germany was emphatically monarchical, as befitted the Hegelian schema. This is very important to grasp because the Prusso-German concept of authority that had been systematized by Hegel was espoused by all conservative elements by the time of Bismarck's ascendency, 1862–90. Ultimate authority derived from almighty

God and was channelled to the world via the monarch, who was God's anointed. And here it should not be forgotten that the German version of the "divine right of kings" lasted until the revolution of November 1918. Hegel had formulated the doctrine of the "organic state" according to which the "powers-that-be," the existing dynasties, were the only legitimate authority. This was transmitted to the subjects via the Estates, that is, the aristocracy and the professional bureaucracy. The effect of this was that Hegel's constitutional concept ruled out both British and French Enlightenment theories of the state, which generally could be said to be based on a social contract in which the citizenry had a legitimate form of representation. In short, German conservatives, the so-called right-wing Hegelians, saw no justification for organs of representative government in which political decision making took place in an elected assembly. Such ideas were considered decidedly inappropriate for Prusso-Germany, not least of all for theological reasons, although Bismarck had to concede to the German national movement, which had always wanted a federal parliament, that there would be a Reichstag, a representative body for the entire Reich, as a weak form of legislature.

It is one of the ironies of history that precisely in the powerful and conservative Bismarckian-Wilhelmine Empire, a military monarchy, the world's largest and best-organized democratic party arose. This was the Social Democratic Party, founded in 1863 and, by 1912, the largest party in the Reichstag. Since the German federal legislature was not a proper parliament that controlled the executive, the government was not based on the party constellation of the lower house but rather formed itself at the chancellor's behest, the holder of the chancellorship being responsible only to the Kaiser.

It would have been surprising had this Bismarckian system not had its internal critics among certain liberal groupings, plus the Roman Catholic Center Party as well as the Social Democrats, but the forces of conservatism were too deeply entrenched for the Wilhelmine Empire ever to have followed the example of Great Britain and adopt a fully developed parliamentary system. In the final analysis, only the Social Democrats were thoroughly committed to the goal of genuine parliamentary government, the hopes of some liberals and members of the Center Party notwithstanding. The Social Democrats, having been regarded since the 1870s as the dangerous revolutionary "internal enemy," remained totally isolated in the Reichstag and were able to participate in government only after constitutional changes were made in the wake of the November 1918 revolution that led to the founding of the ill-fated Weimar Republic. It became so because the right-wing Hegelian conservative elements conspired all through the history of the Republic until 1933 to discredit the parliamentary system as essentially non-German. In doing so they contributed to the ultimate political triumph of the Nazi dictatorship.[27]

From what has just been said, it should be clear that politics in Bismarckian-Wilhelmine Germany were dominated by the concern of the propertied classes, both the old Junkers (land-owning aristocracy) and the new industrial power elites seeking to keep the forces of social democracy at bay. Indeed, Wilhelmine Germany, particularly under the second Kaiser from 1888 on until his enforced abdication in November 1918, was very much a polarized nation. The conservatives were perennially worried about the possibility of revolution, but instead of adopting a policy of accommodation toward the working class—such as recognition of the trade unions in the law, institutionalization of a modernized arbitration system, shortening the working day, and so on—there was permanent confrontation with organized labor both political and industrial. The Social Democratic Party, it should be remembered, had in 1891, having been actually outlawed for the previous twelve years, adopted a Marxist program that, of course, predicted the inevitable collapse of capitalism, the disappearance of the royal houses, and the advent of communism. This ideology instilled deep fear in the middle and upper classes in Germany, as they never forgot the atrocities perpetrated during the proletarian uprising in Paris after the French defeat in the war against Prussia, 1870–71, when the Paris Commune attempted a violent revolution.[28] There was, however, a group of intellectuals, professors in the social sciences called the *Kathedersozialisten*,[29] who did recommend social reform while still retaining the monarchical system, in order to accommodate the more reasonable demands of organized labor, and thus weaken the electoral appeal of the Social Democratic Party. These conciliatory professors were, however, voices crying in the wilderness. The ruling elites preferred a more hard-line authoritarian course in domestic politics, declaring in effect that nothing would induce them to alter the existing monarchical constitution.

The other extremely important factor that inhibited the constitutional modernization of Bismarckian-Wilhelmine Germany was, of course, imperialism. Once Bismarck, in 1884, had agreed to support German chartered companies in Africa and New Guinea, a wave of colonial and imperial enthusiasm was unleashed that led not only to the acquisition of more colonies in Africa and the Pacific but, more ominously, to the building of an ambitious battle fleet. Indeed, one cannot speak of politics in Wilhelmine Germany without addressing both *Weltpolitik* and *Flottenpolitik*, that is, overseas expansion and naval construction on an unprecedented scale. There were three factors driving Germany in this direction. First, the colonial enthusiasm of sectors of German commerce, aided and abetted by missionary societies; second, the ideology of imperialism that was advocated by leading intellectuals such as the famous professor Heinrich von Treitschke (1834–96) in Berlin, and Heinrich Class (1868–1953), chairman of the Pan-German League (1908–39), enthusiastically supported by virtually the entire professoriate;[30] and third, the phenomenon of "social imperialism."[31] The latter concept has been used to explain what had influenced Bismarck, to a large degree, to allow Germany to enter the race for overseas colonies in the first place. It meant that the government could control threatening social movements at home, such as democracy, if it could manipulate public opinion to support patriotic projects overseas. These projects came to include not only more colonial acquisitions but later, after Bismarck's dismissal, the building of a battle fleet that would rival that of Britain. And the justification for the massive expenditure thus incurred was that Britain was opposed to Germany's colonial expansion. But this was not true.[32] There was no real reason for hostility toward Britain, as it was Germany's largest trading partner; and there was certainly no serious unresolvable friction in the field (i.e., out in the colonies). Despite this, however, the German press and the Reich governments from the 1890s right up to 1914 maintained a consistent anti-British propaganda with which to justify the massive naval expenditure.[33]

Finally, on the politics of the Reich, the architect of German naval expansion himself, Admiral Alfred von Tirpitz (1849–1930), was driven by the doctrine that sooner or later there would have to be a clash with Britain because it was the power that stood in the way of Germany's natural ambitions to expand overseas. As well, Britain was obviously declining, as the South African war and difficulties in India, Ireland, and elsewhere, indicated. All that was needed was a little more resistance from Germany, and the British would have to abandon their preeminence in world politics to their more energetic and better-organized Teutonic cousins. In short, Anglo-German antagonism became a key element of the German paradigm.

Next, when we address the question of culture we are really talking about what the Germans meant by *Kultur*. This is not the same as what is commonly understood by *culture* in English, which has to do with education and artistic accomplishment. A cultured individual, in the Anglo-Saxon sense, is understood to be one who is well read, who may also be linguistically proficient—that is, to have a command of one or more foreign languages—and who has some musical abilities and a wide general knowledge. *Kultur* for the Germans, however, meant considerably more. It covered those often mystical elements that went into making up the German national identity, indeed everything that made Germans both unique and superior. It is intimately bound up with the way that Germans in the nineteenth century came to understand their national history.

The famous German historian, Friedrich Meinecke (1862–1954) devoted virtually his entire scholarly life to explaining *Kultur*, and there is no doubt that most of his colleagues agreed with him.[34] The beginning of a unique sense of German self-awareness went back to the writings of such eminent thinkers as Gottfried Herder (1744–1803) and was well established by the time of Goethe's death in 1832. It was very much a literary movement to begin with but it was to develop into *cultural nationalism*. This was Herder's achievement. He observed that all culture was essentially tribal. It had its origins in the soul of the people, the *Volk*, who inhabited a discrete part of the world. Each *Volk* was unique, and their uniqueness was the expression of the tribal spirit, or *Volksgeist*. There was indeed a peculiar *Volksgeist* shared in by all the German-speaking tribes. However, they were politically still fragmented. And this fact caused Goethe (1749–1832) in 1796 to inquire: "Germany? I know not where to find that country. Where learning begins politics ceases to be."[35]

It was a good point, because in Goethe's day there may have been a German *cultural* nation, many people speaking and writing in German, but there was no German *political* nation. By the conclusion of the Napoleonic wars, however, a German national consciousness was being awakened as indicated by the writings of eminent academics and clergy such as Johann Gottlieb Fichte (1762–1814) and Friedrich Schleiermacher (1768–1834), among others, as a patriotic reaction against the French occupation. Indeed, it was in this period from about 1794 to 1815 that the so-called German question was posed. And the German question was simply this: how was Germany to become a nation state like France or Britain? There were two possible solutions: one was that the European Great Power, Roman Catholic Austria, would unite all the middle-size and petty German states into one Reich. That was called the "greater German solution"—*die grossdeutsche Lösung*. The other one was that Protestant Prussia would unite the German principalities *without Austria*: the so-called "lesser German solution"—*die kleindeutsche preussische Lösung*.

In the period from 1815 to 1871, Prussia answered the German question with, as Bismarck phrased it, "blood and iron." This meant that the defining influence on German political culture was going to be Prussian and Protestant. And Prussia was preeminently a military monarchy that had gradually expanded from being an insignificant Electorate in the Holy Roman Empire during the fifteenth century to becoming a European great power by the end of the reign of Frederick the Great in 1786. Moreover, this was achieved largely at the expense of Austria, thus establishing what was called the *German Dualism*, that is, the deadly rivalry between the two largest Germanic states for the ultimate dominance of Germany.

So far in this section we have been talking mostly about history, and for a very good reason. *Kultur* is the product of history. In the course of Prusso-German history in the nineteenth century, we witness a most efficacious example of how history developed in accordance with a schema virtually predicted by a school of historians. As already indicated, there was much public discussion from 1815 at the latest as to which state, Austria or Prussia, should unite Germany. The decision that Prussia should be the unifying power had really been made in the aftermath of the 1848 revolution when a National Assembly convened in Frankfurt had debated the issue until, finally, Austria recalled its delegates, thus leaving the way open for a Prussian solution. Consequently, on 2 April 1849, a deputation of elected members of the Frankfurt parliament traveled to Berlin. On the next day they offered the throne of a united "lesser Germany" to Friedrich Wilhelm IV, King of Prussia. And here a curious but crucial thing happened. The king politely but firmly rejected the honor on the grounds that it would make him merely a constitutional monarch, that is, a head of state bound by the principles of the constitution rather than a leader ruling by the grace of God. In other words, he would have accepted the throne of a united Germany had the delegation consisted of the princes of the other German principalities, all rulers by divine right. However, since it was a group of revolutionaries, albeit very moderate, liberal and essentially nonviolent revolutionaries—they included a strong representation of university professors—the king could still not compromise his principles. A legitimate hereditary ruler derived his authority directly from God and not from a popularly elected assembly claiming that sovereignty resided with the people. This reeked too much of the "ideas of 1789," the French Revolution, for the God-fearing Protestant Prussian king.[36] Consequently, the decision by Friedrich Wilhelm IV of Prussia to reject the offer of the throne of a united Germany from the revolutionary Frankfurt National Assembly prolonged the debate about the solution to the German question until 1866, when Bismarck began to solve it by forcibly ejecting Austria from the German Confederation and thus paving the way for a "Prussian Solution," based strictly on the monarchical principle (monarchy by the grace of God) after the defeat of France in 1870.

There was palpable disappointment caused by Prussia's refusal to accept the crown of a united Germany from the elected Frankfurt National Assembly, thus frustrating the objectives of most delegates. The majority drew the conclusion that there was nowhere to go, and so decided to dissolve the Assembly. Some delegates, however, refused to go along with this and stubbornly continued to advocate radical constitutional change. These delegates were soon forcibly dispersed by a detachment of Prussian troops, led, providentially some would say, by an officer who was destined to become the first German emperor in 1871, Wilhelm I. The great German experiment in parliamentarianism after the 1848 revolution was humiliatingly consigned to one of the most ominous political failures of modern history. Thereafter, a period of reaction set in with a return to the politics of the *German Dualism* within the reinstated German Confederation under Austrian chairmanship. The dilemma concerning which power was to unite Germany remained. Under these circumstances the historian, Johann Gustav Droysen (1808–84), who had been a leading delegate in Frankfurt, revised his constitutional views and began to advocate that Prussia was destined to lead the future united Germany, but under terms convenient to Prussia alone—and that meant the retention of the military monarchy by the grace of God.

Droysen had, in the meantime, abandoned any idea of a Western style constitution with a sovereign parliament. Indeed, he argued that a retrospective view of the history of the Holy Roman Empire of the German Nation up to the eighteenth century, which saw the final emergence of Protestant Prussia as a European Great Power, proved that divine providence was guiding Prussia into this historic role. The Prussian solution to the German question was, in Droysen's portrayal, preordained.[37]

Droysen and the so-called Prussian school of historians that he founded argued, from the 1850's onward, that Prussia should fulfill its historic role in its own way—specifically by preserving the monarchy under the grace of God and by discarding any imported foreign constitutional ideas in forging the solution. This, of course, coincided precisely with what Hegel had advocated about the Prussian constitution. The constitutional ideas had to be homegrown for them to be efficacious—indeed, they had to be unique, "organically" evolved cultural products. Imported ideas of constitutionalism were inadmissible and by definition unworkable. This mind-set proved to be remarkably durable in Germany, and partly explains why it took so long for the German people to feel comfortable as equal partners in the family of European nations given that they had been educated to regard themselves as uniquely superior among the European peoples, having been furnished with a constitution that God had ordained for them.

It needs to be kept in mind that already in 1862, Otto von Bismarck had been appointed minister-president of Prussia by the king (Wilhelm I), given a brief to stifle any liberal Western constitutional ideas and to preserve the military monarchy's supremacy. This Bismarck did with éclat. What his three military victories[38] accomplished was not only territorial expansion for Prussia; they convinced any skeptics within

Germany that the politics of force were wholly justified, or, in other words, that *Realpoltik* was the way to achieve all national political goals. This should be done, moreover, by employing existing political institutions, and in Prussia's case that meant the military monarchy and the bureaucracy that administered it. Consequently, when Germany was united under Prussian leadership in 1871, the tradition of the authoritarian, military, bureaucratic and anti-parliamentarian state was firmly established as the essential German way. Moreover, it was deemed right to claim that God approved it as being consonant with the letter and spirit of the gospel of Christ, rightly understood. Protestant German theologians of immense erudition, with a handful of exceptions, totally endorsed this paradigm.[39]

It was not until after World War II, and in particular until the writings of Dietrich Bonhoeffer had been taken on board by German Protestant leaders, and those mostly in the German Democratic Republic, that what has been called the "German paradigm" finally collapsed. Or perhaps, it is more accurate to observe that German pastors at the beginning of the twenty-first century had become less likely to appeal to outdated and discredited notions of the role of the state in the "history of salvation," given that the political culture of contemporary Germany is that of a modern European parliamentary republic committed to international collaboration and the peaceful resolution of conflict.

Finally, it has been argued that the political culture in which Bonhoeffer was born and educated was definitely "peculiar" in the sense that the *Bildungsbürgertum* perceived themselves as in a real sense "peculiar" or special in a way that set them apart from the bourgeoisie of other Western European countries and of North America. A main contributing factor to this was the religious history of Prusso-Germany that reinforced the concept of monarchy by the grace of God. Although this was not uncontested by large sections of German society, in particular those who voted for the Social Democratic Party, nevertheless the value system of the German power elite, as well as the *Bildungsbürgertum*, effectively lent to the German Empire its unique political cultural identity. It is this situation that needs to be born in mind when trying to evaluate the biography of Dietrich Bonhoeffer.

Notes

1. (Oxford, 1984).
2. Ibid., 291–2.
3. See Gil Bailie, *Violence Unveiled: Humanity at the Crossroads* (New York, 1998).

4. The Book of *Exodus*, chapter 32, verses 25–29.
5. The Gospel according to *Saint Matthew*, chapter 5 verses 43–44.
6. It should be noted that how the crucifixion of Jesus of Nazareth is interpreted as of central importance. The concept of the "penal substitutionary atonement" is here challenged. The question is raised whether we have to do with a vengeful God who can only be appeased by the violent sacrifice of his only son, an idea that is as absurd as it is repugnant. See Bailie, 37, and James G. Williams, *The Bible, Violence and the Sacred: Liberation from the Myth of Sacred Violence* (New York, 1992).
7. The theory of the "penal substitutionary atonement" is central to the paradigm of belief of Christian fundamentalists and teaches that God required the sacrifice of his own son on the cross to "atone" for the sin of the world.
8. Nicolo Machiavelli, *The Prince* (London and New York, 1999). Machiavelli began drafting the text in 1513 and circulated his manuscript in and around Florence some three years later. Publication occurred posthumously in 1531/32.
9. For a useful summary of this issue see, Ernst Weymar, "Martin Luther: Obrigkeit, Gehorsam und Widerstand," *Geschichte in Wissenschaft und Unterricht*, 13, no. 3 (March 1962): 133–51. Luther wrote concerning the world as follows: "Dieweil sie aber ein stal voller böser buben ist, so muss man Gesetze und obrigkeit haben, Richter, hencker Schwerd, galgen und was es dings mehr ist, damit man den bösen kenne were." See, *Weimarer Ausgabe, Predigten*, 152, vol. 20, p. 577. Here Luther was citing St Paul's first epistle to Timothy, chapter 1, verses 8–11: "Now we know that the law is good, if anyone uses it lawfully, understanding this, that the law is not laid down for the just but for the lawless and disobedient, for the ungodly and sinners, for the unholy and profane, for murderers of fathers, for murderers of mothers, for manslayers, immoral persons, sodomites, kidnappers, liars, perjurers, and whatever else is contrary to sound doctrine, in accordance with the glorious gospel of the blessed God with which I have been entrusted."
10. Oliver Janz, *Bürger besonderer Art: Evangelische Pfarrer in Preussen 1850–1914*, (Berlin, 1994).
11. Han Herman Brinks, "Luther and the German State" *The Heythrop Journal* 39 no 1 (1998): 1–17.
12. Lothar Gall, *Bismarck-The White Revolutionary*, 2 vols. (London, 1986), 1: 1815–1871, 317–77 *passim*. Johannes Willms, *Bismarck: Dämon der Deutschen: Anmerkungen zu einer Legende* (Munich, 1997), 203–51 *passim* and 285–86.
13. For a concise examination of the significant differences in political ethos between the Church of England and German Protestantism since the Reformation, see Andrew Chandler, "A Question of Fundamental Principles: The Church of England and the Jews of Germany 1933–1937" *Year Book Leo Baeck Institute* 38 (1993):221–61.
14. This concept was developed by the German theologian Richard Rothe (1799–1867). His understanding was that the state was in fact the church acting in the world. Rothe propagated his ideas first as professor in Heidelberg, 1837 to 1849, and then in Bonn until 1854, returning to Heidelberg as professor of church history and systematic theology until his death. Rothe taught that

the church was to be virtually absorbed by the state and that the nation thus transformed reaches perfection and becomes the Kingdom of God on earth. Not surprisingly, Rothe had been a student of Hegel in Berlin during 1819. See the entry in the New Schaff-Herzog *Encyclopoedia of Religious Knowledge*, vol. 10, under "Rothe, Richard: Theologian." See also his *Theologische Ethik*, 5th ed. (Wittenberg, 1871).

15. Heinrich Ritter von Srbik, *Geist und Geschichte vom deutschen Humanismus bis zur Gegenwart*, 2 vols. (Munich, 1950), 1: 189.

16. See Friedrich Meinecke, *Cosmopolitanism and the National State* (Princeton, 1970), 103. German romantic thinkers about the nature of the state are here investigated. They universally rejected the mechanistic utilitarian notion of the state and prefer an "organic" notion such as that expressed by Adam von Müller (1779–1829) whose ideas had considerable influence on conservative German political thought in the nineteenth century. Essentially for him, "the state is not merely a factory, a dairy, an insurance company or mercantile society; it is the close uniting of the entire physical and intellectual needs, the entire physical and intellectual richness, the entire internal and external life of a nation into a great, energetic, infinitely dynamic and vital totality" (103). This amounts to a mystical evaluation of the state to a degree not found in, say, Anglo-Saxon political theory. This question is also examined by Franz Schnabel in his *Deutsche Geschichte im neunzehnten Jahrhundert*, 4 vols. (Freiburg, 1959), 1: 283–315.

17. Leonard Krieger, *The German Idea of Freedom—History of a Political Tradition* (Chicago/London, 1957), 125–38. Krieger makes the following observation on 129: "In the young Hegel as well as the old the idea of freedom was associated with the concepts of collective bodies in a way which took account of individualistic considerations but subordinated them to higher principles embodied in the nation, the corporation, and the state."

18. Gerhard Ritter, *Sword and Scepter*, 4 vols. (Coral Gables, Florida, 1972), 1: 209–10. It is this idea that became paradigmatic for the *Bildungsbürgertum*. Ritter observed, "This militant philosophy of history won Hegel an astonishing number of converts. The pervasive influence of Hegelian ideas is discernible throughout nineteenth century German historical and political literature. It was an influence that kept on spreading—but even as it spread it grew more and more shallow."

19. Roger Chickering, *Imperial Germany and a World without War: the Peace Movement in German Society, 1892–1914* (Princeton, 1975). See especially, Julian Jenkins, *Christian Pacifism Confronts German Nationalism—The Ecumenical Movement and the Cause of Peace in Germany, 1914–1939* (Lampeter, 2002).

20. An excellent summary of Hegel's teaching with regard to state power is provided by Friedrich Meinecke, *Machiavellism: The Doctrine of Reason of State and its Place in Modern History* (London, 1957).

21. The address was held on 26 July 1932: Bonhoeffer, "A Theological Basis for the World Alliance?" in Bonhoeffer, *No Rusty Swords: Letters lectures and Notes from the Collected Works*, ed. and intro. Edwin H. Robertson (London, 1970), 161. Also *DBW*, 11: 327–44. "Zur theologischen Begründung der Weltbundarbeit."

22. Georg Lasson's introduction to Hegel's *Lectures on the Philosophy of History*, in *Werke*, vol. 8 (Leipzig, 1920), 172.

23. See the work of Hubert Kiesewetter, *Von Hegel zu Hitler: eine Analyse der Hegelschen Machtstaatsideologie und der politischen Wirkungsgeschichte des Rechtshegelianismus*, (Hamburg, 1974.)

24. There is a considerable literature on German "war theology," but see Arlie J. Hoover, *The Gospel of Nationalism: German Patriotic Preaching from Napoleon to Versailles* (Wiesbaden/Stuttgart, 1986); Karl Hammer, *Deutsche Kriegstheologie 1870–1918* (Frankfurt, 1971). The motto, *Gott strafe England* ("May God punish England") that was current during World War I in Germany derived from the pen of the German-Jewish poet Ernst Lissauer (1882–1937). See Rainer Brändle, *Am wilden Zeitenpass: Motive und Themen im Werk des deutsch-jüdischen Dichters Ernst Lissauer* (Frankfurt am Main, 2002).

25. B. W. Pressel, *Die Kriegspredigt 1914–1918 in der evangelischen Kirche Deutschlands* (Göttingen, 1967).

26. Heinrich Missala, *"Gott mit uns" Die deutsche katholische Kriegspredigt 1914–1918* (Munich, 1968).

27. Kurt Sontheimer, *Antidemokratisches Denken in der Weimarer Republik: die politischen Ideen des deutschen Nationalismus zwischen 1918 und 1933* (Munich, 1962), 7.

28. See Francis L. Carsten, *August Bebel und die Organisation der Massen* (Berlin, 1991).

29. The *Kathedersozialisten* were those German professors, mostly in economics, since the 1860s who advocated a state-initiated social service system in order to overcome the dangerous social hostility engendered by *laisser faire* capitalism. Strictly speaking, they were not socialists at all but social reformers who exerted some influence on Bismarck's famous social policy of the 1870s. The most notable were Adolf Wagner (1835–1917), Gustav Schmoller (1838–1917), and Lujo Brentano (1844–1931).

30. Alfred Kruck, *Geschichte des Alldeutschen Verbandes, 1890–1939* (Wiesbaden, 1954), and Roger Chickering, *We Men Who Feel Most German: A Cultural Study of the Pan-German League, 1886–1914* (Boston, 1984). Here the anti-British thrust of German naval policy is amply documented. As well, see the additional works cited in note 19.

31. Hans-Ulrich Wehler, *Bismarck und der Imperialismus* (Cologne/Berlin: 1969). See in particular the section "Die Bedeutung des Bismarckschen Imperialismus," 423–502.

32. See the study by Michael Fröhlich, *Von Konfrontation zur Koexistenz: Die deutsch-englische Kolonialbeziehungen in Afrika zwischen 1884 und 1914* (Bochum, 1990).

33. See the standard work by Volker R. Berghahn, *Der Tirpitz-Plan: Genesis und Verfall einer innenpolitischen Krisenstrategie unter Wilhelm II* (Düsseldorf, 1971), and also Paul M. Kennedy, *The Rise and Fall of British Naval Mastery* (New York, 1976; see the section "The End of the Pax Britannica [1897–1914]"), 205–238. Also, Volker R. Berghahn, *Germany and the Approach of War in 1914*, 2nd ed. (London, 1993, especially chapters 2 and 3, "Tirpitz's Grand Design and "Anglo-German Naval Race." As well, Herman Kantorowicz, *The Spirit of Brit-*

ish Policy and the Myth of the Encirclement, rev. ed., trans. W. H. Johnston, pref., Gilbert Murray (London, 1931).

34. See especially, *Historism: The Rise of a New Historical Outlook* (London, 1972).

35. See Johann Wolfgang von Goethe, *Werke*, ed. on behalf of the Grand Duchess Sophie of Saxony [by Gustav von Loeper et al] (Weimar, 1887–1919), vol 5, part 1, 218.

36. Günter Mick, *Die Paulskirche: Streiten für Einigkeit und Recht und Freiheit* (Darmstadt, 1997), 235–241. See also Theodor Schieder, *Vom Deutschen Bund zum Deutschen Reich*, vol. 15, *Handbuch der Deutschen Geschichte* (Munich, 1975), 96–98.

37. The doctrine that Protestant Prussia had been preordained to unite Germany was called *Borussismus* or the Hohenzollern Legend. See Franz Schnabel, *Deutsche Geschichte im 19. Jahrhundert*, vol. 1, 100–101. The legend was set in circulation by none other than Johann Gustav Droysen (1808–84) in a massive work entitled *Geschichte der preussischen Politik*, 14 vols. (Berlin 1855–86). Droysen had been a deputy at the Frankfurt National Assembly who had vigorously advocated the "Prussian solution" to the German question. He was most disappointed when Friedrich Wilhelm IV rejected the offer of the imperial crown thereby frustrating the objectives of the national movement. Subsequently, as professor of history in Kiel, Droysen began to advocate that Prussia should, despite everything, proceed to unite the German petty states by force (*Realpolitik*) if necessary, as this was Prussia's historic vocation. When Otto von Bismarck accomplished this after the three wars of unification in 1871, it appeared as though Droysen's prophecy had been vindicated, and the legend thereby won many supporters throughout all of Germany, excluding Austria, of course. See Heinrich Ritter von Srbik, *Geist und Geschichte*, vol. 1, 370.

38. The victories were over Denmark in 1864, Austria in 1866, and France in 1870.

39. John A. Moses, "Justifying War as the Will of God: German Theology on the Eve of the First World War," *Colloquium*, vol. 31, no. 1 (1990): 3–20.

2

BONHOEFFER'S FORMATION

An individual's way of comprehending the world is conditioned by where he or she was born, who the parents were, and of course, the peculiarities of the education system. At this point, it is important to recall the Germany of Bonhoeffer's childhood, the values of his parents, and particularly those of the academic teachers who had most influence on him during his university training.

First, the figure of the Wittenberg Augustinian monk, Martin Luther, and the consequences of his rebellion against the papacy in the sixteenth century have been paradigmatic for subsequent German history. The outcome of the German Reformation, the subsequent wars of religion to the Peace of Westphalia in 1648, followed by the revolutionary wars with France and the struggle against Napoleon at the beginning of the nineteenth century, all served to confirm the Protestant Church as one of the chief bastions of monarchism and a sworn opponent of democratic movements. By their very nature these were revolutionary, republican and hostile to the doctrine of monarchy by the grace of God that was central to German thinking about authority and government.

Given the crucial role that the Reformation of Martin Luther has played in German history, God is certainly one of the crucial factors. The present tense may be used, albeit advisedly, because the events of October/November 1989 that led to the opening of the Berlin wall and free elections in East Germany and to ultimate unification, have often been called a "Protestant revolution," one that was certainly prepared "under the umbrella of the church" as was said at the time.[1] Neither should it be forgotten that the God to whom Luther prayed was a "mighty fortress," certainly a warrior God, and this image was strengthened, indeed raised to a fundamental philosophic principle, in the course of German history. Understandably, God could not possibly have been described as a pacifist. Warfare was a given in landlocked central Europe, peopled by nations of very different cultures.[2]

Second, as indicated, the state was very early seen as God's instrument on earth for the achievement of his purposes for humankind. The philosopher Hegel, who had been called to a professorial chair in Berlin from Heidelberg in 1818 to succeed Gottlieb Fichte (1762–1814), became known as the "royal Prussian state philosopher,"[3] and there until his death in 1831 Hegel laid the foundation for the ideology of the *Machtstaat*, the power state. This became the widely accepted understanding of the state in Germany until the end of the Second World War. It was hardly conducive to the reception of democratic ideas because it confirmed Luther's teaching about the "powers that be" (*die Obrigkeit*), in particular that they—i.e., the princes—derived their power from God and were responsible only to him, *not to the people*, as was the case in the political cultures that developed in the West.[4]

Third, the *church*, as we have already seen, in this scheme of things lived under the protective power of the prince, who was designated by Luther a *Notbischof*—literally, an emergency bishop, with the power of oversight over the church, which was relegated to an ancillary role in the kingdom (virtually a department of state)—although in Hegel's philosophy of religion the state is perhaps best understood as the secular arm of the church ensuring security for all citizens and, above all, protection for the church, the custodian of the gospel. In coming to an understanding of German history it is crucial to grasp the importance of this unique relationship between church and state.[5]

Fourth, it will be obvious that the profession of arms, soldiering, in Prusso-Germany was one imbued with the highest of prestige, since the defense of the realm was a sacred duty. A reading of the biography of the Prussian Field-Marshal Helmuth von Moltke (1800–91) will make clear the centrality of this concept. Von Moltke was a man of firm Lutheran piety, evincing a remarkable sense of duty and honor, mental and physical toughness, as well as possessing immense erudition. It was he who, under the chancellorship of Otto von Bismarck, led the Prussian army to victory in the three campaigns (Denmark, 1864; Austria, 1866; France, 1870/71) that led to the Prussianization of Germany in 1871. In doing it for Prussia, von Moltke was serving God in the noblest way imaginable. Indeed, von Moltke's self-perception was that he, as a Field-Marshal, was emphatically a servant of God exercising a unique and critical function. The following report serves to illustrate this in a dramatic way: on 11 December 1880, von Moltke ventured to instruct the Swiss Professor Dr. Johann Kaspar Bluntschli (1808–81), then of Heidelberg university, who had recently edited a handbook of international law, that he had a completely unrealistic understanding of the nature of war. Clearly the Swiss scholar had been formed in a totally different world of ideas from that of the Prussian officer. He appeared to regard peace as the desirable objective of international relations. Consequently, the Field-Marshal wrote to him as follows: "Eternal peace is a dream and not a beautiful one at that, and war is a link in God's ordering of the world. In it are unfolded the noblest virtues of men: courage, self-denial, loyalty to duty, and preparedness to self-sacrifice. Without war the world would sink into a morass of materialism."[6]

This is arguably the most eloquent justification by a practicing Prussian–Lutheran Christian officer for warfare as "the continuation of politics by other means" (Karl von Clausewitz). And there is no doubt that the vast majority of Prussian officers and those of both the Kaiser's imperial army as well as those of Hitler's *Wehrmacht*, perceived themselves as fulfilling a virtually divine calling. Indeed, for many, especially officers during the Third Reich, the state, of which the person of the dictator, Adolf Hitler, was a substitute for the Creator. For those who retained the Lutheran teaching of their childhood and youth, the state was certainly God's instrument on earth.

Fifth, Prusso-German aggrandizement became regarded as a divinely ordained step in the further expansion of the united Germany under Prussian leadership. As the young Max Weber proclaimed in 1895 when giving his inaugural lecture at Freiburg University, the acquisition of overseas territories was but the natural consequence of German unification.[7] As a latecomer among the Great Powers, the new Germany felt an undeniable call to become a leading imperial power. It experienced a burgeoning *Sendungsbewusstsein*, that is, an historic sense of mission. In the Prusso-German scheme of things, this was without doubt divinely ordained. Pan-Germanism became an entrenched ideology from, at the very latest, the 1890s onward. There was only discussion about at what pace and how aggressively German expansion should occur. Opposition to this mindset was only to be found among social democrats and a handful of pacifists. Indeed, the existence of a very large and highly organized political and industrial labor movement in Germany, "the disloyal opposition," as it was regarded by the middle and upper classes, made the ruling elites and the patriotic middle classes extremely apprehensive.[8] The distrust of the social democratic party and the trade unions tended to harden the hearts of the German state and federal governments against making any concessions to the demands of the labor movement for modernization of both the political system, industrial relations, and the social service provisions. Industrialists, in particular, were infused by the idea that they had to be "masters in their own house" (*Herr im eigenem Hause*). They resisted, consequently, all attempts by labor to negotiate on wages and conditions, and persisted in a policy of virtual subjugation of the working class, regarding themselves as *Arbeitgeber*, the German word for employer, meaning those who generously offered the dignity of work to the toiling masses. These were designated the *Arbeitnehmer*, employees, the people who should be grateful for the opportunity to become wage earners.[9]

The Bismarckian-Wilhelmine Empire was consequently a very polarized and authoritarian society, a vivid portrayal of which is provided by Heinrich Mann's famous novel *Der Untertan*, published in 1913 and available in English first as *The Patrioteer* and then as *The Man of Straw*. It was into this world that Dietrich Bonhoeffer was born in Breslau in 1906, fourth son of a professor of psychiatry, Karl and his wife, Paula, neé von Hase. There were eight children in all, and Dietrich had a twin sister, Sabine, who died in Göttingen as recently as 7 July 1999.[10]

In 1912 the family had moved to the leafy Berlin suburb of Grunewald, father Karl having been appointed to a chair at the university of Berlin and placed in charge of his section at the famous hospital, the *Charité*, there. The Bonhoeffers were by family background and father's station in life members of the upper bourgeoisie and in every sense of the word *Bildungsbürger*. Frau Paula Bonhoeffer came from a distinguished pastor's family, and it was she rather than her husband who exerted the religious influence on the children. With eight children within ten years it was a busy household, but by all accounts extremely well organized. Frau Bonhoeffer, a trained teacher herself, supervised the children's education and ensured that they received the highest standard in music and languages, as well religious instruction. It is interesting to note that Dietrich, as a boy, had decided to become a theologian even though his older brothers had chosen to study law and physics, respectively. Dietrich was not just trying to be different; he was genuinely interested in theology from a very early age.[11]

Of significance, also, was the fact that in 1915 the Bonhoeffers had moved house to Wangenheim Strasse in Grunewald, where a number of other professors also lived. Among them was the internationally renowned patristic scholar Adolf von Harnack, who became a family friend. Dietrich knew him from an early age, and as a student regularly accompanied him on the train from the Hallensee suburban station to the university in the center of Berlin. Bonhoeffer became one of Harnack's most outstanding students, though not, as it turned out, one of his life-long disciples. Indeed, after he had begun to read the Swiss theologian Karl Barth, Bonhoeffer gradually distanced himself from his German professors in more than just subtle ways. Indeed, the intellectual/spiritual migration upon which Bonhoeffer had embarked is central to the thesis being advanced here about his revolutionary theological/political career. Certainly, he was able to extricate himself from the methodological strictures imposed by his Berlin mentors. Bonhoeffer was destined to restructure the predominant theological paradigm.[12]

Here it is extremely important to comprehend the political mentality of Bonhoeffer's German professors. Most of them had been, not surprisingly, convinced Prusso-German patriots who unquestioningly understood and supported German imperial expansion as the nation's destiny under God. They unhesitatingly welcomed the outbreak of war in 1914, virtually as a heaven-sent opportunity to realize the preeminence in the world which they believed was Germany's by right. When the dreadful conflict erupted, Bonhoeffer was only in his ninth year. Two of the older brothers, Karl-Friedrich and Walter, had reached military age in 1917 and, although still at school, were required to serve in the army. Walter was fatally wounded in the spring offensive of April 1918, and his death affected the family greatly, making an indelible impression on the younger Dietrich. There is no doubt that the Bonhoeffers were a loyal, patriotic, upper-middle-class German family. It would have been impossible to be otherwise. Nevertheless, as will become clear, they did not share the more extreme attitudes of many of their peer group. One could say that they were patriotic but definitely not uncritically *deutschnational*, that is, uncompromisingly nationalist. After the November Revolution of 1918 that led to the abdication of the Kaiser, and indeed of all the princely houses, Karl Friedrich Bonhoeffer, who survived the war, became a Social Democrat, and the other brother, Klaus, had begun to acquaint himself with the ideas of Karl Marx but finally became a member of the moderately conservative German People's Party, led by Gustav Stresemann (1878–1929). This party came closest to representing the family's political values after the war.[13]

Prior to the war, the element of the *Bildungsbürgertum* that was arguably the most decidedly *deutschnational*, that is, the ultra-patriotic champions of the Prussian solution, was without doubt the professoriate, especially the Protestant theologians, with very few exceptions, and leading among them was the aforementioned Adolf von Harnack as well as all the other professors with whom Dietrich Bonhoeffer studied after the war—with the interesting exception of Adolf Deissmann.[14] Patriotism for them was a central part of their Protestantism. They really believed that the state was the arm of God on earth, the agency through which he expressed his inscrutable will for humankind. And in the decade leading up to the war, many of these professors of theology endorsed Germany's presumed God-given right to expand at the expense of lesser powers, or ones, like Britain, whose empire was deemed to be moribund and in a state of inexorable decline. Consequently, when the war came in August 1914, it was assessed as a *Kairos*. This is a theological term signifying a special intervention of God in the affairs of humanity, similar to the Pentecost event in the lives of Jesus' apostles in the New Testament. At that time, the so-called descent of the Holy Spirit occurred, manifesting itself in the rush of a mighty wind and the appearance of "tongues of fire" on the heads of those present in the upper room (Acts 2:1–4). The preaching of German pastors about the outbreak of war in 1914 was couched exactly in these terms. The cataclysmic conflict had from the beginning an apocalyptic character.[15]

The thrust of the rhetoric of German pastors and professors from August 1914 was that God had called Prusso-Germany to be his hammer to punish those Powers that had misguidedly aligned themselves against it and its undoubtedly righteous historic cause or mission to the world. The professors and other intellectuals had a perception of themselves as the custodians of the national spirit, rather like Old Testament prophets, and were extremely vocal in publishing declarations or manifestos about the nature of the war and about Germany's historic opportunity to fulfill its destiny as the leading cultural nation in the world. Notably, they all expressed the utmost disgust with Britain as a putatively Protestant nation, siding with the barbaric Orthodox Russians and the degenerate papist French, against their Teutonic and Protestant brothers. Hence the aforementioned popular saying, *Gott strafe England!*

There then ensued a spate of manifestos in which the German professors energetically tried to refute the charge of German aggression in invading Belgium and also passionately to defend the German military against allegations of atrocities perpetrated on the Belgian or French civilian populations. At the same time, they proclaimed Germany's right to defend itself against the envious coalition led by Britain. A particularly notable example of these manifestos called *Aufruf an die Kulturwelt* (An Appeal to the Civilized World) was published on 4 October 1914. In this document, ninety-three leading intellectuals, including theologians, gave their rationale for the war. It made a spectacular impact, especially on the British. Renowned German men of letters and learning declared their solidarity with the German military and all its deeds. In particular, the manifesto proclaimed the undoubted superiority of German *Kultur*.[16] The notable Swiss theologian, Karl Barth, who had been trained by some of these same theologians, especially by Adolf von Harnack, was astounded and appalled at the naivety of these notable scholars, and he denounced them as incorrigible imperialists and publicly dissociated himself from what, for him, were outrageous convictions based on a false theology of the relationship of the state to God. In fact, the manifesto in question alienated him forever from his old teachers, among whom were Bonhoeffer's later professors. Barth then went on to pioneer another direction in theology that left the state out of the schema entirely.[17]

Harnack was greatly embittered by what he regarded as a "betrayal" by a former student, and later denounced Barth for being a less-than-rigorous scholar. The paradox is that Bonhoeffer maintained his friendship with Harnack while he moved more and more into alignment with Barth's theology, a process that lasted a good decade. He did not actually meet Barth personally until 1931.[18] Harnack was, indeed, a committed imperialist, so much so that he was the ghostwriter for the Kaiser's famous declaration at the beginning of the war in which Wilhelm II appealed to all sections of society to lay aside all class enmity and to unite behind the war effort. This was clearly directed chiefly at the working class to encourage them to declare solidarity with all other parties that were ideologically hostile to the social democratic movement, and show loyalty to the throne and to the existing political system.[19]

Another paradox is that Bonhoeffer's doctoral supervisor at Berlin was none other than Reinhold Seeberg, who during the war had been a convinced and, indeed, rabid annexationist. In June 1915, for example, Seeberg demanded in a manifesto the permanent annexation of Belgium and northern France so as to enable Germany to build naval bases there from where to threaten Britain and her overseas empire. As well, Seeberg recommended the expulsion of the Slavic peoples in the east from their countries—an early version of ethnic cleansing—so that these territories could be settled by Germans. And, finally, this renowned theologian demanded massive reparations to be exacted from Britain. This was the expression of a conviction that German *Kultur* and *Macht* (power) formed an organic unity; great military power was in fact an expression of cultural superiority, and behind German greatness was the hand of God. Among the professors there were few dissenters from this conviction.[20]

Here, then, was the world of ideas, indeed a "war theology," from which Bonhoeffer would have to extricate himself. As indicated, the Swiss theologian Barth was the most outspoken critic of it within the German-speaking theological world. His main point was that the finite human mind, by means of the discipline of philosophy, no matter how rigorous, could not aspire to know the mind of a transcendent God and predict the schema according to which the deity was working out his design for humanity in history. This was precisely the grandiose project that von Harnack and his associates were convinced they could realize. They were indeed most confident that their uniquely German historical theology had enabled them to do this. It is interesting, in this regard, that Bonhoeffer's biographer and lifelong friend, Eberhard Bethge, in his detailed study of Bonhoeffer's life, gives only very small clues concerning the theological mind-set of these professors and indicates that Bonhoeffer would distance himself from them.[21] As Bonhoeffer was only in his eighteenth year when he first went up to university, it is not surprising that he needed time to mature considerably before he became an autonomous spirit. Indeed, in his first semester at the University of Tübingen in 1923, he joined for a short time the clandestine national army, the so-called *schwarze Reichswehr*, that was formed illegally in defiance of the Treaty of Versailles. One of the most humiliating conditions of the peace settlement was that the regular German army be limited to 100,000 men.[22] Consequently, patriotic youths led by former officers enthusiastically joined the illegal military training organization. If a student associated himself with this movement it would have to be assumed that he was decidedly *deutschnational*, embittered by the harsh peace treaty, and also one who would have endorsed the "stab in the back" legend. Again, this was an explanation of Germany's defeat that was in currency from the beginning of the Weimar republic. It gained widespread acceptance, especially in right-wing circles. According to it, the imperial German army could have won in the end had it not been for the wave of strikes and revolutionary activity inspired by the disaffected left of the Social Democratic Party and the incipient Communist Party. All these disruptive actions on the home front had allegedly crippled the fighting power of the loyal soldiers in the face of the enemy, hence the "stab in the back."[23] The ensuing humiliation of the Treaty of Versailles weighed heavily upon young patriotic Germans, and it was this that led them to support such a movement as the *schwarze Reichswehr*.

As a young student, Bonhoeffer must have encountered these ideas, which have been described as elements of a "pre-fascist" mind-set, but despite his youthful patriotism he soon distanced himself from this position.[24] Not surprisingly, many people of this mind-set came later to be seduced by the nationalist and racist policies of Adolf Hitler. Bonhoeffer, however, was enabled, after significant learning experiences, to tread a decidedly different path. Quite early in his education, then, Bonhoeffer was becoming immunized against an uncritical patriotism.

We have alluded to German "war theology" that looked upon the state as an instrument of God and the motor of history in advancing the cause of true freedom. Clearly, it was inspired by Hegelianism, and advanced by the Prussian school of history that dominated German universities at the time.[25] The interesting thing for German theology at the end of the First World War was that only a few theologians really appreciated that Germany had really lost the war. Curiously, they were unable to draw the obvious conclusion that perhaps God's approval, or endorsement of German policy, had been withdrawn. The judgment of history was plain for all to see. Despite this, many pastors and theologians could not bring themselves to accept this and to revise their theology of the state accordingly. Instead, they consoled themselves that the outcome of the war was the consequence of a constellation of wicked forces, both within and outside Germany that had frustrated

Germany's righteous cause. They eagerly welcomed the "stab in the back" legend and continued to think resentfully and contemptuously of the Allied powers. In short, they would not be reconciled with the post-1919 political realities, at least inwardly.

The brutal fact was that Germany had been most forcefully eliminated from the ranks of the great powers. This weighed heavily upon the minds of the German professoriate in general, and it particularly concerned the historians and theologians who had been at the forefront in delivering a rationale for imperial German expansion. Under these circumstances their previous schema of historical or war theology had to be readjusted. This explains the shift in direction among many Protestant pastors and theologians in Germany towards a so-called *Schöpfungstheologie*, that is, the theology of creation, according to which the world was comprised of various "orders of creation." These were the givens of international life such as the *Volk* or nation, the people of the one blood.[26] This brand of theology, called also *Ordnungstheologie*, or the theology of orders of creation, came into its own during the Nazi period and was championed by a number of high-profile theologians. Their more sober-minded and clear-sighted Swiss colleague, Barth, took a highly critical view of them and perceptively traced their mentality back to the war theology of the prewar era.[27] What they now advocated with considerable fervor was that the *nation of one blood* had been chosen by God to execute His will on earth. It was an extreme form of nationalist theology that needs to be understood if we are to comprehend what happened in the "Church Struggle" after 1933 when Hitler seized power. Awareness of it is also necessary in order to appreciate what Bonhoeffer and the few supporters among his brother clergy had to confront.

After his two semesters at Tübingen where he received a thorough grounding in philosophy, Bonhoeffer and his brother Klaus were enabled through their parents' generosity to spend a semester abroad based in Rome. Dietrich had severely injured himself in a fall while skating and had been unconscious for some time. This alarmed his parents, who traveled to Tübingen to take care of him. The visit coincided with Dietrich's eighteenth birthday, 4 February 1924, and he expressed the wish to travel to Italy, whereupon the Bonhoeffer parents made this financially possible. The brothers crossed the Alps on 4 April. The Rome experience proved to be of major significance. Bethge commented:

> The fascination exercised by Catholic Rome became a permanent influence on Bonhoeffer's thought. It cannot be said to have diminished his critical awareness, but the universality of the Church and its liturgy in its Roman guise made a tremendous impact on him, even before his encounter with Karl Barth's theology.[28]

Compared to the magnificence and cosmopolitanism of the city of Rome and the great Church of Rome, Bonhoeffer assessed his own church as provincial, nationalistic, and narrow-minded, so the sojourn became the first of a series of experiences that enabled Bonhoeffer finally to escape the oppressive and even incestuous ethos of German Protestantism without ever, of course, abandoning the great "catholic insights" that Luther had made in the sixteenth century concerning justification and the forgiveness of sins that became the essence of the Protestant principle. This may sound very confusing if one does not appreciate that Luther's key theological insight on justification is essentially *catholic*, as it is clearly based on a careful reading of St. Paul's Epistle to the Romans—and if it is anchored in the text of Holy Scripture it is by definition "catholic." The Roman Catholic Church and the Lutheran Church have now come to a formal agreement on this in an historic statement entitled "Alle unter einem Christus—All under One Christ."[29]

After Rome, Bonhoeffer began his more focused study of theology at Berlin among the leading scholars of the day. In the case of Adolf von Harnack, he was sitting at the feet of the foremost authority on the world of New Testament and early church history; while with professor Karl Holl he became steeped in Luther studies. With the internationally acclaimed Adolf Deissman, the theologian-archaeologist who had revolutionized biblical studies with his discoveries, Bonhoeffer extended his knowledge of the New Testament and, at the same time, came into contact with the man who would introduce him to the ecumenical movement of the day. However, for his doctoral dissertation supervisor, Bonhoeffer chose Reinhold Seeberg, not because he was an ardent German nationalist but rather because of his competence as a systematic theologian and possibly because of Seeberg's reputation as a doctoral supervisor who allowed his students a certain independence of thought. Certainly, this gave Bonhoeffer the freedom to develop his own ideas. There is, however, a reciprocal relationship between professor and student at this level, and Bonhoeffer won from Seeberg, together with a firm grasp of Hegelian method, the concept of "Christ existing as community," in short, a highly refined comprehension of the church as the body of Christ functioning in human society. And this became the subject of Bonhoeffer's dissertation, *Sanctorum Communio*, "the communion of saints," that is, the church in the world. The subtitle read: "A Dogmatic Enquiry into the Sociology of the Church."[30]

The crucial thing, however, is that Bonhoeffer did not become slavishly dependent upon Seeberg's strongly Hegelian concepts, and so he was able to approached his subject autonomously. Fortunately, Seeberg respected his student's independence of mind and did not interfere excessively in the preparation of the thesis. And here a quote from Bethge provides an important clue that Bonhoeffer had begun to take a stance independent from his mentors:

> But, since he had already begun to be fascinated by Barth when he first sat at Seeberg's feet, criticism of his master set in immediately. He rejected out of hand Seeberg's attempt to harmonize the Bible and the modern spirit, Luther and idealism, theology and philosophy.[31]

This paragraphs needs careful investigation to determine its full meaning. What Bethge seems to be saying here is that the "modern spirit" was expressed in German liberal theology that derived so much from Hegel who bequeathed the schema of seeing the history of the state as the "path of God in the world." But Bonhoeffer, under Barth's influence, came to see that one could not understand the state, the creation of men, as the dynamic product of revelation, that is, the word of God, or bring the two into a creative reciprocal relationship as von Harnack and his many German disciples had tried to do. Karl Barth strenuously opposed this way of thinking, and was adamant that God in his inestimable majesty could never be comprehended and considered to be at the disposal of mere mortals. It was precisely over this point that Harnack so angrily and firmly distanced himself from Barth; but as indicated, Bonhoeffer steered a middle course between the two. Barth had already made his systematic repudiation of Harnack's position, and also that of the majority of his colleagues, in his famous commentary on the Epistle to the Romans, in 1918. This was a work of seminal significance that attacked the basic assumptions upon which the theology of these influential men was based. Essentially, Barth highlighted the untenability of their claim that men, no matter how learned, could comprehend the mind of God. To quote one telling passage: "For when we have clearly perceived that, if divinity be so concreted and humanized in a particular department of history—the history of religion or the history of salvation—God has ceased to be God."[32]

To put it in technical language, Harnack, Seeberg, and their disciples represented the "'genetic-historical" method whereas Barth, abstracting the church from history altogether, employed a "theological-dogmatic" method. That is to say, Harnack, relying heavily on the philosophy of Hegel, insisted upon understanding the church as being embedded, as it were, in the evolving history of humanity, while Barth's point of departure was the plain word of God as bequeathed to humankind in the bible, that is, revelation, and this stood outside human history, abstracted from the affairs of men.[33]

Consequently, in Bonhoeffer's first major theological statement, his doctoral thesis, we find elements of both schools of thought. As his objective was to analyze the essential nature of the church in the world as a unique society, a community of the faithful, Bonhoeffer, true to the "liberal" tradition, made use of the great German sociologists of the day, such as Ferdinand Tönnies (1855–1936), Ernst Troeltsch (1865–1923), and Max Weber (1864–1920), applying their concepts to help define an association—i.e., the church—that is *in* the world but not *of* the world. At the same time, however, he wished to bring sociology into harmony with the theology of revelation, or, in short, to reconcile Troeltsch and Barth. This aim would appear at first glance to be unattainable, but Bonhoeffer imaginatively borrowed a concept from Hegel who had observed that God existed as community; now he transformed it into "Christ existing as community." As Bethge commented:

> To Hegel the community was the dwelling place of the Holy Spirit in the form of the absolute spirit. To Seeberg it was the dwelling-place of the Holy Spirit in the form of absolute will. Bonhoeffer set out to refashion the whole Christologically, believing that he was overcoming the Troeltsch-Barth antithesis by attaining an overriding third position. Later critics regarded this as more bold than successful.[34]

The doctoral thesis was eventually published in 1930, but it made no impact at the time. Indeed, why would it? Bonhoeffer's cousin Hans-Christoph von Hase wrote to him saying, "There will not be many who understand it, the Barthians won't because of the sociology, and the sociologists won't because of Barth."[35] Nevertheless, it was far more than the product of a theological *Wunderkind*. When he presented it in 1927, Bonhoeffer was just twenty-one. He had completed it in eighteen months while leading an extraordinarily full social life alongside the preparation of the seminar papers required by his other professors. The thesis was written, however, with Barth in mind because Bonhoeffer was concerned that Barth's concept of revelation had left too little room for the church in his scheme of things. And so, with Bonhoeffer's identification of Christ with the church, he had established the foundations for a revitalization of the sense of Christian community among the faithful. Revelation only became meaningful within the framework of the community where the proclamation of the gospel took place, where people met to praise God, to pray, and to unite for service to their fellow human beings—in short, to respond to the promptings of the Spirit that took place within the community of the faithful.

In a real sense, *Sanctorum Communio* was the platform for Bonhoeffer's theological take-off, despite its inevitable immaturity. Barth commented on it in 1955—he had not taken notice of it before—and was very positive about it, saying:

If there is one thing that justifies Reinhold Seeberg, it may lie in the fact that there emerged from his school this man and this thesis which, with its broad and deep vision, not only rouses the deepest respect when one looks back at the situation at the time, but also is to this very day more instructive, more stimulating, more enlightening and more truly 'edifying' to read than a great deal of the better-known writing that has since been published on the problem of the church.[36]

This judgment was accurate because Bonhoeffer's early work became obligatory reading for the beleaguered Lutherans in the former German Democratic Republic, where Christians under the communist yoke needed an encouraging doctrine of the church in order to have a basis for standing fast against the hostile church policy of the Communist regime. There, the faithful were forced to realize that the church was not exclusively a community of faith but rather one based on love and service to others, *regardless of their status*—in short, "a church for others."[37]

Without doubt, Bonhoeffer's doctoral thesis signified that here a new Lutheran voice was being raised that was autonomous, not confined to the Procrustean bed of the dominant "liberal" school that imposed a distinct cultural nationalism on its concept of the church. With Bonhoeffer, the church was emphatically an active community grounded in love, placing no restrictions upon who was to be the recipient of that love, certainly not limited to the one specific nation. Indeed, it was the universal community. The intellectual/theological seeds that Bonhoeffer planted in 1927 had struck deep roots. They flourished many years later while he was in prison writing his so-called *Tegel theology*, between 5 April 1943 and his execution on 9 April 1945.

With the acceptance of the dissertation by the theological faculty at the University of Berlin, Bonhoeffer's career as a theologian had begun. And although his supervisor, Seeberg, was never enthusiastic for Barthian ideas, he was well predisposed toward Bonhoeffer. Indeed, the professor was sufficiently magnanimous and grateful to adopt his student's ideas on theological exegesis that Bonhoeffer had presented in a seminar in 1925, and to use them in a paper he published himself.[38] That was certainly a great compliment paid by a master to his brilliant pupil.

It remained for Bonhoeffer to prepare his post-doctoral thesis, the *Habilitation*, as an essential prerequisite for advancement to a full professorial chair in the German university system. However, before that, on 17 January 1928, Bonhoeffer sat for his first theological examination—a preliminary to ordination, but was not ordained because he had not yet reached the canonical age. He therefore took up the post of lay assistant, called in German, *Vikar*, to the pastor in charge of the German congregation in Barcelona, Spain, on 15 February. The sojourn in Spain was to be Bonhoeffer's second significant learning experience outside Germany. Its relevance to our topic lies in the fact that as a twenty-three-year-old German he was ministering to what the Germans call the *deutsche Kolonie* in Barcelona, that is, the German expatriates working there in various commercial, artistic, or consular capacities. It is reported that the pastor in charge was not exactly one of those clergymen who was totally involved in his calling; he had apparently more time for a glass of good red wine and a cigar than he had for preparing his sermons. It appears, then, that Bonhoeffer filled a certain deficit in theological instruction for the congregation during the year he spent in Barcelona. The quality of his sermons and addresses that have survived from that period testify to the diligence of their preparation and to the depth of his commitment, especially those addresses prepared for the youth group. One of these is of particular importance in any attempt to trace Bonhoeffer's intellectual/theological development. It is called *Grundfragen einer christlichen Ethik*, or, "basic questions of a Christian ethic."[39]

What it indicates is that the young patriotic Bonhoeffer was still groping toward a genuine peace ethic that was totally free of patriotic bias. In a real sense, it makes him more credible because one could hardly expect the young man to "jump over his own shadow," as it were, and from one day to the next, to throw off the effect of years of fervent German patriotic education and embrace a full blooded cosmopolitanism. The lecture in question was the last talk he gave to the youth of the Barcelona German community. Bonhoeffer was trying to make the young Germans there more conscious of the impact of the Great War and the subsequent revolution on their fatherland. Clearly, the loss of his older brother in what must have seemed to Bonhoeffer a hopeless cause weighed heavily on him.

The thrust of the lecture was to exculpate Germany from any sense of guilt for the outbreak and duration of the war as was stipulated in the Treaty of Versailles. It should not be forgotten that the peace treaty was regarded in Germany as a brutal *Diktat* and, in conservative and business circles, because of the heavy reparations obligations, was the chief explanation for all of Germany's postwar economic problems.

As mentioned earlier, a particular school of theology had begun to emerge in the early 1920s, the *Schöpfungtheologie* or *Ordnungstheologie* in which the state, and more particularly the *Volk*, were designated as "orders of creation," key elements in God's plan for the salvation of humanity. This was precisely the theology of *national Protestantism* in Germany, from which Bonhoeffer in his doctoral thesis had clearly distanced himself, or at least he appeared to have done so. Now, in

Barcelona, however, a good decade after the war, he seems to have experienced quite a dramatic reversal in his conviction.

In the lecture Bonhoeffer was at pains to stress that Germany's behavior in the Great War could be harmonized with the Christian teaching of brotherly love. As well, he was concerned to defend the church from the reproach that it had failed the nation during the war because it had ardently justified the war. Bonhoeffer now prioritized the *Volk* as an order of creation as follows:

> God gave me to my mother and to my *Volk*; what I have is due to this *Volk*; what I am, I am because of my *Volk* and therefore that which I have belongs to my *Volk*. *That is the divine order of things, because God created the nations. If I remained passive in a dangerous situation that would be nothing less than the betrayal of my neighbor.*[40] [emphasis added]

Bonhoeffer then went on to say that, of course, one would not hate one's enemy because he was in the same situation of having to defend his mother, children, and his *Volk*. Nevertheless, in the dilemma between the New Testament commandment to love one's enemies and the obligation to love one's own *Volk*, one had to decide for the *Volk* because that would undoubtedly conform to the will of God. Further, he argued, it was not a choice between good and evil because, although one took up arms and spilt blood, the love one owed to one's *Volk* would justify the murder one had to commit in the course of protecting one's people; indeed it justified war itself.

As if that were not sufficient, Bonhoeffer in his enthusiasm to inspire his young audience with pride in the fatherland went a step further to justify a war of aggression:

> Every *Volk* perceives a call from God to make history, to involve itself actively in the struggle of the nations. One may not fail to heed this call out of the process of growth and development [of the nations] so that it may happen in the sight of God. Indeed, God calls the *Volk* to a range of actions [*Mannigfaltigkeit*], to struggle and victory. Strength is from God as is the power and the victory, because God creates youth in men as with nations and he loves youth because God is himself eternally young and strong and victorious. Indeed, fear and weakness should be overcome by courage and strength. So then, when a *Volk* that experiences such a call within its own life, to its youth and to its strength, should such a *Volk* now not be permitted to follow that call even if it means doing so at the expense of the life of other peoples? God is the Lord of history; and if a *Volk* submits in humility to this sacred will that guides the history of the world then it is able with God in His youth and strength, to overcome weakness and cowardice.[41]

The assumptions in the mind of Bonhoeffer, as he wrote this lecture, seem to be based clearly on the philosophy of the power struggle as taught by Hegel and which was regarded as paradigmatic for all nationalist German theologians, as well as historians, of the day. One wonders how Bonhoeffer seemed to go into reverse with regard to his theology in *Sanctorum Communio* in which he clearly distanced himself from the nationalist position of his former teacher, Adolf von Harnack, and his school. Now, in Barcelona, however, early in 1929, Bonhoeffer appears to be committed to the Harnack mind-set. There is, of course, the fact that he was still mourning the death of his elder brother at the front, but also to be borne in mind is the nature of the audience to whom he was speaking. Those young expatriate Germans in Barcelona would all have been patriotic and hardly inclined to endorse a pacifist position. Indeed, they would have all been seething with indignation at the humiliating conditions of the Treaty of Versailles. Bonhoeffer would certainly have appreciated that and may have decided to adopt a line of reasoning that he felt would be helpful to his theologically unsophisticated audience. It is hardly likely that Bonhoeffer was guilty of calculated intellectual dishonesty.

Commentators are quick to point out that Bonhoeffer never again used such language. Here his biographer noted that, "he inadvertently moved to a position close to that of those who complained of their nation's lack of *Lebensraum*, space to live in. [But] Neither in his sermons nor in his letters did he ever make any such statements again."[42] Nonetheless, it reflected sharply the mind-set of the ultra-nationalist war theology of orders of creation that welcomed the advent of the Third Reich. This episode, therefore, makes more intriguing the process by which Bonhoeffer very soon after came to abandon that position and become the most determined opponent of war or nationalist theology—indeed, an inspired and doughty advocate of peace among the nations. Decisive experiences and influences came into effect that derived from the advice of his legally trained brother and brothers-in-law, but particularly from the time spent in Union Seminary, New York. All these combined to make possible a complete transformation in values. The Barcelona lecture with its strident nationalism faded like a blip on the screen, never to reappear. It nevertheless represents the disastrous mind-set shared by most of Bonhoeffer's contemporaries, and demonstrates how difficult it was for them to adopt a critical response to the advent of Hitler, whose rhetoric about the will of "Providence" (*die Vorsehung*) for the *Volk* proved to be so universally seductive to Germans still smarting, as they were, under the shame of the 1918 defeat and the perceived injustice of the Versailles *Diktat*.

Notes

1. The volume of literature seeking to explain the "Protestant Revolution" in the German Democratic Republic is extremely large. However, a concise introduction to the witness of the Protestant Church in the former East Germany against the Communist tyranny is provided by Gregory Baum, *The Church for Others: Protestant Theology in East Germany* (Grand Rapids, 1996). The legacy of Bonhoeffer as an inspiration to many among the Protestant leadership in East Germany is duly acknowledged here.

2. Martin Luther's views on the necessity of warfare are contained in his tract *Ob Kriegsleute selig sein können* ("Whether Soldiers, Too, Can Be Saved"). See *Luther's Works* (American edition), vol. 46, ed. R. C. Schultz (Philadelphia, 1967), 87–137.

3. Heinrich Ritter von Srbik, *Geist und Geschichte* (Munich, 1950), vol. I, 189.

4. The renowned German Professor of History at Hamburg post-1945, Fritz Fischer, evaluated this element of German historical development as having been fateful for the political culture of Prusso-Germany. See John A. Moses, *The Politics of Illusion: The Fischer Controversy in German Historiography* (London/New York, 1975).

5. See note 13 in the previous chapter and the section "Hegel and the German Reich."

6. See *Moltke: Leben und Werk in Selbstzeugnissen: Briefe, Schriften, Reden* selected and introduced by Max Horst, Birsfelden bei Basel: (no year), 351. See also Richard Steigmann-Gall, *The Holy Reich—Nazi Conceptions of Christianity* (Cambridge/New York, 2003).

7. Wolfgang J. Mommsen, *Max Weber and German Politics, 1890–1920* (Chicago, 1984), 69.

8. There is an extensive literature on the German working class movement, but see Francis L. Carsten's biography of the Social Democratic leader, August Bebel (1840–1913), *August Bebel und die Organisation der Massen* (Berlin, 1991).

9. For an investigation of the way in which organized labor was perceived by the Prusso-German State, and how the trade unions in particular tried to establish what they perceived to be their rightful position in both the German economy and society, see John A. Moses, *Trade Unionism in Germany from Bismarck to Hitler*, 2 vols. (London/New York, 1982).

10. Bethge, *Bonhoeffer*, 3 [cf. 2000, 3]. See also Sabine Leibholz-Bonhoeffer, *Vergangen Erlebt Überwunden: Schicksale der Familie Bonhoeffer* (Gütersloh, 1995). In addition, see the memoir of Sabine Leibholz by Edwin Robertson, in *Bonhoeffer Rundbrief*, no. 60, (October, 1999): 42–44.

11. Ibid., 20–27 [cf. 2000, 34–31].

12. Ibid., 48 [cf. 2000, 70–71].

13. Ibid., 17 [cf. 2000, 30].

14. On Deissmann, see Albrecht Gerber, *Deissmann the Philologist* (Berlin/New York, 2010).

15. Karl Hammer, *Deutsche Kriegstheologie 1870–1918* (Frankfurt/Main, 1971), 50–57; Klaus Vondung, *Die Apokalypse in Deutschland* (Frankfurt, 1988), 189–207.

16. John A. Moses, "The Mobilisation of the Intellectuals 1914–1915 and the Continuity of German Historical Consciousness," *Australian Journal of Politics and History* 48, no. 3 (September 2002): 336–52. See also Wolfgang J. Mommsen, ed., *Kultur und Krieg: Die Rolle der Intellektuellen, Künstler und Schriftsteller im Ersten Weltkrieg* (Munich, 1996); Jürgen von Ungern-Sternberg and Wolfgang von Ungern-Sternberg, *Der Aufruf "An die Kulturwelt!"* (Stuttgart, 1996); Steffen Bruendel, *Volksgemeinschaft oder Volksstaat: Die "Ideen von 1914" und die Neuordnung Deutschlands im Ersten Weltkrieg* (Berlin, 2003).

17. Bethge, *Bonhoeffer*, 50 [cf. 2000, 73].

18. Ibid., 51; 131 [cf. 2000, 74; 175].

19. Hammer, *Kriegstheologie*, 374.

20. Klaus Böhme, *Aufrufe und Reden deutscher Professoren im Ersten Weltkrieg* (Stuttgart, 1975) 125–37. Seeberg's own collected essays on the First World War are published in *Geschichte, Krieg und Seele: Reden und Aufsätze aus den Tagen des Welkrieges* (Leipzig, 1916).

21. Bethge, *Bonhoeffer*, 48 [cf. 2000, 70–71].

22. Ibid., 32–34 [cf. 2000, 51–53]. See also Hanfried Müller, *Von Kirche zur Welt* (Hamburg-Bergstedt, 1961).

23. On the "stab-in-the-back" legend, see John W. Wheeler-Bennett, *The Nemesis of Power-The German Army in Politics 1918–1945* (London, 1961), 3–82 passim.

24. Hanfried Müller, "Dietrich Bonhoeffer—Christuszeuge in der Bekennenden Kirche für die mündige Welt," *Bonhoeffer-Studien*, ed. Albrecht Schönherr and Wolf Krötke (Berlin, 1985) 37, 40. Müller is careful to isolate Bonhoeffer from what he terms here the "clerical-estate." These cultivated so-called *faschistoid* ideals that were shared by many of the Protestant clergy of the day. Müller's critique of the Protestant *clerus* of the time is, of course, colored by his Marxist-Leninist commitment. He occupied a chair in theology at the Humboldt University in East Berlin until the collapse of the communist regime there.

25. This Hegelian-inspired outlook certainly dominated the German intellectual world at the time. See Hubert Kiesewetter, *Von Hegel zu Hitler*. Here is carefully documented just how extensively Hegel's philosophy of the state had permeated the thinking of German social scientists, including historians, jurists, and politicians as well as theologians.

26. Klaus Scholder, *The Churches and the Third Reich* (London, 1988), vol. 1, 99–100. For an illuminating study of this school of theological thought, see Robert P. Eriksen, *Theologians under Hitler. Gerhard Kittel, Paul Althaus and Emanuel Hirsch* (New Haven /London: 1985).

27. Karl Barth, *The German Church in Conflict* (London, 1965), 8.

28. Bethge, *Bonhoeffer* 38. [cf. 2000, 59].

29. See, *Roman Catholic/Lutheran Joint Commission Statement on the Augsburg Confession*, signed at Augsburg, 23 February, 1980 *Lutheran World Information*, December, 1980.

30. For an in-depth analysis of the essential nature of Bonhoeffer's theology see Clifford J. Green, *Bonhoeffer—A Theology of Sociality*, 2nd rev. ed. (Grand Rapids, 1999).

31. Bethge, *Bonhoeffer*, 48. [cf. 2000, 70–71].

32. See the translation of the sixth edition of the *Epistle to the Romans* by Edwyn C. Hoskyns (Oxford, 1968), 79. As well, see Thomas Albert Howard, *Protestant Theology and the Making of the Modern German University* (Oxford, 2006), 410–18, where the conflict between Harnack and Barth is examined from a mainly theological standpoint.

33. Eckhard Lessing, "Die theologischen Anfänge" in *Verkündigung und Forschung* 46, no. 2 (2001): 5.

34. Bethge, *Bonhoeffer*, 59 [cf. 2000, 83].

35. Ibid., 58–59 [cf. 2000, 83].

36. Ibid., 60 [cf. 2000, 180].

37. John A. Moses, "Bonhoeffer's Reception in East Germany," in *Bonhoeffer for a New Day: Theology in Transition*, ed. John W. de Gruchy (Grand Rapids, 1997), 278–97.

38. Bethge, *Bonhoeffer* 57 [cf. 2000, 80].

39. In *Barcelona, Berlin, Amerika 1928–1931*, DBW, X (Munich, 1991), 323–345. A partial English translation of this lecture exists, entitled "What Is a Christian Ethic?" in *No Rusty Swords*, 39–48. However, it is precisely the crucial passages dealt with here that are deleted from the shortened translated version.

40. Ibid., 337; emphasis added.

41. Ibid., 339–40. Cf. Clifford Green, *Bonhoeffer—A Theology of Sociality*, 127–28. Note that Green translates *Mannigfaltigkeit* as "manliness" whereas the dictionary gives it as "multiplicity," "variety," and "diversity." It may well be that Bonhoeffer was thinking of Paul's first Epistle to the Corinthians, chapter 12, in which Paul speaks of the variety of gifts that derive from the one Holy Spirit. The power and strength required to engage in the eternal struggle for survival are ultimately gifts from God.

42. Bethge, *Bonhoeffer*, 86 [cf. 2000, 119]. Clifford Green (see previous footnote) affirms this and goes on to point out that the "orders of creation" theology that underpinned the Barcelona address was also not long after discarded by Bonhoeffer as an "adequate foundation for Christian ethics" (128).

3

THE PROBLEM OF ANTI-SEMITISM IN GERMANY FROM LUTHER TO HITLER

At this point it is necessary to introduce the Jewish Question, as it is central to Bonhoeffer's development as a revolutionary in the context of the Third Reich.[1] Indeed, it is the key to understanding Bonhoeffer's new kind of Lutheran theology. As will be shown, Bonhoeffer, reacting to the persecution of the Jews in Nazi Germany as he did, with very little support from his coreligionists, overthrew centuries of Christian prejudice and theological debate on the role of the Jews in the history of the church. In doing so he had built a theological bridge for Christian-Jewish reconciliation, the construction of which will be investigated in the penultimate chapter. Here the concern is to trace the evolution of Christian anti-Judaism and anti-Semitism, focusing on Germany where it culminated in the Holocaust.

Hostility to the Jews was a Europe-wide phenomenon with a history that went back to the Roman Empire and is, indeed, found already expressed in the New Testament. One of the chief aims of St. Luke writing the Acts of the Apostles was to describe the gradual separation of the Church from Israel as two quite discrete entities. At that time a process of defamation set in that peaked in the famous passage in John 8:44, where Jesus is reported as saying to Jews who were questioning him, "You are of your father the devil, and your will is to do your father's desires. He was a murderer from the beginning, and has nothing to do with the truth." And again there are two passages in the Book of Revelation, 2:9 and 3:9 that identify the Synagogue with Satan.[2]

These inflammatory statements are hard to reconcile with the rabbi Jesus' own Jewish identity, and are more likely to be part of the agenda of the unknown authors of the Acts of the Apostles and the fourth gospel.[3] However, even if the statements were *viva voce* those of Jesus, they could be interpreted as a consequence of his Jewish interlocutors refusing to afford him hospitality, that is, to give him a hearing. There were many competing factions or parties among the Jews at that time, and here Jesus could only have been reproaching those Jews who had turned their back on the heritage of Abraham. Scholars such as the

American Episcopalian Bishop John Spong have investigated in detail all the anti-Semitic expressions in the New Testament (and subsequently, by church leaders) and concluded that the New Testament passages cannot be held up as signs of Jesus' own anti-Semitism. He was, after all, an extremely pious rabbi whose agenda was solely to purify the Jewish tradition.[4] However, the New Testament sayings were no doubt portentous, given the subsequent interpretations. Certainly, there are Jewish scholars today in Germany who have no difficulty in asserting that Christianity in its very essence is anti-Semitic. There is a difference, however, between anti-Judaism and anti-Semitism.[5]

If one visits Strasbourg cathedral in Alsace, finally completed in 1439, which is a German Gothic edifice with a strong family resemblance both to the nearby Freiburg minster and Ulm cathedral, there are located on a pillar in the nave two small female figures in stone facing each other. One is the bent and blindfolded *Synagogia* and the other the radiant and upright *Ecclesia*. This is the expression of the long tradition of Christian anti-Judaism, not to be confused with anti-Semitism. Anti-Judaism, as the Strasbourg statues portray, is based on the notion that the New Covenant superseded the Old Covenant, rather than augmenting it, and that the church became the sole repository of all revelation and therefore inherently superior to Judaism. This is called *Theologia Gloriae*, and as Spong's study illustrates, it dominated the Christian church down through the centuries until our own time. The only way in which Jews could avoid the persecution that characterized Jewish-Christian relations for so long was for them to become baptized. In short, the Christian church was always anti-Judaistic, and at many phases of history quite violently so.

Anti-Semitism is a relatively recent concept derived from the notion that Jews were racially and biologically inferior and that their presence within the nation was corrosive and ultimately socially disintegrating. Moreover, there arose the absurd accusation that Jews were conspiring to take over the world and that their presence within host societies was a form of "racial poison." A certain number of writers went into print demanding the expulsion and/or extermination of Jewish communities.[6] That, of course, was a product of nineteenth century racial theories.[7] Such theories were made popular in Germany by several writers, but the one who first used the term *anti-Semitism* was the Hamburg journalist Wilhelm Marr in 1873, and he was the first also to demand the physical extermination of the Jewish population by means of pogroms.[8] There has recently been much discussion of this subject owing mainly to the publications of Daniel Goldhagen, who distinguished between two kinds of anti-Semitism. The first he called eliminationist, which was the demand to eliminate the Jewish cultural and religious presence from the host society either by getting Jews to convert to Christianity or to emigrate. The second is exterminatory, meaning the physical murder of Jews.[9] The one eventually led to the other in Nazi Germany, as will be shown.

Saul Friedländer explains the background to this by identifying the concept of "redemptive anti-Semitism."[10] This, he argues, was born of the fear of racial degeneration on the one hand, and the religious belief in redemption in Germany, on the other. Indeed, the main cause of racial degeneration was, as Friedländer observes, "the penetration of the Jews into the German body politic, into German society, and into the German bloodstream. Germanhood and the Aryan world were on the path to perdition if the struggle against the Jews was not joined; this was to be a struggle to the death. Redemption would come as liberation from the Jews—as their expulsion, possibly their annihilation."[11]

With hindsight, we can observe that this kind of anti-Semitism became especially virulent in Germany. Indeed, it is impossible to conceive of the Holocaust without there having been a long history of peculiar hostility towards Jews that was justified in both pseudoscientific and religious/theological terms.[12] It appears that peoples in many countries the world over and throughout history have been and are susceptible to a variety of racial theories that demonize the "other" for the sake of promoting national cohesion, and thereby they have justified and condoned genocide.[13]

Further, with regard to the phenomenon of anti-Semitism it would have to be observed that there were virulent examples of it elsewhere in nineteenth-century Europe, as evidenced by the pogroms in czarist Russia and the Dreyfus affair in France. Recent research has also drawn attention to violence against Jewish minorities in a number of other European countries.[14] Interestingly, however, in Bismarckian-Wilhelmine Germany the upsurge of anti-Semitic propaganda did not at the time result in officially sanctioned violence against Jews because it would have been unconstitutional. Indeed, as the late Israeli scholar Walter Grab has pointed out, the Reich constitution of 1871 had *graciously* granted to the Jewish minority in Germany equality before the law, but these privileges were *ungraciously* withdrawn under the Third Reich some sixty years later. That was a phenomenon of the Nazi era when the concept of law and constitutional rights applying equally to all citizens, regardless of race or religion, had been discarded under the new, "folkish" (*völkisch*) dictatorship which made blood kinship the principle of citizenship. It was a concept that produced disastrous consequences.

In the anti-Semitic writings that Hitler, for example, had read voraciously in his youth, the existence of Jews in German society was likened to the presence of bacillae that would infect the main body of the people if intermarriage with Jews was allowed to go unchecked. Jews did not have to be present in vast numbers; like all kinds of bacillae, a small infestation was sufficient to wreak irreparable damage on a body. An essentially healthy body could be gradually infected, and the "pure" Germanic racial heritage would be diluted and weakened.[15] In the writings of the nineteenth-century anti-Semites, then, it was simply the fact that there were Jews present in German society, some occupying high-profile positions in the world of commerce, banking, education, and the professions, especially journalism, that gave cause for an alarm that lacked any basis in fact.

The Peculiar Status of Jewish Subjects in Imperial Germany

In order to achieve a right perspective on the history of the Holocaust in the Nazi era it is necessary to establish the facts relating to the Jews within the self-styled "pure" Germanic host society. Overcoming ignorance in this regard is an essential precondition to achieving a measure of understanding. Scholars such as Thomas Nipperdey, late professor of modern history at the University of Munich, have pursued this question in some detail, precisely to establish how hysterical the views of anti-Semitic publicists and activists were.[16] The actual number of Jews in Germany in 1871 was some 512,000, rising to 615, 000 in 1910. That was a growth of about 20 percent; but in relation to the growth of the entire population it represented a significant decline from 1.25 to 0.95 percent. So the Jews were in fact a tiny minority. What was it, then, that aroused such hostility toward them? The fact is that, as indicated, Jews in Germany occupied a special status within German society of the late nineteenth and early twentieth centuries. A breakdown of their professional employment statistics shows that, in the industrial society that Germany had become, Jews still practiced their traditional professions from earlier times. With passage of time, however, they had become increasingly more established within the prosperous middle class, having adjusted to a large degree to the mores of the host population. Their involvement in agriculture remained minimal as before, while the number of Jewish tradesmen continued at around 15 percent of the overall Jewish workforce. On the other hand, the number of Jews in commerce and banking was disproportionately high, even though statistics show a slight regression from 52.1 percent of the total Jewish number of employees in 1895 to 49.4 by 1907, which meant, looking at the entire population, 10.2 to 11.5 percent respectively. But in Berlin, 1907, it was 25 percent, which made the Jewish presence in the commerce and banking sector in the national capital somewhat more visible. The presence of Jews in trade and industry was correspondingly smaller, specifically, 19.3 percent (1895) and 21.9 percent (1907).[17]

Further statistical breakdown indicates that while the majority of Jews were not rich, there was a notable number of Jews among the very well-to-do in German society—and that among *them* there were some who were very rich indeed. As Nipperdey demonstrated, this development started in the middle of the nineteenth century, or, in other words, co-terminus with Germany's industrial revolution, and took off significantly after the unification of Germany in 1871. For example, in commerce there were a number of Jewish-owned giant companies in the department store, mail order, and wholesale sectors, among which were the nationally reputed houses of L. H. and later O. Tietz as well as the house of Wertheim, all highly successful enterprises.

In the banking sector there were a considerable number of Jewish-owned private banks, but they fell in number between 1895 (1977) and 1907 (1851). On the other hand the number of Jewish bank directors and branch managers rose in the same period from 2,528 to 3,179. In Berlin, in 1895, 37 percent of the owners and directors of banks were Jews. Correspondingly, the Jewish proportion of the entrepreneurial class as well as the leading employees of firms grew considerably. Almost 20 percent of the textile industry was in Jewish hands, while Jews were prominent in the electrical, metal and machinery, and manufacturing industries. L. Loewe's engineering works and E. Rathenau's General Electric Company (AEG) were prominent examples. And there were others, less well known. Only in the mining and iron and steel industries were Jews minimally represented.

It has been estimated that by 1910/11 Jews occupied 13.3 percent of 808 directorships and 24.4 percent of 2092 company boards, figures that mirror the Jewish component in the banking sector. In addition to these there were the prominent Jewish personages such as Albert Ballin, director of what became the world's largest shipping line, Hamburg-Amerika (Hapag); the Berlin Press barons Mosse and Ullstein; and the founder and owner of the *Frankfurter Zeitung*, Leopold Sonnemann. And among the one hundred richest men in Prussia in 1910 there were twenty-nine Jews, while in Frankfurt, the house of Rothschild was the fourth richest in the country. In Berlin itself ten out of the eleven wealthiest firms were in Jewish hands. As Nipperdey points out, some of these Jewish magnates belonged to the "establishment" of the empire as the names Fürstenberg, Rathenau, Warburg, and the Kaiser's special friend, the above-mentioned Albert Ballin, indicated.[18]

To this extent, Jews in imperial Germany had come to occupy a unique status. Certainly, a peculiar elite had become exceptionally outstanding players in those sectors of the economy described above, that is, as members of the *haute bourgeoisie*. In addition, observing the broader Jewish population, on the basis of their middle-class social status they had become better off than the remainder of the population, as a breakdown of tax returns demonstrated.[19]

To sum up, then, the social profile of Jews in imperial Germany indicated a broad upper and middle class, a small, very rich upper class, and a small, poor lower and lower middle class. And this profile was fundamentally different from that of the remainder of the population. Consequently, Jews stood out from the host population, even if they were "assimilated" in the sense that they had abandoned the observance of their religion, or even if they had become in some instances baptized Christians and wished to identify with the majority population of Germans. Clearly, Jews expected to be able to participate fully in German culture in spite of the social discrimination that undoubtedly occurred. They adjusted to and adopted the educational ideals of the German bourgeoisie; indeed, they were especially concerned not to be outdone by their fellow burghers in acquiring the cultural goods of the *Bildungsbürgertum* and immersed themselves as fully as possible in the vast German literary, musical and artistic heritage.[20] However, this intensive identification of Jews with German culture was never acknowledged or appreciated by the *Bildungsbürgertum*, as will be demonstrated below.

Thomas Nipperdey has judged that Jews in imperial Germany could be considered integrated as individuals, but not, however, as a group. They were "insiders" with regard to education and culture, for example, but "outsiders" in their professional status both within the state and in sections of society. As Nipperdey observed, it was difficult in the light of the barriers erected on both the Jewish and the non-Jewish sides of German society for a Jew to live as both German and Jew, indeed, even to be absolutely certain of an identity, and it was especially difficult for those who had cut their ties with the Jewish religion. Latent and open anti-Semitism frustrated further assimilation and the yearned-for symbiosis with the German bourgeois world. The effect of this situation in which Jews were never either able or allowed to detach themselves from their background resulted in the end in the strengthening of their Jewish cultural identity within Wilhelmine society.[21] And this exceptional status was the background to the blame heaped upon the Jews in particular, alongside communists and social democrats, for the German collapse in the Great War in 1918—the "stab in the back" legend (*Dolchstosslegende*) of which Hitler made such great play of in his autobiography, *Mein Kampf*.[22] The views he expressed there about the deleterious effect of Jews in German society and how they had deliberately hindered the German war effort, were, it has to be observed, not simply confined to one Bohemian outsider but rather were the convictions of wide sections of the German middle and upper classes.[23]

The litmus test of this deep-seated rejection of Jews in German society was provided by a decree of the Prussian war minister (11 October 1916) ordering a census of all Jews in the armed forces, "to determine ... how many Jews subject to military duty were serving in every unit of the German armies."[24] The census was held on 1 November 1916, but the results of the census were not published during the war. Only rumors were circulating about it, alleging that Jews were shirkers. In the early 1920s, however, a systematic study of the data revealed the census to have been fraudulent. In actual fact Jewish participation in frontline service was the equivalent to that of the general population, with a minimal deviation due to age and occupational structure.[25]

Here was a situation in which anti-Semitic authorities, officials, and army officers, were determined to make scapegoats of an unpopular section of the population that had a reputation for profiteering, or if they were in the army, to have secured themselves safe desk jobs. The mystery is why the authorities would want to do this at such a time. Such behavior fits neatly into Friedländer's notion of "redemptive anti-Semitism." The Jewish minority was being maligned, especially during the crisis situation of the war when the initial expectation of a rapid victory ("home before Christmas" 1914) for Germany had evaporated. Instead, a long and costly conflict ensued, the victorious outcome of which was by no means certain. Some group had to be made responsible, and the Jews fulfilled this requirement. In this way, they, beside the social democrats and communists, became an integral part of the stab-in-the-back legend of 1918–19. That myth continued to have its negative impact throughout the ill-starred Weimar Republic. Consequently, after the enforced signing of the Treaty of Versailles, most middle- and lower-middle-class Germans, at least, regarded the Jews more than ever as "Germany's misfortune" (*Deutschlands Unglück*). Without this atmosphere it is hard to imagine how the Nazi party would have been able to launch itself as it did. It was certainly Hitler's most effective rallying cry that among those responsible for the misery of the German people after the lost war and the dictated peace treaty, the Jews were most prominent. In this way the seeds planted by the nineteenth-century anti-Semitic writers sprouted and became noxious plants which spread and bore their most pernicious fruit.

The concern at this point is to trace the evolution of anti-Judaism, particularly from the time of Martin Luther (1483–1546) up until its transformation into anti-Semitism and to explain why the Nazis called for the "final solution", the eradication of all Jews from Europe.

The Historic Roots of Anti-Judaism

Prior to the Protestant Reformation of the sixteenth century, the relationship of Jews to Christians had alternated between virulent mutual suspicion and hostility on the one hand, and phases of remarkable tolerance and even good will on the other. The start, as noted, did not augur well for the future. At the beginning, the early fathers of the church taught a theologically based anti-Judaism in order to legitimize the new teaching. John Chrysostom (347–407), for example, preached extremely hostile sermons against the synagogue in the Eastern church, while Augustine of Hippo (354–430) did the same in the West, though not in the same inflammatory way. Nevertheless, Judaism was for Augustine a heresy and the Jews a "thorny and barren people"—"barren" meaning, presumably, not able to bear the right spiritual fruit.[26]

Under the Emperor Justinian (527–565), Jewish religious services were disrupted and Jews were forbidden to use the formula in Deuteronomy 5:4, "Hear O Israel: the Lord our God is one Lord," as it was seen as conflicting with the doctrine of the Trinity. Justinian then promulgated the landmark Codex Justinianus in 529 that formed the basis for further canon law governing church/state relations. Therein legal disabilities were imposed on Jews.

However, with the collapse of the empire in the West in 476, a period of tolerance was ushered in, with the exception of Spain where persecution of Jews continued until the Arab invasion in 711. Interestingly, from today's vantage-point, the Jews and Arabs in Spain lived in peaceful coexistence alongside the Christians. And under the Emperor Charlemagne (768–814), this relative harmony was fostered and continued by subsequent Carolingian emperors so that the epoch from the sixth to the eleventh century in the West witnessed not only peaceful Jewish-Christian relations, but also a flourishing of learning and culture. With the beginning of the Crusades, however, which were ostensibly directed against Islam, the Jews again came under attack. Many crusading knights became convinced that their notion of Christian duty extended beyond the annihilation of Moslems to include the destruction of oriental Jewry.

Then in the fourth Lateran Council in Rome (1215) laws were codified requiring Jews to identify themselves by wearing a badge on their clothes to hinder them from socializing with Christians, to isolate, stigmatize, and separate them, and to enforce social segregation—and this led to the Jews concentrating themselves in ghettos and alleys in the towns. Intermarriage between Jews and non-Jews was religiously impossible. For Christians, marriage was a sacrament that could be entered into only with another Christian. Similarly, the Jews, for their part, would not mix with non-Jews unless the latter became Jews. By this time in the Middle Ages the hostility between church and synagogue had reached its peak. Heinrich Heine (1797–1856), the German-Jewish poet, summed it up with his characteristic irony as follows:

> The great persecution of the Jews began with the Crusades and raged most violently to around the middle of the fourteenth century. Then came the black death, which, as with every other public misfortune, was attributed to the Jews because they had called down the wrath of God, and with the help of lepers poisoned the wells. Then the angry mob, especially the hordes of flagellants, half naked men and women, who, whipping themselves in penance, all the while singing an ecstatic hymn to the Virgin Mary, marauded through the Rhineland and South Germany, murdering many thousands of Jews . . . or forcefully baptizing them. . . . [The result was] the more the hate from outside oppressed them, the more they withdrew into their private sphere and the more deeply rooted became the piety and fear of God among the Jews of Bacharach.[27]

The Reformation contributed nothing to solve this problem. At first, though, the young Luther was not only tolerant but showed genuine good will. In his middle age, however, he became filled with the burning desire to convert the Jews by theological disputation, but when this had no effect he lost all patience, and in the last year of his life he wrote his notorious anti-Jewish pamphlet, "Von den Juden und ihren Lügen" (Concerning the Jews and Their Lies). And in this pamphlet, Luther anticipated the vocabulary and practice of the later pogroms, demanding the destruction of all synagogues and Jewish houses, the confiscation of their prayer books and Talmudic scriptures, the abolition of the rabbinate, the prohibition of Jewish commerce, the removal of legal protection for their caravans, and finally he recommended the enslavement of all Jewish men and women capable of work, and if they did not submit they were to be forcibly exiled.[28]

For Luther, the only way for a Jew to become an acceptable burgher was to submit himself to baptism. Otherwise, Jews were condemned to remain an oppressed minority. The only exception in Germany in this period was in the Duchy of Cleves, where the Prussian Statthalter Johann Moritz von Nassau-Siegen (1604–1679) was governor; under him all religious confessions enjoyed freedom of worship, including Jews. Then, however, the most important development in the emancipation process occurred as a result of the French Revolution of 1789. In the National Assembly in Paris, 1791, all Jews were granted citizenship rights—a democratic decision, and a fact of far reaching significance. Subsequently, when the armies of Napoleon I occupied Germany, the local princes began piecemeal to emancipate Jews by royal decree. In 1812, Prussia ruled the abolition of ghettoes, but there were still disabilities imposed; complete civic rights were not yet accorded to Jews. They were barred from becoming officers in the army and from entering the civil service.[29]

Despite such discrimination, it was, compared to the situation previously, undeniably an improvement. There developed, especially in Berlin, an unprecedented flourishing of intellectual and cultural life that in turn led to the widespread assimilation of Jews. This came, though, not without cost. Assimilation into bourgeois life meant also a loss of Jewish identity, since many Jews gradually began to neglect and forget their religious beliefs and practices. The period of relative acceptance, however, did not last very long.[30]

What is remarkable is that from the mid-nineteenth century, when gradually all the Germanic principalities decreed the toleration of Jews, there began, paradoxically, a renewed hatred of them that manifested itself in politics and society.[31] There is no ready and completely satisfactory explanation. Certainly, it had something to do with the internal social crisis in Germany that was triggered by the rapid industrialization, a consequence of which was the unprecedented growth of organized labor. The fact that Karl Marx, a secular Jew, had become the intellectual leader of the working-class movement, led the bourgeois mind always to associate social democracy and communism with Jews.[32] And it is true that not a few leaders of the trade unions and social democratic movement were Jews. Apart from Marx there were other outstanding figures such as Stephan Born (1824–98), Ferdinand Lassalle (1825–64), and Eduard Bernstein (1850–1932), to name but the most famous ones. And, of course, organized labor in Germany as elsewhere engendered considerable disquiet within the middle and aristocratic classes.[33]

Following Reinhard Rürup, it can be said that this modern anti-Semitism was essentially a movement against Jews who were seeking to integrate into the evolving industrial society, and, as such, it was of a different character entirely from the old religious anti-Judaism. As Rurüp succinctly puts it, the "Jewish question" arose in the process of transformation from a feudal to a bourgeois-capitalist society that began in the late eighteenth century.[34] In this era many Jews had "assimilated"—that is, abandoned links with Judaism and lived as secular Germans. Others became "acculturated"—meaning they adopted German culture but continued the practice of their religion.

Whereas formerly, in the preindustrial era, it was the church that perceived the Jewish presence as inimical to the well-being of a Christian German community, now anti-Jewish attitudes took root in bourgeois secular society. Previously, the Jew was regarded as the "murderer of

Christ." Now he became at once the enemy of the people, a revolutionary, and a threat to the Christian-Germanic way of life. An irrational hatred towards Jews entered into the collective unconscious. Once again, despite the legal emancipation and their successful entry into bourgeois society, the Jews became the scapegoats for a range of social problems with which, of course, they had nothing to do. They were despised as a foreign, unassimilable, and destructive race rather than as members of a religious community that had rejected Christ and Christians. The late Werner Jochmann, one of the foremost authorities on the phenomenon of German anti-Semitism, observed that

> anti-Semitism in the Wilhelmine era [1871–1914] was chiefly an issue for the Protestant majority of the German people. The collapse of the old social order, the forced and often quite violent transformation of society from a feudal-agrarian to a modern industrial one resulted in serious disruptions. People reacted very differently according to the degree of their religious convictions. Indeed, it must be observed that the social behavior of people was not solely determined by economic factors but also by their basic religious attitudes and church affiliation.[35]

So while there was always a residual consciousness in the minds of non-Jews of the medieval resentment of Jews on religious grounds, now in the industrial age modern anti-Semites came to hate Jews for things they allegedly did in the economic and social spheres, such as exploiting and cheating non-Jews, taking their jobs from them, and gaining control over the stock market, the press, and even the state itself.[36]

Anti-Judaism and Anti-Semitism

Scholars, particularly since the end of the Second World War, have puzzled over this phenomenon. Why were the Jews victimized as "Germany's misfortune," as Heinrich von Treitschke (1834–1896) formulated it: *Die Juden sind unser Unglück*? That was a particularly virulent slogan; it was used with deadly effect by the Nazis decades later. Thus, one has to enquire how this anti-Jewish mentality became virtually paradigmatic for German society and particularly for the *Bildungsbürgertum*, and how it developed into exterminatory anti-Semitism.

The name Wilhelm Marr, as an anti-Jewish agitator, has already been mentioned. He was the first to coin the word *anti-Semitism* and to recommend the extermination of the Jews in Germany. An active publicist, he had written a book called *Der Sieg des Judentums über das Germanentum* (The Triumph of Judaism over Germandom) in 1873 that went through over a dozen editions. Anti-Semitic journalism flourished, and publications began to appear from a cluster of racially inspired authors, Austrian, French and even one Germanophile Englishman who became a naturalized German, named Houston Stewart Chamberlain (1855–1927), Richard Wagner's son-in-law. All these people believed that their racial theories were unquestionably scientific. Chamberlain's writings in particular served as a specific source for later Nazi propagandists.[37] The so-called *Judenfrage* had been posed. At that time, in the second half of the nineteenth century, no one could have imagined that the definitive German answer to the Jewish question would be given in Auschwitz.

The decision on precisely when to intensify the persecution of Jews to actual annihilation of all European Jews was the result of a long and complex bureaucratic process. It had partly to do with how the Nazi leadership responded to the military situation in the East during the second half of 1941, more specifically between 16 September and 25 October.[38] After a meeting between Heinrich Himmler and the Führer on 16 September, Himmler communicated Hitler's wish to the Gauleiter Greiser on 18 September to evacuate all Jews from the Reich as soon as possible.[39] This meant, of course, that those Jews, regardless of age or gender, who had been already rounded up and incarcerated within the confines of German-occupied Europe would be transported to the East and exterminated in special camps. This means that the earlier widespread understanding that the decision for the "Final Solution" had been taken at the Wannsee Conference held 20 January 1942, in a villa on the outskirts of Berlin is untenable.[40] Indeed, by that time daily gassings of Jews had already been taking place at Chelmno in western Poland for more than two months. The purpose of the Wannsee meeting was not to determine the nature of the "Final Solution" but rather to coordinate department policies and generally to facilitate the mechanics of the plan for the Europe-wide deportation of Jews—in short, to remove any bureaucratic obstacles that might impede Himmler's SS from carrying out the extermination process. Over a specially arranged lunch on that January day in 1942, the leading SS officers and high-ranking career civil servants from the Foreign Office, the Ministry of the Interior, the Ministry of Justice, as well as representatives of the governments of Nazi-occupied Eastern Territories and the Reich Security Main Office, were convened by *Obergruppenführer* and *General der Polizei* Reinhard Heydrich (1904–42). Heydrich opened the meeting by announcing that he had been appointed by Hermann Göring as Plenipotentiary for the Preparation of the Final Solution, explaining that all European Jews were to be included in the murder program, the responsibility for which was assigned to a desk in the Gestapo headquarters led by *Obersturmbannführer* Adolf Eichmann (1906–62).[41] This officer was the mastermind behind the deportation of the European Jews to extermination camps in the East where the mass killing would be carried out systematically, employing the tools of modern science and technology.[42] This was the uniquely German contribution to the history of genocide.

The Function of the Educated Upper Middle Class

The volume of published literature that tries to explain this phenomenon is considerable. However, in order to make sense of it, one has to try to explain how anti-Semitism became paradigmatic for the *Bildungsbürgertum*. If the educated elite had been able to counter the absurdities of the fanatical anti-Semitic pamphlet writers, then, arguably, the genocidal consequences might have been avoided. But, as shall now be seen, even the educated elite was infected with racism, indicating how even the most intelligent people had succumbed to obscurantist and irrational ideas.[43]

One can begin to answer this question by referring to the work of the German American scholar Fritz Ringer of the University of Pittsburgh. His research field is the history of European education, wherein he has observed a crucial uniqueness in the German educational tradition from the beginning of the nineteenth century that sets it apart from the educational traditions of France and Britain. Ringer's thesis rewards investigation.

In Britain and France, the universities of the eighteenth and nineteenth centuries had the task of educating young men to serve in the church, the civil service, and the world of commerce, especially after the industrial revolution—in short, to provide them with the knowledge to carry out specific functions in the state, the economy and in society. Education was primarily utilitarian, and it was determined by the way in which Britain and France modernized.

In Germany, where entrepreneurial capitalism was still comparatively underdeveloped, the universities educated, apart from Protestant clergy, candidates for the various state public services. Men were recruited for postings in these areas on the basis of their educational achievements. And the point is that for the middle classes to become upwardly mobile, there being little private enterprise, they looked to the church and to the bureaucracy in which to pursue a profession. These two fields provided the opportunity for social advancement. And if one's chances of recruitment depended upon one's university record, education, particularly a classical education, was prioritized. The class of people that this system produced was the

Bildungsbürgertum, to which reference has already been made. And the elite of this group were, of course, the professors themselves. As Fritz Ringer observed:

> I continue to be interested in the German university professors of the late nineteenth and early twentieth century centuries, whom I call 'mandarin intellectuals'. The prominent place of the university professors in nineteenth century German society still seems to me to be more than an accident. Their role, their sense of self, and their conception of learning, I would continue to argue, were deeply affected by a primary identification with *Bildung*. After all, they stood at the apex of the crucial hierarchy of education in nineteenth century Germany. Almost by definition, they were the foremost representatives of the *Bildungsbürgertum*, of what were called the 'academic' professions. They understandably claimed the right to speak for the educated classes as a whole, and thus in effect to articulate the cultural aspirations of the nation. At the same time they largely defined and filled role of the intellectual in modern Germany....
> It therefore continues to seem to me possible and causally important to understand certain common assumptions of German university scholars as outgrowths of a 'mandarin' ideology of *Bildung*.[44]

It is their concept of *Bildung*, their formation as cultivated individuals, that set the German scholars apart from everyone else in the civilized world. The reason is that it is based on a mystical, certainly spiritual, understanding of the racial community. The definition of *Bildung* as Fritz Ringer reports, gives us the clue. It "means forming the soul by means of the cultural environment. *Bildung* requires: (a) an individuality which, as the unique starting point, is to be developed into a formed or value-saturated personality; (b) a certain universality, meaning richness of mind and person, which is attained through the understanding and experiencing (*Verstehen und Erleben*) of objective cultural values; (c) totality, meaning inner unity and firmness of character."

The philosopher and sociologist Georg Simmel (1858–1918) elaborated on this definition by observing that it was possible that a person might develop learning, virtuosity, and refinement that derive from a normative external realm. Thereby, a person might acquire cultivated attributes yet remain uncultivated. Cultivation came only, "*if the contents absorbed out of the supra-personal realm (of objectified cultural values) seem, as through a secret harmony, to unfold only that in the soul which exists within it as its own instinctual tendency and as the inner prefiguration of its subjective perfection.*"[45]

This is language that is freighted with various—indeed, "peculiar"—assumptions that demand to be investigated. It says the learner absorbs the "contents of the supra-personal realm," that is, the cultural products that exist, to become a "value-saturated" personality. Obviously, the individual's comprehending or experiencing is not simply an analytical or intellectual activity because his whole being, body, mind, and soul, are involved in the process. And here is the mystical part: *Bildung* is supposed to transform a unique "individuality" into a unified "totality." This happens by virtue of the "secret harmony" with which the cultural products interact with that which already exists within the individual soul. It is argued, in effect, that the individual possesses a prior "instinctual tendency" to enable this process to take place. In short, "the cultivated individual is at once a unified totality and in harmony with his prior "instinctual tendency."[46] When one reads this definition from the hand of Georg Simmel, one is struck by its frankly tortuous and obscurantist language, and one wonders whether Simmel, a Jew who had suffered considerable discrimination during his academic career, was being justifiably ironic about the obscurantism of the "Teutonic" colleagues who had made life difficult for him.[47]

The point has been made that a person may acquire from the external world certain accomplishments, virtuosity and skills that give him or her cultivated attributes, but that person is still not necessarily cultivated—that is, he or she still lacks *Kultur*. That is a serious question. The answer is that one would have to be of the *Volk*, of the blood, a member of the racial community as an essential precondition to becoming cultivated. This is the mystical *conditio sine qua non*, of becoming genuinely cultivated. In a word, one would have to be born with the instincts peculiar to the *Volk* to enable the spiritual reciprocal relationship between the external cultural products one is, say, reading or participating in, for the so-called secret harmony to result.

Ringer's reflections, based on Georg Simmel's definition, have revealed the frankly obscurantist assumptions upon which leading German educators in the nineteenth century and much later, as well, based their definition of *Kultur*—indeed, in what precisely distinguished the German from, say, his French neighbors and English cousins, and indeed his fellow citizens of Jewish origin. Curiously, the German thinkers were excessively concerned with identifying what made up the unique German identity, as such scholars as Friedrich Meinecke (1862–1954) through their numerous works demonstrated.[48]

From Herder's teaching we know already that the *Volk* is something that has emerged out of history as a unique cultural community. It is not an artificial construct based on Enlightenment concepts of the universality of reason. Rather, it is an organic outgrowth of the interaction of environment, both physical and spiritual, on the tribal group. This group is a discrete racial entity that is by definition exclusive, preserving its identity from dilution from the influx of foreign influences and, above all, foreign blood. It is distinguished by its unique *Volksgeist* or national spirit and cannot be imitated or reproduced elsewhere than where it is located. If a member emigrated, he or she would eventually lose identity as a member of that particular *Volk*.[49] By the same token, if foreigners entered into the midst of a *Volk*, they may indeed learn the language and imitate many of the customs, even adopt the religion, but it would still never be possible for them to be absorbed into the *Volk*, no matter how much they tried; it would be a spiritual impossibility.

This type of thinking about how the national community was formed became paradigmatic for the Germans once the teachings of Herder, and particularly of Hegel, had been received in German education. Only within the community of the *Volk* could the complex process of *Bildung* begin to work and take its unique effect. So, by definition, outsiders, no matter how clever they might be, could never become part of the process. And Jews were obviously outsiders in Germany—outsiders of an especially pernicious kind. Their presence in the community was judged by anti-Semitic writers to be especially corrosive. Because they had such a highly developed sense of their own cultural identity, rooted as it was in the practice of their ancient religion, and because they were at the same time adept at imitating the intellectual environment, their presence was seen to defile the purity of the German *Volksseele*, the national soul, which was understood to be Nordic and Teutonic.[50]

Here we witness a collision between Enlightenment thinking about the essential equality of human beings by virtue of their common rationality (i.e., cosmopolitanism) and the avowedly irrational folkish ideology that had its roots in Herder's doctrine of cultural nationalism expressed in the *Volksgeist*. We have just seen this documented in the definition of *Bildung* that most German academics endorsed. That said, not all German professors during the era 1871–1933 were openly anti-Semitic. Some Jews even became professors themselves in this period, but comparatively few. As a rule, German professors accepted Jewish students, and some even fostered them because of their ability, and kept their anti-Semitic convictions to themselves.[51]

However, not all members of the *Bildungsbürgertum* were so tolerant, and these formed a link with the fanatical pamphleteers who demanded the elimination or extermination of Jews. Some were so worried about the presence of Jews who were allegedly getting a stranglehold of German commerce, the press, banking, the theater, and even politics, that a political party was founded in 1878, called the *Christlichsoziale Partei*, under the leadership of the court preacher Adolf Stöcker (1835–1909) with a program demanding active discrimination against Jewish involvement in the public sphere. Stöcker's anti-Semitism, like that of Heinrich von Treitschke at the same time, was a curious mixture of prejudices based on a fear of the loss of what they considered true Germanic culture if the Jews succeeded in taking over key positions in society while retaining their Jewish identity. If, however, they submitted to baptism, that would assure complete equality between Christian and converted Jew.[52] But Stöcker's movement constituted a minority manifestation of anti-Semitism that really harked back to Luther. As Uriel Tal observed, "his [Stöcker's] demands and proposals for the solution of the Jewish question constitute a complex system of theological, biblical, pietistic, and racial motifs."[53]

Nevertheless, Stöcker's anti-Semitism was not yet exterminatory. And his party, in any case, never gained wide public support, not because of any opposition to his anti-Semitism, but because of its social program aimed at trying to win over the working class to so-called Christian social values.[54] The workers by this time were virtually alienated from the church and were committed social democratic voters in so far as they were not Roman Catholics, and the conservatives regarded the policies of the fiery pastor as utopian nonsense. Furthermore, Stöcker had made the mistake of singling out Bismarck's most successful banker, Gerson Bleichröder, who was Jewish, for special criticism, as an example of a Jew in a highly influential position. This, however, had to backfire because it could be construed as indirect criticism of the highly revered founder of the Reich.[55] Given Bismarck's standing in the eyes of the *Bildungsbürgertum* generally, Stöcker's position could never have achieved widespread endorsement. Consequently, his movement was a failure, but his Christian social criticism of Jews, which was frankly eliminatory anti-Semitism, did fertilize the soil for the growth of exterminatory anti-Semitism, as did Treitschke's anti-Semitic slogans. Already, such a publicist as Paul de Lagarde (1827–91) writing before the end of the nineteenth century, used a vocabulary that anticipated the Nazis, calling the Jews vermin and bacillae in society, claiming that they were obviously impossible to reeducate, and that, therefore, the only solution was eradication.[56]

Despite such antipathy, however, it was still possible for some outstanding Jews to reach the highest levels of the bureaucracy and society by virtue of their expertise, such as the aforementioned Bleichröder. As well, the Colonial Secretary between 1907 and 1912, Bernhard Dernburg (1865–1937), was Jewish, but his laudable service to the Reich did not save him and his family from Nazi discrimination.[57] Others, such as the already mentioned Albert Ballin (1847–1918), enjoyed the confidence of the Kaiser, but Ballin was never invited to court with his wife, precisely because he was Jewish.[58] He committed suicide when Germany lost the Great War. The famous chemist Fritz Haber (1868–1934), the inventor of poison gas in the First World War, and a convert to Christianity, had served Germany as a patriotic scientist, but with the advent of Hitler in 1933 he went into voluntary exile to live with former enemies in Cambridge, England. His Jewishness disqualified him from remaining a German.[59] Many thousands of German Jews who identified ardently with German culture experienced the same fate.

Anti-Semitism in imperial Germany and in the postwar Weimar Republic, then, had various levels of manifestation. It ranged from the barbaric and vulgar to the ultra-refined version as represented among the *Bildungsbürgertum* whose members could be so gentlemanly that they would not want to be seen in association with the more outspoken fanatics; but nevertheless they still believed in the essential superiority of *Kultur* and therefore always harbored reservations about the Jewish element in German society.

However, sweeping generalizations about the *Bildungsbürgertum* must be avoided. This is because prominent examples can be identified who were not anti-Semitic, or who were at least sufficiently liberal in outlook as to tolerate family members marrying burghers of Jewish descent. Among the most famous families, of course, was that of the author Thomas Mann, whose wife was Jewish.[60] The same was true of the Bonhoeffer family. Both had Jewish in-laws. And both opposed the anti-Jewish policies of the Nazi regime. As indicated, many scholars have tried to explain why there was so much resentment in Germany toward Jews of both the assimilated, secular kind and those who practiced their ancient religion, especially in view of the fact that Jews were so integrated in the world of commerce and the professions.

Hitler and the Jews

Adolf Hitler had, of course, made no secret of his hatred of Jews and to what extent he held them responsible for Germany's misfortunes. In *Mein Kampf*, his autobiography written while in Landsberg prison in 1924, the future German dictator simply regurgitated all the prejudices and clichés that had been in circulation about Jews for decades past. There was nothing original in his accusations. Essentially, Jews were cunningly clever vermin with the innate ability to insinuate themselves into influential positions in society, thereby defiling the German race. The implication was clear that in the future, reborn Germany, there would be no place for them.[61]

When Hitler joined the German Workers' Party in Munich in October 1919, he was appalled by its weak leadership. Immediately he began to impose his own worldview on it, and by virtue of his charismatic oratory finally got himself elected leader furnished with dictatorial powers on 29 July 1921. The party was renamed the National Socialist German Workers' Party (NSDAP), a so-called Führer party, or a party subordinated to the sole will of the leader, driven by a blatantly racist ideology and a social-Darwinist understanding of history. Right-wing Hegelians had no difficulty in endorsing it.[62]

Owing to a chain of drastic political misjudgements by all the other parties, especially during the end-phase of the Weimar Republic, Hitler found himself, by July 1932, leading the strongest single party in the legislature, with 230 Nazi deputies. At the beginning of 1933, despite losing thirty-four seats in the November 1932 election, he was still in a position to form a coalition government with the ultra-conservative German National Peoples Party as well as members of the Center Party and the Bavarian Peoples Party. Reich President Hindenburg saw no alternative to appointing Hitler chancellor, on 30 January 1933.

Initially, Hitler was preoccupied by the more pressing need to secure himself in office so that he could rule not only his party but also the nation as a dictator. This he achieved by having a bill passed by the Reichstag called the Enabling Law on 23 March 1933. It gave Hitler the sweeping powers he wanted in order to rule without constitutional restraints. Relying on the mass support of the loyal brown shirt legions of uniformed thugs (the *Sturmabteilung,* S.A.) that dominated the streets of Germany's cities, Hitler was able to bully the parties in the Reichstag into submission, threatening civil war if the other parties did not support his projected legislation. All succumbed, except the Social Democratic Party. (The hitherto very strong Communist Party, the KPD, had already been outlawed under the Emergency Decree of 28 February and so was no longer represented in the Reichstag for the debate on the Enabling Law).

In the ensuing vote, Hitler received 441 votes to 94 (the Social Democratic Party) against. As a two-thirds majority was needed, the Catholic Center Party, with 71 seats, the third strongest party, through a monumental lack of political judgement, was happy to guarantee it. The bill was officially called "An Act for the Removal of Distress from People and Reich," its purpose being, allegedly, to give Hitler a free hand to deal with all the economic problems plaguing the country.[63] A week later a "Law against the New Construction of Parties" was passed. All other parties were abolished if they had not already disbanded themselves, and this left the NSDAP as the only legal party. The Nazis now proceeded with their policy of *Gleichschaltung,* that is, systematically bringing every organization in the country under their control—including the armed forces, the trade unions, the universities, and the churches. But precisely the churches were going to prove problematic, as shall be seen.

Not even the old conservatives who had "jobbed Hitler into office" (Allan Bullock) could have imagined what the National Socialist revolution, also called the "sliding revolution," had in store for Germany.[64] The future program was all in Hitler's head, and now that he had complete control of the nation, he and his party ideologues could begin to turn their attention to solving the Jewish problem—the major item on the domestic political agenda. All the while Jews were being subjected to discrimination, boycotts of their businesses, and persecution throughout the country. There was no police protection for them. Intimidation of all citizens not of "Aryan" descent was the first step in dealing with the Jewish question. The next step was to pass the requisite discriminatory legislation to abrogate normal citizenship rights for non-Aryans.

The first of these came on 7 April 1933, a "Law for the Restoration of the Professional Civil Service." This included the notorious "Aryan Paragraph" that excluded non-Aryans, meaning Jews, from holding public office. Initially, it did not apply to persons already in office prior to 1914 or who had fought for Germany in the Great War. But they, too, were excluded in the Nuremberg laws, passed on 15 September 1935, after the party rally there at which the Reich doctors' leader, Dr. Gerhard Wagner, announced that legislation would be introduced to prevent the further "bastardization" of the German people.[65] The first measure was called the *Reichsbürgergesetz* (national citizenship law), and it expressly excluded all Jews from citizenship. It was augmented by regulations promulgated in November 1935 that arbitrarily defined who was a Jew, either by religious profession or through Jewish ancestry. The second law was entitled "A law for the protection of German blood and honor." This prohibited intermarriage with Jews and also made sexual relations with Jews a crime designated as *Rassenschande* ("racial defilement").

The intention was to implement Nazi racial doctrines through the systematic exclusion of Jews from public life, and the laws incidentally were applied to pastors in the church who had been born Jews, a factor of key significance in creating opposition in the church. In this way Jews and persons of Jewish descent were denied the protection of the law and participation in the economy. They had nowhere to go except to try to emigrate. Why more did not try to do this than actually did is a question much debated by scholars.

As indicated, the form of the final solution to the Jewish question had not been determined until the second half of 1941 and then bureaucratically coordinated at the Wannsee conference in January 1942. But long before that, there had been vicious examples of anti-Semitic actions in Germany beginning with the boycotts of Jewish-owned businesses, including wanton destruction of their premises. These pogrom-like actions, which were unfolding all over the country, were reined in only for the period of the Berlin Olympics in 1936, so as not to give foreign visitors a bad impression of the "New Order" in Germany. However, the brutality resumed soon after, and peaked in the so-called *Reichskristallnacht* from 9–10 November 1938, a massive operation conceived by Josef Goebbels and implemented by the SA.[66] The excuse for such brutal action was the assassination of a German diplomat in Paris by a seventeen-year-old Polish-Jewish youth, Herschel Grynspan, on 7 November 1938. Indeed, the German propaganda at the time stated that it was the Jews who had declared war on Germany. Goebbels had expected that the operation would spark off a national uprising against all Jews, but that did not materialize. Still, the results were catastrophic. Ninety-one former citizens were murdered, hundreds rounded up and transported to their death in concentration camps, 35,000 arrested, 191 synagogues razed, and 7,000 shops destroyed. Government decrees of 12–13 November 1938, completed the exclusion of Jews from economic life by confiscating Jewish property and assets, and, as well, imposed a fine of 1 billion marks on the Jewish community.[67]

So, what had happened since the Nazis seized power in Germany? First, Jews were openly discriminated against and intimidated; they were then deprived of all basic rights, and finally they were dehumanized, treated as *Untermenschen*—subhuman—in accordance with Aryan racial doctrine. It remained only to determine what form the final solution would take: emigration or resettlement to Palestine or Madagascar? When such eliminatory options were eventually closed off, the Nazi leadership had no qualms in resorting to exterminatory solutions. Quasi-military *Einsatzgruppen* (task groups) followed the invading German forces, systematically shooting captured Jews, partisans, and other civilians in all the German-occupied territories in the East. Initially, the *Einsatzgruppen* shot captives into mass graves or gassed them in specially equipped vans. This was but the prelude to the highly organized "industrial annihilation" by means of Zyklon B gas carried out in camps designed for that purpose, such as at Auschwitz.[68]

Here it should be recalled that in Hitler's first political statement in 1919, he had written that the Jews had to be removed from Germany.[69] Although at the time he had no clear idea how this might be accomplished, he and his henchmen were not overly concerned by the means. After all, if one is dealing with vermin, killing by means of poison gas would serve quite well as it saved the trouble of transporting the victims overseas. In their particular aim of making Germany and Europe *Judenfrei* (free of Jews), the Nazis succeeded to an appalling extent, murdering six million of the nine million Jews within Nazi-controlled areas.[70]

The question is commonly posed, why was it the Nazis who accomplished the extermination of six million Jews, bearing in mind that anti-Semitism was rife in other European countries? The answer lies, following Raul Hilberg, in the bureaucratic coordination and continuity of purpose that had been the characteristic of the German public service in all of its branches.[71] Obviously, in such a massive operation many government departments would be required to cooperate and to align their efforts toward achieving the overall continuity. In retrospect, it is clear that there occurred a kind of inexorable process beginning with the initial Nazi legislation to segregate the Jews. This led next to their expulsion and finally to their annihilation. Thus, first the right to live as Jews in German society was revoked. This resulted in the well-known legal disabilities that deprived Jews of citizenship rights. Thereafter a phase of emigration was initiated when many German and Austrian Jews sought to flee to more accommodating countries. Then Jews in Nazi-occupied Europe were rounded up for extermination, all being destined to perish in the gas chambers. So Nazi policy accelerated from a denial of the right of domicile to a denial of the right to live. That there were only a few voices of protest, such as Bonhoeffer's, poses considerable questions about the phenomenon of the *Bildungsbürgertum* and their values that contributed to the shaping of German political will during the Third Reich.

Notes

1. Most relevant to this question is Michael Meyer, ed., *German-Jewish History in Modern Times*, 4 vols. (New York, 1996–98). See especially vol. 4, *Renewal and Destruction, 1918–1945*.

2. A useful introduction to this subject is provided by Asta von Oppen, *Der unerhörte Schrei-Dietrich Bonhoeffer und die Judenfrage im dritten Reich* (Hannover, 1996). See also, Karl A. Schleunes, *The Twisted Road to Auschwitz: Nazi Policy towards German Jews, 1933–1939* (Urbana, Ill., 1990) and more recently, Christopher R. Browning, *Nazi Policy, Jewish Workers, German Killers* (Cambridge, 2000).

3. See Elaine Pagels, *Beyond Belief: The Secret Gospel of Thomas* (New York, 2004). The Apostles' names by which the four gospels are identified were appropriated by the real authors in order to lend them authenticity.

4. See John Shelby Spong, *The Sins of Scripture* (San Francisco, 2005), 183–212 passim.

5. Julius Schoeps is a German scholar of Jewish descent who understands National Socialism virtually as an outgrowth of Christianity. See *Der*

Nationalsozialismus als politische Religion edited by Michael Ley and Julius Schoeps (Bodenheim bei Mainz, 1997), especially 262–71.

6. Hans-Ulrich Wehler, *Deutsche Gesellschaftsgeschichte*, vol. 3, *Von der "Deutschen Doppelrevolution" bis zum Beginn des Ersten Weltkriegs 1849–1914* (Munich, 1995), 924–34. Thomas Nipperdey, *Deutsche Geschichte 1864–1918* (Munich, 1993), 396–413.

7. For a survey of the scholarly writing on this subject, see Shulamit Volkov, "Anti-Semitism as a Cultural Code: Reflections on the History and Historiography of Antisemitism in Imperial Germany," in *The History of the Holocaust*, ed. Dan Stone (Houndsmill Basingstoke, 2004), 307–28.

8. Paul W. Massing, *Rehearsal for Destruction—A Study of Political Anti-Semitism in Imperial Germany* (New York, 1949), 6. Further, on Marr see Peter Pulzer, *The Rise of Political Anti-Semitism in Germany and Austria* (Cambridge, Mass., 1988), 47–50. See also, Moshe Zimmermann, *Die deutschen Juden 1914–1945* (Munich, 1997) and Uriel Tal, *Christians and Jews in Germany: Religion, Politics and Ideology in the Second Reich, 1970–1914* (Ithaca, 1975).

9. Daniel Goldhagen, *Hitler's Willing Executioners: Ordinary Germans and the Holocaust* (London, 1996). Goldhagen delineates the concepts "eliminationist" and "exterminatory" anti-Semitism on p. 44 to 128. See also his *A Moral Reckoning: the Role of the Catholic Church in the Holocaust and its Unfulfilled Duty of Repair* (London, 2002), 23–25. There is considerable controversy about Goldhagen's thesis, mainly because he argues that *all* Germans were essentially complicit in the extermination of the Jews: since there was no protest against it, they endorsed it. This undifferentiated judgement has not gone unchallenged. See Geoffrey Eley, ed., *The "Goldhagen Effect": History, Memory, Nazism—Facing the German Past* (Ann Arbor, 2000). See Eley's introduction, 5, where he observes that Goldhagen argued that eliminationist anti-Semitism had become by the last third of the nineteenth century a cultural norm in Germany that led to the majority of ordinary Germans becoming willing to kill Jews. Also critical of Goldhagen's lack of differentiation is Oded Heilbronner, "German or Nazi Antisemitism," in *The Historiography of the Holocaust*, ed. Dan Stone. It could not be argued that the German people fanatically supported the Nazi anti-Jewish policy until the later 1930s, see p. 19.

10. Saul Friedländer, *Nazi Germany and the Jew: The Years of Persecution, 1933–1939*, vol. I. (New York, 1997), 87.

11. Ibid.

12. See also other key works on Christian-Jewish relations such as Uriel Tal, *Christians and Jews in Germany: Religion, Politics, and Ideology in the Second Reich, 1870–1914* (Ithaca, 1975); and Zygmunt Bauman, *Modernity and the Holocaust* (Cambridge, 1991).

13. See the works of the French scholar René Girard on the theme of "sacred violence": *Things Hidden since the Foundation of the World* (Stanford, 1978) and *Violence and the Sacred* (Baltimore, 1979).

14. Christhard Hoffmann, et al., eds., *Exclusionary Violence: Antisemitic Riots in Modern German History* (Ann Arbor, 2002).The introductory chapter contextualizes the question by drawing attention to examples of anti-Semitic violence in other European countries during the nineteenth century, and proceeds to examine instances of it in Germany from the early nineteenth century

up until the Weimar Republic, i.e., prior to the advent of the Third Reich. See especially the chapter by Richard S. Levy, "Continuities and Discontinuities of anti-Jewish Violence in Modern Germany, 1819–1938," 185–202. On the Dreyfus affair, see Albert S. Lindemann, *The Jew Accused: Three Anti-Semitic Affairs—Dreyfus, Beilis, Frank, 1894–1915* (Cambridge, 1991), 57–128.

15. See the relevant passages in *Mein Kampf* (See footnote, no. 23).

16. Nipperdey, *Deutsche Geschichte*, 396. See also Werner E. Mosse, *Jews in the German Economy* (Oxford, 1987), 298, who shows that "The German-Jewish economic elite . . . played a prominent part in German economic development over the course of four generations from the age of early industrialization to the emergence of fully industrial capitalism in the twentieth century."

17. Ibid., 398.

18. Nipperdey, *Deutsche Geschichte*, 1: 399. See also David Sorkin, "Enlightenment and Emancipation: German Jewry's Formative Age in comparative perspective," in *Comparative Jewish Societies*, ed. Todd M. Edelmann (Ann Arbor, 1997), 274–86. Here, Sorkin carefully documents how earnestly the German Jewish community identified with the German host society and concludes with a witticism attributed to Heinrich Heine that "The Jews are like the people among whom they live, only more so."

19. As Nipperdey illustrates, the average tax paid by Jewish taxpayers was seven times higher than the Roman Catholics and three and a half times higher than the Protestants. Nipperdey, *Deutsche Geschichte*, 1: 399.

20. Ibid., 405. See also, Eugene Kamenka, "The Holocaust: Explaining the Inexplicable?" in *Why Germany? National Socialist Anti-Semitism and the European Context*, ed. John Milfull, (Providence/Oxford, 1993), 2–6. Kamenka discusses the question why the Germans under Hitler so vehemently attacked a minority who wanted nothing more than to be as thoroughly German as possible, and concludes that there is no satisfactory explanation.

21. Nipperdey, *Deutsche Geschichte*, 408.

22. See Adolf Hitler, *Mein Kampf* (London, 1939) 172; 286; 448.

23. On the stab-in-the-back legend from a Marxist-Leninist viewpoint, see, Joachim Petzold, *Die Dolchstosslegende* (Berlin–Ost, 1963). See also: John A. Moses, "The Effect of the Stab-in-the-Back-Legend (*Dolchstosslegende*) on German Historical Awareness," *Teaching History* 16, no. 2 (July, 1982): 1–17.

24. Friedländer, *Nazi Germany*, 73, and Robert S. Wistrich, *Hitler and the Holocaust* (London, 2001), 26. Wistrich reports that 12,000 Jews fell in the service of the Reich and a relatively high number won awards for bravery on the battlefield.

25. Ibid., 75.

26. Von Oppen, *Der unerhörte Schrei*, 18. The information following is derived also from the same work. This subject is treated most lucidly by John Spong, *The Sins of Scripture*, 183–212.

27. From Heine's text, *Der Rabbi von Bacharach* written in 1840. Cited after von Oppen, *Der unerhörte Schrei*, 21.

28. Ernst Ludwig Ehrlich, "Luther und die Juden" in *Antisemitismus—von der Judenfeindschaft zum Holocaust* edited by Herbert A. Strauss and Norbert Kampe (Frankfurt/Main, 1984), 59–60. Heiko A. Oberman, *The Roots of Anti-Semitism in the Age of the Renaissance and Reformation*, trans. James I. Porter (Philadelphia, 1984) and also his *Luther: Man between God and the Devil* (New

Haven, 1989). See especially the section entitled, "Darkness at Noon: Luther and the Jews," 292–97.

29. Reinhard Rürup, *Emanzipation und Antisemitismus* (Göttingen, 1975), 20.

30. David Sorkin, *The Transformation of German Jewry, 1780–1840* (New York/Oxford, 1987). Here the author investigates the character and meaning of Jewish integration into German society and argues that their Jewish identity did not thereby disappear, but was transformed. In fact, German Jews came to share in a subculture that created a unique separate identity evidenced by the way in which they thought and acted. This subculture resulted from the particular way the Jews became part of modern Germany. However, in the eyes of the German *Bildungsbürgertum*, as is discussed below, their identification with German culture did not ensure their total acceptance in German society.

31. See Steven Beller, *Vienna and the Jews 1867–1938: A Cultural History* (Cambridge, 1989).

32. See Werner Mosse, *German-Jewish Economic Elites 1820–1935: A Socio-Cultural Profile* (Oxford, 1989).

33. Massing, *Rehearsal*, 151–69.

34. Rürup, 75–76. See also the other contributions by the same author: "Emanzipation und Krise: zur Geschichte der 'Judenfrage' in Deutschland vor 1890," in *Juden im wilhelminischen Deutschland 1890–1914*, ed. Werner Mosse and Arnold Pauker (Tübingen, 1976), 1–56; "The Tortuous and Thorny Path to legal Equality—'Jew Laws' and Emancipatory Legislation in Germany from the late Eighteenth Century," in *Year Book—Leo Baeck Institute* 31 (London, 1986): 3–34.

35. Werner Jochmann, "Struktur und Funktion des deutschen Antisemitismus 1878–1914," in *Antisemitimus* 120. Uriel Tal, by way of endorsing Jochmann's assessment wrote, "it is clear that the social, political, and spiritual factors that determined the status of the Jews in the German society of the Second Reich, into which they desired to integrate fully without, however, forfeiting their Judaism, had their roots in the Christian heritage": *Christians and Jews in Germany*, 223.

36. Albert S. Lindemann, *The Jew Accused: Three Anti-Semitic Affairs—Dreyfus, Beilis, Frank, 1894–1915* (Cambridge, 1991), 16.

37. Von Oppen, *Der unerhörte Schrei*, 25.

38. Christopher R. Browning has painstakingly examined the various explanations and investigated all the extant sources in a chapter entitled "The Decision-Making Process," in *The Historiography of the Holocaust*, ed. Dan Stone (London, 2004), 173–96. See also Browning, *Nazi Policy, Jewish Workers, German Killers* (Cambridge, 2000), 1–25.

39. Ibid., 188.

40. See Mark Roseman, *The Wannsee Conference and the Final Solution: A Reconsideration* (New York, 2002), 92–126.

41. Roderick Stackelberg, *Hitler's Germany: Origins, Interpretations and Legacies* (London, 1999), 224–25; Robert S. Wistrich, *Hitler and the Holocaust* (London, 2001), 109–10. Roger Manvell and Heinrich Frank, *Göring* (London, 1962), 244 where Göring's instructions to Heydrich are published.

42. Wolfgang Scheffler, "Wege zur 'Endlösung," in *Antisemitismus*, 209–212. Ulrich Herbert, ed., *National Socialist Extermination Policies: Contemporary German Perspectives and Controversies* (New York, 2000).

43. Bernhard Giese, *Intellectuals and the Nation: Collective Identity in a German Axial Age* (Cambridge/New York, 1998). Here the author explains how the German educated bourgeoisie of the nineteenth century (the *Bildungsbürgertum*) set the agenda for national unity under the leadership of Protestant Prussia to the exclusion of Roman Catholic Austria. The point is that Wilhelmine Germany perceived itself as a quintessentially Protestant nation in which Roman Catholics, not to mention the Jewish minority, had to struggle for recognition and justify their right to be accorded recognition as German subjects.

44. Fritz Ringer, "*Bildung*: The Social and Ideological Context of the German Historical Tradition," *History of European Ideas* 10, no. 2 (1989): 195–96.

45. Ibid; emphasis added. See also the writings of Norbert Elias on the question of *Bildung*: *Norbert Elias on Civilization, Power and Knowledge: Selected Writings*, edited with an introduction by Stephen Mennell and John Goudsblom (Chicago, 1998).

46. Ringer, "*Bildung*," 196.

47. Georg Simmel (1858–1918) was a scholar of wide-ranging expertise in the social sciences who remained for most of his academic life a *Privatdozent* and then *ausserordentlicher Professor* in Berlin. In 1914 he finally secured a full professorship at Strasbourg where in the wartime situation there were virtually no students. Simmel then tried in 1915 to gain an appointment in Heidelberg but was again passed over. Despite his brilliance, Simmel remained an academic outsider in his homeland. See David Kim, ed., *Georg Simmel in Translation: Interdisciplinary Border-Crossings in Culture and Modernity* (Cambridge, 2006).

48. Friedrich Meinecke, *Weltbürgertum oder Nationalstaat* (1907); English: *Cosmopolitianism and the National State* (Princeton, 1970).

49. Herder's thought on this issue is summarized by Friedrich Meinecke, *Historism—The Rise of a New Historical Outlook* (London, 1971), 295–372.

50. Jeffrey S. Librett, *The Rhetoric of Cultural Dialogue: Jews and Germans from Moses Mendelssohn to Richard Wagner and Beyond* (Palo Alto, 2000). This is a perceptive analysis of the question why Jews could embrace German culture but were never really accepted, even by the most enlightened of German thinkers. Librett's analysis strongly confirms the findings of Fritz Ringer in this regard. As well, see Michael Mack, *German Idealism and the Jews—The Inner Anti-Semitism of Philosophy and German Jewish Responses* (Chicago, 2003). Mack investigates what he calls the "anti-Semitic fantasies" of such notable German idealist thinkers of the eighteenth and nineteenth centuries as Immanuel Kant, G.W.F. Hegel, and others, and summarizes the "counter narratives" of German Jewish intellectuals such as Moses Mendelssohn, Heinrich Heine, and Abraham Geiger. In doing so Mack reenforces the findings of Librett's work.

51. Ernest Bramsted, a German-Jewish refugee from Nazi Germany and who during his student days in Berlin studied under Friedrich Meinecke, was a member of the Department of History at the University of Sydney, Australia, 1952–69. In a private conversation Dr. Bramsted related to the author how Meinecke treated him, as a student, in a most friendly manner, even on one occasion offering him a cigar.

52. Massing, *Rehearsal*, 76–77.

53. Uriel Tal, *Christians and Jews in Germany*, 252.

54. On Stöcker's political career, see Pulzer, *The Rise* 83–97; and Günter Brakelmann, Martin Greschat, and Werner Jochmann, *Protestantismus und Politik: Werk und Wirkung Adolf Stoeckers* (Hamburg, 1982). Uriel Tal, *Christians and Jews in Germany*, 248–59.

55. Fritz Stern, *Gold and Iron: Bismarck, Bleichröder, and the Building of the German Empire* (New York, 1977). Of particular importance is Stern's analysis of the phenomenon of anti-Semitism. Bleichröder, despite his position in the banking world and his importance to the Reich Chancellor, Otto von Bismarck, was always a victim of latent anti-Semitism, even among highly educated and reputable Germans. See especially the chapter "The Hostage of the New Anti-Semitism," 494–531.

56. Hermann Graml, *Antisemitism in the Third Reich* (Oxford, 1992), 56–57.

57. Werner Schiefel, *Bernard Dernburg 1865–1937: Kolonialpolitiker und Bankier im wilheminischen Deutschalnd* (Zurich: Atlantis Verlag, no date).

58. Lamar Cecil, *Albert Ballin: Business and Politics in Imperial Germany* (Princeton, 1967). Ballin was discriminated against by the Prussian nobility, despite his close association with the Kaiser, in a way similar to that experienced by Gerson Belichröder under Bismarck, a fact that ruled him out of contention for a post in cabinet. 112.

59. Fritz Stern, "The Scientist in Power and Exile," in *Dreams and Delusions: The Drama of German History* (London, 1987), 51–76.

60. Martin Travers, *Thomas Mann* (London, 1992). This study succinctly investigates the changing cultural values of the famous author as they were made manifest in his successive novels.

61. Ian Kershaw, *Hitler, 1889–1936*: vol. I, *Hubris* (London, 1998). The following account of the evolution of Hitler's anti-Jewish legislation follows Kershaw's narrative which is the most up-to-date and thorough examination of the Führer-State that Hitler based on his anti-Semitic prejudices. In short, anti-Semitism was essentially what Nazi Germany was about.

62. Kiesewetter, *Von Hegel zu Hitler*, 257–292 *passim*.

63. Kershaw, *Hitler*, vol. I, 466–68.

64. See Larry Eugene Jones, *German Liberalism and the Dissolution of the Weimar Party System* (Chapel Hill, N.C., 1988) for a full account of the complicity of the bourgeois liberal and conservative parties in Hitler's rise to power.

65. Kershaw, *Hitler*, vol. I, 567.

66. Anthony Read and David Fisher, *Kristallnacht: The Unleashing of the Holocaust* (New York, 1989). See also Graml, *Antisemitism*, 16–29, and Wilfred Fest, *Dictionary of German History 1806–1945* (London, 1978), 30–31, under the heading "Crystal Night (*Kristallnacht*, Night of Broken Glass)."

67. Kershaw, *Hitler*, vol. 2, 146.

68. Ibid. 463–477 *passim*. See also Richard Breitman, *The Architect of Genocide: Heinrich Himmler and the Final Solution* (Hanover, N.H., 1992).

69. Kershaw, *Hitler*, vol. 1, 570. This is the famous letter to Adolf Gemlich, 16 September 1919. It was composed by Hitler at the request of Captain Karl Mayr, his superior in the office of the *Reichswehr* (Army) News and Enlightenment Department of Munich, where Hitler held a minor posting. At that time Hitler advocated that the state of Bavaria introduce laws discriminating against Jews for their deleterious influence on German society. Here he wrote

that the ultimate objective of such legislation must be the irrevocable removal of the Jews in general. At that time it was considered simply as a call for the forced expulsion of Jews from Germany. However, Hitler himself may indeed have meant it to be a call for genocide. See Ernst Deuerlein, "Hitler's Eintritt in die Politik und in die Reichswehr," *Vierteljahrsheft für Zeitgeschichte* 7 (1959): 203–205.

70. The statistics of the number of Jews exterminated show that of the approximately nine million Jews in 1933 who lived in the twenty-one countries occupied by the Nazis, over six million were killed by 1945. In addition some 1.5 million Gypsies and at least 250,000 mentally or physically disabled persons were exterminated. More than three million Soviet prisoners of war were also killed. Further, other undesirables such as Jehovah's Witnesses, homosexuals, Social Democrats, Communists, partisans, trade unionists, and Polish intelligentsia, among others, all became victims of the Nazi genocide. See the following website: http://www.deathcamps.info/testimonies/victims.htn>

71. Raul Hilberg, *The Destruction of the European Jews* (Chicago, 1962), 639.

4

BONHOEFFER'S OPENING TO THE WEST AND THE INVOLVEMENT IN ECUMENISM

It is important to grasp that by mid-1932 at the latest—that is, some six months prior to Hitler's appointment as Reich Chancellor—Bonhoeffer had become extremely allergic to National Socialism as a political ideology. As far as his fellow pastors were concerned it would be quite fair to say that the vast majority had been at that time deeply unhappy with the Weimar Republic, chiefly because a Lutheran church without a hereditary monarch as *summus episcopus* who epitomized the ancient union of "throne and altar" (church and state) was an unaccustomed and possibly heretical novelty. As a professional group the pastors had always been traditionally conservative and had tended, during the Republic, to support the more right-wing parties, especially the DNVP (The German National Peoples Party).[1] Given a choice, they would have preferred to have the Kaiser back again. And it was this dissatisfaction with the current secular state and the nostalgia for the monarchy, added to their *deutschnational* sentiments, that made them susceptible to the blandishments of the Nazi movement once it was in power. Bonhoeffer, on the other hand, had gathered crucial experiences from outside Germany, and these coupled with his developing theological radicalism, plus the values derived from his family, had immunized him against the possibility of seduction by Hitler.

We now have to inquire how this happened. Theologically, Bonhoeffer had, through his encounter with Karl Barth's ideas, distanced himself from his mentors who had identified revelation with history, a fact that caused them not only to overestimate but also to allocate a central role to the state in God's plan for humanity. Already in his commentary on *The Epistle to the Romans*,[2] Barth had repudiated the concept so crucial to the theology of the liberal Protestants, namely, that the German Empire had become God's chief instrument in the "history of salvation." He observed, "There is no fragment or epoch of history which can be pronounced divine. The whole history of the church and of all religion takes place in this world. What is called the 'history of salvation' is not an event in the midst of other events, but is nothing less than the KRISIS of all history."³ This is a most telling passage since Barth clearly confronts a key assertion of Leopold von Ranke's, formulated in his 1854 lecture "On the Epochs of Modern History," that "every epoch was immediate to God" (*jedes Zeitalter ist unmittlebar zu Gott*).⁴ This latter assertion had become paradigmatic for both German nationalist historians and Protestant theologians. Perhaps Barth's most significant reproach to his German liberal Protestant peers with regard to the "history of salvation" is as follows: "For when we have clearly perceived that, if divinity be so concreted and humanized in a particular department of history—the history of religion or the history of salvation—God has ceased to be God, and there can be no relation with him, then we are able to see that the whole occurrence of the known world derives its content and significance from the Unknown God."⁵

Significantly, all Bonhoeffer's teachers had been "liberal theologians," which meant, among other things, a preparedness to engage in serious debate with the secular world in order to deal openly with truly controversial things. Certainly, in a real sense Bonhoeffer himself remained a kind of liberal theologian, as he wrote to Eberhard Bethge from prison on 3 August 1944.⁶ But he decidedly repudiated Harnack's firmly held position, shared also by the other mentors (with the notable exception of G. A. Deissmann), that God favored the power state, the *Machtstaat*, as Hegel had taught. It had not been entirely easy for Bonhoeffer himself, as has been seen, to overcome this concept so favored by the then dominant school of theology, as the stridently nationalist content of his Barcelona lecture on Christian ethics illustrated. However, when he returned to Berlin from his year of service in Spain in February 1929, Bonhoeffer devoted himself to completing his post-doctoral thesis as a prerequisite to gaining an academic post, the *Habilitationsschrift*. This was called *Akt und Sein*, that is, *Act and Being*, essentially an extension of the doctoral thesis that had advanced the concept of the church as actualizing Christ's presence in the world—in short, how revelation becomes concrete. *Act and Being*, however, was an extremely erudite, not to say abstruse, attempt to answer some of the main issues raised by the theologians Karl Barth and Rudolf Bultmann as well as by the philosopher Martin Heidegger. Bonhoeffer was exercised by the problem of the doctrine of the transcendence of God and his ultimate remoteness and unknowableness, issues that Barth in particular had focused upon. The young, aspiring academic theologian was concerned that this would make God unavailable to humanity, so he wanted to establish that although God is totally unbounded he, nevertheless, had placed himself at man's disposal—not, of course, to allow himself to be manipulated by man but in the sense that God sustains humanity and Creation generally. A key passage in *Act and Being* reads as follows:

In revelation it is a question less of God's freedom on the far side from us, i.e. his eternal isolation and aseity, than of his forth-proceeding, his given Word, his bond in which he has bound himself, of his freedom as it is most strongly attested in his having freely bound himself to historical man, having placed himself at man's disposal. God is not free of but for man. Christ is the Word of his freedom. God is there, which is to say: not in eternal non-objectivity (but looking ahead for the moment) 'haveable', graspable in his Word within the church. Here a substantial comes to supplant the formal understanding of God's freedom.[7]

As with *Sanctorum Communio*, *Act and Being* was about the absolute reality of the church through which the act of God in sending Christ affects the essential being of humankind, in German, das *Dasein*, or actual existence of the children of God.

The reception history of the book need not detain us here, but it has to be appreciated that the ideas contained in it reappeared fifteen years later in Bonhoeffer's letters from prison.[8] His ability cheerfully to survive under the conditions of incarceration by the Gestapo is, in the main, attributable to both the strength of mind and the radical faith that Bonhoeffer was able to express in theological terms. In a real sense a Christian cannot be imprisoned because the mind imbued by faith keeps him or her aware that ultimately nothing is outside the dominion of God. This, of course, presumes a particular faith combined with extraordinary mental discipline.

Bonhoeffer had thus established a substantial theological/philosophical basis from which he was enabled to confront the palpable evils of National Socialism. *Act and Being* was completed in February 1930, accepted by the faculty, and on 31 July he was invited to give his inaugural address. He chose the subject "The Question of Man in Contemporary Philosophy and Theology." In this Bonhoeffer drew on his post-doctoral thesis, making the point that, "God is nearer to me than my existence is, in as much as it is he who first discloses my existence to me," and he went on to affirm that, "in reflexive theological thought I have no closer reference to my existence than to God."[9]

The inaugural lecture was a remarkably formidable statement for so young a theologian, rigorously locating true human existence in relationship to God. It was a kind of highly intellectual sermon on two Biblical texts; one from Psalm 8, verses 5–6: "What is man that you should be mindful of him: or the son of man that you should care for him? You have made him little less than a god: and have crowned him with glory and honor." The other was taken from Job 7, verse 17: "What is man that thou dost make so much of him, and that thou dost set thy mind on him?"

In this essay on Christian anthropology, Bonhoeffer makes the theologically incontrovertible observation that fallen humanity cannot on its own comprehend itself or the purpose of humankind in this world without reference to Christ, who exists as the Christian community, and indeed does not exist without the community.¹⁰ And he concluded by saying, "Thus not only does every individual theological problem lead back to the reality of the church of Christ, but theological thinking discovers itself in its totality to be of such a nature that it belongs to the church alone."¹¹ Again and again Bonhoeffer reiterated the proposition that fallen humanity can exist, can be "saved," only by being incorporated into the Body of Christ, the community that is the hidden Christ among us. The community brings Christ to humanity, and humanity in Christ is humanity in the community. Bonhoeffer was now *habilitiert*, that is, qualified to teach at a German university.

In retrospect, we can see that Bonhoeffer had been acquiring the spiritual weapons with which to equip the German church to survive the onslaught of National Socialism, a movement that Bonhoeffer, more clearly than most of his contemporaries, recognized as serving the Antichrist. Indeed, as we shall see, Bonhoeffer's theological justification for resistance to this evil flowed from his insight that the church is Christ's presence in the world and is therefore automatically at enmity with the forces of the Antichrist.¹² Obviously, this insight was not shared by most of the Protestant church leaders and laity alike, whose judgment was clouded by the deeply entrenched Lutheran culture of regarding the head of state as an authority ordained by God himself. Although it now sounds incomprehensible, at the time the vast majority of German pastors found it difficult not to regard Hitler as the *Obrigkeit*, the "powers that be" ordained by God, as expressed in St. Paul's *Epistle to the Romans*, Chapter XIII. Bonhoeffer's significance lies in the fact that he had laid the theological foundations for overcoming this fateful notion. In this, of course, he was far ahead of his time. Only a few sympathetic contemporaries were able to share his radical new insights. Then, before Hitler seized power, the newly minted academic was to gain invaluable experiences from a sojourn in America, from September 1930 until June 1931, based at New York's famous ecumenical Union Theological Seminary, for which he had been awarded a fellowship.¹³

The New World Experience

In the United States, Bonhoeffer's theological and political views were simultaneously confirmed and questioned. That means, as indicated, that although the young theologian was already developing along a path he had himself pioneered, one different from that of most of his German mentors, he remained, in spite of his reservations about trends in Protestant theology, an unshakable Lutheran. From this vantage point he was able to subject what he experienced in America to a stringent criticism. Theologically, he was not impressed by what he called Anglo-Saxon theology, which he regarded more as religious philosophy.[14] Indeed, after listening to numerous sermons he expressed the opinion that in New York one could hear preaching about almost anything and everything except the real gospel. In all the time Bonhoeffer was there, so he claimed, he had not succeeded in hearing anything on the gospel of Jesus Christ, of the cross, of sin and forgiveness, or of life and death. Instead of the Christian message, what one got to hear was about faith in ethical progress and social idealism, and Bonhoeffer wondered just how these Americans assumed the right to designate any of that as specifically "Christian." And in place of the church as community of believers in Christ, there was the church as a social corporation.[15]

These were views that Bonhoeffer reported back to the head office of the federated Protestant Churches in Berlin (*Kirchenbundesamt*) on 25 August 1931. They were very critical opinions which Bonhoeffer reiterated after his second, very brief visit to New York in 1939. The Christian denominations of America were not known for their theology but rather for their practical work in the community and their public effectiveness. This, he said, was also true of almost all Anglo-Saxon churches, a fact that constituted a great problem for members of the Confessing Church.[16] Essentially, the difficulty was attributable to the fact that, "God had granted American Christianity no Reformation. He had given it strong revivalist preachers, churchmen and theologians but no Reformation of the church of Jesus Christ by the Word of God."[17] This was a perceptive insight that illustrates Bonhoeffer's distinguishing characteristics as a systematic theologian.

Above all, Bonhoeffer was appalled by the lack of theological rigor. The Americans had reduced Christianity to religion and ethics. The result was that "the person and work of Jesus Christ must, for theology, sink into the background and in the long run remain misunderstood, because it is not recognized as the sole ground of radical judgment and radical forgiveness. The decisive task for us today is the dialogue between Protestantism without Reformation and the churches of the Reformation."[18]

This was indeed cutting criticism, and it illustrates supremely well Bonhoeffer's strictly Christ-centered focus. It was the same rigor that enabled him critically to dissect the sinister implications of *Schöpfungordnungs-theologie* ("orders of creation theology") when confronted with the machinations of the "German Christians" back home after Hitler's rise to power. There were, nevertheless, very positive experiences from the sojourn at Union Theological Seminary that deeply influenced Bonhoeffer, despite the negative impression of American theology.[19]

Most importantly, Bonhoeffer befriended other foreign students as well as, significantly, black students and pastors in New York. The two non-American students that were particularly influential in Bonhoeffer's life were the Frenchman Jean Lasserre and the Swiss Erwin Sutz. As a Frenchman, Lasserre represented Germany's longstanding national enemy (*der Erbfeind*). But Bonhoeffer found him more committed to the gospel, especially to the Sermon on the Mount, than he was to patriotism. Indeed, he made Bonhoeffer understand that the gospel transcended all national boundaries, and that the idea of a nationalist theology was inconsistent with the gospel, as a serious reading of the Sermon on the Mount would make abundantly clear.[20] This insight, of course, contributed to debunking further the entire *Volkstum* (nation-centered) school of theology represented by men such as Paul Althaus, Emanuel Hirsch, and Gerhard Kittel that had quite seriously identified the German people (*Volk*) as an instrument of God in the history of salvation. For them, the Sermon on the Mount had no relevance to the present world but was located in the eschatological sphere; the requirement to love one's enemies would become applicable, as far as nations were concerned, only after history, that is, in the next world. Through Jean Lasserre, then, Bonhoeffer learned that, "the people of God are one Christian people, that no nationalism, no race or class hatred, can strike effective blows if we are one."[21] Essentially, it was impossible to be a Christian and a nationalist, and as Eberhard Bethge has pointed out, this was a very unfamiliar idea to German theologians in 1930.[22]

Erwin Sutz, Bonhoeffer's Swiss friend, turned out to have been a student of Karl Barth, and he was instrumental in setting up a meeting between Barth and Bonhoeffer in Bonn immediately on Bonhoeffer's return to Germany in July 1931. A link was thus forged that was to have crucial historical significance for the later struggle of the church against National Socialism. Erwin Sutz also remained a key contact for Bonhoeffer in Switzerland during the latter's function as a double agent working for German counter-espionage, after the outbreak of war in September 1939.

All told, the sojourn in New York came to have immense significance for Bonhoeffer's later career, not least by virtue of the fact that there he was introduced to the "Negro question." Through a black fellow student at the theological seminary, Frank Fisher, Bonhoeffer established a warm solidarity with the struggle of black Americans for equality. Fisher's friendship enabled Bonhoeffer to gain invitations to the homes of the "outcasts of Harlem." It stimulated him also to read voraciously about the black struggle and even to become an avid collector of recordings of Negro spirituals, which he later introduced to his students in the "illegal" seminary at Finkenwalde, an institution that Bonhoeffer directed from mid 1935 until its enforced closure in September 1937.

Indeed, Bonhoeffer developed a particular admiration for black Americans despite the fact that their religious culture was so utterly different from mainstream Lutheranism. The closest manifestation in Germany to Negro religion would have been that of the Moravians, with which Bonhoeffer certainly was not unfamiliar because his mother, Paula, in her youth had spent some months at Herrnhut whence the Moravians came; and also through his childhood governess Käthe Horn, also a Moravian, though she exerted no particular religious influence over her charges.[23] However, it was important in Bonhoeffer's formation that he was aware of alternative forms of religiosity. Consequently, in the enthusiastic preaching and singing of black American congregations, Bonhoeffer began to appreciate their unique spirituality, so vastly different from that of the formal world of German Protestantism. As well, Bonhoeffer observed the vigorous outreach to the urban proletariat, something that did not happen in Germany apart from rare exceptions. There, church membership was predominantly bourgeois, as Bonhoeffer noted in his doctorate. If the church was what Bonhoeffer understood it to be, then it was essential for the gospel to be brought to the masses who had turned away from it.[24]

In the large Abyssinian Baptist Church in Harlem, Bonhoeffer observed impressive numbers of people from the neighborhood not only worshipping but participating in a variety of different clubs, some recreational and social but others devoted to improving the educational standards of members as well as promoting charitable work. This was especially noticeable at that time of the Great Depression when the church had maintained a soup kitchen and organized relief for the unemployed.[25]

This behavior by such an educated German, a *Bildungsbürger*, of that time would have to be regarded as fairly atypical. In Germany, one did not normally go out of one's way to befriend colored people whose culture would have to be automatically considered, if not inferior, then so alien as to contain nothing worth appropriating. Bonhoeffer's curiosity, however, about things foreign, combined with his growing conviction that in Christ all distinctions were done away with, allowed him to transcend the general prejudices of his class and identify with the plight of the marginalized. This became eloquently manifest in a sermon that Bonhoeffer preached in New York on Armistice Day (11 November 1930) on 1 John 4:16: "God is Love; and he that dwelleth in love dwelleth in God, and God in him." And to this he added that striking text from St. Paul's Epistle to the Galatians, chapter 3:28: "There is neither Jew nor Greek, there is neither slave nor free, there is neither male nor female; for you are all one in Christ Jesus."

In a word, the experiences gained in America enabled Bonhoeffer to overcome the parochialism and cultural aloofness that was characteristic of so many Germans who would have seen themselves as *Bildungsbürger*. This was attested to emphatically by Bonhoeffer's student friend at Union Theological Seminary, Paul Lehmann, in whose house Bonhoeffer had been a frequent guest. Lehmann, who was of Russian-German ancestry, made very perceptive observations about the *Bildungsbürger* Dietrich Bonhoeffer that highlighted the latter's uniqueness: "His aristocracy was unmistakable yet not obtrusive, chiefly, I think, owing to his boundless curiosity about every new environment in which he found himself and to his irresistible and unfailing sense of humor. [He manifested the] capacity to see oneself and the world from a perspective other than one's own. This paradox of birth and nationality in Bonhoeffer has seemed to me increasingly during the years since to *have made him an exciting and conspicuous example of the triumph over parochialism of every kind*."[26] These observations about the 25-year-old Bonhoeffer by an American with the background to be able to make such judgments certainly define him as an unmistakable *Bildungsbürger*, but one in whom the reappropriation of the gospel in the American environment enabled him to appreciate the value of very different cultures.[27]

Finally, with regard to America, Bonhoeffer became more aware of the ecumenical movement, not least through Jean Lasserre, and of the willingness of Americans to revise their views on German "war-guilt" on which some church groups had passed resolutions favorable to Germany. Indeed, Bonhoeffer had frequently lectured on the ill effects on Germany of the Treaty of Versailles generally, and of Article 231 in particular. This had required that Germany accept sole responsibility for the outbreak of the war and its consequences. He very much rejected this as a miscarriage of international justice but still acknowledged Germany's main, if not sole, guilt in these words:

> Before the war we [i.e., the Germans] lived too far from God; we believed too much in our own power, in our almightiness and righteousness. We attempted to be a strong and good people, but we were too proud of our endeavors, we felt too much satisfaction with our scientific, economic and social progress, and we identified this progress with the coming of the Kingdom of God. We felt too happy and complacent in this world; our souls were too much at home in this world.
>   Then the great disillusionment came. We saw the impotence and weakness of humanity, we were suddenly awakened from our dream, we felt the wrath of God upon us, and we recognized our guiltiness before God and we humbled ourselves under the mighty hand of God.[28]

This passage could only have been written in the light of Bonhoeffer's changed theological position, for it is a clear indictment of the prevalent "folkish" thinking and of the values of cultural Protestantism. On his return home, apart from spending the first crucial few weeks attending Barth's lectures and seminars in Bonn, Bonhoeffer accepted nomination to attend a conference in Cambridge, England, in August 1931, as youth secretary from Germany to the World Alliance for the Promotion of Peace through the Churches.

The Ecumenical Involvement

From now on Bonhoeffer became committed to strengthening the ecumenical movement because he saw in it a great potential for intensifying agitation for peace at an international level. This had become acute because just as Bonhoeffer had departed for New York, the Nazis had risen to become a mass party in the September 1930 national elections, advancing from a mere 12 to a formidable 107 seats in the Reichstag. This development convinced Bonhoeffer that war would become inevitable if the Nazi movement succeeded in becoming the dominant force in German politics. The only way to avoid this was to mobilize world opinion for peace by means of the ecumenical movement, and this became Bonhoeffer's all-consuming project until 1937, by which time political events had made such hopes totally illusory. Nevertheless, his ecumenical agitation at that time has remained a great challenge to all churches even to this day.[29] The world situation back in the 1930s, however, had compelled Bonhoeffer to focus more intensely on ecumenical issues. He had already defined what he meant by Christendom when he wrote that

> Christendom is the great congregation of people who humble themselves before God and who put their hope and faith in the love and help of God. Christendom is the community in which men stand together for each other, as a brother stands for his brother. Christendom is one great people composed of persons of every country in concord in their faith and their love because there is one God, one Lord, One Spirit, One Hope. That is the marvellous mystery of the people of God. Above all differences of race, nationality, and custom there is an invisible community of the children of God.[30]

Mobilizing Christendom initially seemed a distinct possibility through the agency of the World Alliance conference in Cambridge, but it was going to prove more problematic than Bonhoeffer at first anticipated. The ecumenical movement was dominated by Anglo-Saxons whose theology he had already found far too sentimental and theologically superficial. Certainly, the World Alliance was an organization that had peace as its main objective, but Bonhoeffer saw in it far more potential for energetic and positive action if the member churches could have been more radical. They seemed to think that peace would reign in the world if more nations were prepared to treat each other charitably, arrange periodic conferences, and pass innocuous resolutions that gave the illusion of unanimity. In fact, the prevailing Anglo-Saxon attitude was not to tackle any issues that could prove divisive. The main thing for them, so their behavior indicated to Bonhoeffer, was to avoid controversy over the hard questions. For him and his German colleagues, the British and American theologians were, frankly, intellectually lazy, lacking in rigor and largely starry-eyed. On this problem Bonhoeffer commented in a letter to his friend, Helmut Rössler, after his return from the United States in October 1931 as follows:

> My stay in America ... made one thing plain to me: the absolute necessity of cooperation and at the same time the inexplicable gap that seems to make such cooperation impossible. Looked at from across the Atlantic, our standpoint and our theology look so local, and it seems inconceivable that in the whole world just Germany, and in Germany, just a few men, have understood what the Gospel is. And yet I see a message nowhere else.[31]

The few Germans to whom Bonhoeffer here was referring would have been those followers of Karl Barth, like himself, and as arrogant as it might sound, Bonhoeffer's observation was essentially correct—at least with regard to those Anglo-Saxons he encountered, who were dominant in the ecumenical movement. They simply lacked both the scholarship and the rigor.

A significant thing about the World Alliance was that one of its more prominent founders was the German theologian Friedrich Siegmund-Schulze (1885–1969). He was one of the very few pacifists within the German pastorate,[32] and his collaboration with British theologians before the war had led to the foundation of the Alliance. Given the right-wing Hegelian mind-set of many German theologians, however, it was far from popular among them. Consequently, Bonhoeffer, by virtue of his support for ecumenism and the peace movement, was taking a minority position. That this was the case was evidenced by expressions of hostility among German theologians prior to the Cambridge conference scheduled for 1–5 September. There had been a preliminary meeting in Hamburg, 1–3 June, of the German branch of World Alliance supporters for the purpose of preparing the agenda that was to include national and international obligations and disarmament.[33]

It was well known in German theological circles that a German delegation would be attending the Cambridge meeting, and this Hamburg gathering of a preliminary committee—Bonhoeffer was still in America—provoked a vehement reaction from the nationalist opposition. It is vital to bear in mind that such hostility existed toward the very idea of ecumenism among many German theologians. Two of the most uncompromisingly "folkish" theologians, Professors Paul Althaus and Emanuel Hirsch, protested in the pages of the *Hamburger Nachrichten* as follows under the headline "Protestant Church and International Reconciliation":

> In this situation there can in our opinion be no understanding between us Germans and the nations that were victorious in the World War; we can only show them that while they continue the war against us, understanding is impossible. . . . This gives full force to the demand that all artificial semblance of cooperation should be broken and that it should be unreservedly recognized that Christian and churchly understanding and cooperation on questions of rapprochement between the nations is impossible so long as the others conduct a policy lethal to our nation. He who believes that understanding can be better served otherwise than by this denies the German destiny and confuses consciences at home and abroad, because in this matter he does not honor the truth.[34]

The article was reproduced on the front page by all the right-wing newspapers throughout Germany. The national Lutheran paper, *Allgemeine Evangelische Lutherische Kirchenzeitung*, also endorsed it. Certainly, there was very little sentiment in Germany for reconciliation with former enemies or for international understanding. At that time Germany was in the throes of massive unemployment and difficulties meeting the repayment of foreign loans, the blame for which was attributed to the intolerable conditions imposed by the Treaty of Versailles.[35]

Clearly, Bonhoeffer would have to do some energetic persuasion among his coreligionists if the ecumenical movement were ever to appear theologically justifiable to them. Indeed, he stated quite categorically that, "because there is no theology of the ecumenical movement, ecumenical thought has become powerless and meaningless, for example, at the present time in Germany, because of the political wave of nationalism among German youth."[36] This he attempted to remedy at a youth peace conference in Czechoslovakia, on 26 July 1932, with a long address entitled "Zur theologischen Begründung der Weltbundarbeit" (A Theological Basis for the World Alliance's Work).[37]

An Ecumenical Theology at Last

This address is a milestone in ecumenical theology. In introducing the subject, Bonhoeffer said,

The concern of youth deeply involved in the Ecumenical movement is this: how does our ecumenical work, or the work of the World Alliance, look in the mirror of the truth of the Gospel? And we feel that we cannot approach such questions in any other way than by a new strict theological work on the biblical and Reformation basis of our ecumenical understanding of the church in complete seriousness and without regard for its consequences or for its success. We ask for a responsible theology of the ecumenical movement for the sake of the truth and certainty of our cause.[38]

Bonhoeffer went on to reproach the Anglo-Saxons for having a "static concept of peace," as follows:

Under the predominant influence of Anglo-Saxon theological thought in the World Alliance, the peace envisaged here has previously been understood as the reality of the Gospel, we may well say, as part of the kingdom of God on earth. From this standpoint the ideal of peace is made absolute, i.e. it is no longer regarded as something expedient, as an order of preservation, but as a final order of perfection, valid in itself, as the penetration of another order into the fallen world. External peace is a "very good" condition in itself. It is thus an order of creation and the kingdom of God and as such must be preserved unconditionally. But this conception must be repudiated as religious enthusiasm, and therefore untrue to the Gospel. International peace is not a reality of the Gospel, not a part of the kingdom of God, but a command of the angry God, an order for the preservation of the world toward the coming of Christ. International peace is therefore no ideal condition, but an order which is directed towards something else and is not valid in itself. . . . There can only be a community of peace when it does not rest on lies and on injustice. Where a community of peace endangers or chokes truth and justice, the community of peace must be broken and the battle joined.[39]

The admonition here directed at the British and American theologians concerning their "static concept of peace" implied strongly that they should devote more rigorous thought to what it meant and how to achieve it. At the same time, Bonhoeffer reproached those German theologians who were hostile to ecumenism—for believing in a "static concept of truth." These men, as we have seen, were so preoccupied with repudiating what they considered to be the lie of sole German war guilt as fixed in the Treaty of Versailles, that they were blind to the ways in which Germany had not lived up to the vision of Christ as expressed in the Sermon on the Mount. Bonhoeffer's problem with those of his colleagues who regarded the state and the German *Volk* as "orders of creation" was essentially that they did not take into account the *fallenness* of creation. They would not acknowledge that neither state nor *Volk* were immune from sin.

Consequently, in his address of July 1932 Bonhoeffer was at pains to find a rationale for the ecumenical movement that lay between the extremes of Anglo-Saxon sentimentalism of ineffectual "good fellowship," on the one hand, and the angry and embittered nationalism of many of his fellow countrymen, on the other. Of course, behind the address lay the theology already expressed in *Sanctorum Communio*, namely, that the church was Christ's presence, *Christus praesens*, in the world. That being the case, the word of the church was the word of the ever-present Christ, and as such ought to be comprehended as gospel and commandment at the same time. Indeed, the church's obligation in the world was courageously to proclaim the gospel for the sake of world peace. And the precondition for this was the most extensive knowledge of the realities of this world.

Here, however, was a problem: could the church ever know completely or sufficiently the realities of the world? Bonhoeffer conceded that it would not be adequate for all situations; there would be errors of judgment and that the name of God would even be misused. This should not, however, paralyze the church into resignation. On the contrary, the central fact that the church possessed the assurance of the forgiveness of sins enabled it to pronounce fearlessly on the realities of the world. This has been analyzed by the German theologian Martin Heimbucher, as follows:

> Reality becomes for the church according to Bonhoeffer an ethical sacrament, and that in a twofold sense: as certain as the forgiveness of sins is bestowed upon the church in word and sacrament, so with the same certainty may the church pronounce its commandment in the world. And as the Gospel is concretely appropriated via the sacrament, so the commandment is defined and actualized in reality.[40]

As Bonhoeffer analyzed the realities of the world in 1932 there was an urgent need for the proclamation of the gospel of peace and reconciliation by the church. This was the commandment that ought to be proclaimed. The problem was to get the divided church to act as one. And here Bonhoeffer developed a highly creative vision for the World Alliance. It should no longer perceive itself as an organization to facilitate occasional ad hoc meetings among the various churches; rather, because it was the embodiment of the *Oekumene* it had a commission actually to be a real manifestation of the church, *eine Lebensform der Kirche*, on the world stage. As such, its task was to exert itself to proclaim the gospel in order to meet present day demands. And this proclamation was directed to the state, which for the Lutheran Bonhoeffer amounted to a reformulation of the neo-Lutheran doctrine of the two kingdoms that quite emphatically allowed the state to function autonomously without any reference to the moral law. This type of thinking was disastrous, as Bonhoeffer understood, because there was no sphere of life that was not under the revealed word of God in Christ. For this very reason there was no longer any separate sphere of political life in which the state operated according to its own laws of existence. *Everything* was under the lordship of Christ.[41]

This, of course, raised the question of how should the church behave toward the state. And here Bonhoeffer came from a distinctly German understanding of the state in contrast to the Anglo-Saxon for whom the state was a mere facilitator for commerce and enforcer of the law. It needs to be kept in mind that in the Lutheran-German tradition, the state was taken seriously as the agency in the world to which God has allocated authority in the secular affairs. The distinction with regard to Anglo-Saxons lies in the fact that they rather perceived the state as a man-made expedient to regulate life in accordance with the wishes of men, though Christians obviously preferred their politicians to be essentially driven by the values of the gospel of Christ. In Germany, of course, it was never the role of the church to tell the state what to do; it could claim no power over the state. Nevertheless, the church had the task of reminding the state of the eschatological new creation of the world. That meant where men had the capacity, as in the First World War, to wreak total destruction on nations, to violate the created order, the church had the duty to demand a change in present circumstances, in short to admonish the nations to put an end to war. To this extent the church did set a limit to the autonomy of the state, and although the church, strictly speaking, may normally make only apolitical statements, it did become eminently political when it proclaimed that the order of international peace was God's command for the world today. Bonhoeffer's view was expressed as follows:

> The church, which comes together in the World Alliance, speaks to Christendom, telling it to hear its word as the commandment of God, as it stems from the forgiveness of sins. But it speaks also to the world, telling it to alter its conditions. The world cannot hear the true voice of the church, nor can the state. The voice of the church cannot be authoritative towards it, but the state finds in the church a critical limit to its possibilities and thus will have to take notice of it as a critic of its actions.

Finally, Bonhoeffer made his most devastating criticism of the World Alliance. He wanted it to perceive itself as the church proclaiming the gospel in accordance with the truth, but it was precisely the question of the truth, he believed, that divided the member churches and rendered them impotent in the struggle for peace. And here Bonhoeffer became most impatient:

> The churches included in the World Alliance have no common recognition of the truth. It is precisely here that they are most deeply divided. When they say "Christ" or "Gospel" they mean something different. That is at present the most pressing problem in ecumenical work. We can only speak as the church, which proclaims the truth of the Gospel. But the truth is divided. And that must make our word powerless, indeed false. But almost more fearful than this fact is the way in which we gladly set ourselves above it. We may not play with the truth, or else it will destroy us. Here we are on the edge of the abyss. If we would only open our eyes! But of course that will not do away with the fact of the division of the one true church, which alone would be in a position to speak. . . . I know of no solution here. I can only point to one thing, namely that where the church recognises the guilt of its division and where it feels it must still speak out under the commandment of God, the forgiveness of sins is held out and promised to the humble. Of course this cannot be a *solution* of our need, but only the expression of the waiting of the whole church for *redemption*. The last message that can be given here is that the church should remain humble in its need and live from forgiveness alone.[42]

Surely this statement had made Bonhoeffer a prophet in his time. Indeed, the current ecumenical movement is still wrestling with the problem how precisely to implement Bonhoeffer's initial admonition from July 1932 because the demand for peace is still at the top of the world's agenda. After the Nazis had seized power, Bonhoeffer had further occasion to reiterate his demand that the ecumenical movement constitute itself as the universal church. That was at a conference in Fanø in Denmark in August 1934, where he called for nothing less than an ecumenical council for peace. Division among the member churches and theological weakness in assessing reality combined to frustrate this vision, as it still does today.

To this point we have learned that Bonhoeffer had made the pilgrimage from being a patriotic *Bildungsbürger* to becoming a radical critic of the prevailing nationalistic theology of his peers as well as being equally critical of what he called Anglo-Saxon sentimentalism and lack of theological rigor. Crucial to this process was the theological impact of Karl Barth as well as the experience gathered in America. The sojourn at Union Theological Seminary also forced Bonhoeffer to "look over the fence," an essential prerequisite for any ecumenical dialogue. One had to cooperate with the "separated brethren" provided a common theological language could be negotiated. First, though, all sides had to agree on the importance of the search for this language. Dialogue was essential.

Bonhoeffer believed, justifiably, in the event, that German theological rigor, as he expressed it in the address "A Theological Basis for the

World Alliance," was the way to promote this dialogue. Of crucial significance in Bonhoeffer's pilgrimage was the conviction, in contrast to that of his nationalistic peers, that war could have no further place in God's plan for humanity. This was a frontal attack on the deepest convictions of the vast majority of German *Kulturprotestanten* whose worldview was formed by the Hegelian/neo-Rankean schema. In the event, Protestants of this mind-set rejected Bonhoeffer—and even today they are struggling to come to terms with him.[43]

By the year 1932, Bonhoeffer's spiritual/intellectual life had reached a turning point. His statements subsequent to that year indicate that he had been forced to rethink many things when he was enrolled at Union Theological Seminary in New York between 1930 and 1931 where he had encountered the "Negro problem" and "Anglo-Saxon theology." As well, the encounter with Jean Lasserre and the Erwin Sutz, led Bonhoeffer to alternative views. By then, too, the ecumenical movement had become a field of endeavor in which Bonhoeffer was challenged to revise the previously dominant "nationalist" theology of many of his German colleagues. On his return to Germany, the first thing he did was to go to Bonn for the purpose of finally meeting and hearing Karl Barth. All these elements in Bonhoeffer's experience must have had their effect, as his many public statements attest. At the same time, the blatant brutality of the Nazi movement clearly confirmed in his mind the absolute necessity of opposing it with the gospel of Christ, as it were, reappropriated. This is eloquently expressed in a lecture to students at the Berlin Technical University on 4 February 1932.

On close examination this lecture must be regarded as a window into the mind of Bonhoeffer in this phase of his development, immediately prior to the advent of the Third Reich. In it he has left us with a major statement of his reassessment of the nature of the world of nation states that underlines yet again his total disenchantment with the Hegelian-Rankean system of permanent power struggle as the essence of the history of salvation. As such, it is revolutionary in the context of a German Protestantism that accepted, by and large, the Hegelian philosophy of history as paradigmatic. Early 1932 was a time of acute internal political crisis in Germany, engendered largely by the impact of the Great Depression, the consequent massive growth in unemployment, and the government's impotence to master this gigantic problem. There were over six million breadwinners out of work. Bonhoeffer, as then student chaplain, contributed to a series of lectures being held at the Technical University in Berlin, and he chose the subject of "Das Recht auf Selbstbehauptung," the right to self-assertion, delivered on 4 February 1932.[44]

"The Right to Self Assertion"

The significance of this address lies in the fact that it is a radical rejection, not only of the Hegelian schema but also of the entire Western capitalist system and the kind of ruthlessly competitive society that it produced. It stands in stark contrast to the Barcelona lecture on "Basic Questions of a Christian Ethic" examined earlier. This new address on the right to self-assertion signifies a "revolution" against capitalism and all forms of political violence that derive from it. Unrestrained capitalism, as Bonhoefffer had come to believe, was a system based on the exploitation not only of labor but also of the environment. It was the cause of much human suffering as well as the spoliation of nature, but Bonhoeffer's solution was not Marxism-Leninism but Christianity rightly understood.

He began his address by speaking to the students about the dire situation of unemployment with which many of them would be confronted on completion of their courses. Bonhoeffer understood the Marxist terminology correctly in that he referred to labor power as a commodity, in German, *Ware,* similar to the English word "ware" as used in commerce for items for sale. As a consequence of the Depression and the mass unemployment, this "ware," human beings, was becoming increasingly devalued both as individuals and as a class. The worker was confronted with the harrowing question: how did one have the right to be employed and earn a wage when thousands of others had nothing and had to survive on the dole. In holding down a job that thousands of others could do, one was in a social-Darwinist situation of the survival of the fittest, and one had to look on while others were deprived of any prospect of survival with any human dignity. If one insisted on the "right to self-assertion," then that is what happened.

Survival was a question not only for individuals but also for professional groups and classes. Tradesmen were locked into a despairing struggle for their existence. The community was really split into warring classes as Marx described, where the bourgeoisie felt threatened with ruin while the proletariat believed it could only survive and establish its rights at the cost of the bourgeoisie. All this hostility endangered the very basic institutions of civil society. For example, the institutions of marriage and family that had existed for centuries were threatened with dissolution, and Bonhoeffer inquired whether the defenders of these institutions had a right to protect themselves in such a situation.

Everything was confronted with or involved in a struggle for survival. Here Bonhoeffer had clearly in mind what would happen if out of the industrial chaos of the Depression the Communist Party actually triumphed and imposed their scheme of human society on the nation.

Obviously, the church would disappear and in place of it there would arise private religious associations. As well, the universities would be reconstituted as mere trade schools. It was a strange prospect that confronted humanity at that time when every element of society was locked in a struggle for survival, whether to assert its right to continue as before or simply give up the struggle and go under.

Bonhoeffer then observed that the struggle not only affected society as a whole in all its sectors but that nations, too, were confronted with the same question of survival. What right to existence did nations have? Did an old established nation have the right to prevent the rise of a young flourishing one? Or, alternatively, did a young and strong people have the right to overrun an old neighboring nation by force and to eject it from the community of nations? Further, did a nation have the right to expand its borders to win *Lebensraum* for its people who were suffocating for lack of space, simply to survive? And did a nation have the right to destroy the flourishing culture of a neighboring country? The great question of the time was whether it was a case of each nation insisting on its rights or of simply abandoning the struggle and being cast on to the dung heap of history.

Bonhoeffer then posed the rhetorical question by stating that none of the above questions were questions of rights but simply of historical development, questions of how power relationships were adjusted throughout the history of the world. That was one possibility, he said, but it was not a moral possibility. To this point Bonhoeffer portrayed the situation as Hegel might have done. These issues were the simple realities of history but this situation left the radical Christian Bonhoeffer with a great challenge. He wanted to show that the "right to self assertion" was sub-Christian.

The difficulty with the American-European world, predicated as it was on the capitalist system, was that it could not envisage a workable alternative. Bonhoeffer saw just such an alternative operating in India, at that time under the British Raj against which the Indian idealist, Mahatma Gandhi, with his principle of nonviolence, was inspiring a liberation movement. Clearly, Bonhoeffer had been very impressed by Gandhi's principles of nonviolent opposition to the ruling power, and in this lecture projected an idealized and simplified image of the situation in India with the aim of inspiring his German student audience with Gandhi's way of surviving against seemingly overwhelmingly hopeless circumstances. Indeed, Bonhoeffer was pointing out in a somewhat oblique way that if the non-Christian Indian could suffer in such a heroic manner, enduring such immeasurable humiliation with patience and dignity, it should be all the more feasible for Germans who had the example of the crucified Christ ever before them.

Behind Gandhi, so Bonhoeffer argued, was an ancient civilization that arose in a country where it was possible for an ordinary worker's family to survive relatively easily because the basic means of life were readily available. These circumstances engendered a style of life that was self-sufficient, contented, and that led to an identification of the individual with the forces of nature. This taught the people a reverence for the sacredness of all life. As a result, killing anything was wrong; there should be no violence done to any living thing. Indeed, the individual should fight against any desire to kill, to impose his own will by force, should strive to overcome hatred with love, and so on. In a word, the individual had to learn to suffer, learn to suppress violent urges, and, finally, learn to die, because all this was better than asserting oneself and descending into violence. In this way the individual soul, which was at one with the soul of the universe, remained whole and holy. Indeed, human beings, by virtue of love and suffering, were made one with the universe and survived.

As Bonhoeffer pointed out, in order to understand this kind of thinking it was necessary to appreciate that in Hindu culture the individual encapsulated the universe in himself or herself; a person was a microcosm of the universe. The practical consequence for life was that the individuals were self-sufficient, solely responsible for themselves. It had been Gandhi's greatest achievement to extend this teaching that was directed first to the individual person and then to an entire nation, placing the community under one commandment: thou shalt not destroy any life form; suffering is better than to live by violence. This, of course, happened: Gandhi's followers, for example, at the infamous Amritsar massacre at the hands of the British authorities, suffered with great human sacrifice for their nonviolent protest. In this way the question concerning the "right to self-assertion" in India at the time of the Raj was expressed.

Bonhoeffer then went on to make observations on what the civilization of the West was based. It found the solution to its problems in war and industrial production. Here Bonhoeffer was appalled at the *Konzeptionslosigkeit*, that is, the inability to devise alternative solutions regarding this problem. Indeed, the history of the West taught us that it was essentially a history of wars. There humanity was locked in a veritable social-Darwinistic struggle for survival that had disastrous consequences. The history of India, Bonhoeffer argued, on the other hand, was a history of passive suffering. Further, war in European historiography had a quite different significance from, say, war between two indigenous (or primitive) tribes. And here Bonhoeffer made a reference to "modern historiography" which had remained committed to the recognition of violence as essentially endemic to the human condition.

That is to say, war between two putatively civilized European states had an advanced cultural significance as Hegel sought to show. Bonhoeffer did not here mention Hegel by name, but it is reasonably clear that when he used the German word *Geschichtsschreibung*, "historiography," he meant the German historical profession that practically to a man assumed the Hegelian understanding of the function of the power struggle in history.[45] Bonhoeffer then went on to affirm that war was, so to speak, the forerunner of the machine in its spiritual significance. In the age of the machine, one might have expected that war had been rendered obsolete. He then suggested that war, and then the machine, had been the typically Western ways of solving the problem of human society. The spiritual implications of this demanded to be understood.

Having thus juxtaposed the Indian with the Western solutions to life, Bonhoeffer postulated that the Indian way was the more truly human way, and the Western way was that of brutes—in short, the subhuman way, the long history of Christianity notwithstanding. It was a distinguishing characteristic of the East that human beings were able to suffer for the sake of the soul, whereas in the West men strove to master nature in order to force it into their service.

From these observations, Bonhoeffer concluded that the basic theme of European-American history was man's struggle for mastery over nature. On the other hand, Bonhoeffer regarded the Indian's assessment as deeper and stronger because he maintained an attitude of passivity or resignation. This was certainly not a feature of Western man's attitude to nature, which, for him, posed a permanent challenge. Indeed, in contrast to the Indian attitude to nature, Bonhoeffer argued, the European could not love nature without perceiving in it the demonic forces that threatened him. Western man's relationship to nature was thus a divided one. Nature denied him everything and therefore he had to win things from it against its will. The Indian, by contrast, received everything from nature and therefore loved it; life was not a struggle against nature but a continual receiving from it, so Bonhoeffer observed.

At this point Bonhoeffer made a profoundly chilling observation: the European had to win his right to life not only against nature but also against other human beings by struggle. His life meant essentially "killing." Here, in Bonhoeffer's thought, the Hegelian schema for human behavior, illustrated in the repeated clash of nations, is unquestioningly apparent. This had never before been made so tragically clear as in the previous fifteen years, that is, since the First World War. Indeed, the behavior of Western humanity bore this out with brutal force.

As well, it was not only the attitude to nature that distinguished the European but also his attitude to history and to other people. His comprehension of life was driven by the "right to self-assertion," and this was in fact the right to life. Life, however, was not something that human beings gave to themselves; rather it was something they received, and something that was suffered and endured. Through the passive experience of birth human life was determined. The individual's lifelong commitment to family and country was a consequence of the accident of birth. Life for Western man meant being bound by history and his community, the product of history, and that meant to be bound to other human beings. The individual grew into a world that he did not create himself. It defined him, and he acknowledged himself bound to it. Indeed, life meant to be bound simultaneously both toward the past and toward the future, to be obligated to others in the environment in which one found oneself, and that demanded an attitude of responsibility.

Bonhoeffer recognized that great individualists regarded the commitments imposed by birth and environment as a curse. In the Old Testament story, Jeremiah cursed the day he was born, and in a comparable way so did Nietzsche's Zarathustra. These were examples of human beings striving for the right to self-assertion, to free themselves from the bonds of their history and their community. One demanded to be free from nature, indeed to assert the right to the great human possibility of the individual's freedom from nature, his superiority over the animal world. Man in such an autonomous status had the ability and the right, so argued Bonhoeffer, freely to choose death in whatever cause he deemed to justify it, and included the possibility of self-sacrifice.

Bonhoeffer's thought here is certainly confronting and can only be comprehended through coming to grips with his theology of service, of *being there for others*. This derived, of course, from his understanding that being a Christian, a member of the Body of Christ, the church, preordained that the individual was called to die after the example of Jesus of Nazareth who sacrificed himself for others. Bonhoeffer went on to assert that man was only free over nature and history if he were likewise free for death. And here is his insight: the right to self-assertion became the right to a death freely chosen. And this was the one possibility that remained unchallengeably valid: that man only became truly human, and was capable of really asserting himself, if he is free for death. This truth, however, would be heard and received only where the individual human being responsibly grasped his historical commitment, if he understood that he was not master of his own fate. Instead, he had to comprehend own life solely in terms of responsibility to his fellow human beings. Indeed, it demanded the cheerful surrender of self. The individual lived not in isolation but essentially through and for others. And here Bonhoeffer established a rule by which he himself lived and died: only out of this responsibility did the individual life derive the right to self-assertion, not because the life belonged to him but because it belonged to the community, to others—in short, to his fellow human beings. Indeed, this relatively early (1932) explanation of what being a Christian implied turned out to be truly prophetic in the case of Bonhoeffer's own death. He was being rigorously logical within the framework of his theology of life that meant, essentially, being of service to others. The following qualification makes this clear: man was free only in death; indeed the right to self-assertion meant the right to death, freedom to die, but this did not affirm any right to self-destruction *but rather the freedom to sacrifice one's own life*. A right to life existed only through the capacity to die for others.

As Bonhoeffer had tried to show, to live in an industrial society meant inevitably the death of others who went under in the competition for livelihood, and so life had to be led in openness to the certainly of death, not as glorification of the individual but as sacrifice for fellow human beings. Indeed, only when the individual was capable of comprehending and valuing his life from the standpoint of death could he answer the question concerning his right to life and his right to self-assertion.

From this observation Bonhoeffer went on to affirm that people were not simply individuals but rather members of a community that encompassed the family unit, the church, the various groups that comprised modern industrial society, right up to the nation itself. No one group could live unto and for itself; one was compelled to live in relationship with others, indeed in responsibility for fellow human beings including neighboring nations. There was simply no such thing as an isolated life; interdependence was to be an accepted given. But then Bonhoeffer added an interesting observation that can only be understood as a critical reference to the Nazi Party program. Of course, he said, even for the nation there was that demonic possibility of it tearing itself from the historical context to attempt to live absolutely alone, turned in on itself, in denial of its responsibility. The nation received its power and energy from the possibility of the free death of the entire nation.

Then, however, Bonhoeffer went on to affirm, only when a nation responsibly endorsed its historical context, that is, its obligation to its brother nations, which of course could include a deadly enemy, did it live solely for the death of sacrifice for the brother. In short, only if a nation were prepared to die for its brother, may it live. War (and machines) as the means of self assertion of the community demanded the sacrifice of the individual,[46] but the nation derived its sole right to exist from its preparedness for sacrificial death on behalf of the other, and that meant also for the enemy who is also a brother. At no time may the nation become the expression of selfishness and self-adulation. Whenever that happened, affirmed Bonhoeffer, it was a debasement, and one had to protest.[47]

The reference to the Nazi movement and its ideology is very clear. Hitler and his followers had brought Germany, Europe and the world in general, to the crossroads that Bonhoeffer saw as a time for crucial decision. He affirmed that war came from an epoch of European history when nations were persuaded that only in the killing of the other could *Lebensraum* be won. As far as machines were concerned, and here is clearly meant modern industrial society, the struggle was primarily against nature rather than men per se. And for this reason its modus operandi was much more ruthless. The real catastrophe was when machines were consciously employed in the destruction of human life. And here Bonhoeffer made an observation that reappears in his statements about the role of the ecumenical movement as essentially an instrument for promoting peace. The machine, designed originally to subjugate nature in the service of humanity, now, through its destructive potential, had really made war something impossible to contemplate. This was clearly because of the damage that could be inflicted on all combatants, regardless of who emerged victorious. This prospect would make it function as the ultimate deterrent.[48]

The Nazi menace was judged by Bonhoeffer to presage another great war. He was clearly desperately concerned that this should be avoided, and was trying to instruct his fellow Germans not only what another war would cost the nation but also the entire civilized world. For this reason he asked whether the time had come that all humanity, forming a unity, would no longer need sacrifice and openness to death. In the past, humanity had lived according to the schema of the sacrifice that individuals and communities made. Now, Bonhoeffer proposed that the time had come when, since, in a sense, the entire human race formed a unity, sacrifice and openness to death was no longer needed because there would be no further point to it.

These thoughts bring Bonhoeffer to remind his audience that behind this image of humankind, which was essentially a Western image, was the Christian tradition that derived from the person of Jesus of Nazareth, the son of man and the son of God, the Christ. By his death on the cross he accomplished the substitutionary sacrifice on behalf of humanity out of which alone humanity could live. Indeed, since the events on Calvary, humanity had lived from Christ's sacrifice for his brothers, that is all humanity. Jesus really lived, but the faithful saw his life in the shadow or light of what was accomplished at Golgotha: Jesus' death for his brothers. Since he was free for death he could live because he sacrificed himself for the brotherhood of humankind. For this reason was Jesus' life essentially in the service of the sacred brotherhood: "that they all may be one" (John 17:11). And also for this reason the gospels spoke of the necessity of taking up one's cross and following him; his death sanctified his life, and his and our death sanctified our life. And only where people became free for sacrifice for the most sacred brotherhood of humankind for which Jesus of Nazareth died, had human beings become free to live.

In this way Bonhoeffer had sought to convince his listeners at the height of the great unemployment that engendered the political crisis in the Reichstag that in turn would lead to the Nazi seizure of power, that the way to the future being offered by the Nazis was a recipe for disaster. The only way was to accept the suffering that the mass unemployment caused, and to seek to build up the European brotherhood, especially, among former enemies. That was the way of Christian *Realpolitik*.

What this address by Bonhoeffer revealed was his intense, indeed revolutionary, Christ-centered prophetic calling and how he sought to apply it in the crisis situation of the time. In a very real sense, Bonhoeffer had distanced himself radically from the dominant Lutheran-Hegelian view of the nation in the world that was regarded as paradigmatic among most German Protestant theologians. The German community, however, at that time had been so traumatized by the war, Versailles, and now the economic crisis that Germans attributed to the unjust peace treaty, that the thought of asking people to bear their suffering in the true Christian spirit, as Bonhoeffer was indeed asking, was frankly utopian. The persuasive power of the demagogue Hitler rested on his ability to conjure up and manipulate the image of undeserved German victimhood. This, in the end, proved immeasurably more powerful than the attempts of a far-sighted and gifted young pastor to get his fellow subjects to apply the principles of the Sermon on the Mount reinforced by referring to the teaching of the non-Christian Indian Gandhi, who Bonhoeffer would have regarded as embodying the content of the Sermon on the Mount to a fuller extent than his Lutheran-Christian contemporaries.

The Wedding Experience

Eberhard Bethge relates that Bonhoeffer's university chaplaincy at that time had been a less than edifying experience for the young intellectual pastor. In retrospect it is not surprising that he may have felt this, given the acute socioeconomic conditions engendered by the unprecedented mass unemployment. The apparent hopelessness of the situation must have caused many a compassionate pastor to despair, but Bonhoeffer's vocation to serve stood him in good stead. Even at this early stage of his ministry when he was responsible for university classes and involved in the ecumenical movement, he could respond readily to the church authorities' (consistory) directive to take over a confirmation class in the Zion parish in the working-class suburb of Wedding in Berlin for which purpose he had rented a room in the house of a local baker from January 1, 1932, as his temporary accommodation.

Bonhoeffer was in fact being required to step into a role for which he was, as a particularly upper class *Bildungsbürger*, socially ill-equipped to fulfill, namely the ad hoc task of instructing a class of fifty particularly unruly and underprivileged boys for confirmation, an obligation that lasted until mid-March 1932. It was a case of not only being obedient to the church authorities but of having to redirect his pedagogic gifts in a situation for which he had previously no training or experience. It was especially daunting because the pastor whom Bonhoeffer replaced had found the task so intimidating that he had to resign on health grounds—and was in fact so stressed that he died several weeks later. Bonhoeffer wrote to his Swiss friend Erwin Sutz that the boys had "quite literally harassed [that pastor] to death."[49] Nevertheless, Bonhoeffer embraced this duty with vigor and sensitivity. He confided to Sutz that he was really looking forward to meeting the fifty sets of parents though it meant real work (*wirkliche Arbeit*). Their domestic conditions were, he said, mostly indescribable due to poverty, chaotic conditions and immorality. Despite this, however, Bonhoeffer could comment that the boys were still open, with the potential to surmount their circumstances. He was astounded that under such conditions they did not completely degenerate, and he wondered how he himself might behave in such an environment, and concluded that these people, the Berlin proletariat, possessed great inner strength to be able to resist the demoralizing effects of their living conditions.[50]

These thoughts stamp Bonhoeffer as a particularly sensitive *Bildungsbürger*. Indeed, he was experiencing an aspect of working-class life that normally he would never have encountered. Only the "diaconal structure" of the church which he served enabled this experience, which is warmly recounted by the Danish Bonhoeffer scholar Jørgen Glenthøj.[51] Here we see the young man from such a privileged background, initially anxious about how he could relate to the boys of the poorest parents, boys who were wild and extremely difficult to manage—and we see *them* being won over by Bonhoeffer's personality and generosity, both materially and especially with his time. The young pastor even purchased the cloth from which the boys' confirmation suits were tailored, and after the confirmation (13 March 1932) had actually built a club shack for the boys on land he had rented in Biesenthal. Here

Bonhoeffer spent weekends with newly confirmed boys as well as with students. In addition, he took some of the confirmees to his parents' country house at Friedrichsbrunn.[52] All this was remarkable given the fact that Bonhoeffer's predecessor failed to make any impression on his charges. His relationship to the boys' parents Bonhoeffer did, however, find difficult. Visits to their homes, he reported, were very strained occasions, doubtless because of the obvious social gulf separating the *Bildungsbürger* and the proletariat. Eberhard Bethge reports, however, that Bonhoeffer learned a great deal from this enforced engagement with the working class. It was valuable experience that he was able to pass on to his theological students later in Finkenwalde. And five years later, while in Tegel prison, Bonhoeffer found he was able to put fellow inmates at ease in speaking to them because many were not unlike the people he had come to know in Wedding.[53]

W. D. Zimmermann comments also on this encounter with the working class at Wedding and notes that these people were "red," meaning that at the very least they would have voted Social Democrat and even more likely Communist. So Bonhoeffer had been taken considerably outside his "comfort zone." This, however, was his way of coping with the existential crisis of the unemployed. Indeed, the episode at the Zion parish in Wedding was but one example of Bonhoeffer's social involvement during the great unemployment. In the summer of 1932 he also participated in the founding of a short-lived youth club in Charlottenburg, Berlin, but that did not survive the Nazi seizure of power in January 1933. In addition Bonhoeffer had associated himself with Professor Friedrich Siegmund-Schultze's social work in East Berlin (*Soziale Arbeitsgemeinschaft Berlin-Ost*) that had been running since 1911. Again this too fell victim to the Nazi takeover, as Siegmund-Schultze was one of the very first opponents of Nazism forced to flee into exile in Switzerland where he was forced to remain until after the war.[54]

Siegmund-Schultze and Bonhoeffer would scarcely have perceived themselves as being engaged in the political class struggle. Neither social democracy nor the dictatorship of the proletariat were ideals that could have moved politically conservative theologians, no matter how concerned they were for the plight of the working class. Indeed, socialism was not an issue with which the younger pastor was at all familiar at first hand, although, as we have seen, Bonhoeffer was very sympathetic to the cause of black emancipation when he attended Union Theological Seminary in New York. And, as recounted above, Bonhoeffer was moved by the plight of the unemployed in the great economic crisis in a way that would have frankly disturbed most of his coreligionists. Despite all this, however, radical political change emanating from a politicized working class was not something Bonhoeffer envisioned. Certainly, he came to endorse the necessity of removing by assassination the barbaric dictator, but this he justified on uniquely theological and by no means political grounds. As well, Bonhoeffer had not considered himself personally competent to devise a constitution for a post-Nazi Germany. In that regard he tended to rely on established conservative Lutheran professors of history and law of his acquaintance. This issue will be dealt with in chapter 8.[55]

Notes

1. J.R.C. Wright, *'Above Parties': The Political Attitudes of the German Protestant Church Leadership 1918–1933* (Oxford, 1974), 57–8; Daniel R. Borg, *The Old-Prussian Church and the Weimar Republic: A Study of Political Adjustment 1917–1927* (Hanover/London, 1984), 184–87.
2. See the translation of the 6th edition in Oxford University Press paperback from 1968.
3. Ibid., 57.
4. See the translation in the selection of Ranke's key theoretical statements edited by Georg G. Iggers and Konrad von Moltke, *The Theory and Practice of History* (Indianapolis/New York, 1973), 5.
5. Barth, *Epistle to the Romans*, 79.
6. At that time Bonhoeffer wrote to Bethge that the church had to come out of its stagnation and engage with the world and the great existential issues confronting mankind. "I feel obliged to tackle these questions as one who, although a 'modern' theologian, is still aware of the debt that he owes to liberal theology". See *Letters and Papers from Prison* (1971 edition) 336, and *DBW* VIII. 555.
7. *Act and Being* (London, 1962), 90–91, and *DBW* II, 85. See also, *Letters and Papers from Prison* (London, 1971), 10, and *DBW*, VIII, 30.
8. *Letters and Papers*, Dietrich Bonhoeffer in letters to Eberhard Bethge, 3/4/1944; 29/5/1944; 16/7/1944; 25/7/1944 and in notes penned in July/August 1944. Of course, the overwhelming thrust of what Bonhoeffer wrote in the desolate isolation of Tegel prison was that even there he was still sustained under the protection of a benign and loving father. See Bethge, *Dietrich Bonhoeffer*, 99 [cf. 2000, 135]. See in this regard *DBW*, X, 357–378.
9. *DBW*, II, 90. See the commentary on the relationship between the post-doctoral dissertation, *Act and Being* and the inaugural lecture by Clifford Green, Dietrich Bonhoefffer: *A Theology of Sociality* 74; 115. See also *DBW*, X, 357–78 for the full text of the inaugural lecture.
10. *Antrittsvorlesung* (Inaugural lecture, 31/7/1930), *DBW*, X, 377.
11. Bethge, *Bonhoeffer*, 99 [cf. 2000, 135], *DBW*, X, 378.
12. See Larry Rasmussen, *Dietrich Bonhoeffer: Reality and Resistance* (Louisville, 2005), 15–24. passim.
13. See Bethge, *Bonhoeffer* 104–05 [cf. 2000, 142–43] and *DBW*, X, 423, Note 5.

14. Ibid., 116 [cf. 2000, 157].
15. *DBW*, X, "Studienbericht für das Kirchenbundesamt," 272, and *DBW*, XV, 459–60.
16. In *No Rusty Swords*, 114. See the German original, "Protestantismus ohne Reformation," in *DBW*, XV, 431–60.
17. Ibid., 117–18.
18. Ibid., 118.
19. Ruth Zerner, "Dietrich Bonhoeffer's American Experiences: People, Letters and Papers from Union Seminary," *Union Seminary Quarterly Review* 31, no. 4 (1976): 261–82. See also, Elizabeth Raum, *Dietrich Bonhoeffer: Called by God* (New York, 2002), 44, 50, 53–54.
20. Bethge, *Bonhoeffer*, 112–13 [cf. 2000, 154].
21. Ibid., 113 [cf. 2000,154].
22. Ibid.
23. Ibid., 21 [cf. 2000, 35].
24. *Sanctorum Communio DBW*, I. See notes on page 290. Cf. Mark Ellingsen "Bonhoeffer, Racism and a Communal Model for Healing," *Journal of Church and State* 43, no. 2 (2001): 238.
25. Zerner, "Dietrich Bonhoeffer's," 270.
26. Bethge, *Bonhoeffer*, 114 [cf. 2000, 155] (emphasis added).
27. Of relevance here is a black American pastor's appreciation of Bonhoeffer's theology as essentially color blind; a real achievement for the gospel of Christ in an environment where white Christians had a long way to go to understand that Christianity is meant precisely to be to be "color blind." See Josiah Ulysses Young III, *No Difference in the Fare: Dietrich Bonhoeffer and the Problem of Racism* (Grand Rapids, 1998).
28. *No Rusty Swords*, 79, and *DBW*, X 579. The very same passage was used by Bonhoeffer in a lecture he gave at Union Seminary on the subject of the Great War held presumably in November 1930, i.e., close to Armistice Day. But he gave many talks to a variety of audiences in New York at this time. See *DBW*, X , "Vortrag zum Thema 'Krieg'," 381–88.
29. Wolf Kroetke, "Nur das ganze Wort ist mutig: Oekumene als Ernstfall theologischer Existenz. Das Beispiel Dietrich Bonhoeffers," *Bonhoeffer Jahrbuch* (2004/5): 125–145.
30. From the sermon on Armistice Day, 1930, taking 1 John 4:16 as his text. See, *No Rusty Swords*, 76–78. See also *DBW*, X, 577.
31. Bethge, *Bonhoeffer*, 122 [cf. 2000, 166]. See Bonhoeffer to Helmut Rössler, 18/10/1931, *DBW*, XI, 33.
32. On the significance of Siegmund-Schulze generally, see Julian Jenkins, *German Pacifism Confronts German Nationalism-The Ecumenical Movement and the Cause of Peace in Germany, 1914–1933* (New York, 2002). See his account of Bonhoeffer's critique of the World Alliance for its lack of theological rigor on pages 205–213. Specifically on the origins of the World Alliance, see John A. Moses, "The British and German Churches and the Perception of War, 1908–1914," *War and Society* 5, no. 1 (1987): 23–44. On Siegmund-Schultze's social work among the Berlin working class, see Hartmut Sander, ed., *Friedrich Siegmund-Schultze 1885–1969. Begleitbuch einer Austellung des Evangelischen Zentralarchivs* (Berlin, 1985), 42–65.

33. Bethge, *Bonhoeffer*, 148 [cf. 2000, 195].
34. Cited after Bethge, *Bonhoeffer*, 148–49 [cf. 2000, 195–6]. On the political/theological views of Althaus and Hirsch, see, Robert P. Erickson, *Theologians under Hitler: Gerhard Kittel, Paul Althaus and Emanuel Hirsch* (New Haven, 1985).
35. Bethge, *Bonhoeffer*, 148–49 [cf. 2000, 195–96]. When Bonhoeffer got back to Germany he became deeply involved in chaplaincy work at the Technical University, Berlin, and in a spiritual address (*Andacht*) based on Luke 4:3f. to unemployed students on February 4, 1932, he formulated ideas that challenged the established presuppositions of his "folkish" (*völkisch*) contemporaries. See *DBW*, XI, 394–96.
36. Bonhoeffer, "A Theological Basis," in *No Rusty Swords*, 159, and *DBW*, XI, 328–29, 330, 338–39.
37. Edwin Robertson's translation of this title in *No Rusty Swords* (previous footnote) is slightly inaccurate. A better rendering for *Begründung* would be "foundation" or "justification."
38. Bonhoeffer, "A Theological Basis," in *No Rusty Swords*, 160. *DBW*, XI, 330.
39. Ibid. 168–69. *DBW*, XI, 338–39.
40. Martin Heimbucher, *Christusfriede*, 108. See Bonhoeffer's elaboration of this in "A Theological Basis," in *No Rusty Swords*, 164. *DBW*, XI, 334.
41. Bonhoeffer, "A Theological Basis," in *No Rusty Swords*, 161. *DBW*, XI, 337. This constituted a breakthrough in Lutheran thought about the state that Bonhoeffer elaborated later in *Ethics*.
42. Ibid., 172–73. *DBW*, XI, 343–44.
43. See Wolfgang Huber, "Ein ökumenisches Konzil des Friedens—Hoffnungen und Hemmnisse," in *Ökumenische Existenz Heute*, ed. Wolfgang Huber, D. Ritschl, and T. Sundmeier (Munich, 1986), 110–11.
44. See *DBW*, XI, 215–26. Also, Larry Rasmussen, "The Ethics of Responsible Action," in *The Cambridge Companion to Dietrich Bonhoeffer*, 208–9. See also Bethge, *Dietrich Bonhoeffer* 166–68 [2000, 224].
45. Georg G. Iggers, *The German Idea of History* (Middletown, Conn., 1968). Iggers, of course, has drawn attention to this critically in contrast to von Srbik, who in his *Geist und Geschichte* endorsed the idea of the *Machtstaat*. See, above, chapter 1.
46. *DBW*, XI, 224.
47. Ibid.
48. Ibid. 225.
49. Ibid.
50. Bonhoeffer to Sutz, 28 February, 1932, *DBW* XI, 64–65.
51. *Dokumente zur Bonhoeffer-Forschung, 1928–1945* (Munich, 1969), 28–9.
52. Bethge, *Bonhoeffer*, 168–71 [2000, 227–28].
53. Ibid. 171[2000, 228]
54. Ibid. 171–74 [229–34]; Schlingensiepen, *Dietrich Bonhoeffer*, 103; On Siegmund-Schultze's career, see Stefan Grotefeld, *Friedrich Siegmund-Schultze. Ein deutscher ökumenischer und christlicher Pazifist* (Gutersloh, 1995); *Biographisch-Bibliographisches Kirchenlexikon*, entry on Friedrich Siegmund-Schultze (1885–1969).
55. Wolf-Dieter Zimmermann, *Bruder Bonhoeffer* (Berlin, 1995), 27–28.

5

THE CHURCH STRUGGLE TO 1937

Bonhoeffer's intellectual-spiritual biography has been traced up to 1933 in order to show on what basis he was able to critique the Nazi regime, and to do so, moreover, in such a unique way. Numbers of other fellow pastors and theologians also saw the threat to the church's existence, but none were able to articulate it as consistently as Bonhoeffer did. It is here crucial to keep in mind that Bonhoeffer's critique derived not from having absorbed Anglo-Saxon ideas of constitutional freedom and the rule of law, although he certainly had every opportunity to do so from his sojourns in both the United States and England. Rather, the critique, as the previous chapter demonstrated, arose out of his theological development and his essentially German-Lutheran understanding of the correct role of secular authority, of governance and civic order.[1]

The Nazi movement, based as it was on the leadership principle and the extreme racialist doctrine of blood and soil (*Blut und Boden*), rejected out of hand all Western ideas of parliamentary government, political pluralism, the rule of law, basic rights, and the equality of the individual citizen before the law.[2] All these concepts, according to Nazi ideology, were held to be incompatible with the true Germanic spirit. Citizens of different persuasion or race such as liberals, social democrats, communists, but particularly people of non-Aryan descent, were considered not to be truly German. Consequently, ideas of universal human brotherhood, say, as derived from Christianity or the Enlightenment, were rejected out of hand. The Nazis made membership of the *Volksgemeinschaft*, the national community of people of the same blood, conditional on both ideological and racial considerations. People had not only to cultivate the "right" *Gesinnung*, or mental attitude, they had also to be demonstrably of Germanic blood.

This posed a problem for the Christian churches both of which, Roman Catholic as well as Protestant, Hitler and his associates considered to be obstacles to the spread of Nazi ideology. In fact it is now quite obvious that Nazism perceived itself virtually as a religion that aimed to capture the hearts and minds of all Germans. And it was to be a religion that not only justified the absolute rule of a "folkish" demagogue but also the creation of a greater German power state that would subjugate all European nations to its will.[3] Christianity, in either manifestation, was eventually to be eliminated. Certainly that was the Nazi agenda, but it took some time for the churches to realize this because of the deep-seated nationalism and anti-Semitism of their hierarchies and adherents.[4] In the end, however, the Nazi church policy had to fail. The history of the Church Struggle in Germany is really the history of a painful learning process that taught the churches that it was irreconcilable with the gospel of Jesus of Nazareth to allow the state to assume the role of almighty God in the world. As will become clear, Dietrich Bonhoeffer was the most perceptive and far-sighted German churchman of his day in analyzing the danger that Nazism posed for both church and nation.[5]

The Evil of Nazism

The two issues that initially caused Bonhoeffer to discern the fundamental evil of Nazism were, first, the "leadership question," the *Führerprinzip,* and, secondly, the "Jewish question."[6] Bonhoeffer, like his entire family, particularly his brother and brothers-in-law, who were lawyers, was highly critical of the Nazis rejection of the constitution, their contempt for the law, and their brutal racialism. This caused Bonhoeffer to prepare a long statement on what constituted true political leadership in the German context. It was entitled "The Leader and the Individual in the Younger Generation." Obviously, the question had been exercising Bonhoeffer's mind for some time, and it had been arranged that he present it in an address on Berlin radio on 1 February 1933. President Hindenburg, however, had just appointed Hitler Reich Chancellor on 30 January, and so the nightmare that Bonhoeffer feared had materialized.

Bonhoeffer's radio talk, however, would have exceeded its allocated time and had to be interrupted but not because of any suspected subversive intent. The Nazis had not yet begun to monitor radio broadcasts until 25 March 1933. Despite this, though, Bonhoeffer was able to give the full lecture the next month at the German College for Politics (Hochschule für Politik), then under the direction of the man destined to become first postwar German president, Theodor Heuss (1884–1963). Heuss was politically a liberal as well as being a committed Protestant from the southern German state of Swabia, a traditionally pietistic region. What is crucial here is that Bonhoeffer subjected Hitler's demand for unconditional loyalty on behalf of the people to a radical theological and historical critique.[7] Obviously, though, given his Lutheran commitment, Bonhoeffer, could only mount a critique from within that established German tradition, as will become clear.

Central to the argument was that although political leadership was necessary in all societies, it had to be responsible to the established constitutional traditions. It was also understood that, in Germany, such leadership was traditionally responsible to God and that leaders perceived their office as service to the subjects over whom they ruled. In the postwar situation, when the Weimar Republic had tried unsuccessfully to master the massive economic and political problems that beset the nation, Bonhoeffer conceded that the youth of Germany had come to yearn for a charismatic, indeed messianic, leader to restore dignity to the fatherland. Here, Bonhoeffer warned that in the emotion-charged German situation there was a danger of the leader becoming intoxicated by the expectations placed in him by overenthusiastic youth. He wrote:

> Men, particularly young men, will feel the need to give a Leader authority over them as long as they themselves do not feel mature, strong, responsible enough themselves to realize the claim misplaced in this authority. The Leader will have to be conscious of this clear limitation of his authority. If he understands his function in any other way than as it is rooted in fact, if he does not continually tell his followers quite clearly of the limited nature of his task and of their own responsibility, if he allows himself to surrender to the wishes of his followers, who would always make him their idol—then the image of the Leader will pass over into the image of the misleader, and he will be acting in a criminal way not only towards those he leads but towards himself.[8]

What is significant about this passage is Bonhoeffer's play on the words "leader" and "misleader." The original German for "leader" is *Führer*. But the word that is translated here as "misleader" is *Verführer*, which means "seducer." Clearly, the courageous pastor was accusing Hitler of seducing the German people by his hysterical nationalistic diatribes. Bonhoeffer then went on to elaborate the true qualities of a responsible German leader. Above all he should be someone able to dismantle illusions to keep his subjects focused on realities. He should refuse to become an idol and should exercise self-restraint. Indeed, "he must limit himself to his task in all soberness." As well, the office was only a temporary one, and the leader served his office, not the reverse. Further, as Bonhoeffer elaborated:

> Only when a man sees that office [of Leader] is a penultimate authority in the face of an ultimate, indescribable authority, in face of the authority of God, has the real situation been reached. And before this authority

the individual knows himself to be completely alone. The individual is responsible before God. And this solitude of man's position before God, this subjection to an ultimate authority, is destroyed when the authority of the Leader or of the office is seen as ultimate authority.[9]

For Bonhoeffer, what Hitler had been saying about himself was heresy in two respects; it was contrary both to God's law and to the true German political tradition. Here the young pastor became quite forthright; it is little wonder that his broadcast was cut off by the anxious station management.

The fearful danger of the present time is that above the cry for authority, be it of a Leader or of an office, we forget that the man stands alone before the ultimate authority and that anyone who lays violent hands on man here is infringing eternal laws and taking upon himself superhuman authority which will eventually crush him. The eternal law that the individual stands alone before God takes fearful vengeance where it is attacked and distorted. Thus the Leader points to the office, but the Leader and office together point to the final authority itself, before which Reich or state are penultimate authorities. Leaders or offices, which set themselves up as gods mock God and the individual who stands alone before him, must perish. Only the leader who himself serves the penultimate and ultimate authority can find faithfulness.[10]

Bonhoeffer thus perceived Hitler as the incarnation of evil, indeed the complete antithesis to the ideal of a true leader; in reality a seducer of the people. This was already a far-sighted and perceptive assessment of Hitler that few of Bonhoeffer's fellow pastors shared. In arguing as he did, Bonhoeffer placed himself at odds with many in the Evangelical Church, particularly those who went so far as to advocate acknowledging Hitler as the Messiah of the German people. With hindsight this idea seems utterly absurd, but there were those Protestants at the time who called themselves "German Christians" whose project was to align Christianity with Nazism, thus sacrificing the essence of the gospel on the altar of "blood and soil" nationalism. The Church Struggle was initiated with the aim of preventing the "German Christians" from gaining control of the entire church, something they almost achieved with the endorsement of the Nazi party. This theme will be picked up again later in this chapter.[11]

Confronting the Jewish Question

The other key issue on which Bonhoeffer based his critique of the Nazis was the Jewish question. He felt compelled to address this once the

Nazis had decreed the exclusion of citizens of Jewish blood from being appointed to public office, and that included baptized Jews from holding office in the church as ordained pastors, the so-called Aryan paragraph. That was on 7 April 1933. Already on 15 April Bonhoeffer's manuscript "The Church and the Jewish Question" had been completed, and it was published in June 1933. Again the critique is mounted from a purely theological standpoint within the German-Lutheran historical context. That is to say, Bonhoeffer's point of departure was the "doctrine of the two kingdoms" according to which the state exerted its sovereignty in secular matters while the church had the exclusive task of preaching the gospel without interference from the state.[12] Bonhoeffer had perceptively observed that the state in its handling of the Jewish question had clearly violated this doctrine, because in excluding baptized Jews from the ranks of the clergy the state would be prescribing who could be baptized and who could not. It was exclusively the church's role to determine that. A genuinely German state would be one rooted in the national heritage: it could not violate the "doctrine of the two kingdoms" and remain true to itself.

In this address, Bonhoeffer was really instructing the Nazis about the true Germanic idea of the state and of legitimate church-state relations within the German historical context. And, of course, he was rebuking the "German Christians" whose chief aim was to conform the church to Nazi policy in the conviction that the church, too, had to be purged of all non-Aryan elements in order that it should become and remain a genuinely "Germanic Church."

The real question at issue was whether the church must submit to the state's ruling here as if the "doctrine of the two kingdoms" no longer applied. Indeed, Bonhoeffer defiantly proclaimed that "the state which endangers the Christian proclamation negates itself." He went on:

> All this means that there are three possible ways in which the church can act towards the state: in the first place, as has been said, it can ask the state whether its actions are legitimate and in accordance with its character as state, i.e. it can throw the state back on its responsibilities. Secondly, it can aid the victims of state action. The church has an unconditional obligation to the victims of any ordering of society, even if they do not belong to the Christian community. "Do good to all men." In both these courses of action, the church serves the free state in its free way, and at times when laws are changed the church may in no way withdraw itself from its two tasks. The third possibility is not just to bandage the victims under the wheel, but also to put a spoke in the wheel itself. Such action would be direct political action, and it is only possible and demanded when the church sees the state fail in its function of creating law and order, i.e. when it sees the state unrestrainedly bring about too much or

too little law and order. In both these cases it must see the existence of the state, and with it its own existence, threatened. There would be too little law if any group of subjects were deprived of their rights, too much where the state intervened in the character of the church and its proclamation, e.g. in the forced exclusion of baptized Jews from our Christian congregations or in the prohibition of our mission to the Jews. Here the Christian church would find itself in *statu confessionis* and here the state would be in the act of negating itself. A state which includes within itself a terrorized church has lost its most faithful servant.[13]

It is important to note that Bonhoeffer had communicated his thoughts on the issue of *status confessionis* to the churches abroad directly in English. His text was reproduced by the American ecumenist C. S. Macfarland in his study *The New Church and the New Germany* (1934). In it he noted succinctly, quoting Bonhoeffer:

> The exclusion of the Jewish Christians from our communion of worship would mean: The excluding church is erecting a racial law as a prerequisite of Christian communion. But in doing so, it loses Christ himself, who is the goal of even this human, purely temporal law. The Christian church cannot deny to any Christian brother the Christian communion which he seeks. A church which excludes the Jewish Christians puts itself under the Law; it is then a church of Jewish-Christian type.
>
> A Christian church cannot exclude from its communion a member on whom the sacrament of baptism has been bestowed, without degrading baptism to a purely formal rite to which the Christian communion that administers it is indifferent. It is precisely in baptism that God calls man into this concrete church and into its communion.[14]

Here we have the essential idea of Protestant Christian resistance against the Nazi regime which, clearly, for Bonhoeffer was emphatically not a legitimate German state as it was regarded by the heretical "German Christians." This illustrates how important it was to Bonhoeffer that there should be a right theology of church-state relations. As he would later point out, the "German Christians" were not genuine representatives of the church because they served in reality the Antichrist. Indeed, that Bonhoeffer regarded Hitler as the agent of the Antichrist is abundantly clear from the correspondence he conducted with the English theologian Canon Leonard Hodgson in Oxford from 18 July 1935.[15] In it the young German theologian was at pains to explain that it was impossible for the Confessing Church in Germany to be associated with the pro-Nazi Reich Church at a forthcoming ecumenical meeting in England. He wrote:

The teaching as well as the doctrine of the responsible leaders of the Reich Church has clearly proved that this church does no longer serve Christ but that it *serves the Antichrist*. Obedience to the only heavenly Lord Jesus Christ continues to be coordinated, nay, subordinated to obedience towards worldly masters and powers. . . . No member of the Confessional Church (and much less one of her ministers) can thus recognize in the Reich Church a church which pays homage to our Lord Jesus Christ as God and Savior; he must rather beseech God that He may confound the Reich Church Government as an instrument of the Antichrist.[16]

Another point to make about "The Church and the Jewish Question" is that, as it was for Luther, so too was it for Bonhoeffer and his coreligionists in 1933: the Jewish question would cease to exist once all Jews were baptized. There was, indeed, a Jewish problem to be solved, but the Nazi way of addressing it violated the church's way. Bonhoeffer came in time to revise his position on this, and instead of demanding that Jews become Christians he developed a theology of ecumenical outreach toward the Jewish community according to which there was no requirement for them to submit to baptism. This position, however, was not reached without a considerable learning experience. In fact, Bonhoeffer in his essay "The Church and the Jewish Question" had only taken the first, but nevertheless crucial step, in developing a revolutionary solution to this age-old problem, which was, of course a problem for the church only because it had made it a problem.

It is essential here to trace the steps by which Bonhoeffer moved toward a theological reconciliation between church and synagogue. First, virtually alone among his colleagues, Bonhoeffer saw the consequences for the church of Nazi Jewish policy. And, of course, the church for Bonhoeffer was the Lutheran church, and it is out of the tradition bequeathed to it by the sixteenth century Reformer that Bonhoeffer mounted his own protest against the Nazi state in the twentieth century. Not surprisingly, his comprehension of the Jewish question had not yet gone beyond Luther's, and that was, Jews needed to be baptized, made members of the Christian church, in order to inherit the benefits of Christ's salvific promises; in short, they needed to leave the fellowship of the synagogue and embrace the church. It is the assumption upon which this demand was based that has incensed certain commentators, not only Jewish ones. For example, the Roman Catholic writer Eva Fleischner, writing in *Judaism in German Christian Theology since 1945*, observed that even Dietrich Bonhoeffer held to the belief that Jews were contemptible.[17] To support her view, Fleischner cited the following passages from Bonhoeffer's essay "The Church and the Jewish Question":

> The Church of Christ has never lost sight of the thought that the "chosen people," who nailed the redeemer of the world to the cross, must bear the curse of its action through a long history of suffering. "Jews are the poorest people among all nations upon earth, they are tossed to and fro, they are scattered here and there in all lands, they have no certain place where they could remain safely and must always be afraid that they will be driven out . . ." (Luther, *Table Talk*). But the history of the suffering of this people, loved and punished by God, stands under the sign of the final home-coming of the people of Israel to its God. And this home-coming happens in the conversion of the people of Israel to Christ. . . . The conversion of Israel, that is to be the end of the people's period of suffering. From here the Christian church sees the history of Israel with trembling as God's own, free, fearful way with his people. It knows that no other nation of the world can be finished with this mysterious people, because God is not yet finished with it. Each new attempt to solve the "Jewish problem" comes to nothing *on the saving historical significance of this people*; nevertheless, such attempts must continually be made.[18]

Fleischner left out the passage here in italics from her text, and Eberhard Bethge points out that while she paid tribute to Bonhoeffer's heroic resistance against the Nazis, she was adamant that there was no documentation that indicated Bonhoffer ever repudiated the curse of God upon the Jewish people. This, of course, is not correct because Bonhoeffer does so in *Ethics* (1940), as shall be seen. However, if these sentences from 1933 (omitted by Fleischner) are scrutinized again, it will be clear that Bonhoeffer could already see the Jewish question in a new light, in contrast to the vast majority of his coreligionists. Indeed, the passages indicate that he had appreciated that the traditional anti-Judaistic theology—namely, that the Jews had to submit to conversion—was in need of revision. This is precisely what Bonhoeffer went on to do. Another crucial point is that in 1933 Bonhoeffer was confronting fellow churchmen who were steeped in the traditional anti-Judaistic theology of the time, and by suggesting to them that they should now suddenly embrace secular and non-baptized Jews as well as baptized ones would have to be seen as unrealistically premature.

Indeed, the historian looking back on Bonhoeffer's intellectual-theological pilgrimage would have to observe that, given the theological milieu out of which he came, it is not surprising that he initially came to confront the "Jewish Question" within the established, traditional Lutheran theological framework. What is significant is that Bonhoeffer possessed the intelligence, humanity, and moral courage to begin to reassess the issues that the Third Reich's racial and church policy raised for German subjects of Jewish faith. He thought them through, as will be shown, to bequeath to the church a revolutionary new theology, indeed, an ecclesiology that saw Judaism and Christianity in a creative, reciprocal relationship and not at irreconcilable loggerheads as in the past. As one Israeli scholar has phrased it, "From the Jewish point of view he [Bonhoeffer] is the pioneer and forerunner of a gradual re-judaizing of the churches in our day."[19]

Some scholars have sought to contrast Bonhoeffer's obvious commitment in 1933 to a theology of punishment of the Jews for the crucifixion of Jesus with his active aid for Jewish refugees from the Third Reich when he was a pastor in London. Attention is drawn to the passages in "The Church and the Jewish Question" (from April 1933) where Bonhoeffer can be said to be ambivalent about the persecuted, non-baptized Jews. There is no doubt that he is clearly still committed to the doctrine of the two kingdoms that accords to the state the right to deal with the "Jewish Question" as it sees fit. However, and this is highly significant, Bonhoeffer warns the state not to overstep the limits of its responsibilities. It may not, for example, encroach on the right of the church to baptize whomsoever it will. This is a radically rigorous exegesis of the doctrine of the two kingdoms whereby Bonhoeffer insists on the autonomy of the church in the spiritual sphere. Both state and church had clearly delineated areas of responsibility from God that were discrete. One did not encroach on the sphere clearly reserved for the other. A state that interfered in this right of the church to exercise its spiritual responsibility to humanity was no state at all, certainly not one that could command the loyalty of Christians.

Indeed, the significance of "The Church and the Jewish Question" is that it was the statement of a traditional Lutheran who was confronted by a state that had betrayed the long-established, putatively inviolate principles of church-state relations. In a word, the Nazi "state" violated the bounden duty of the state to protect all subjects regardless of racial origin or religious background. In this regard the Third Reich constituted a permanent attack on the doctrine of the two kingdoms because it persecuted instead of protecting sections of its subjects. Here the church was justified in taking a stand; more than that, it was obliged to do so. Consequently, Bonhoeffer first affirms the right of the church to interrogate the state about the legitimacy of its policy in regard to the Jews. This was to remind the state of its traditional responsibilities. Second, Bonhoeffer insisted that the church had to behave charitably toward all victims of the state's illegitimate policies—in short, to "do good to all men" unconditionally. And these two tasks were the church's inescapable duty. Third, if the state did not respond, then men of conscience had to consider vigorous opposition to the illegitimate state by taking direct political action because the state was failing in its function of creating law and order.[20]

This final point is an unequivocal appeal to conspiratorial action, something that Bonhoeffer came to take up in 1939. Prior to that, however, we see him engaged in passive opposition, primarily on behalf of the persecuted Jews. This is a crucial factor in evaluating "The Church and the Jewish Question." At a first reading Bonhoeffer appears to be uncompromisingly committed to the established Lutheran theology based on the conviction that the Jews, because of their call for the crucifixion of Jesus, were permanently cursed by God. Certainly, that was the position of most Lutheran pastors. However, a closer scrutiny of the text reveals that Bonhoeffer wanted to overcome that position, hence the above three recommendations for action against the Nazi state. The entire thrust of these is clearly to preserve the dignity and citizenship rights of Jewish fellow subjects. It is obvious that Bonhoeffer saw in the situation an inescapable challenge to the church. He wrote: "In the Jewish problem the first two possibilities will be the compelling demands of the hour. The necessity to direct political action by the church is, on the other hand, to be decided at any time by an 'evangelical Council' and cannot therefore ever be casuistically decided before hand."[21]

As Eberhard Bethge pointed out concerning this issue, Bonhoeffer boldly used the situation to remind the Nazi state that it had exceeded the boundaries of its competences, especially in the way it was "solving" the Jewish problem.[22] And further, as Bethge correctly indicated, Bonhoeffer's recollection was that the judgment of God hung *not only over the Jews but also over the Church for its unfaithfulness*. This was a particularly subtle aspect of Bonhoeffer's critique. He may indeed still have seen the conversion of Israel as the long term necessary outcome, but he had also a warning for the church:

> From here the Christian Church sees the history of the people of Israel with trembling as God's own, free, fearful way with his people. It knows no nation of the world can be finished with this mysterious people, because God is not yet finished with it. Each new attempt to "solve the Jewish problem" comes to nothing in the saving historical significance of this people; nevertheless, such attempts must continually be made. The consciousness on the part of the church of the curse that bears down upon this people, raises it far above any cheap moralizing; instead, as it looks at the rejected people, it humbly recognizes itself as a *church continually unfaithful to its Lord* and looks full of hope to those of the people of Israel who have come home, to those who have come to believe in the one true God in Christ, and knows itself to bound to them in brotherhood.[23] [emphasis added]

Here it is clear that Bonhoeffer had located the church, because of its unfaithfulness, also under the judgment of God. He was emphatic that this "mysterious people," the Jews, had an ongoing saving-historical (*heilsgeschichtliche*) significance. That means that the synagogue still played a role in God's plan for the salvation of the world. Consequently, both church and synagogue were jointly under judgment. Furthermore, no nation in the world could be finished with this "mysterious people" because God was not finished with them. This may be reasonably assessed as a demand upon Christians to see Jews in a kind of fraternal relationship, certainly not hostile, awaiting the historic judgment of almighty God when church and synagogue would be reconciled. Certainly, this came to be Bonhoeffer's position by 1940.

As Eberhard Bethge affirms, it indicated that Bonhoeffer saw the "Jewish Question" as much less a problem for the Jews than for the Christians and the Nazi regime. Admittedly, the demand for Jews to be baptized remained as before, but Bonhoeffer initiated a new phase of church-synagogue relations in that he required Christian solidarity with the persecuted Jews because the state has become derelict, having abdicated its traditional responsibilities. Indeed, he prioritized the need for the church to stand up courageously for all Jews, something that was a totally new departure from long-established attitudes. And in this Bonhoeffer was virtually a voice crying in the wilderness. His colleague, Walter Künneth (1901–97), who produced an "opinion" on the Jewish question around the same time as Bonhoeffer's essay, certainly defended the church's right to baptize Jews, but then he insisted that baptized Jews should not become so visible that their presence could lead to an alienation process in the church. Essentially, Jews were a foreign element in the nation. And the nation was an "order of Creation," a unique part of God's ordering of the world. Consequently, Künneth's proposal consigned baptized Jews to an inferior category in the church. They could not enjoy full and untrammeled membership.[24] Bonhoeffer could never have endorsed such a position because of its totally unacceptable racial and hence theological assumptions, founded as it was on the flawed "orders of creation" theology. At this point of Bonhoeffer's development toward a revolutionary position one may identify four aspects, as follows.

First, Bonhoeffer was still committed to a constitutional order that set a clear dividing line between the respective historic roles of church and state in Germany. The Nazis, however, in their determination to establish a new kind of state were in the process of revising the historically established order to replace it with a political system that was solely dependent upon the political will of a tyrant; instead of order and even handed justice there was caprice and arbitrariness of action.

Second, the old order that presumed obedience to God and service to him was hierarchically organized. This system was now negated by the Führer, who assumed that he alone was the source of all political will and authority, arrogating to himself the status of virtual Savior.[25]

Thirdly, following from this, the new state and its supporters were godless although in their rhetoric they employed frequent references to God or "Providence." In reality, their objective was the destruction of the Christian church.

Finally, the new regime was irresponsible with regard to the German people and other nations as well, frivolously and arrogantly risking the possibility of collective suicide in another war.[26]

These insights of Bonhoeffer stamp him as a highly perceptive analyst who can already see in 1933 that National Socialism was in fact a secular religion, and Hitler its diabolical Messiah who was able to seduce the German people at a time of particular confusion, desperation and humiliation. Resistance to this impending calamity was the duty of all Christian people. However, apart from Bonhoeffer and a handful of his coreligionists very few Germans, Christians or otherwise, could perceive the danger.[27]

Viewed in this light, Bonhoeffer's two statements "The Leader and the Individual in the Younger Generation" and "The Church and the Jewish Question" stamp him as uniquely far-sighted. The latter essay, however, despite the assumption that the Jews still needed to be baptized because of an assumed curse from God, was a necessary first step forward to a revolutionary new ecclesiology based on Christian-Jewish collaboration. Such a position, however, was not worked out by Bonhoeffer until after he had begun writing *Ethics* in 1940. Prior to that, however, he made valiant attempts to reeducate his coreligionists, for example in his contribution to the production of the two "Confessions" that led to the formation of the "Confessing Church" in opposition to the pro-Hitler *Reichskirche*.

The "Jewish Problem" in the Bethel Confession

The Bethel Confession was finally formulated about six months after the publication of Bonhoeffer's essay "The Church and the Jewish Question." And the notable thing is that Bonhoeffer, although he had considerable input into its formulation, in the end refused to sign it. The reason for this was because it was watered down in its final form against Bonhoeffer's wishes in order to comply with the more conservative proclivities of the other consultants, not only with regard to the Jewish question. The initial draft formulated by Wilhelm Vischer (1895–1988) was completed in full consultation with Bonhoeffer, and so had his unqualified endorsement, but the revised published version did not.[28]

Eberhard Bethge comments that while the Bethel Confession, in the form in which Bonhoeffer approved it, exhibited a curious mixture of strong anti-Nazi and anti-"German Christian" sentiment and doctrine, it still retained the traditional Lutheran position with regard to the "people of the Jews" who had rejected Christ. Further, it referred to the replacement of the covenanted people of Israel in the Old Testament, by the Christian church. This is known as *Enterbungslehre*, the doctrine of disinheritance of the Jews, whereby the church is substituted for the synagogue. And it is this doctrine that gave the church the commission to convert and baptize the Jews, literally to embark on a mission to the Jews—*Judenmission*.[29]

All this looked very anti-Judaistic, but Bethge reminds us that the Bethel Confession was directed at the "German Christians" who had in August and September 1933 secured the dominant position in the church's synods and had announced their intention to introduce the Aryan paragraphs into the church. It had to be borne in mind that the "German Christians" claimed that from then on it was the German master race which was the "chosen people" with a special mission to the world and who demanded therefore a "national church" and an expression of Christianity that conformed to the unique characteristics of the German people. Against this background, observed Bethge, the inclusion of "the doctrine of disinheritance" took on a new perspective. What is to be kept in mind here is that the very fact that the Confessing Church insisted, against the stand of the "German Christians," on the continued practice of baptizing Jews, they were defending an existing right of the church in opposition to the Nazi "state" which was in the process of usurping those traditional Lutheran rights. To that extent, argues Bethge, the Bethel confession was a modestly courageous step toward embracing all Jews at that time of acute crisis. This was brought on by the fact that the "German Christian" dominated synod was about to apply the Nazi Aryan paragraph excluding all baptized Jews from the pastorate.

To oppose this by upholding the right of the church to baptize whomsoever it chose without racial restriction of any kind was, under the circumstances, an act of considerable defiance against a blatantly aberrant government and heretical state church that wanted to exclude all Jews from the racial community, and that meant also the church proper. It should be noted that the section of the Bethel Confession in the unpublished August draft which was entitled, "The Church and the Jews" began with the proclamation: "The Church teaches that God from among all the peoples of the earth chose Israel to be His people." So we have a rediscovery of Romans 9–11,[30] where St. Paul reaffirms his solidarity with his kinsmen, stating clearly that, "They are Israelites, and to them belong the son-ship, the glory, the covenants, the giving of the law, the worship, and the promises; to them belong the patriarchs, and of their race, according to the flesh, is the Christ, who is God over all, blessed for ever" [Romans 9:4–5]. The August draft of the Bethel Confession went on to comment:

> God wants the redemption of the world which He began with the call to Israel and who will complete it with the Jews. For this reason He preserves a sacred remnant of Israel according to the flesh who neither by means of emancipation or assimilation are absorbed into another nation nor through Zionist or similar movements are a nation among other nations nor who can be exterminated by Pharaoistic measures. . . . And it can never ever be the task of any nation to take revenge on the Jews for the murder of Golgotha . . . we reject all attempts to misuse the miracle of God's especial love towards Israel according to the flesh as a proof for the religious significance of the Jewish or any other people.[31]

As Bethge reports, such sections as these were edited out of the final published version of the Bethel Confession, and it was this that caused Bonhoeffer to withhold his signature to the document.[32] Nevertheless, the final version of the Bethel Confession, despite its flaws and weaknesses, did not deny that the Jews were God's elect and therefore worthy to be held in respect. And this respect was grounded not simply in humanitarian values, but based in a reevaluation of traditional Christian theology. The crucial point, however, is that Bonhoeffer remained adamant that the future of the church in Germany depended upon declaring unequivocal solidarity with the Jews; indeed the church stood or fell depending on which way it voted on the Jewish question. And in this it experienced great difficulty.

Few of Bonhoeffer's coreligionists in 1933 were as advanced as he was on the Jewish question with regard to the church. It could scarcely be said that he held the Jews in contempt. The more typical attitude of pastors not associated with the "German Christians" who were openly anti-Semitic, was the idea that you could baptize Jews and admit them to the Christian fellowship but that they should not be too prominent because their presence would make the proclamation of the gospel in the German context more difficult. That means simply, so deeply rooted was hostility towards Jews, that even baptized ones were still a stumbling block. Indeed, Jews should really be excluded from the national community because they were foreign. The process of exclusion, however, should take place in such a way that did not contradict "the Christian ethos,"[33] which meant while there should not be violent persecution there would still be social ostracism.

It is, therefore, crucial to note the difference between Bonhoeffer's analysis of the Jewish question and that of the vast majority of his colleagues. In practice they found themselves unable, as a group, to oppose the Nazi policy of exclusion, persecution, and annihilation. But for Bonhoeffer it was a case of finding the church in a situation of *in statu confessionis*. This meant the church had been confronted with a challenge to its very existence to preserve and preach the gospel, and that, therefore, one had no alternative but to make a stand for the truth against the alien regime of violence and hostility toward the true church. This was the essential basis of the church struggle. Other pastors came on side but not exactly for the defending their Jewish brothers so much as a protest against the claims of the "German Christians" with regard to the unity of Holy Scripture and their endorsement of state control of church affairs, as shall be seen.

The Ambitions of the German Christian Movement

As indicated, this group among German Protestants regarded Hitler as the second Savior. For them the *Volk*, the nation, was an instrument of God's plan for salvation, and therefore the Führer's role in protecting the *Volk* was a sacred commission from on high. Hitler, despite the exalted status accorded him by them, was probably not overly impressed by the "German Christians" but found their presence convenient for realizing the initial phase of Nazi church policy, specifically, to coordinate the churches into the National Socialist revolution. In practice that meant checkmating any political influence of the churches. That was important in the case of Rome since the Roman Catholics had been represented by a large political party in Germany, namely, the Center Party (*Zentrum*), at first in Prussia, since 1870. In 1933, this very large nationwide party was effectively rendered politically impotent by a *Konkordat* that Hitler had concluded with the Vatican on 20 July that year which guaranteed the freedom of the Roman Church in Germany to regulate its own affairs *provided in did not engage in any political activity*.[34]

With regard to the Protestant churches the situation was more complex because they were organized in twenty-eight territorial churches. Hitler wanted them fused together into one big *Reichskirche*, a national Church under a *Reichsbischof*. And this is precisely what the "German Christians" wanted to effect. If they could gain control of the various synods then that objective could be achieved. They had already won a majority in the synod of the "Church of the Old Prussian Union," and it had endorsed the Aryan paragraph which the "German Christians" had enthusiastically advocated.[35]

Already on 1 April 1933, the "German Christians" held their national rally in Berlin, where they demanded, in addition to a unified national church, submission to the "leadership principle," the dismissal of all "non-Aryan" pastors, and the unrestricted collaboration with the state in all political and social issues. They behaved, in short, as if the doctrine of the two kingdoms was no longer relevant.[36] This is what alarmed Bonhoeffer, in particular, especially so when the Nazis granted their wish in proclaiming the Aryan paragraph a week later. There then arose a struggle for the leadership of the future Protestant Church of Germany. Hitler's preferred option was for a national church led by someone totally submissive to him. That man was a former navy and army chaplain, distinguished by his virtually complete lack of theological sophistication, Ludwig Müller (1883–1945). When on 23 July after the nationwide church synod elections the "German Christians" in most of the territorial churches gained the majority, they dominated the national synod at Wittenberg on 27 September. On that occasion Ludwig Müller was elected unanimously *Reichsbishof*.[37]

This event unleashed widespread consternation among traditional Lutherans. Bonhoeffer, who was negotiating to go to London at the time, had been in collaboration with Hermann Sasse at the famous Lutheran hospice in Bethel in August 1933 trying to formulate, as we have seen, a definitive oppositional statement against the "German Christians," the Bethel Confession. Bonhoeffer's position on this was concisely spelled out in a letter to his grandmother on 20 August:

> Our work here gives us much pleasure but also much trouble. We want to try to make German Christians declare their intentions. Whether we shall succeed I rather doubt. For even now if they officially make concessions in their formulations, the pressure they are placed under is so powerful that sooner or later all promises are bound to be broken. *It is becoming increasingly clear to me that what we're going to get is a big, popular, national church whose nature cannot any longer be reconciled with Christianity and that we must be prepared to enter upon entirely new paths which we will have to tread.* The question really is: Germanism or Christianity. The sooner the conflict comes out into the open, the better. Nothing is more dangerous than concealing this.[38] [emphasis added]

In Berlin, at the end of September 1933, Pastor Martin Niemöller founded the Pastors' Emergency League (*Pfarrernotbund*), which by January 1934 had acquired a membership of some 7,000 pastors, almost half of those in office in the entire country, signifying that Protestantism in Germany was in the deepest crisis of its history. It had to be recognized that the arrival of the Nazis to power raised crucial existential questions for the church, and Bonhoeffer saw the issue quite clearly. The true church had to oppose all efforts of the regime to pervert Christianity, and that meant to fight the control of the "German Christians" who wanted desperately to be recognized at home and abroad as the only true and legal custodians of the Christian church in Germany.

Then, on 13 November 1933, in Berlin, a rally was held at the Sport Palace of some 20,000 "German Christians." In their boundless enthusiasm for the Nazis, however, they committed a tactical blunder that resulted in a severe loss of support from among the traditional Lutheran rank and file church people. The chief Berlin representative of the "German Christians," Dr Reinhold Krause, took it upon himself in the keynote speech to spell out what the "German Christians" stood for, since many people had not yet fully understood their agenda. In a complete distortion of history and theology, Krause portrayed Luther as the great nationalist forerunner to Hitler's Nazi revolution and declared that what was now happening in Germany was really the logical completion of Martin Luther's original work from the sixteenth century and that what was going on was really the second German Reformation. The aim now was to create a genuine *Volkskirche*, a "people's church," in contrast to a "pastors' church" that was hitherto unattractive to the German masses.

Krause went on by saying that the masses would only find their way to the church when all non-German elements were eradicated. That meant that the Old Testament had to go, and that also the New Testament had to be purified from all superstition and other distortions. In particular the theology of sin and unworthiness which was found in the writings of the Rabbi Paul had also to be eliminated. Instead of all that, the "pure" Jesus doctrine—namely, the heroic figure of the Messiah—had to be the basis of the new proclamation, and, moreover, this doctrine of Jesus conformed to the objectives of National Socialism.[39] It was also resolved by the rally that all pastors who did not endorse this prescription be summarily dismissed. As well, it was demanded that the Aryan paragraph be adopted by all synods that had not yet done so in order to get rid of any pastors who had been baptized Jews.

Needless to say, such views had to offend all traditional believers, and indeed, it proved to be an embarrassment to the new *Reichsbischof* who was at this point concerned to project a more moderate image in order to consolidate the gains already made and win the trust of the broader laity. Krause's speech was diplomatic blunder of massive proportions. The "German Christians" had revealed themselves as wolves in sheep's clothing and had thus conjured up more opposition than they had reckoned with. The effect of the Sport Palace debacle was to accelerate the Confessional movement, since it challenged ordinary Christians to state plainly what it was they really believed in—indeed, what in fact was the substantive basis of their faith. Consequently, from early 1934, all over Germany in the territorial churches, independently of each other, concerned Christians began to set down the essentials of the faith in a series of so-called Confessions, which were statements intended to define what it meant to be a Christian under a tyranny of an unprecedented kind. National Socialism demanded in the end that all individuals submit mind and soul to the leadership of one man as though he were the Savior in person.[40]

At this point, Karl Barth, still at his university post in Bonn, raised his voice with a "Declaration on the right understanding of the reformed confession in the German Evangelical Church," 3–4 January 1934.[41] Finally, after protracted and, at times, acrimonious negotiations, the confessional statements in the various territorial churches were effectively unified for the entire Reich at synods of oppositional churchmen held at Barmen and Dahlem (Berlin) in May 1934. So was formulated the Barmen Confession that was endorsed by many Lutheran, United and Free Churches from all over Germany, and this new church was from then on known as the "Confessing Church," *die bekennende Kirche*. The de facto schism in the German church was now open and official. The Nazis now found themselves in a curious position. Their preferred option, of course, had been a totally subservient Reich church. The "German Christians" had perceived themselves as being able to furnish a version of Christianity acceptable to the new political masters. They had not reckoned with the degree of opposition they encountered. It was imagined that all Protestants would endorse the ultra-patriotic agenda, and this would enable them to surmount any "minor" theological reservations, and declare unequivocal solidarity with the "German Christians."

The reality was, of course, that most German Protestants had quite enthusiastically acclaimed the Führer and his policies, both domestic and foreign. The sticking point was that rigorous Lutherans could not endorse a violation of the doctrine of the two kingdoms. This posed a dilemma for the Nazis, who now found it impossible to persecute thousands of people who were unequivocally "Aryan" in blood and who even declared unswerving loyalty to the Führer, but who wanted to remain traditional German Protestants. This is what was behind the Barmen Confession.

It has to be said, though, that the Barmen Confession was a relatively weak consensus document that in Bonhoeffer's view could have been more forceful in denouncing Nazi racial policy. Instead, it was content to establish basic theological principles. These derived again chiefly from Karl Barth's influence. The first of six theses stated: "Jesus Christ as witnessed to in Holy Scripture is the one Word of God to which we listen and in whom we trust in life and death and whom we have to obey."

That was certainly an excellent point of departure. There then followed a series of repudiations, the most important being, "We repudiate the false teaching that the church can and must accept as sources of her proclamation apart from and beside the one Word of God as well other events and powers, individuals and truths as God's revelation."[42] This, at least, was a an unequivocal statement about the integrity of holy scripture as containing all that was necessary for salvation.

The fifth thesis repudiated the totalitarian claims of the state on both church and in the political sphere, stating:

> We reject the false doctrine that the state, over and above its special commission, should and could become the single and totalitarian order of human life, thus fulfilling the church's vocation as well.
>
> We reject the false doctrine that the church over and above its special commission, should and could appropriate the characteristics, tasks, and the dignity of the state, thus itself becoming an organ of the state.[43]

The intention was clearly to draw a line in the sand with regard to the "German Christians" and their agenda, and it was done by appealing to the heritage of the founder of German Protestantism, Martin Luther. However, as will become clear, the Barmen Declaration was hardly a call to heroic resistance. Apart from Bonhoeffer and a few of his supporters most pastors and theologians were loyal in principle to Hitler as an authentic German head of state, and hence were reluctant to criticize his domestic and foreign policies where these did not touch the church. As late as 1938 the Confessing Church could voluntarily still make a public oath of loyalty to the Führer on his successful occupation of Austria, the Anschluss on 12 March of that year. Only a handful of pastors refused to sign it. They were not, however, persecuted, as the Nazi authorities chose to regard their opposition as a purely internal church affair. And that in itself is an indication that the Nazis at that stage saw no advantage in further persecution of the Confessing Church.[44]

Winning Recognition for the Confessing Church in the Ecumenical Movement

Against this background then, Bonhoeffer's personal stand appears as that of an isolated outsider. Prior to his departure for London, however, Bonhoeffer had the opportunity to attend a meeting of representatives of the World Alliance (15–30 September 1933) in Sofia, Bulgaria. Immediately before that, however, between 9–12 September, a conference of the executive committee of Life and Work was held just outside Sofia at Novi Sad. To that conference the Reich church had sent their delegate, Dr. Theodor Heckel, who was to become, as head of the foreign service section of the church, technically Bonhoeffer's superior. Heckel's task was to justify what had happened in Germany to the international ecumenical movement. In the event he was quite unsuccessful because the conference refused to accept any cover up of the by now well-known outrages that were occurring in Germany. Bishop George Bell as chairman was deputized to make an official remonstration to the Reich bishop.[45]

This would have pleased Bonhoeffer because immediately after, in Sofia, he was to address the World Alliance on "Racial Minorities." When he had done so, he won a resolution condemning Nazi Jewish policy, and as well, he successfully posed another resolution protesting against the Aryan paragraph as irreconcilable with the teachings of Christ. It appeared, then, that the ecumenical movement was unequivocally on Bonhoeffer's side since Heckel's diplomatic overtures on behalf of the Reich church had been met with significant opposition. This had been an unequivocal slap in the face for the Reich church, but it was not going accept defeat, and continued, as shall be seen, to try to win the recognition of the international Christian community *as the one true German church*.

It was at Sophia that Bonhoeffer had made his first acquaintance with Bishop Bell, with whom he was to develop a close collaboration in their joint struggle against the Reich. As indicated, Bonhoeffer was already exploring the option of taking over two German-speaking parishes in London. This appointment was made already for August 1933, though he did not actually take up residence in London until 17 October. The point is that this decision was made prior to the promulgations of the Bethel and Barmen Confessions when there was technically no split in the church. Consequently Bonhoeffer went with the official, though grudging approval of the Reich bishop who was fully aware that Bonhoeffer was an opponent of the "German Christians." Of course, there was the apprehension among the Reich church leadership that the overseas parishes could break away, so they needed to send a pastor who clearly wished to preserve the unity of the German Evangelical Church, and on this score Bonhoeffer could not be faulted. He had been required to declare his allegiance to Germany, but he would not promise to abandon the ecumenical movement.[46]

The eighteen-month sojourn in England was exploited by Bonhoeffer to intensify the church struggle not least through his connection with Bishop Bell. If the Reich bishop had hoped to manipulate Bonhoeffer to add credibility to the new official church administration in Germany he was grossly mistaken. Together, Bonhoeffer and Bell became the spearhead of an ecumenical campaign against the Reich church.[47]

Exercising his role as a leader of the ecumenical movement, Bell issued an Ascension-tide message to all member churches in May 1934 in which he denounced the required submission of the church in Germany to the "leadership principle" as unprecedented in the history of the entire church.

Such a situation made it impossible for the church to receive the guidance of the Holy Spirit. As well, he condemned racial discrimination in the church as a denial of the universal fellowship of all humanity in Christ.[48] The Reich church was left in no doubt that it was out of step with the rest of Christendom, but this, of course, made no impression on the Nazis.

Soon after, as has been seen, the Confessing Church with its Barmen Confession served notice that it was no longer the opposition in the national Church *but the one and only true church* because it alone was unequivocally based on the entire gospel of Christ. Bonhoeffer's concern from now on was to enlist the support of the entire ecumenical movement in solidarity behind the Confessing Church, and he made such expression of solidarity the touchstone of their true Christian commitment because he saw the Confessing Church as the unequivocal custodian of the full gospel, alone confronting the representatives of the Antichrist.[49]

The first opportunity to do this arose at a joint preliminary meeting of the World Alliance and Faith and Order planning committees to be held on the Danish island of Fanø 27–30 August 1934. The Reich church was determined to be the only German representative. Bishop Bell had arranged the agenda so that the situation in Germany would receive full attention, but unfortunately could not avoid accepting bishop Heckel again as the official nominee of the church who was to give an address on "The Problem of the State and the Church of Christ." Bonhoeffer was appalled and initially refused to attend if Heckel were allowed to speak. However, Bell prevailed on him to come and to advocate the case of the Confessing Church.

Heckel's address again was denounced because there was no way he could deny the truth about the suppression of free speech and the racial discrimination occurring in Germany. The meeting, nevertheless, did not go so far as to rule out any future invitations to the Reich church. This was to test Bonhoeffer's persuasive skills to the fullest. As he was convinced that the Nazis would drive Europe and the world again into war he decided to address the issue of world peace in a paper entitled "The Church and the Peoples of the World." In it he challenged the World Alliance to accept the task of proclaiming God's commandment to peace to all the world:

> How does peace come about? Through a system of political treaties? Through the investment of international capital in different countries? Through the big banks, through money? Or through universal peaceful rearmament in order to guarantee peace? Through none of these, for the single reason that in all of them peace is confused with safety. For peace must be dared. It is the great venture. It can never be safe. Peace is the opposite to security. To demand guarantees is to mistrust, and this mistrust in turn brings forth war. To look for guarantees is to want to

protect oneself. Peace means to give oneself altogether to the law of God, wanting no security, but in faith and obedience laying the destiny of the nations in the hand of Almighty God, not trying to direct it for selfish purposes. Battles are won not with weapons but with God. They are won where the way leads to the cross. Which of us can say he knows what it might mean for the world if one nation should meet the aggressor, not with weapons in hand but praying, defenseless, and for that very reason protected by "a bulwark never failing"?

Once again, how will peace come? Who will call us to peace so that the world will hear, will have to hear, so that all peoples may rejoice? The individual Christian cannot do it. When all around are silent he can indeed raise his voice and bear witness, but the powers of this world stride over him without a word. The individual Church, too, can witness and suffer—oh, if it only would!—but it is also suffocated by the power of hate. Only the one great Ecumenical council of the Holy Church of Christ over the entire world can speak out so that the world, though it gnashes it teeth, will have to hear, so that the peoples will rejoice because the church of Christ in the name of Christ has taken the weapons from the hands of their sons, forbidden war, proclaimed the peace of Christ against the raging world.

Why do we fear the fury of the world powers? Why don't we take the power from them and give it back to Christ? We can still do it today. The Ecumenical Council is in session; it can send out to all believers this radical call to peace. The nations are waiting for it in the East and in the West. Must we be put to shame by non-Christians in the East? . . . The trumpets of war may blow tomorrow. For what are we waiting? Do we want to become involved in guilt as never before? . . . We want to give the world a whole word, not half a word—a courageous word, a Christian word. We want to pray that this world may be given to us today. Who knows if we shall see each other again another year?[50]

This prophetic statement was reportedly greeted with great applause.[51] Bonhoeffer's point of departure was that since Hitler's rise to power, all diplomatic, economic, and military strategies to ensure peace had failed. The only hope of the nations now lay in the unprecedented action of an ecumenical council where Christians would take a binding decision against the looming war. Indeed, the church should not wait until the victims of this war were brought to it for pastoral care and healing but should seize the initiative to "put spoke in the wheel."[52]

For Bonhoeffer, the Fanø conference had two distinct functions. First, it had to condemn the heresy and the endorsement of force by the Reich church, and secondly the member churches had to proclaim to their respective governments that peace was a universal promise and commandment from God. In the event, however, this task was not taken up, at least not in the unequivocal sense that Bonhoeffer intended.

Obviously, the delegation from the Reich church had to see in Bonhoeffer's speech a provocation, but by the same token, neither could a majority be found to denounce the use of force in international relations. The only comfort for Bonhoeffer was the resolution, strongly supported by bishop Bell, on an unequivocal declaration of sympathy for the brethren of the Confessing Church. Bonhoeffer took it as the judgment of the ecumenical movement.

There was, however, still much to be done, and another opportunity presented itself at the world conference scheduled for Edinburgh in 1937 of Faith and Order. Unfortunately, Bonhoeffer, who was by 1935 back in Germany, realized that the planners intended to invite delegates also from the Reich church as well as the Confessing Church. In that event, Bonhoeffer told the organizing secretary, Canon Leonard Hodgson, the Confessing Church would not attend, because as he wrote:

> The teaching as well as the action of the responsible leaders of the Reich Church has clearly proved that this church no longer serves Christ but that it serves the Antichrist. Obedience to the only heavenly Lord Jesus Christ continues to be coordinated, nay subordinated to worldly masters and powers. The Reich Church government has dissociated [itself] from the Church of Christ.[53]

Canon Hodgson had clearly little or no idea of how the Reich church had Aryanized Christ, nor apparently did he understand the implications of its endorsement of Nazi racial policy, because despite Bonhoeffer's earnest remonstrations, he insisted on still inviting both German churches. This rebuff led Bonhoeffer to formulate his most systematic statement on ecumenism, "The Confessing Church and the Ecumenical Movement," written in August 1935. It was a vigorous, and in some sections, angry reiteration of the appeal he made for an ecumenical council at Fanø, but more theologically underpinned. He wanted the ecumenical movement to perceive itself as a united church, and as indicated, he made the unequivocal recognition of the Confessing Church as the only true German church the touchstone of the ecumenical movement's sincerity as a church. Basically, one could not dialogue with a church that served the Antichrist and still be the church! In the end, it was a question of how to recognize the truth. And here Bonhoeffer returned to his perennial criticism of Anglo-Saxon Christianity, which he accused of cultivating a "romantic, aesthetic, liberal idea of the ecumenical movement" that failed to take truth seriously and thus nullified the possibility of making the ecumenical movement comprehensible as a church.[54]

If there could be no agreement as to the truth in this situation, Bonhoeffer predicted that the ecumenical movement would founder. In the event, his plea was not registered at the time, but no German delegation attended the Edinburgh conference in 1937. The *Oekumene* had lost its chance to grasp a historical moment. It is at this point that Bonhoeffer withdrew from the ecumenical arena of conflict. He then focused his attention more and more on developing an "Ethic of Responsible Action," and this led him ultimately into the conspiracy to overthrow the Hitler regime.

Notes

1. Ann L. Nickson, *Bonhoeffer on Freedom: Courageously Grasping Reality* (Aldershot, Hampshire, 2002), 179. This work underlines the fact that Bonhoeffer's concept of freedom is entirely a radical theological one that he arrived at by relating his Christology to his experience of the "unfreedom" of the Third Reich. In *Ethics* he wrote, "The cross of reconciliation is the setting free for life before God in the midst of a godless world; it is the setting free for life in genuine worldliness." Cf. *Ethik* in *DBW*, VI, 404. It rather affirms the notion that a Christian with the right *Gesinnung* ("attitude," "values," "mental disposition") can be free regardless of the regime in which he or she lives. Only when the state is captured by evil men and forced into the service of the Antichrist is "responsible action"—for example, the forceful elimination of the Führer—demanded. This is clearly a very different concept of freedom from that generally understood in the Anglo-Saxon world.

2. Adolf Hitler's value system is spelled out in considerable detail in his autobiography, *Mein Kampf*, which he composed while in prison at Landsberg, Bavaria, and published in 1925. It gives frank expression to the author's beliefs about race and particularly the effects of the presence of Jews in Germany. For a systematic analysis of Hitler's values, see Eberhard Jäckel, *Hitler's World View* (Cambridge, Mass., 1981).

3. Robert A. Pois, *National Socialism and the Religion of Nature* (London/Sydney, 1986). See also Woodruff D. Smith, *The Ideological Origins of Nazi Imperialism* (New York/Oxford, 1986).

4. See John S. Conway, *The Nazi Persecution of the Churches 1933–1945* (London, 1968). In this context see also Wright, *"Above Parties,"* and Borg, *The Old-Prussian Church*. Being anti-Semitic was paradigmatic for most German Protestants and also Roman Catholics of the era. Ursula Büttner focuses on the effects of deep-seated anti-Semitism and anti-Semitic theology in the German Protestant Church during the Third Reich in "The Jewish Problem becomes a Christian Problem: German Protestants and the Persecution of Jews in the Third Reich," in *Probing the Depths of German Anti-Semitism: German Society and the Persecution of the Jews, 1933–1941*, ed. David Bankier (New York/Oxford, 2000), 431–62.

5. Close to Bonhoeffer's position was also the pastor Hans-Joachim Iwand, whose collected works have now been published in three volumes by Christian Kaiser Verlag, Gütersloh: *Kirche und Gesellschaft*, vol. I (1998); *Christologie-Die Umkehrung des Menschen zur Menschlichkeit*, vol. II (1999); *Theologiegeschichte des 19. und 20. Jahrhunderts*, vol. III, (2001).

6. The definitive work on Bonhoeffer's struggle against the Nazi persecution of the Jews is by Christine-Ruth Müller, *Dietrich Bonhoeffers Kampf gegen die nationalsozialistische Verfolgung und Vernichtung der Juden* (Munich, 1990).

7. Bonhoeffer explained this incident to his colleagues and friends in a circular letter dated 2 February, 1933. It should be noted that the Nazis had not yet begun to oversee the content of radio broadcast until 25 March 1933.

See DBW XII, 47. See *No Rusty Swords*, 190–204 (the original is in *DBW*, XII, 242–59). For a detailed analysis of Bonhoeffer's ideas with respect to the nature of the state which this lecture reveals, see the following essays by Ruth Zerner, "Dietrich Bonhoeffer's Views on the State and History," in *A Bonhoeffer Legacy—Essays in Understanding*, ed. A. J. Klassen (Grand Rapids, 1981), 131–60, and "Church, State and the Jewish Question," in *The Cambridge Companion to Dietrich Bonhoeffer*, ed. John W. de Gruchy (Cambridge, 1999), 190–205.

8. *No Rusty Swords*, 202. The English translation of the German original renders it impossible to experience the full effect of the two German words *Führer* (leader) and *Verführer* (seducer)! See the original in *DBW*, XII.

9. *No Rusty Swords*, 203.

10. Ibid., 203–204.

11. The standard work in English on the *German Christian* movement is by Doris L. Bergen, *Twisted Cross: The German Christian Movement* (Chapel Hill/London: 1996).

12. There is a considerable literature on this subject. However, an incisive and informative source of information on it is provided by the former East German pastor and theologian Günter Krusche, "The Church Between Accommodation and Refusal: The Significance of the Lutheran Doctrine of the 'Two Kingdoms' for the Churches of the German Democratic Republic," *Religion, State and Society* 22, no. 3 (1994): 323–32.

13. "The Church and the Jewish Question," in *No Rusty Swords*, 225.

14. C. S. Macfarland, *The New Church and the New Germany* (London, 1934), 69–71, cited in *DBW*, XII, 359–60.

15. *DBW*, XIV, 54–55.

16. Ibid. Emphasis added.

17. Here I am following Eberhard Bethge's commentary "Dietrich Bonhoeffer und die Juden," in *Die Juden und Martin Luther—Martin Luther und die Juden*, ed. Heinz Kremer (Vluyn, 1988), 211–48. See Eva Fleischner, *Judaism in Christian Theology since 1945: Christianity and Israel considered in Terms of Mission* (Metuchen/New Jersey, 1975), 24–25.

18. Cited after "The Church and the Jewish Question" as it appears in English translation in *No Rusty Swords*, 226–27.

19. Pinchas Lapide cited after Eberhard Bethge, "Dietrich Bonhoeffer und die Juden," 215. But see the work of Stephen Haynes in this regard: *The Bonhoeffer Legacy: Post Holocaust Perspectives* (Minneapolis, 2006). This work has the virtue of having investigated the most relevant scholarly opinions on Bonhoeffer's motivations for coming to the defence of Jews during the Third Reich. Assessments vary from deep reluctance on the part of some authorities to acknowledge Bonhoeffer's efforts on the behalf of Jews (e.g., "he was the best of a bad lot"—of Germans) to high praise in having laid the foundations for a new theology of Jewish-Christian relations. In a real sense, Haynes plays "devil's advocate" with regard to Bonhoeffer's record in thought and action on behalf of the Jews.

20. Bonhoeffer "The Church and the Jewish Question," in *No Rusty Swords*, 224–25. Cf. Kenneth Barnes, "Dietrich Bonhoeffer and Hitler's Persecution of the Jews," in *Betrayal: German Churches and the Holocaust*, ed. Robert P. Erikson and Susanne Herschel (Minneapolis, 1999), 114. In this context, see Geffrey B. Kelly, "Bonhoeffer and the Jews: Implications for Jewish-Christian

Reconciliation," in *Reflections on Bonhoeffer: Essays in Honour of F. Burton Nelson*, ed. Geffrey B. Kelly and C. John Weborg (Chicago, 1999), 133–68.

21. "The Church and the Jewish Question," in *No Rusty Swords*, 226.

22. Bethge, "Dietrich Bonhoeffer und die Juden," 223.

23. Bonhoeffer, "The Church and the Jewish Question," in *No Rusty Swords*, 227–28.

24. Bethge, "Dietrich Bonhoeffer und die Juden," 226. Richard Gutteridge, *Open Thy Mouth for the Dumb–The German Evangelical Church and the Jews 1879–1950* (Oxford, 1976), 97–99.

25. See Andreas Pangritz, "Dietrich Bonhoeffers theologische Begründung," 505. Here Pangritz notes, "Bonhoeffer was appalled by the Nazi doctrine that the individual had to surrender his or her conscience to the Führer. This would be unconditionally abandoning one's will or individual autonomy to an alien agency, that is, allowing one's will to be determined by something other than the moral law. For a Christian to do this would be like substituting Hitler as the person in whom one seeks personal integrity instead of Christ. So, to allocate to the man Hitler the function of one's redeemer would be to submit to the most devastating contradiction to the Christian truth." See, John A. Moses, "Dietrich Bonhoeffer as Conspirator against the Hitler Regime: the Motivation of a German Protestant Revolutionary," *War and Society* 17, no. 1 (May 1999): 25–40.

26. Cf. Hannes Heer, "'Die grosse Maskerade des Bösen': Dietrich Bonhoeffers Bild und Bewertung des Nationalsozialismus," *Zeitschrift für Geschichtswissenschaft*, no. 49 (December 2001): 1082.

27. Ibid., See also Michael Burleigh, *The Third Reich: A New History* (London, 2001), 674–76.

28. See the account of the Bethel Confession by Ferdinand Schlingensiepen, *Dietrich Bonhoeffer 1906–1945: Eine Biographie* (Munich, 2006), 153–61.

29. Bethge, "Dietrich Bonhoeffer und die Juden," 228. Cf. *DBW*, XII, 403.

30. Bethge, "Bonhoeffer und die Juden" 229. See *DBW*, XII, 362–407, for the original draft of the *Bethel Confession* alongside the edited August version. See also Kurt Dietrich Schmidt, ed., *Die Bekenntnisse und grundsätzlichen Äusserungen zur Kirchenfrage des Jahres 1933* (Göttingen, 1934), 105–30. The latter contains an even more severely attenuated version, and for Bonhoeffer a totally unacceptable weakened text. See *DBW*, XII, 488. For a comprehensive investigation of the production of the *Bethel Confession*, see the 1987 dissertation by Guy Christopher Carter of Marquette University (Wisconsin), "Confession at Bethel, August 1933: Enduring Witness: The Formation, Revision and Significance of the First Full Theological Confession of the Evangelical Church Struggle in Nazi Germany."

31. Bethge, "Dietrich Bonhoeffer und die Juden," 229, and *DBW*, XII, 403.

32. See *DBW*, XII, 505–507.

33. Von Oppen, *Der unerhörte Schrei*, 44. See also Wolfgang Gerlach, *And the Witnesses were Silent; the Confessing Church and the Persecution of the Jews*, trans. and ed. Victoria J. Barnett (Lincoln, Neb. 2000).

34. Conway, *The Nazi Persecution of the Churches*, 24–25. Emphasis added. German Roman Catholics were also not free of anti-Semitic prejudice. See Walter Zwi Bacharach, "The Catholic Anti-Jewish Prejudice, Hitler and the Jews," in Bankier, *Probing the Depths of German Anti-Semitism*, 415–30.

35. Bethge, *Bonhoeffer*, 237 [cf. 2000, 304–6]. See also Bergen, *Twisted Cross*, 90, and Büttner, "The Jewish Problem becomes a Christian Problem," 431–459 passim.
36. Klaus Scholder, 'Kirchenkampf' in *Evangelisches Staatslexikon*, ed. Hermann Kunst *et al* (Stuttgart/ Berlin, 1975), 1182.
37. Kurt Meier, *Kreuz und Hakenkreuz-Die Evangelische Kirche im Dritten Reich* (München, 1992), 47–48.
38. Bethge, *Bonhoeffer*, 232 [2000, 302]. See *DBW*, XII, 117–18.
39. Meier, *Kreuz und Hakenkreuz*, 49–51. Cf. Schlingensiepen, *Bonhoeffer*, 164–68.
40. *Die Bekenntnisse und grundsätzlichen Äusserungen zur Kirchenfrage des Jahres 1933*, intro. Kurt Dietrich Schmidt (Göttingen, 1934). A second volume covers the year 1934 with the same publication details published in 1935.
41. Scholder, "Kirchenkampf" 1182.
42. Ibid.
43. Conway, *The Nazi Persecution of the Churches*, 84.
44. Ibid., 221.
45. Edwin Robertson, *Unshakable Friend: George Bell and the German Churches* (London, 1995), 25–26.
46. Bethge, *Bonhoeffer*, 250–51 [cf. 2000, 321–22].
47. Robertson, *Unshakable Friend*, 24–45 passim.
48. Ibid., 33.
49. See note 12.
50. "The Church and the Peoples of the World," *No Rusty Swords*, 289–92. See the perceptive commentary hereto by Krötke, "Nur das ganze Wort is mutig."
51. Jørgen Glenthøj, "Dietrich Bonhoeffer und die Ökumene," *Mündige Welt* (1956): 153–54.
52. See the commentary by Heimbrucher, *Christus Friede—Welt Frieden*, 165.
53. See note 15 for fuller reference to this letter of Bonhoeffer's to Canon Hodgson.
54. "The Confessing Church and the Ecumenical Movement," in *No Rusty Swords*, 336.

6

THE ETHICS OF CONSPIRACY

The Betrayal of the *Bildungsbürgertum*

One of the remarkable features of the advent of the Hitler dictatorship in Germany was the rapidity with which the professions welcomed the "New Order" as signaling a rebirth of genuine Germanic culture and values. These had been supposedly perverted by foreign imports such as liberalism, parliamentary democracy, and communism. And, of course, Jews had been accused of spearheading all of these supposedly deleterious influences.

Consequently, the birth of the Third Reich heralded a reassessment among all the professions of their role in this revitalized fatherland. There were now such things as German physics, German medicine, German engineering, German law, German philosophy, German history, and, of course, German theology. All of these disciplines had been brought into line with the ideology of National Socialism, though it would be more accurate to observe that there was an across-the-board self-surrender of the German scientific world to their new political masters. There exists now a considerable number of scholarly studies on how each of these disciplines actually behaved during the Third Reich. What Bonhoeffer had observed about the objectives of the "German Christians" being more concerned with Germanism than with Christianity was generally true for all other disciplines in that they proceeded from obscurantist, irrational premises about the innate mental and physical superiority of the Aryan race. It was a phenomenon that in the end destroyed the scientific and scholarly credibility of the German universities at that time, and what is more, crippled the ability of German scientists to compete on the world stage.[1] By submitting to the Nazi *Weltanschauung*, German scientists and scholars effectively stultified true scientific inquiry and thereby put learning back decades, the technical excellence of individuals such as Werner Heisenberg and Werner von Braun notwithstanding.[2] Here, most decidedly had the *Bildungsbürgertum* "lost both their heads and their bibles," as Bonhoeffer once observed despairingly to his Swiss friend Erwin Sutz.[3]

Well might we ask, then, what is distinctive about German physics? The answer was that scientists of pure Germanic blood could only do German physics. German-Jewish scientists such as Albert Einstein or Max Born had nothing to offer the new Germany. German doctors saw their objective in the production of "human material" (*Menschenmaterial*) of such a quality that would best serve the purposes of the Führer. They supported Hitler's racial policy, including euthanasia, and the "Final Solution" to the Jewish question as absolutely necessary for the health of the master race. In this Hitler was apostrophized as the great surgeon of the people.[4] Similarly, the legal profession assumed the validity of Hitler's racial theories as the basis of German jurisprudence.

Historians prostituted their discipline by interpreting German history in a deterministic way to plot the evolution of the master race to world domination.[5] For this, of course, there had been a highly influential precedent in the so-called Prussian school that dominated German universities from the second half of the nineteenth century to the Third Reich which had, as has been seen, imposed the "orthodoxy" that Prussia had been destined by providence to unite Germany.[6] Soon after Hitler's seizure of power, there occurred in German universities a voluntary *Gleichschaltung*, that is, all disciplines allowed themselves to be coordinated into ideological conformity with National Socialism. Intellectual activity took place within a straightjacket of official irrationalism. Such intellects as the Freiburg philosopher Martin Heidegger (1889–1976) prostituted their intellect to provide a "scientific" justification for what had occurred.[7]

It is difficult to comprehend how otherwise intelligent persons could submit themselves to such obscurantism. An approximate analogy today would be the phenomena of racial and religious fundamentalism that is seen being expressed in international terrorism. The Nazi movement was nothing more or less than an earlier version of organized terror based on a quasi-religious fundamentalism that enthroned a fictitious or alleged purity of the *Volk* or nation as the highest value.[8] And, as stressed, leading representatives of all university disciplines endorsed this *Weltanschauung* as self-evident truth. Obviously, there were individuals whose innate rationality resisted such a prostitution of the human intellect, but their choice was either to emigrate or to conform at least outwardly in order to protect themselves.

The disturbing thing was that all this occurred in a country which was over 95 percent Christian. And here the larger church, the Protestant, found itself in an ethical dilemma. It was assumed that Luther had solved the problem of church-state relations with his version of the doctrine of the two kingdoms. This, as we have seen, neatly allocated discrete roles to church and state in the life of the nation according to which, as St. Paul spelled out in Romans 13, the state was responsible for the good order of society and the protection of the nation. The church, as it evolved since New Testament times, had the task of preaching the gospel and was responsible for the cure of souls.

During the Third Reich, and more recently during the communist dictatorship in East Germany, most Protestants thought that the old Lutheran formula would cover all circumstances. The state had its function and responsibilities clearly delineated that did not interfere with the role of religion. In both instances, however, under National Socialism and Communism, the state had changed the rules by becoming de facto a rival religion. In fact, National Socialism has been classified as a "religion of nature" that demanded that humanity be regarded as a part of nature and thus subject to the pitiless judgments of the laws of nature.[9] Such teaching had to violate the self-perception of the church; indeed it violated every principle upon which German religious and political culture had hitherto been predicated. In addition, as indicated above, all scientific disciplines including the humanities submitted to the prevailing ideology in the conviction that the aims and objectives of the Führer were "scientifically" justified. By now it will be clear that the men of the world of scholarship and science did this by acquiescing in the Nazi deification of the *Volk*. Anything was legitimate that could be shown to be done in the interests of the *Volksgemeinschaft*, the national community. This was, in short, the organizing principle of Nazism. As such, it had to collide with every precept in the New Testament.

Bonhoeffer's Lonely Stand

Curiously, only Bonhoeffer, supported by a few close colleagues, could articulate this problem and advance some means of opposing it. Eberhard Bethge, just prior to his death (18 March 2000), commented on this by saying that there were two phases in Bonhoeffer's opposition. The first, the organizational-agitational phase, covered the years 1933 to 1939, and the second, the conspiratorial phase, from 1939 to 1945.[10]

We have seen that Bonhoeffer first tried to persuade his fellow citizens that the Nazi doctrine called the "leadership principle" that demanded unconditional submission to the will of the Führer was both incompatible with the gospel and traditional German political culture. As well, he tried to convince fellow Germans that Nazi racial policy was also in stark violation of the message of human equality in the New Testament. Very few were listening because they were mesmerized by Hitler's charisma with which he proclaimed his message of national renewal based on his concept of "blood und soil."

Bonhoeffer at the same time had tried to enlist the support of the ecumenical movement for the Confessing Church in the belief that through its organizations and the holding of a great ecumenical peace council it would be possible to mobilize the nations of the world collectively to stand up to the Nazis. This would rescue both world peace as well as the church in Germany from being seduced by the Antichrist.[11]

Clearly, in all this Bonhoeffer was far in advance of his time, and being largely isolated from his peer group, his efforts had no chance of success. Whether they deserve the description of naïve is another matter. History has shown that his analysis of the situation was perceptive and accurate. Further, the remedy he prescribed was logical. It was not his fault that neither his coreligionists in sufficient numbers nor the international community would listen and lend their support.

It was mentioned above that Bonhoeffer's response to the Third Reich and its criminal policies can be divided into two phases; initially verbal and written protest, followed by conspiratorial action to subvert the system and finally to plot the elimination of the Führer. The first phase was when Bonhoeffer tried to persuade his coreligionists and fellow countrymen and women that they had "lost their heads and lost their Bibles." He did this in his formal teaching at the University of Berlin (winter semester 1932–33), in his preaching in London (October 1933–April 1935), in his teaching again at the illegal seminary at Finkenwalde (April 1935 to autumn 1937), and through the books he published as a result of his reflections during that time. All these writings can be evaluated as an attempt to develop a new political ethic to replace, or at least adjust, the one bequeathed by Luther.[12] In the course of history Luther's doctrine of the two kingdoms had been distorted into meaning that the state had complete freedom to disregard the ethics of the gospel in the pursuit of its aims and that, moreover, the church had no right of admonition of the state if it considered the state had gone beyond its brief and violated human rights.

A first step in bringing the German people back onto the right path was, of course, the Barmen Declaration (29–31 May 1934), sections of which, referred to in the previous chapter, emphatically denied that there was any sphere of life that was not under the ultimate sovereignty of God. Basically, the Barmen Declaration was a reiteration of the *original* Lutheran doctrine of the two kingdoms because the Nazis and the "German Christians" had blatantly violated it. The second step was the synod held at Berlin-Dahlem (19–20 October 1934) that openly declared that the Confessing Church had decided to establish a separate organizational identity. Bonhoeffer had, of course, championed this move wholeheartedly as the only possible course of action under the circumstances.

Unfortunately, the Confessing Church never lived up to the high expectations to become a source of vigorous opposition. It remained for Bonhoeffer to use his considerable theological acumen in a heroic effort to change German political-religious culture. He embarked on this mission after having himself experienced a kind of "secondary conversion" that equipped him both spiritually and mentally to proceed on his revolutionary path. There is no doubt that Bonhoeffer's mental-spiritual attitude had gone through a distinct change after he returned to Germany from Union Theological Seminary in 1932. He had discussed this later with his brother Karl-Friedrich in 1935 and an earlier girlfriend and distant cousin, Elizabeth Zinn, in 1936, reflecting on the circumstances of the intervening years and their effect on him. He confided in Zinn that in the past he been quite egoistic in his ministry; he had never really submitted himself obediently to the bible. This led to his reappropriation of the Sermon on the Mount and its call for peace, especially the command to love one's enemies, as has been seen.[13]

It has already been mentioned that Bonhoeffer's encounter with Jean Laserre, his French fellow student at Union Seminary in New York, encouraged Bonhoeffer to reassess the meaning of the Sermon on the Mount with its key admonition to love not only one's neighbor but, more importantly, one's enemy. Laserre had further brought home to Bonhoeffer that the prioritization of one's own country over another, nationalism, was incompatible with the gospel.[14] These insights bore rich fruit in the book *The Cost of Discipleship* (*Nachfolge*) published in 1937, the distillation of his lectures at Finkenwalde. The work is not only a brilliant and radical reinterpretation of the Sermon on the Mount but also a thundering indictment of the values of cultural Protestantism and the *Bildungsbürgertum*.

First of all, *Nachfolge* teaches that unconditional obedience to the will of God liberates humanity for discipleship. People really do have to comprehend the commandments and precepts of both the Old Testament and of Jesus who fulfills them in the New Testament, quite literally. There has to be "single-minded obedience" before true discipleship can begin. Bonhoeffer deals with this in a paradoxical way. He argues that Jesus really does intend that His followers love their enemies. Consequently, it could not be argued that it was an act of love to punish enemies for their wickedness in order to teach them better behavior in future. German theologians prior to the First World War seriously advanced the concept that to wage war to bring your enemy—read "errant neighbor"—around to your way of thinking was essentially an act of love. As absurd as it sounds, it really was the mental attitude of many German Protestant theologians prior to the First World War.[15]

Bonhoeffer's point was that the basic commandments and precepts that Jesus enunciated had to be regarded as utterly binding. Even the advice given to the rich young man to sell all his goods and give the proceeds to the poor was meant to be taken literally [Matthew 19:21]. Other disciples had done so. The rich young man could not submit to this because he loved his wealth, and went away sorrowful. What Jesus demanded was a radical change of disposition on the part of the young man. This demand, according to Bonhoeffer, is still in force. It meant that today, living in the expectation of Jesus' second coming, Christians should retain their goods in stewardship and be spiritually detached from them because it is not wealth that gave essential meaning to life, only faith in the Savior did so. As Bonhoeffer phrased it: "In the last resort what matters is not what the man does, but only his faith in Jesus as the son of God and Mediator."[16] Consequently, Bonhoeffer teaches the so-called *paradoxical* understanding of the commandments and precepts. The faithful have to be prepared to render single-minded obedience when called to do so, hence the power of the saying from the Sermon on the Mount in Matthew 5:43–45: "You have heard that it was said, 'You shall love your neighbor and hate your enemy.' But I say to you, Love your enemies and pray for those who persecute you so that you may be sons of your Father who is in heaven; for he makes his sun rise on the evil and on the good, and sends rain on the just and unjust."

Clearly, Bonhoeffer wanted this to be understood by his countrymen as a commandment for here and now. The previous belligerent disposition that had become paradigmatic, even for theologians, had to be abandoned and replaced by a disposition of single-minded obedience. After all, as Bonhoeffer insisted, "Only he who believes is obedient and only he who is obedient believes."[17]

All this was a demand for a radical change of heart. Indeed, in the German context it was virtually a demand for revolutionary change. And here is where the indictment of his contemporaries comes in. The corrupted mentality, values, and attitudes of the *Bildungsbürgertum* were the consequence of their exploitation of so-called "cheap grace."

In *The Cost of Discipleship* Bonhoeffer attacks the misuse by his contemporaries of the central issue of Luther's theology, justification, to avail themselves of "cheap grace" as follows:

> We Lutherans have gathered like eagles round the carcass of cheap grace, and there we have drunk the poison which has killed the life of following Christ. It is true of course that we have paid the doctrine of pure grace divine honors unparalleled in Christendom, in fact we have exalted that doctrine to the position of God himself. Everywhere

Luther's formula has been repeated, but its truth perverted into self-deception. So long as our Church holds the correct doctrine of justification, there is no doubt whatever that she is a justified Church! So they said, thinking that we must vindicate our Lutheran heritage by making this grace available on the cheapest and easiest terms. . . . We justified the world, and condemned as heretics those who tried to follow Christ. The result was that a nation became Christian and Lutheran, but at the cost of true discipleship. The price it was called upon to pay was all too cheap. Cheap grace had won the day. But do we realize that this cheap grace has turned back upon us like a boomerang? The price we are having to pay today in the shape of the collapse of the organized church is only the inevitable consequence of our policy of making grace available to all at too low a cost. We gave away the word and sacraments wholesale, we baptized, confirmed, and absolved a whole nation unasked and without condition. Our humanitarian sentiment made us give forth unending streams of grace. But the call to follow Jesus in the narrow way was hardly ever heard.[18]

The harrowing honesty of this statement would be hard to surpass. Bonhoeffer had pronounced a savage indictment on his coreligionists who had gone so far as deify the state and enthrone the man Hitler in the place of the true Savior. It was a demand for an ethical revolution.

The Gestapo finally closed down the "illegal" seminary at Finkenwalde in the autumn of 1937. Soon after, in Advent, *Nachfolge* (*The Cost of Discipleship*) was published, the product of his lectures to his students at Finkenwalde. Not many people were ready to appropriate inwardly the central message. In any case the church was under siege. Already on 1 July 1937 Hitler had given the order to have Martin Niemöller arrested as his personal prisoner. And when Finkenwalde was closed Bonhoeffer and Bethge moved for four weeks to Göttingen to his twin sister's Sabine's empty house as she and her non-Aryan husband, Gerhard Leibholz, had already fled to England for safety.[19] There in that short time, Bonhoeffer wrote the second of his major theological statements about what was missing from his church, namely, *Life Together* (*Gemeinsames Leben*). This work had been clearly very much influenced by Bonhoeffer's experience of the three Anglican theological colleges that he visited in 1935, Kelham, Cowley, and Mirfield, all of which were monastic institutions. Again, this little book was an appeal to his coreligionists to adopt a more collective or intrapersonal form of piety, to be more concerned with the well-being of others and less self-absorbed. To quote an American Bonhoeffer scholar, in *Life Together*,

Christ is depicted as the embodiment both of God and Christians, who are moved to do what, without Christ, they would be unable to accomplish: to live together, sharing faith, hope, and self-giving love in a community as representative of God's graced outreach to God's children and the incarnate embodiment of all those who crave in their faith for community with God. The Christ of *Life Together* is the binding force of that community in its "togetherness," gracing Christians to go beyond the superficial, often self-centered, relationships of their every day associations toward a more intimate sense of what it means to be Christ to others, to love others as Christ loved them.[20]

These ideas should not have been revolutionary, but they were when we consider that the German community was being defined solely in terms of an obscurantist ideology of "blood and soil" that brutally excluded not only citizens of different race but also citizens of different political persuasion. *Life Together* is a very subtle critique of the Nazi idea of *Volksgemeinschaft* (national community) because it was essentially based on emotion fired by aggressive and exclusionist objectives, and as such utterly alien and inimical to Christianity. It was a bad dream. As Bonhoeffer wrote, "Every human idealized image that is brought into the Christian community is a hindrance to genuine community and must be broken up so that genuine community can survive."[21] Bonhoeffer warned Christians here that what the Nazis were offering was irreconcilable with the idea of Christian community although many Christians in Germany obviously had been deceived into believing that *Volksgemeinschaft* was the equivalent to genuine Christian community.

In criticizing the Nazi idea of community by contrasting it with the essential idea of Christian community, Bonhoeffer was in a real sense instigating revolution against the Nazi regime. Indeed, he reminded his people that their true identity was imparted to them by their baptism into Christ and certainly not by membership in a *Volk*, a concept derived from frankly obscurantist "blood and soil" mysticism. Against this Bonhoeffer was instructing Germans where their true citizenship lay. One had to think very clearly to distinguish between the Nazi idea of community and the Christian idea of community. Bonhoeffer wrote:

> Christian community is not an ideal we have to realize, but rather a reality created by God in Christ in which we may participate. The more clearly we learn to recognize that the ground and strength and promise of all our community is in Jesus Christ alone, the more calmly we will learn to think about our community and pray and hope for it.
>
> Because Christian community is founded solely on Jesus Christ, it is a spiritual [*pneumatische*] and not a psychic [*psychische*] reality. In this respect it differs absolutely from all other communities. . . . The basis of all pneumatic, or spiritual, reality is the clear, manifest Word of God in

Jesus Christ. At the foundation of all psychic, or emotional, reality are the dark, impenetrable urges and desires of the human soul. The basis of spiritual community is truth; the basis of emotional community is desire. The essence of spiritual community is light. . . . The essence of emotional, self-centered community is darkness.[22]

Bonhoeffer was proposing a model for Christian togetherness and reconciliation that clearly struck at the roots of what the Nazi propaganda was tying to instill into the hearts and minds of all Germans. And although at this stage of his ministry Bonhoeffer was isolated, still he persevered. He took a parish in Berlin but in January 1938 he was placed under a ban from residing in Berlin and Brandenburg. Despite that, however, he resumed teaching his "expelled" Finkenwalde students secretly on a Pomeranian farm (Sigurdshof) until 18 March 1940, when the Gestapo struck again. We should note that in all there had been 113 students at Finkenwalde and 68 in Sigurdshof. Bonhoeffer was indeed pushing his fortunes to the limit when one considers that not a few pastors at this time were being arrested and imprisoned. And, of course, many of Bonhoeffer's students were forced into military service. Some 53 had been killed before the war ended.[23]

During this period Bonhoeffer was experiencing great anguish about how he should continue resistance. Obviously, training all those students at least ideologically-theologically to oppose the system was one significant way. This option, however, had been brutally closed off. And Bonhoeffer had to consider that by 1939 all men of his birth year (1906) were going to be conscripted for military service. He definitely did not want to be forced to fight for the Führer, the agent of the Antichrist; but there was no provision for conscientious objectors in Nazi Germany. If men refused to fight they were summarily executed. Consequently, after considerable soul-searching, Bonhoeffer opted to return to the United States where a friend from his Union seminary days, Paul Lehmann, had arranged a post for him. With the intention, then, of continuing opposition from outside, Bonhoeffer left for America a second time. It should be noted here, though, that he had already, since the beginning of 1939, been in touch with the conspirators through his brother-in-law, Hans von Dohnanyi, who was the link to the circle of conspirators around Admiral Canaris. However, by 2 June Bonhoeffer was on a ship bound for New York. It was to be a very short trip. By 27 July he was back in Germany.[24] Barely a month later, on 1 September, the *Wehrmacht* commenced the invasion of Poland. Everything that Bonhoeffer had predicted about Hitler now materialized. The Second World War had been unleashed.

The attenuated sojourn in the United States had been enough to convince Bonhoeffer that his true place was back with his countrymen.

Before he left New York he wrote to his former American professor, Reinhold Niebuhr:

> I have made a mistake in coming to America. I must live through this difficult period of our national history with the Christian people of Germany. I will have no right to participate in the reconstruction of Christian life in Germany after the war if I do not share in the trials of this time with my people. . . . Christians in Germany will face the terrible alternative of either willing the defeat of their nation in order that Christian civilization may survive, or willing the victory of their nation and thereby destroying our civilization. I know which of these alternatives I must choose; but I cannot make the choice in security.[25]

After March 1940 when the Pomeranian seminary had finally been closed, the Confessing Church's Council of Brethren (*Brüderrat*) through its chairman, Wolfgang Staemmler, to whom Bonhoeffer reported, encouraged Bonhoeffer now to carry on with his research. That was on 15 November. The next day Staemmler himself was arrested as part of the ongoing persecution of the Confessing Church. Bonhoeffer to this point had only been banned from Berlin-Brandenburg; further bans were to come; on 22 August 1940, he was banned from public speaking, and later, on 19 March 1941, a ban was placed on his publishing.[26]

Plotting Tyrannicide

In order to live with the situation, Bonhoeffer took up residence in the Bavarian Alps to pursue his plan to write a detailed work on Protestant ethics. Retrospectively, Bonhoeffer described this period as follows:

> [While in Bavaria] I reported to the state police as required by regulations, so in this place there was nothing more to fear. People in the church advised me that they were interested in a book on "concrete Protestant ethics" to follow from *The Cost of Discipleship*. Because I had always worked predominantly as an academic theologian I felt an inner satisfaction that I was fulfilling my vocation in the church. . . . Consequently at that time my church-related activity was restricted to this research and writing, and I adhered strictly to the ban on public speaking.[27]

This passive form of resistance was complemented by Bonhoeffer's active contribution to the conspiracy to overthrow Hitler. He had moved into the second phase of his opposition without abandoning the first. It was essential for Bonhoeffer's continued existence in Nazi Germany that he had an official task that exempted him from being drafted into the army. That was created for him through the mediation of Hans von Dohnanyi who had gradually insinuated Bonhoeffer into the circle of conspirators around Admiral Wilhelm Canaris, head of military counter-intelligence in foreign countries, and Colonel Hans Oster who was chief of the central section in which Dohnanyi was an official (*Referent*). This was an ideal cover for the conspirators, especially for Bonhoeffer, as he was given identity papers and allocated to the Munich office in October 1940. In this position he was no longer liable for war service. The pretext for enrolling Bonhoeffer was that he had special contacts in foreign countries, and these he would most certainly exploit in Switzerland, Italy, and especially Sweden—but against the policies of the regime that for him was emphatically a criminal organization bent on the ultimate destruction of Christian civilization.[28]

It needs, of course, to be understood that the conspirators intended not only the overthrow of the regime, they also envisioned initially the arrest and trial of Hitler; and for the realization of these aims they would need the cooperation of high-ranking army officers. The difficulty here, however, was that every army officer had sworn an oath of personal allegiance to Hitler, to render him unconditional obedience and to be prepared at any time to sacrifice his life for the oath.

Consequently, as long as the officers could not be persuaded that Hitler was not a legitimate head of state they would certainly keep their oath, as indeed most of them did. And this is the key issue in Prusso-German political culture. People were brought up to believe that their word was their sacred bond. That presumed, of course, that one was giving one's word to a God-fearing, honorable head of state. In addition to that, however, there was the neo-Lutheran ethic that understood the state as an order of creation, a manifestation of the will of God, regardless of its obviously brutal and inhumane activity in the world. Bonhoeffer was fundamentally opposed to this, but only very few individuals in the Third Reich could, as he did, comprehend that Hitler was never a legitimate head of state, that he was, if not the Antichrist, then his agent.[29]

Hans Dirk von Hoogstraten has made in this regard the perceptive observation that "all citizens of Nazi Germany were objects of the life-threatening control of the Nazi state. Most of them joined the oppressing forces, serving the system ideologically, whether in the military service or in the bureaucracy." The Dutch scholar went on to point out that the Führer's claims on individuals were based on fear and terror, to which most people submitted in a mood of hopeless religious resignation. A few, however, refused to submit to the system. These, too, were not free from fear, but their conscience, inspired by hope as well as their outrage at the criminality of the regime, overcame their fearful attitude, and so they sought the resort to "righteous action."[30] Having come to this conclusion, Bonhoeffer was clear in his own mind that he had no alternative but to embark on the course he did, namely, to endorse tyrannicide; but as we shall see, it was far from a clear-cut issue for the conscientious and perceptive Lutheran theologian. This was because before Hitler's could be arrested and tried, a sufficient number of the highest-ranking officers would have to agree and lend their support; but this was not possible. Most could not bring themselves to participate in what amounted to a coup d'état that involved the murder of the head of state. In these circumstances, Bonhoeffer and the other conspirators were unanimous that Hitler had to be assassinated. For Bonhoeffer, however, with his commitment to the validity and binding character of the word of God, especially the Ten Commandments, murder was a moral problem of the highest order. How this could be justified under the circumstances was for him a major theological issue. His reflections on this come under the heading, the "ethics of responsibility." It was Bonhoeffer's way of solving the dilemma posed by the unequivocal significance of the seventh commandment, "Thou shalt do no murder."

The Ethics of Responsibility

A good year had elapsed since Bonhoeffer had made his fateful decision in New York to return and become active in the opposition against Hitler. As indicated, he now combined his two methods of resistance, writing and conspiracy. The writing consisted of the first draft of the manuscript, "Ethics of Formation." He was also deeply involved in the plans for the subversion of the Nazi dictatorship that originated in the office of Admiral Wilhelm Canaris. What had brought Bonhoeffer to this stage was his profound disappointment, indeed anger, that many otherwise honorable men, *Bildungsbürger*, had fallen under the spell of Hitler. They had either conformed for the sake of security or had become at least outwardly, diligent collaborators in the system. It concerned Bonhoeffer deeply that subsequent generations would want to question the conscience of these men who had witnessed so many Nazi atrocities such as the pogroms of November 1938, the invasion of Poland that was carried out on fraudulent pretexts and followed by acts of wanton destruction. Much worse, of course, was to come. [Bonhoeffer's thoughts on these issues were penned in his memoir, "After Ten Years" written at the end of 1942, and the full content of this will be dealt with in greater detail in chapter 8.]

Here it is essential to notice that Bonhoeffer was not so much concerned about the mindless riff-raff in the SS and Nazi party generally, or the unprincipled opportunists who never possessed an informed conscience anyway, but rather with the men who had considered themselves to be the highest manifestation of humanity, the elite of the *Bildungsbürgertum*. How, inquired Bonhoeffer, could these men bear to witness the atrocities of the regime, accept the absolute claim on their person that Hitler made on them, forcing them daily into unbearable dilemmas of conscience? Bonhoeffer described the effect on the "man of conscience" as follows:

> The innumerable honorable and alluring masks and costumes in which evil approaches him makes his conscience anxious and uncertain, until he finally is content with a soothed rather than a clear conscience, until he finally lies to his own conscience so as not to despair; because a man whose only security is his own conscience will never be able to understand that a bad conscience can be stronger and more salutary than a deceived conscience.[31]

How did this state of affairs come about? In the first place, the regime had been very successful in depicting Germany as the victim who was only demanding historical and social justice, giving the impression that despite all the evil deeds, it represented an essentially honorable cause in the best interests of the German people. And here it might be conceded that given the hegemony of misinformation at the time, it was just possible that even persons of integrity and learning were deceived by the system.

Once having been taken in, so to speak, the man of conscience was troubled by the dilemmas in which he found himself forced to make decisions. And being in a dilemma means that whatever choice one made it would violate one's conscience. The choice was always between the greater and lesser evil, and that was the temptation of those who remained in their influential positions under the Nazi regime, who collaborated with it against their convictions and who placated their conscience by referring to their basically good intentions. Objectively, in adopting this position, they became accomplices to unimaginable atrocities to which they closed their eyes.

This outraged Bonhoeffer, who railed against them, saying, if only they had the honesty to have a bad conscience for their complicity in wickedness instead of lying to themselves. These *Bildungsbürger* could not manage that, observed Bonhoefffer, because their life was kept stable by the need at all times to have a good conscience. They could not live without what they deemed to be self-respect and personal honor. The result was that they played down the evil reality in order to escape the salutary pressure of a bad conscience that would urge them to turn from their collaboration in order seriously to face the dangers of opposition.[32]

Here, Bonhoeffer had located precisely the "neuralgic point" about the entire worldview of the *Bildungsbürgertum*. They had the incomparable capacity to bludgeon their conscience into submission. Was this the ultimate effect of their addiction to "cheap grace"?

In "After Ten Years", Bonhoeffer declared that only that man would remain steadfast "whose final standard is not his reason, his principles, his conscience, his freedom, or his virtue, but who is ready to sacrifice all this when being called to obedient and responsible action in faith and in exclusive allegiance to God—the responsible man, who tries to make his whole life an answer to the question and call of God. Where are these responsible people?"[33]

Bonhoeffer was saying simply that the addiction to cheap grace had crippled the individual's ability to be guided solely and alone by the example of Jesus of Nazareth. What was missing in the behavior of the *Bildungsbürgertum* was this basic requirement in a Christian person. In the same text, Bonhoeffer observed that his fellow countrymen with their in-bred readiness for subordination to what they regarded as lawful authority lacked the basic capacity for the discernment of political wickedness. This crippled them from advancing to what he called, "free and responsible action, even in opposition to his task and his calling; in its place there appeared on the one hand an irresponsible lack of scruple, and on the other a self-tormenting punctiliousness that never led to action. Civil courage, in fact, can grow only out of the free responsibility of free men."[34]

Considering this deficiency, which proved even more disastrous under Hitler than under the Kaiser, Bonhoeffer in his *Ethics* manuscript addressed the issue of "the structure of responsible life."[35] Clearly, what was exercising him was the planning of the assassination of the Führer. Given the eternal validity of the commandment "Thou shalt do no murder," it was obvious that the conspirators, Bonhoeffer included, were going to incur guilt for their action. The theologian nevertheless concludes that "the readiness to accept inevitable guilt is a prerequisite of responsible action." In short, one could not place one's personal innocence above responsibility for others. This has to be a key observation. Those who wanted to preserve their personal innocence were blind to the more pernicious guilt with which they burdened themselves through their failure to identify with the plight of the victims. The only way was to enter into the community of guilt for the sake of others.

Bonhoeffer's thesis here is that acting as demanded by personal responsibility meant the acceptance of guilt. This position, though, has to be ethically controversial. Can a person incur guilt for killing the instigators and perpetrators of unprecedented genocide in order to save the lives of further millions of innocent people? As well, there were huge risks involved in such an action. It could have unleashed a civil war with unforeseeable consequences. Further, an execution without trial and no recourse to law would remain an offence, since good ends cannot justify evil means. In short, Bonhoeffer considered tyrannicide an action that burdened those responsible for it with guilt, even though in that crisis situation the elimination of an insane despot was the demand of the hour, indeed a practical and eminently humanitarian necessity. The peculiar circumstances created by Hitler made it so. And here is the crucial point: Hitler had to be killed because the oath of allegiance made to him by officers under his command frustrated arriving at a clear decision to overthrow the regime.[36] The elimination of Hitler would at a stroke render the oath null and void, immediately releasing the officers from commitment to it. Their conscience would then be made open to new possibilities. Behind Bonhoeffer's conviction was Luther's admonition that one may not act against one's conscience. If conscience is protesting against any act that endangers a person's integrity, conscience remains a binding authority. Hence we have here a very "Protestant ethic." The liberated conscience "unites with responsibility grounded in Christ to bear guilt for our neighbor's sake."[37] In the year 1941, guilt was incurred by the violation of the law against high treason and assassination.

This was, of course, asking too much of most military leaders, who could not be expected to be able to reason in this way. To intervene personally in the course of history and to take upon themselves the guilt associated with such action was far more than their own inner convictions would allow. And here it has to be remembered that without the concurrence of the German army in the very beginning, and their oath of allegiance to Hitler, the Third Reich and the Second World War would never have eventuated. These people were a class apart, having been formed in a very inflexible tradition of unconditional obedience to secular authority, something that in the end that led to the suppression of any remnant of Christian conscience. They were not able, with few exceptions, to comprehend that, as Bonhoeffer observed, "The final responsible question is not how I can heroically extricate myself from the affair, but how a coming generation might continue to live?"[38]

Bonhoeffer clearly understood the dilemma of his military contemporaries. They lacked the encounter with Christ that would have made it possible for them to accept responsibility for the neighbor and for the continuing life of future generations. That was indeed possible in Christ because the responsible human being did not have to carry the burden of guilt alone but stood always under the promise of forgiveness, the essence of the Protestant ethic.

Bonhoeffer saw clearly that the existing state law and mock justice that sustained the barbaric Nazi regime in power had indeed to be broken in order to make true justice prevail again. But to accomplish this incurred guilt. The responsible individual would, however, accept the concomitant guilt because he felt obliged to act in free responsibility. As Bonhoeffer phrased it, "Before the others, the person of free responsibility is justified by need; before self, the conscience acquits, but before God the responsible person hopes for grace alone."[39]

The question provoked here is, how can it be that conscience acquits one in one's own eyes when one must admit before oneself that one is entangled in guilt? Bonhoeffer answered, one was acquitted because the guilt incurred was inevitable, and because the liberated conscience hopes for the forgiveness of guilt.[40]

Finally, and this is what makes Bonhoeffer unique among his peers, there is no question that Bonhoeffer's concept of conscience was an outright rejection of all variants of the neo-Lutheran concept of conscience that exerted hegemony over the *Bildungsbürgertum*. They had become accustomed to submitting their conscience to the law in the mistaken belief that the secular law expressed the ultimate will of God. At the very best it was the penultimate will of God because there had to be law and order, but this, as we have seen, could be perverted by a dictator who had exalted himself in the place of the Savior. The ultimate authority, as Bonhoeffer demonstrates in his study of the Protestant ethic of responsibility, was none other than the person of Christ himself.

Notes

1. There is a considerable literature on this phenomenon. Some representative examples are as follows: Allan Beyerchen, *Scientists under Hitler: Politics and the Physics Community in the Third Reich* (New Haven, 1977); Paul Weindling, *Health, Race and German Politics between National Unification and Nazism, 1870–1945* (Cambridge, 1989); Monika Renneberg and Mark Walker eds., *Science, Technology and National Socialism* (Cambridge, 1994).

2. Thomas Powers, *Heisenberg's War: The Secret History of the German Bomb* (London, 1993).

3. *DBW*, XII, 58 (Bonhoeffer to Sutz, Berlin, 14 April 1933).

4. Weindling, *Health, Race and German Politics*, 493. "On the one hand the Führer was to be an 'iron surgeon' to cure national ills. The national leader was to renew and regenerate a decaying and degenerating nation, conceptualized as a social organism."

5. Karl-Ferdinand Werner, *Das NS Geschichtsbild und die deutsche Geschichtswissenschaft* (Stuttgart, 1967).

6. Georg G. Iggers, *The German Conception of History* (Middletown, Conn., 1968).

7. See Hannah Arendt, *The Origins of Totalitarianism* (New York, 1966).

8. See Hitler's discussion of these ideas in *Mein Kampf* (London, 1939), 323–34. On page 332, Hitler affirms his belief that the "folk concept of the world is in profound accord with Nature's will; because it restores the free play of forces which will lead the race through stages of sustained reciprocal education towards a higher type, until finally the best portion of mankind will possess the earth and will be free to work in every domain all over the world and even reach spheres outside the earth."

9. Pois, *National Socialism as a Religion of Nature*, 55.

10. Eberhard Bethge, "Zwei Formen von Widerstand. Ein Brief: Wird Bonhoeffer richtig verstanden?" in *Bonhoeffer Rundbrief-Mitteilungen der Internationalen Bonhoeffer-Gesellschaft Sektion Bundesrepublik Deutschland*, no. 59 (June 1999): 5–6.

11. John A. Moses, "Dietrich Bonhoeffer as Conspirator against the Hitler Regime: The Motivation of a German Protestant Revolutionary," *War and Society* 17, no. 1 (May 1999): 25–45; Moses, "Dietrich Bonhoeffer's Prioritization of Church Unity (Oekumene)," *The Journal of Religious History* 24, no. 2 (June 2000): 196–212.

12. André Dumas, *Dietrich Bonhoeffer: Theologian of Reality*, trans. Robert McAfee Brown (New York, 1968), 69–76, where Dumas examines the question whether, in the course of Bonhoeffer's development as a theologian, he experienced phases in which he moved out of one mind-set into another, i.e., whether there was continuity or discontinuity.

13. See Bethge, *Bonhoeffer*, 154–55 [2000: 204–06]. See also Schlingensiepen, *Dietrich Bonhoeffer*, 113.

14. Bethge, *Bonhoeffer*, 112–113 [2,000, 153–54].

15. John A. Moses, "Justifying War as the Will of God," *Colloquium* 31, no. 1 (1999): 3–20.

16. *The Cost of Discipleship*, rev. ed. (London, 1959), 71. *DBW*, IV, 72.

17. Ibid., 54. *DBW*, IV, 56.

18. Ibid., 44–45. *DBW*, IV, 40.

19. Bethge, *Bonhoeffer*, 492 [cf. 2000, 587].

20. Geoffrey B. Kelly's editor's introduction to Dietrich Bonhoeffer, *Life Together* (Minneapolis, 1996), 8.

21. Ibid., 36. The original is "Jedes menschliche Wunschbild, das in die christliche Gemeinschaft mit eingebracht wird, hindert die echte Gemeinschaft und muss zerbrochen werden, damit die echte Gemeinschaft leben kann," *DBW*, V, 23–4.

22. Ibid., 38–39.

23. Ilse Tödt, "Paradoxical Obedience: Dietrich Bonhoeffer's Theological Ethics, 1933–1943" *Lutheran Theological Journal* 35, no. 1 (May 2001): 9.

24. Bethge, *Bonhoeffer*, 554–66 [cf. 2000, 650–662].

25. Ibid., 559 [cf. 655].

26. Tödt, "Bonhoeffer on Paradoxical Obedience," 9.

27. Ibid.

28. Bethge, *Bonhoeffer*, 626–687 passim [cf. 2000: 722–87].

29. Ibid. See Bethge's discussion about whether Bonhoeffer meant that Hitler was the Antichrist in person or was merely his agent, 627 [cf. 2000: 722–23]. Bethge reports here that Bonhoeffer told him quite clearly on this question:

"No, he is not the Antichrist; Hitler is not big enough for that; the Antichrist uses him, but he is not as stupid as that man."

30. Hans Dirk van Hoogstraten, "The Enemy and Righteous Action," in *Bonhoeffer for a New Day*, ed. John W. de Gruchy (Grand Rapids, 1997), 188.

31. Cited after Heinz Eduard Tödt, "Conscience in Bonhoeffer's ethical Theory and Practice," in *Bonhoeffer's Ethics*, ed. Guy Carter, et al. (Kampen, 1991), 50. The quotation is from "After Ten Years," Bonhoeffer's reflections at the end of 1942, central to which was the concern that the educated upper middle class as a group had failed in their assessment of the Nazi regime and betrayed their conscience by at least outwardly supporting it. See note 28 above which identifies sections of Bethge's biography that elaborates this issue.

32. Ibid., "After Ten Years."

33. *Letters and Papers from Prison*, enlarged ed. (London, 2000), 5.

34. Ibid., 6.

35. Bonhoeffer, *Ethik, DBW*, VI, 256.

36. Heinz Eduard Tödt, "Conscience in Bonhoeffer's Ethical Theory," 53.

37. Bonhoeffer, *Ethik, DBW*, VI, 279.

38. Heinz Eduard Tödt, "Conscience in Bonhoeffer's Ethical Theory," 54; "After Ten Years," 7.

39. *Ethik, DBW*, VI, 283.

40. Heinz-Eduard Tödt, "Conscience in Bonhoeffer's Ethical Theory," 55.

7

Bonhoeffer and the Jewish Question

If there was one single issue that set Bonhoeffer apart from his contemporaries, his coreligionists, and the *Bildungsbürgertum* generally, it was the Jewish question. This chapter seeks to flesh out a number of the points raised in chapter 3. Attention has already been drawn to the tradition of anti-Judaism and anti-Semitism in German history, particularly as it developed in the nineteenth century. At that time, the ideals of *Kultur* were being enunciated by leading German philosophers and educationalists, who taught that a person had to be of German blood in order to be able to participate in and appropriate true German culture. These thinkers, anticipating the Nazis, had thus made membership in the racial community an essential prerequisite for becoming a true German. This enabled a certain development called "formation" to occur. As we have learned, this process was called *Bildung*. The key issue here is that a person of non-German blood might indeed become learned, that is, scholarly in Germany, by virtue of going through the education system and, as a result, manifest a high proficiency in appropriating the products of the German mind, for example in literature, the arts, music and philosophy, the *Geisteswissenschaften* (sometimes translated as "mental or moral sciences"), but it was impossible for them to become formed as only a racially pure German could be. German Jews, then, by definition, were excluded from the cultural community, although the manner of this exclusion would have mostly been in the form of a mental reservation on the part of the "genuine" *Bildungsbürger*. In the period since 1871 when the federal constitution was imposed on all the Germanic states, excluding Austria, all previous legal exceptions affecting Jews were lifted and full citizenship rights were accorded to "citizens of Jewish faith." However, legal emancipation did not equate with social acceptance as such contemporary Jewish scholars as the late Walter Grab have eloquently demonstrated.[1] Here, Grab makes the point that anti-Semitism, in spite of the emancipation of the Jews in Germany from 1871 onward, remained fashionable in educated and aristocratic circles (*salonfähig*), and as conditions after the First World War became increasingly more difficult in Germany, so the level of the latent hatred of Jews grew, and this was exploited most intensively by the Hitler movement. Grab's central thesis is that the emancipation of the Jews in Germany had been *granted*, as it were, *graciously* by the Prusso-German state under Chancellor Otto von Bismarck, and had not been *won* as it was in France and elsewhere through democratic struggle, through popular uprisings against the old state authorities that demanded democratic rights for all people, indeed, the abolition of privileges and disabilities simultaneously. These changes, as a result, became constitutionally anchored and hence could not be removed without another revolution. Consequently, when the Nazis seized power in 1933 in Germany, the so-called national socialist revolution, the rights that had been *graciously* accorded the Jews in 1871 and confirmed in the Weimar Constitution of 1919, were now most *ungraciously* withdrawn. In short, the Jews were the victims of the failure of democracy in Germany.

With regard to the churches in Germany there had always been a "Jewish Problem." This was owing to the fact that despite the external emancipation of Jews, there remained a theologically grounded, deep-seated anti-Judaism that was a question of doctrine. Indeed, clerical anti-Judaism, and ultimately, anti-Semitism were predicated on the assumption that the New Covenant established by Jesus of Nazareth had abrogated the Old Covenant of Moses entirely. And the consequence of this was that Jews, to have any chance of salvation, would have to be baptized. That, of course, was essentially the view expressed by the older Martin Luther, and it was held to be valid until Karl Barth and Dietrich Bonhoeffer, independently of each other, effectively repudiated it.[2] This will be dealt with in greater detail below.

What must be established at this point is just how deep-seated the anti-Semitism and anti-Judaism was among the vast majority of Protestant clergy. The Roman Catholic clergy were by no means immune from it.[3] As has been seen, Bonhoeffer, in his spirited defense of fellow German citizens of Jewish faith, was virtually alone among his colleagues. This indisputable fact illustrates beyond any shadow of doubt that anti-Semitism was paradigmatic for the vast majority of the *Bildungsbürgertum*, and it is this that first hindered the development of a vigorous liberal tradition in Germany and hence made it virtually impossible for most of its members to develop a critical stance toward the criminal Nazi racial policy.[4]

It will be necessary at this point to examine in greater detail how difficult it was for the Confessing Church, Bonhoeffer's church, to revise the existing paradigm regarding the Jewish question, to eliminate once and for all the prejudice, and so come to a new theologically purified assessment of the issue. We will see that it was not until the ideas of Karl Barth and Dietrich Bonhoeffer were enunciated that the issue could be isolated and finally clarified. This process could only take place, after much deliberation, in a series of postwar synods. [See chapter 9.]

The bid for control of the church mounted by the "German Christians" in the early stages of the Third Reich, with the aid of the Nazi authorities, challenged many local and regional churches to formulate various confessions of faith in an effort to define the essence of true reformed and Protestant Christianity.[5] The "German Christians" had been trying to align Christianity with Nazi ideology, and that meant in practice the exclusion of even baptized Jews from the fellowship of the church. As already noted, they even advocated the elimination of the Old Testament and the Pauline epistles from the bible. This attempt to bowdlerize the holy scriptures, understandably, had to bring most traditional Lutherans to the barricades. If Luther stood for anything it was surely for the unity of the scriptures, and the offer of the sacrament of baptism to all people unconditionally. The first Christians were indisputably baptized Jews. To demand in 1933 that the church should refuse to baptize Jews and admit them to full membership of the church, including the pastorate, was a blatant theological absurdity. This, however, did not hinder the Prussian Synod of 5/6 September 1933 (known as the "brown synod" (because of the number of Nazi uniforms among the delegates) from adopting this position formulated in the so-called Aryan Paragraph that was a component of Nazi anti-Jewish legislation passed already in April 1933. This had excluded persons of Jewish descent and belief from holding positions in the public service. Instead of maintaining theological orthodoxy, the Prussian Evangelical Church had prioritized the bizarre Nazi concepts about racial purity over the central doctrine of Christianity. This, as we have seen, amounted to a *status confessionis* for Bonhoeffer: the church had failed to meet a challenge to its essential beliefs. A stand had to be taken.

This situation gave rise to the above-mentioned confessional movement in which Bonhoeffer was directly involved. It became, therefore, crucially important to enunciate the orthodox position of the church before the meeting of the National Synod scheduled for the end of September 1933, where a deadly theological confrontation with the "German Christians" was expected. To further this aim Bonhoeffer traveled to the famous Lutheran hospice at Bethel as the venue chosen to consult with the Erlangen systematic theologian Hermann Sasse[6] in order to draft a confession that highlighted the church's duty to protect the Jews. In the book of Leviticus 19:34, it states: "The stranger who sojourns with you shall be to you as the native among you, and you shall love him as yourself; for you were strangers in the land of Egypt: I am the Lord your God."

Both Bonhoeffer and Sasse were agreed that the confession had to state unequivocally that there could be no backing down on the question of admitting baptized Jews to the full fellowship of the church, otherwise the church would have betrayed the essence of the gospel. Unfortunately, there were some twenty theologians involved in formulating the confession, and most of these were not prepared to be as theologically rigorous as Bonhoeffer and Sasse. Consequently, the final draft, as we have seen in chapter five, intentionally avoided any declaration of solidarity with the tiny minority of pastors who were of Jewish descent, something that Bonhoeffer regarded as a matter of principle. Both he and Sasse in the end refused to sign the statement that they themselves had practically initiated.[7]

It must be remembered that the team of theologians who had formulated the Bethel Confession were not "German Christians." They were representatives of the mainstream who rejected the innovation that the state had a right to interfere in church matters. Nevertheless, most of them, including at the time Martin Niemöller, still regarded the German Jews, because of their racial origin, as non-German. They stressed the line that the "people of the Jews" had rejected the Messiah and that therefore, in place of the Old Testament people of the covenant, came the new people of God, namely the Christian church based on the New Covenant that was sealed by the saving act of Jesus' self-sacrifice on Calvary. The only approach to the Jews from then on was to demand their conversion, and for that purpose the church maintained a so-called Jewish mission (*Die Judenmission*).[8]

The mission to the Jews, precisely at this time, was a not an insignificant gesture. It was a minimalist way of defying the "German Christians" who, of course, being fanatically pro-Nazi, had no time for Jews, baptized or otherwise. It was derived, however, from a theology that taught that the entire history of Jewish Israel was merely a preliminary experience to the advent of the true Israel of God, the Christian Church (*Vereinnahmungs-Theologie*). This was not the position that Bonhoeffer came to espouse, or that of Karl Barth, as shall be seen; hence Bonhoeffer's refusal to sign the Bethel Confession. His theological approach was rather to emphasize the "diaconal structure" of the Church, namely, the commandment actively to show compassion for the victim, the excluded, and the helpless stranger. In the German situation at the time it meant defying the Nazis in order to protect the Jews from persecution. As indicated, the efforts of both Bonhoeffer and Sasse to get this expressed unequivocally in the Bethel Confession were in vain.[9]

What the Bethel Confession illustrates quite emphatically is the virtually universal contempt among middle-class Germans for their fellow citizens of Jewish faith. If the Christian church could show no sensitivity or compassion to them in a situation in which they were being brutally and criminally victimized, then it is highly unlikely that more secular-minded Germans would go out of their way to come to their aid. The anti-Judaistic culture had become deeply rooted in Germany. And this, of course, was confirmed some nine months later in the Barmen Declaration that had been initiated by Karl Barth. This document, the foundational statement of the Confessing Church, was also a compromise. Its aim had been to delineate the orthodox position in opposition to the "German Christians," but it could only win support from among the wider Protestant clergy by avoiding confrontation with the Jewish question, and the result was that the statement failed to formulate any protest against the marginalization of the Jews and even failed to protect pastors of Jewish origin from deportation to concentration camps.[10]

However, already after the promulgation of the Aryan Paragraph, Bonhoeffer was so incensed that in August 1933 he published a pamphlet entitled "The Aryan Paragraph in the Church" designed to influence opinion at the coming Prussian Synod and the later National Synod. It clearly drew upon his earlier statement "The Church and the Jewish Question," discussed previously in chapter 5. Bonhoeffer now focused more sharply on the central issue, namely, the theological significance of excluding baptized Jews from the pastorate. The "German Christians" had on 23 July won a majority of synod seats at the national church elections, and Bonhoeffer was concerned that they would adopt the Aryan Paragraph for the church. It was therefore urgent that the implications of this be spelled out. Bonhoeffer's key point in the pamphlet was that if Jewish Christians were excluded from the fellowship of the church, then the substance of the church of Jesus Christ, as he put it, would have been destroyed. Certainly, the credibility of the church would have been placed in question. Indeed, the continuity of the church was only to be found in the church where the Jewish Christians had not been excluded. The kind of "ethnically cleansed" church that the "German Christians" wanted ceased to be the church. Consequently, the only theologically honest thing to do was to walk out of such an association.[11] This position did not achieve much resonance among the vast majority of pastors, as the number of baptized Jewish colleagues would not have exceeded two in a thousand—and there were some 18,000 pastors in Germany at the time.

There was initially, even among the theologians who agreed with Bonhoeffer in principle, a certain reluctance to make such an issue of the Aryan Paragraph because so few pastors were in reality affected, but Bonhoeffer and his half-Jewish pastor friend Franz Hildebrandt would not give up the fight, and they continued to lobby among their high-profile associates such as Martin Niemöller and Friedrich von Bodelschwingh, making the point that the Aryan Paragraph was a breaking of the faith, a *status confessionis*. These efforts resulted in the formulation of a declaration by Bonhoeffer and Niemöller that stated that whoever supported the Aryan Paragraph automatically excluded themselves from the Christian communion. This was duly communicated to the Reich bishop, Ludwig Müller, on whom, not unexpectedly, it clearly made no impression.[12]

At this point Martin Niemöller, having drawn closer to Bonhoeffer's radical position, took the initiative with like-minded pastors to found the Pastors' Emergency League, (*Pfarrernotbund*) and, using the declaration already sent to the Reich bishop as his guidelines, formulated the following four-point set of principles to stand as the basis of their opposition to the German Christians. It was called the *Notbundverpflichtung*:

1) I oblige myself to discharge my office as a servant of the Word solely on the basis of Holy Scripture and the Reformation confessions as the correct exegesis of Holy Scripture.
2) I oblige myself without reservation to protest against all violations of such confessional positions.
3) I oblige myself to the best of my ability to be co-responsible for all those who are being persecuted for their stand regarding these confessions.
4) Aware of these obligations I bear witness to the fact that a violation of the Reformation confessions has been made by virtue of the introduction of the Aryan paragraph within the Church of Christ.[13]

Within two weeks of the circulation of the *Notbundverpflichtung*, until the eve of the National Synod on 27 September, some 2,000 signatures had been collected so that there was a solid basis on which to protest against the endorsement of the Aryan Paragraph. At this point Bonhoeffer and Niemöller with twenty other Prussian oppositional pastors composed an appeal to the National Synod in which it was stated that the Aryan Paragraph was a flagrant violation of the church's confession and was by implication a denial of the true Reformation heritage.[14] Bonhoeffer, who was not a member of the synod, had sent a telegram to the Reich bishop inviting him to a public debate on the Aryan Paragraph. Not surprisingly, there was no response, and Bonhoeffer in a final act of desperation resorted with two friends to fixing protest placards on trees and buildings, a not unprecedented measure in the "Luther city" of Wittenberg. However, in Bonhoeffer's case there were less dramatic immediate or long-term consequences from this act of defiance against the errors of the church hierarchy than was the case with Luther's posting of the ninety-five theses on All Souls' eve in 1517. What can be said, however, is that persistent opposition of Bonhoeffer and his tight circle of friends did hinder the adoption of the Aryan Paragraph at the National Synod, simultaneously arousing the conscience and challenging the theological integrity of sufficient numbers of pastors to enable the formation of what eventually became the Confessing Church. In its self-perception this church claimed to be the only one in Germany that remained in confessional continuity with the original Lutheran heritage.

The situation as it appeared to Bonhoeffer, Niemöller, and their supporters after the National Synod was as dismal as it was potentially dangerous. Continued opposition to Nazi church policy could result in arrest for treason, as it eventually did in many cases. Meanwhile, in October 1933 Bonhoeffer retreated with a certain sense of resignation to his appointment in London to the cure of souls in two German parishes there. It was during this period that circumstances developed to the extent that the *status confessionis* had to be invoked.[15]

Bonhoeffer's remoteness in London from the center of action in Berlin in no way lessened his concern for the fate of the church in Germany. He continued to be anxious that his theological allies should continue steadfast, and wrote in this sense to Niemöller urging him to remain radical on the question of the Aryan paragraph and to be prepared for conflict that could have the direst consequences. There could be no side-stepping the consequences of maintaining theological integrity. In short, the principles enunciated in the *Notbundverpflichtung* had to be upheld at all costs.[16] Bonhoeffer had good reason to write to Niemöller in this sense because back in anti-Semitic Berlin, Niemöller gave every indication that he was going to weaken on the Aryan paragraph because on the tenth Sunday after Trinity, 1935, the famous pastor of Dahlem Church was still preaching in decidedly anti-Judaistic terms. Using as his text Matthew, 23:29–36,[17] Niemöller clearly indicated that he comprehended the current persecution of the Jews as a fulfillment of Jesus' prophecy. In short, Niemöller's historical theology was driven by a fixed notion that the Jews were no longer a covenanted people and thus deserved what was happening to them.[18]

Bonhoeffer, on the other hand, was inspired by a different theology and was preaching in London in the spirit of Proverbs 31:8–9, "Speak up for people who cannot speak for themselves. Protect the rights of all who are helpless. Speak for them and be a righteous judge. Protect the rights of the poor and needy." At that time many Jewish refugees from Nazi Germany were arriving in London, mostly destitute and in need of accommodation and work in order to survive. Bonhoeffer saw in the persecution of Jewish Christians and Jews, both of which groups were rendered homeless by the Nazis, a *Kairos*, an opportunity sent by God calling the church to declare solidarity with the persecuted and if necessary not only to alleviate their suffering but also to suffer alongside them. This was a stand far removed from that of Niemöller who, because of what he called the "weaker brethren" in the church, demanded that the Jewish Christians should keep in the background and remain as invisible as possible. He was admitting that the average Lutheran in the pew had an in-built aversion for even converted Jews, and this should be taken into account. Bonhoeffer, personally, was acutely aware of the plight of baptized Jews because his twin sister, Sabine, was married to one—namely, Dr. Gerhard Leibholz—and he had personally, together with Eberhard Bethge, assisted in helping the Leibholz couple to flee first to Switzerland and then to England. And in London, Bonhoeffer was daily involved in meeting the calls for help from refugees who sought him out in his parishes.

So, by contrasting the approaches of Bonhoeffer and Niemöller to the Jewish question it becomes clear that Bonhoeffer prioritized the diaconal aspect/structure of the church in the world in line with the ideas already systematically expressed in both his doctoral dissertation, *Sanctorum Communio*, and his postdoctoral thesis, *Act and Being*, in which the central theme is that the church is Christ acting in the world, the essential task of which is to serve the needs of others. Niemöller, representing in fact the vast majority of Lutheran pastors at the time, could see only the falsely understood theology of substitution and punishment, namely, the teaching that the synagogue had been replaced by the church in God's plan for salvation and that the Jews, in failing to accept Jesus of Nazareth as the Messiah, merited eternal punishment. Consequently, what was happening to them under the Nazis was theologically explicable. Bonhoeffer increasingly saw his task in overcoming this mind-set, although at this relatively early stage he had yet to revise the views expressed in "The Church and the Jewish Question" in which he had stated unequivocally that the Jews were a "mysterious people both loved and punished by God."

By April 1935 Bonhoeffer was back in Germany, having responded to the call of the Council of Brethren of the Church of the Old Prussian Union to lead a seminary to train ordinands for the Confessing Church, and since it would not be recognized by the state, it was technically illegal and had to be financed independently by the Confessing Church. This was started first at a remote farming property outside the Pomeranian village of Zingst on the Baltic coast, and then more permanently at Finkenwalde, east of Stettin in the vacant house of a former country estate of the von Katte family. As the Confessing Church had been founded in defiance of the Reich Church it could not call upon institutional funding. The planned seminary had therefore to be entirely supported by sympathetic members of the Confessing Church throughout the country. Consequently, the ordinands had to be convinced opponents of Nazi church policy and loyal disciples of Dietrich Bonhoeffer, who had made them understand the theological fallacies of anti-Judaism and anti-Semitism.

In order to illustrate just how militant Bonhoeffer and his students had become regarding the Jewish question, they were prepared to travel to Berlin-Steglitz for a synod, scheduled for 23–26 September 1935. The Aryan paragraph would be on the agenda, a topic of particular concern at that time as the Nazi government had just promulgated the so-called Nuremberg Laws (15 September) that had defined the degree of Jewish blood an individual had to have in order to be classified a Jew. It would have been an opportunity, indeed, the last one, as it transpired, for the Confessing Church to confront the state with its discriminatory anti-Jewish policies. To assist in this a "Memorandum on the Obligations of the Confessing Church toward non-Aryan Protestants" had been prepared and tabled. It drew graphic attention to the effects of the discriminatory actions of the state on Christians of Jewish origin and to their marginalization by the church and society, and the consequences of the loss of their property and dignity.

Despite the clarity of the memorandum, the leading synod officials simply refused to be moved. They lacked the conviction that Bonhoeffer and his students had hoped they would show, and failed, therefore, to raise the question of the infamous Nuremberg laws. All that the synod conceded was that no Jews were to be denied the sacrament of baptism and that the charity of Christ was to be made available to non-baptized Jews. It was a weak formulation that reflected the fear of the church of new Nazi regulations to monitor the finances of the church and its organization. Bonhoeffer, of course, was less interested in institutional questions than in issues of theological principle, and he saw the outcome of the Steglitz synod both as a capitulation before the power of the criminal regime and as a further example of the theological bankruptcy of the Confessing Church. They had missed the opportunity "to put a spoke in the wheel" of the state, as Bonhoeffer had hoped.

This experience was yet further indication of the deep-rooted anti-Judaism among most Protestant theologians and pastors. They were clearly not capable of "jumping over their own shadow" to "open their mouth for the dumb," as Bonhoeffer had desired. Indeed, Bonhoeffer was so far in advance of the majority of his colleagues that he could argue that the way in which the church dealt with the Jewish question would determine whether the church was still the church of the Christ present within it. "Are we still the church of the ever-present Christ?"[19]

he urgently inquired. Only few were listening. Indeed, within three months of the promulgation of the Nuremberg laws, the Confessing Church leadership sent an appeal to all affiliated parishes to celebrate the centenary of the birth of the notorious anti-Semitic pastor Adolf Stöcker, 11 December 1935.[20] In doing so, the Confessing Church was emphatically endorsing Stöcker's views that the Jews were a deleterious influence within German society.

On the other hand, some more perceptive members of the Confessing Church leadership had mustered up sufficient moral courage to compose a memorandum to Hitler in which they complained that the state was compelling the church to hatred of the Jews, stressing that this was a violation of the commandment to love one's neighbor. The memorandum had been composed by a lawyer, Friedrich Weissler, with the collaboration of two of Bonhoeffer's former students. One of these took it upon himself, unbeknownst to Dr. Weissler, to provide a copy of the memorandum to the Swiss newspaper, *Basler Nachrichten*, which published it before the text reached the Führer. This move had dire consequences because Weissler was subsequently arrested and murdered and the two collaborators arrested and incarcerated for two years in a concentration camp.[21]

After this debacle, Bonhoeffer and Franz Hildebrandt, with a view to encouraging the church to reassess its failure to be more outspoken on the Jewish question, composed a further memorandum urging both clergy and laity to reflect on the church's obligation to listen to the prompting of the Holy Spirit—it was Pentecost—and not to be swept away in the wave of hatred. Indeed, the two energetic pastors in opposition wrote that the Holy Spirit through the word, sacraments, and prayer, would in the end bring peace.

These efforts had no visible effects, as the one of the most distinguished leaders of the Confessing Church, Hans Asmussen, was still preaching the old established line as late as the tenth Sunday after Trinity, 1937, as follows:

> The age of the Jews is passed. Israel failed to recognize God's great hour. . . . It came to this because they distorted their service to God. The Jews made out of the house that was rightly God's house, a temple in which they worshipped money. For this reason the advent of Christ incarnate was something alien. They had to hate him because he made manifest their end.
>
> The new covenant knows no peace with Jews or heathen. Both stand with regard to the church in irreconcilable hostility as long as the church is still the church.[22]

Again, we have a graphic example of the distance separating Bonhoeffer's understanding of the Jewish question from that of the majority of his coreligionists. He saw the possibility of overcoming the seemingly unbridgeable gulf separating church and synagogue that was fixed in the mind of German Lutherans by locating the church and synagogue in a reciprocal relationship whereby the church kept permanently in mind its Jewish roots from which it could not be separated and still be the church. To do this Bonhoeffer reevaluated Romans 11:17–18:

> Some of the branches of the cultivated olive tree have been broken off, and a branch of a wild olive tree has been ... joined to it. You gentiles are like that wild olive tree, and now you share the strong spiritual life of the Jews. So then, you must not despise those who were broken off like those who were broken like branches. How can you be proud? You are just a branch; you don't support the roots. The roots support you.[23]

The logic of this assessment was patently clear to Bonhoeffer, though not, of course, to most of his coreligionists. It expressed his position unequivocally but failed to convince anyone else other than his closest collaborators and disciples.

On the night of 9 November 1938, *Reichskristallnacht*—when the synagogues were burnt down, Jewish shops vandalized, and hundreds of Jews maltreated and even killed—Bonhoeffer marked in his bible Psalm 74:8: "They wanted to crush us completely; they burnt down every holy place in the land." [24] Again, the majority of the Lutheran theologians saw in these events the proof that the Jews were under a curse for having rejected Christ. Bonhoeffer, on the other hand, predicted that "if today the synagogues burn, tomorrow the churches will be set on fire."[25]

At this time Bonhoeffer began very seriously to reflect on the biblical sources that gave insight into the relationship between church and synagogue, the key passages being in Romans, 9:4 and 11:11–15. What was happening in Germany now reversed the traditional criticism by the church of Israel into a criticism of the church. Indeed, only a church that took the part of the persecuted Jewish brothers of Jesus would be consistent with the Jewishness of Jesus and aware of the significance that his people had for him.[26]

Gradually, but only gradually, others in the Confessing Church were beginning to evaluate the situation along these lines and to preach accordingly. This led inevitably to the arrest of those pastors who were accused of treason for simply pointing out that what was happening was a violation of the Ten Commandments, or for calling the nation to repentance and for praying for forgiveness, and that the nation might be spared the judgment of almighty God. Under these circumstances the church leadership had to take a stand, and at a church rally in Berlin-Steglitz on 10–12 December 1938, sufficient moral courage was manifested in a declaration protesting against the arrest of pastors and at the same time urging solidarity with converted Jews, calling them brothers and sisters. This had been a difficult learning process for many Protestants. Initially, in 1933, they had demonstrated only the desire to be rid of Jews of all persuasions. Five years later, they had to face the probability of being arrested for speaking out for them. If the church in 1933 had taken on board what Bonhoeffer had upheld as the role of the church—namely, to admonish the state regarding its duty toward all citizens regardless of racial origins—the situation could conceivably have developed differently. For the Protestant Church in Germany, however, given the deeply embedded tradition of obedience to the powers that be, the idea of assuming the role of conscience of the state was still far too remote. Further, the possibility that the church, under certain circumstances, might embark on a path of active opposition by "putting a spoke in the wheel" of the state was beyond comprehension at the time. Bonhoeffer occupied a lonely outpost.

Here it must be reiterated that Bonhoeffer's idea of opposition to the state, triggered off by the Nazi Jewish policy, was entirely theologically derived. Initially, he saw that state authority was being misused against a defenseless minority, and that violated not only the traditional notion of the state as being instituted by God to maintain law and order and dispense justice without fear or favor, to all subjects, regardless of their religion. It also conflicted with basic Christian ethics. Under these circumstances, the church could not stand idly by without admonishing the state about its true role in history. This, indeed, was Bonhoeffer's point of departure. And the more he pleaded for the Jews, the more he got to hear from his coreligionists the theological rationale for *not* intervening on their behalf—namely, that the Jews had incurred the wrath of God by rejecting the crucified Jesus as Messiah. Therefore, what was happening to them was the natural consequence of their original willfulness.

Until 1939, Bonhoeffer had proceeded by establishing a theological rationale for opposition to Nazi policy as his protests at various synods illustrated. Disappointingly, the only fruit that such protest had harvested was the above-mentioned communiqué issued by the church rally held at Berlin-Steglitz 10–12 December 1938, and this was little more than the pathetic cry of the now embattled and powerless church. It symbolized the limit of the traditional church's capacity to demand any realistically effective change in the policy of a regime that had nothing but contempt for the rule of law.

It was at this point in Bonhoeffer's career that he made the transition from theological protest and agitation within the church to conspiratorial action against the Godless tyranny that held the nation in thrall. Crucial in explaining this was Bonhoeffer's family tradition of upper-middle-class liberalism. Certainly, both sides of his family were *Bildungsbürger* imbued with a high sense of decency and justice that included an abhorrence of all manifestations of discrimination and violence against defenseless fellow citizens, including Jews. As well, alongside his brother Klaus and his brother-in-law Hans von Dohnanyi, Bonhoeffer had always been critical of the Nazi contempt for the constitution. Dohnanyi was already involved in clandestine opposition to the Nazis and it was he who introduced Bonhoeffer into the circle of conspirators around Admiral Wilhelm Canaris, head of military counter intelligence (*Abwehr*).

This occurred at a time in 1939 when Bonhoeffer was experiencing doubts about his ability to effect a change of heart among his coreligionists. It appeared to him for a short time, as has been seen, that it would be best to continue the struggle from outside Germany in the United States, where he had the opportunity take a teaching post and also to act as chaplain to the American Committee for Christian-Jewish Refugees in New York, an instance of binding up the wounds of the victims.[27] This option, as we have seen, was, after only a few weeks in New York (June–July 1939), rejected in favor of returning to Germany to identify with his people and to fight for the preservation of Christian civilization. He therefore seized the opportunity to work as an agent of the *Abwehr*, and that allowed him to travel abroad to intensify contact with the Ecumenical movement. The position also exempted Bonhoeffer from obligatory military service. In addition, it enabled him to assist some Jews to escape to safety in Switzerland, the action designated, "Operation 7".[28]

Asta von Oppen has commented perceptively on this transition in Bonhoeffer's life, as follows:

> The task he fulfilled in the seminars on behalf of the church Bonhoeffer now exchanged for the role of an underground political activist. The ecclesiastical reformer became a political conspirator. Whereas his theology had caused him to become active in the church he now reflected upon his bourgeois roots *that he saw as co-responsible for the current political situation in Germany. This led to his recognition of the shared guilt of the upper bourgeois caste for the political devastation and confusion, and persuaded him of the necessity to conspire with like-minded citizens to undermine those in power in order, either peacefully or with violence if necessary, to eliminate them.*[29]

This insight into the shared guilt of the *Bildungsbürgertum* by Bonhoeffer was at the core of his conspiratorial/revolutionary behavior. But unlike his fellow conspirators who wanted a Germany restored to a political order more reminiscent of the Reich that Bismarck had created,

Bonhoeffer wanted a spiritually completely reconstructed Germany that had done harrowing penance for the evil it had perpetrated on the world and on the Jews in particular.[30] And central to achieving this change of heart among his contemporaries was a revised theology of the relationship between Christianity and the Jewish religion. He had already been thinking about this since 1933, and in the years following, accelerated by the increased discrimination and atrocities perpetrated against the Jews, Bonhoeffer's thoughts on this age-old subject began to crystallize in a remarkable way. After becoming an agent in the *Abwehr*, Bonhoeffer had the opportunity between his traveling assignments to intensify his work on systematizing a Protestant ethic. During this time he began formulating his ideas on this project. In retrospect, the following theological route of progress in Bonhoeffer's mind can be made out:

Christ came to proclaim the Kingdom of God. The universality both in time and space of the Kingdom of God led inexorably to the discipleship of Christ in this world. And this world is the penultimate sphere standing in need of justification. For this purpose Christ came into the world as the incarnate Son of God, and the Incarnation compels historical responsibility. This is because the Incarnation, being an historical event, directed human attention to the continuity of history. And here we are reminded of the fact that the figure of Jesus of Nazareth is a product of Jewish history which itself, because of the ministry of Jesus of Nazareth, flowed seamlessly into European history. In *Ethics* Bonhoeffer expressed it as follows:

> The historical Jesus Christ is the continuity of our history. But Jesus Christ was the promised Messiah of the Israelite-Jewish people, and for that reason the line of our forefathers goes back beyond the appearance of Jesus to the people of Israel. Western history, is by God's will, indissolubly linked with the people of Israel not only genetically but also in a genuine uninterrupted encounter. The Jews keep open the question of Christ. He is the sign of the free mercy-choice and of the repudiating wrath of God: "Behold, therefore, the goodness and severity of God." [Romans 11:22]. An expulsion of the Jews from the West must necessarily bring with it the expulsion of Christ. For Jesus Christ was a Jew.[31]

Bonhoeffer's language here is, admittedly, not completely perspicuous, especially the sentence "The Jews keep open the question of Christ" (*Der Jude hält die Christusfrage offen*). Despite this, however, the tone, feeling, and intention are absolutely clear. He was at pains to establish an indissoluble organic bond between ancient Israel and Christianity, a bond that had been expressly and wrongly repudiated. The German theologian Andreas Pangritz has perceptively pointed out that the recognition of this bond placed the German-Jewish relationship in an entirely new perspective; one could justifiably say the former relationship of irreconcilable theological enmity could now be seen in a "revolutionary" new light with ground-shaking historical and political implications. For Christians, Jews were not an alien *Volk*, but through the historical significance of Christ inextricably part of European and world history.[32]

Significant for this development in Bonhoeffer's thought is the timing of this formulation. It has been dated as having been written in 1941 after the first deportation of Jews had occurred. Over six thousand Jews had been transported to the concentration camp in Gurs in the south of France in October 1940. Bonhoeffer had been made fully aware of this through his contacts with the offices of the ecumenical movement in Geneva (Committee for Refugee Services) while he was in Switzerland from 24 March to 24 April 1941, ostensibly on behalf of the *Abwehr*. This office of the World Council of Churches had begun to monitor Nazi Jewish policy and its implementation in occupied Europe. Then on 21 June 1941, Nazi Germany began the fateful campaign against the Soviet Union, Operation Barbarossa. This resulted in the opening up of the East as a region in which ostensibly to resettle Jews. The first deportations from Berlin eastward occurred between 29 August and 26 September when Bonhoeffer was again in Switzerland.

The *Abwehr*, as a separate government agency, was not privy to these decisions but its personnel such as Dohnanyi and Bonhoeffer were gaining more and more information about the Nazi violation of human rights, and they used this material to compile comprehensive reports to pass on to those military officers who were known to be involved in the anti-Hitler conspiracy. The intention was to mount a case against Hitler to justify his arrest and for use in the trial that was expected to follow.[33] The time had indeed come in which to "put a spoke in the wheel," that is, actively to intervene to put a stop to the regime's criminal activities. And clearly it was the sum of anti-Jewish measures and atrocities to 1939 that had accelerated Bonhoeffer's determination to embark on political opposition. It was no longer sufficient to pray piously and to "sing Gregorian chant." The time had come for responsible action. Indeed, as we have seen, since 1933, the awareness had been growing in Bonhoeffer that the hatred of the Jews that the state had instituted as official policy had its roots in the history of the church and in its theological distortions. These he now—that is, in the period 1939–40—set out to correct.

The deportations in 1941 sparked the insight that the expulsion of the Jews from the West meant also the de-Christianization of the West, since Jesus was a Jew. The expulsion was the policy of a criminal regime that had taken control of a Christian country. Consequently, if Christians stood aside and condoned such a policy, they would be betraying their heritage. This, according to Bonhoeffer's insight, was a sure sign that Christianity had been abandoned in Germany. The descent into barbarism could not have been more graphically illustrated. And, interestingly, at this point Bonhoeffer was unaware that the deportations were but the prelude to the "final solution" that had been coordinated among the various relevant ministries at the notorious Wannsee Conference in January 1942, as already explained. Expulsion led to annihilation. And the guilt for all this weighed upon the Christian church.

In *Ethics*, Bonhoeffer devoted a chapter to "Guilt, Justification and Renewal," in which he pursued the question of a necessary confession of guilt by the church.

> It is a sign of the living presence of Christ that there are men in whom knowledge of the apostasy from Jesus Christ is kept awake not merely in the sense that this apostasy is observed in others but in the sense that these men themselves confess themselves guilty of this apostasy. They confess their guilt without any sidelong glance at their fellow offenders. Their confession of guilt is strictly exclusive in that it takes all guilt upon itself. Wherever there is still a weighing up and calculation of guilt, there the sterile morality of self justification usurps the place of the confession of guilt which is made in the presence of the form of Christ.... With this confession the entire guilt of the world falls upon the church, upon the Christians, and since this guilt is not denied here, but is confessed, there arises the possibility of forgiveness.[34]

And further Bonhoeffer accused the church in these words:

> The church confesses that she has not proclaimed often and clearly enough her message of the one God who has revealed Himself for all times in Jesus Christ and who suffers no other gods beside Himself. She confesses her timidity, her evasiveness, her dangerous concessions. She has often been untrue to her office of guardianship and to her office of comfort. And through this she has often denied to the outcast and to the despised the compassion which she owes them. She was silent when she should have cried out because the blood of the innocent was crying aloud to heaven. She has failed to speak the right word in the right way at the right time. She has not resisted to the uttermost the apostasy of faith, and she has brought upon herself the guilt of the godlessness of the masses.[35]

There had, of course, been ample opportunity between 1933 and 1938, the period between the first boycott of Jewish shops and the pogrom of the *Reichskristallnacht*, for the church to raise its voice, but it could not overcome millennia of anti-Judaism, even when the monstrous fruits of its error were manifest daily, at least to those with eyes to see and ears to hear. There had indeed occurred a catastrophic decline of faith, the thundering proof of which came in a circular dated two days before Christmas 1941 from the Chancellery of the German Evangelical Church. This document, sent to all offices throughout the country, emphasized that the break-through of the racial idea within the nation had required the expulsion of the Jews from the community, and in the light of this appropriate measures were to be taken to ensure that baptized non-Aryans did not participate in the life of the church. Those concerned would have to make what arrangements they could for church services and pastoral care.[36]

Here the leadership of the Confessing Church conformed almost completely to the demands of the regime and demonstrated thereby the hardness of heart and accompanying decline of faith that Bonhoeffer observed. Thus he could write in *Ethics*:

> The church confesses that it has witnessed the lawless application of brutal force, the physical and spiritual suffering of countless innocent people, oppression, hatred and murder, and that it has not raised its voice on behalf of the victims and has not found ways to hasten to their aid. It is guilty of the deaths of the weakest and most defenseless of the brothers and sisters of Jesus Christ. . . . The church confesses that it has witnessed in silence the spoilage and exploitation of the poor and the enrichment and corruption of the strong.[37]

Whereas the Confessing Church only reserved the term "brothers and sisters of Jesus Christ" for baptized Jews, Bonhoeffer here includes all Jews as deserving the protection of Christians. And consistent with his youthful thoughts on the nature of the church in the world, Bonhoeffer then affirms that the role of a truly penitent church would be actually to suffer in sympathy with the non-Aryan victims. Genuine discipleship demanded this level of solidarity with the Jews. Further, to suffer in sympathy in the discipleship of Christ, as Jesus Himself did on Calvary, meant also to enter into the community of guilt of all and to bear the burden of that guilt. Such action would be genuine Christian responsibility. Indeed, Bonhoeffer's theology is a theology of responsibility that is not limited to the ecclesiastical sphere but encompasses the entire world. That included, as well, taking the part of the Jews, the baptized and the non-baptized, without distinction. This would be obligatory particularly because of the revised relationship between church and synagogue, which is now seen by Bonhoeffer as one of interdependence whereas previously it was thought to be one of irreconcilable hostility based on the old supersessionist idea. This, Bonhoeffer emphatically refutes.

The implications of this are revolutionary. The former Protestant attitude, not to mention the Roman Catholic, was that Jews had to be converted; that was the church's role in history. Hence the German Protestants had maintained their *Judenmission*, mission to the Jews, whose point of departure was that the Jewish revelation on Sinai had been abrogated by the revelation in Christ. With Bonhoeffer, this no longer made any sense because the God of the Jews was also the God of the New Testament; indeed, the God of Creation was also the God of Redemption. Further, the God of the Old Testament is the father of Jesus Christ and the God revealed in Jesus Christ is the God of the Old Testament. He is a triune God. However, the holy incarnation and the cross—that is, the revelation made to the gentile world—required that the Old Testament be read anew, otherwise humanity would be restricted to a Jewish or heathen understanding of the Old Testament. It made complete sense only if read in relation to the advent of the Christ. In short, the Old Testament had to be read as a prelude to the New Testament, or, in other words, Christo-centrically.

It needs to be asked here, then, where did Bonhoeffer's "Confession of Guilt" on behalf of the church leave the great theological issue of the still abiding Old Covenant and its relation to the New Covenant, given that both have a role to play in the further history of salvation? But all that can be said is that the church has only recognized the so-called witness-people tradition that the synagogue has played in laying the foundation for the coming of the Messiah. This, of course, signifies a massive qualitative change with regard to the former prevailing attitude to the synagogue. It means at least that the church may finally reassess the history of ancient Israel, recognizing that Israel has been the witness pointing to the advent of the Savior, as Bonhoeffer spelled out in *Ethics*.[38] And, as Andreas Pangritz rightly observes, nations in general, and Germans in particular, who reappropriate the significance of Jesus' Jewishness arrive at a new understanding of what true patriotism should be, namely, the abandonment of all racially instigated nationalism and the embracing of the role of the suffering servant.[39] When this point is taken on board, Bonhoeffer's reassessment of the Jewish question has considerable political implications for the Christian world; indeed, something that would challenge the self-described Christian nations if they developed the perception to abandon all nationalistically driven politics. But there are further concerns.

Stephen Haynes has pursued this question in his book *The Bonhoeffer Legacy: Post Holocaust Perspectives* (2006), and has subjected both Bonhoeffer's statements and actions with regard to the Jewish question to a rigorous scrutiny. He has inquired in the light of Bonhoeffer's acknowledgement that the Old Covenant is still in force whether there is a new basis for a dialogue between *Synagogia* and *Ecclesia*. And he agrees that the next logical step would be for the church, having at last rejected that old theology of supersessionism, to engage in such a dialogue. If, as Bonhoeffer pointed out, "the Jew keeps open the question of Christ," he may well have meant that Jesus' Jewishness compels the Christian to accept the existence of the synagogue and wait for divine guidance as to how the church should relate to observant Jews. One may observe that the forgiveness spoken by Jesus from Calvary would be a sufficient basis for such a theological dialogue. However, it is all very well for those Christians who have at last overcome their anti-Judaism to seek a dialogue, but if such a project were to bear fruit, it would presume a Jewish preparedness to engage in such an encounter. The fact that some indeed do would vindicate Bonhoeffer's hope.

From the Christian standpoint, or more precisely through Bonhoeffer's perception so eloquently spelled out in *Ethics*, the Jew is always the other who is also Christ's brother—the other with whom the fate of the West is inextricably bound. This observation is reiterated by Stephen Haynes: the Jew is the "other" who is also Christ's brother, the other with whom is tied up the fate of the West; the other whose suffering reflects God's providence and whose treatment by the church exposes the latter's moral condition as well as that of society as a whole. Bonhoeffer came to see that from this point on there must be solidarity and not enmity between Christians and Jews.[40] Indeed, Bonhoeffer, we may acknowledge, has posthumously ushered in a new dialogical age.

This involved a progression in Bonhoeffer's thinking from the views expressed in April 1933 which were undeniably ambivalent. On the one hand, he used the Nazi maltreatment of Jews as an occasion to denounce Hitler as an *"anti-Obrigkeit"* in Prusso-German history; a true German "authority" or state would not persecute or make an exception of a particular group of its own citizens on racial or religious grounds. So, then, because the Hitler dictatorship did precisely that it was not a legitimate Germanic authority and therefore it ought to be resisted by "jamming a spoke in the wheel" of the regime. And so, although the Jews were a people both loved and punished by God throughout history, it was no state's prerogative to carry out any such punishment; that right was reserved to God alone.

The theology behind this early statement of Bonhoeffers was clearly based on the still-prevalent notion of supersessionism, that is, that the Old Covenant had been superseded by the New. But Bonhoeffer later in the history of the Third Reich, provoked by the continued maltreatment of Jews by the state—as, for example, in the Night of Broken Glass (*Reichskristallnacht* 9/10 September 1938)—begins to see that the only attitude that Christians could manifest toward the Jews in their persecution, being driven out of the West by the "anti-state," a truly diabolical force, was one of solidarity with the Jews in their sufferings. This is expressed most eloquently in the above-cited passages from *Ethics*.

Now it is a case of he who has ears to hear, let him hear. William Jay Peck has suggested in a perceptive article from 1973 that Bonhoeffer had begun already by May 1933 to criticize his own church, which saw itself as bearer of the Teutonic spirit that evinced only contempt for the Jews and hence had lost it's way completely, save of course, for the few pastors like Bonhoeffer who formed out of the confrontation with the diabolical force of the Third Reich a new and complex cultural vision.[41] Central to that was solidarity with the Jews—not only those baptized but also secular and observing as well. Clearly, this is initially a political solidarity, but it has far-reaching and dramatic theological implications. In a word, if the Old Covenant has not been abrogated and superseded by the New Covenant, then there must be a formula for Christian–Jewish collaboration in the world. Sinai and Calvary coexist and have been efficacious throughout history, admittedly, separately, and that must mean that God continues to work out his purpose for the salvation of the world through both the church and the synagogue simultaneously. The implications of this are extremely potent. It would appear that there is an imperative for producing a theology of ecumenism between church and synagogue. However, since Bonhoeffer did not survive the war, we are left only with those passages in *Ethics* that demand repentance by the church for centuries of rejection and maltreatment of the Jews, the sisters and brothers of Jesus Christ. Is there here, then, a basis for Christian-Jewish reconciliation that really does acknowledge the ongoing validity of the Old Covenant? Was this, indeed, where Bonhoeffer was headed? The problem posed here places a question mark over the Christian doctrine of the Trinity, which insists that Christ is coequal and consubstantial with God the Father, something that would constitute a stumbling block for Jews.

Clearly, for millennia the church has in its various manifestations assumed that the Lordship of Christ implied that all other monotheistic faiths had no covenant with God. Now, if the Old Covenant with the Jews is recognized as being still, as it were, in force, as Bonhoeffer insisted, an interfaith dialogue is an inescapable imperative. The central issue is, then, how can a Christianity based, as it is, on the doctrine of the Trinity engage ecumenically with Jews for whom Jesus of Nazareth, Christ, *cannot* be regarded as the Messiah? Does this apparent exclusivity of both Christianity and Judaism rule out such a dialogue? The answer must be emphatically, No. Bonhoeffer's reappraisal of the Jewishness of Jesus makes this possible. To borrow Hans Küng's phrase from another context, there has occurred a "paradigm change in theology" on a broad front,[42] and Dietrich Bonhoeffer's witness with regard to Christianity and Judaism has contributed to it significantly, even though such a transformation in Christian attitudes toward Jews encountered considerable resistance among his coreligionists in the immediate postwar period, as shall be seen.

As indicated above, the American Bonhoeffer scholar Stephen Haynes has pursued this question in exemplary detail, subjecting Bonhoeffer's statements relating to Jews and the Holocaust to an exacting scrutiny. As well, he has reviewed the work of virtually the entire range of Bonhoeffer scholars, and questions just how rigorous they have been in explaining Bonhoeffer's alleged change of heart toward the role of the Jews in the history of salvation. Haynes, has, as indicated, played devil's advocate with Bonhoeffer on this issue, because not a few have uncritically lauded Bonhoeffer, not only for overcoming centuries of Christian anti-Judaism and prejudice, but also for allegedly having established the foundation for an ongoing dialogue between *Ecclesia* and *Synagogia*. Obviously, such an exercise is a *disideratum* of the highest priority in order that unjustifiable mythologies about Bonhoeffer's achievements in the sphere of Christian-Jewish reconciliation are not perpetuated in human memory.

The main issue dealt with by Haynes is Bonhoeffer's theology regarding Jews or the synagogue. Bonhoeffer courageously stood up to the Nazis as early as 1933 by unequivocally pillorying their criminal treatment of fellow citizens of Jewish faith. As already stressed in detail, Bonhoeffer's point of departure here was that a legitimate German authority (*Obrigkeit*) would never declare war on its own citizens on grounds of race or religious affiliation. The dictator Adolf Hitler did this and disqualified himself as true German head of state. As we have seen, the Nazi Jewish policy eventually drove Bonhoeffer into conspiratorial opposition against the regime and active plotting for its overthrow. However, this political defense of the persecuted minority did not equate to a theological reassessment of the role of Jews in the history of salvation. As Haynes relentlessly demonstrates by subjecting all of Bonhoeffer's extant statements to a rigorous analysis, the "reluctant revolutionary," despite his fearless declarations of guilt and solidarity with the persecuted brothers and sisters of Jesus Christ (*Ethics*), remained anchored in the "witness-people" theology.

So, what is "witness-people" theology? In a word, it is the recognition from an exclusively Christian standpoint that the role of the Jews in salvation history was to prepare the coming of the Messiah, Jesus of Nazareth. This, of course, is a considerable advance on the previously dominant Christian view, that is, that the Old Covenant was superseded and hence extinguished by the New Covenant at Calvary, and that because the Jews rejected Jesus as the Messiah they were "cursed" by God and had accordingly to suffer exclusion and persecution throughout history. This was the view that Bonhoeffer had clearly espoused. It amounted to a theological delegitimization of Judaism, a view he had then clearly overcome—certainly by the time he had begun to compose the *Ethics* manuscript at the latest. Therein the Jews are Christ's brothers and sisters and cofounders of Western civilization, for the persecution of the Jews was tantamount to driving Christ out of the West, a cultural-historical catastrophe of the highest order. What is patently clear, then, is that Bonhoeffer opposed the Holocaust on both theological and cultural-historical grounds. He was able to transcend his cultural conditioning as a *Bildungsbürger* and oppose not only Hitler and National Socialism but also his unreconstructed coreligionists.

The difficult question that must now be posed is whether Bonhoeffer's benevolence toward Judaism, based, as it was, in "witness-people theology," would be sufficient grounds for a "normalization" of Christian-Jewish relations. Rigorous German theologians such as Andreas Pangritz argue strongly that this would be an illusion cultivated by "liberals." Indeed, he wrote that there is no possibility of "normal" Jewish-Christian relations after the Holocaust. The reason for this is that the "witness-people myth" will remain indispensable as long as the bible has any relevance to theology "because it is closely related to the theological concept of Israel as God's Chosen People."[43] Stephen Haynes agrees with this, saying unequivocally:

> As a Christian I share Pangritz's suspicion of the "liberal notion that the church ought to respond to the Holocaust by exchanging an emphasis on its unique relationship with the Jews for a universal obligation to protect the vulnerable. As a theologian, I agree with Pangritz that the obligation to think theologically cannot be forfeited because Christians have failed in the past to discharge it responsibly. As an interpreter of Bonhoeffer, I share the view that he was correct in maintaining that the church cannot fathom the Jewish Question entirely in categories of social morality.
>
> Finally as a student of the Christian-Jewish encounter, I concur that after the Holocaust it is misleading for Christians to speak of "normalizing" relations between the two peoples. For as long as Christians approach the relationship with a biblical-theological mindset, the witness-people tradition will indeed remain "indispensable" for the church's reflection on the mystery of Israel. If there is another base from which to approach Jewish people, I am not aware of it. If there is another way to construct a Christian theology of Israel completely apart from the witness-people tradition, I have not discovered it. If there is an obvious solution to the tension between universalism and exceptionalism in Christian apprehension of the Jews, it remains obscure.

Haynes observes further that post-Holocaust theologians such as Paul van Buren and Franklin Littell, who have paid close attention to Jewish self-understanding, also see no alternative to the "witness-people" understanding by Christians of Jews.[44] The question now is whether it rules out an inter faith dialogue. In view of the changed, post-Holocaust theological situation, there would seem to be an *obligation to dialogue* among all world religions. In chapter 9, the issue of the Protestant Church's acceptance of guilt will be investigated, followed by the question of reparation.

Notes

1. Walter Grab, "The German Way of Jewish Emancipation," *Australian Journal of Politics and History* 30 (1984): 224–35; *Der deutsche Weg der Judenemanzipation 1789–1938* (Munich/Zürich, 1991), 8.
2. See Jochen-Christoph Kaiser and Martin Greschat, eds., *Der Holocaust und die Protestanten: Analyse einer Verstrickung* (Frankfurt am Main, 1988).
3. See Georg Denzler, *Widerstand ist nicht das richtige Wort: katholische Priester, Bischöfe und Theologen im dritten Reich* (Zürich, 2003).
4. Fritz Stern, "The Political Consequences of the Un-political German," in *Dreams and Delusions: The Drama of German History* (London, 1987).
5. The various confessions produced at that time are collected in, *Die Bekenntnisse und grundsätzlichen Äusserungen zur Kirchenfrage des Jahres 1933* gesammelt und eingeleitet von Kurt Dietrich Schmidt (Göttingen, 1934) and *Die Bekenntnisse und grundsätzlichen Äusserungen zur Kirchenfrage des Jahres 1934*, gesammelt und eingeleitet von Kurt Dietrich Schmidt (Göttingen, 1935).
6. On Hermann Sasse, see Maurice Schild, "Hermann Sasse," in *Profile des Luthertums: Biographien zum 20. Jahrhundert* (Gütersloh, 2000): 591–603; and "Sasse and Bonhoeffer: Churchmen on the Brink," *Lutheran Theological Journal* 29 (1995): 3–10.
7. Bethge, *Bonhoeffer*, 231–36 [cf. 2000, 300–04].
8. Christopher M. Clark, *The Politics of Conversion: Missionary Protestantism and the Jews in Prussia, 1728–1941* (Oxford, 1995).
9. The draft and final text of the Bethel Confession are in *DBW*, XII, 362–408. See Guy Christopher Carter, "Confession at Bethel, August 1933." See especially the investigation of the formulation of the Bethel Confession in Stephen Haynes, *The Bonhoeffer Legacy*, 74–82, in which the continuity of Bonhoeffer's thought with his position on the Jewish question from April 1933 is confirmed.
10. Von Oppen, *Der unerhöte Schrei*, 48.
11. Ibid., 50–51.
12. Cf. "Die Erklärung Berliner Pfarrer 'An die Nationalsynode der Deutschen Evangelischen Kirche'," 27 September 1933, in *DBW*, XII, 141–44.
13. Karl Herbert, *Der Kirchenkampf—Historie oder bleibendes Erbe?* (Frankfurt am Main, 1985), 79.

14. Von Oppen, *Der unerhörte Schrei*, 56. The full text and the names of all signatories is in *DBW*, XII, 141–144. See also Jørgen Glenthøj, *Dokumente zur Bonhoeffer-Forschung, 1928–1945* (Munich, 1969), 80–91 for a detailed account of the events leading up to the National Synod and explanation why an adoption of the Aryan Paragraph would have constituted a *status confessionis*.

15. See Glenthøj, *Dokumente*, Section VII, "Auslandspfarrer in London 1933–1935," 112–21, for a detailed account of how Bonhoeffer continued the church struggle while discharging his pastoral duties in London.

16. Ibid., 64.

17. The text from the translation the Revised Standard Version of the Bible is: "Woe to you scribes and Pharisees, hypocrites! For you build the tombs of the prophets and adorn the monuments of the righteous, saying 'If we had lived in the days of our fathers, we would not have taken part with them in shedding the blood of the prophets.' Thus you witness against yourselves, that you are sons of those who murdered the prophets. Fill up then the measure of your fathers. You serpents, you breed of vipers, how are you to escape being sentenced to hell? Therefore I send you prophets and wise men and scribes, some of whom you will kill and crucify, and some you will scourge in your synagogues and persecute from town to town, that upon you may come all the righteous blood shed upon earth, from the blood of innocent Abel to the blood of Zechariah the son of Barachiah, whom you murdered between the sanctuary and the altar. Truly, truly I say to you, all this will come upon this generation."

18. Eberhard Röhm and Jörg Thiefelder, *Juden—Christen—Deutsche*, vol 2, Part 1 (Stuttgart, 1992), 68.

19. Ibid., 71.

20. Ibid, 70.

21. Schlingensiepen, *Bonhoeffer*, 215–19.

22. Von Oppen, *Der unerhörte Schrei*, 76

23. *Good News Bible*. Cited after Bethge, "Dietrich Bonhoeffer und die Juden."

24. *Good News Bible*.

25. Von Oppen, *Der unerhörte Schrei*, 77.

26. Cf. Robert O. Smith, "Reclaiming Bonhoeffer after Auschwitz," *Dialog: A Journal of Theology* (Fall, 2004): 212. In this perceptive article the author traces the steps of the so-called "Hebraization" of Bonhoeffer's theology, meaning how he refocused on what the Old Testament had to say about God's call to the children of Israel and its implications for the church. Smith quotes the Israeli scholar Pinchas Lapide here who observed, that, "From a Jewish perspective Bonhoeffer was the pioneer and the forerunner of a plodding re-Hebraization of the churches in our days," 213. The so-called "Jewish Question" as posed during the Third Reich was really a "Christian Question," viz., a challenge to the Church to reassess its Hebraic roots. See Ursula Büttner, "'The Jewish Problem Becomes a Christian Problem'—German Protestants and the Persecution of the Jews in the Third Reich," in *Probing the Depths of German Antisemitism-German Society and the Persecutuion of the Jews, 1933–1941*, ed. David Bankier (New York/Oxford, 2000). Here Büttner gives arguably the earliest example of a pastor who recognized already at Easter 1933 that the maltreatment of

the Jews, viz., "the Jewish problem has become a Christian problem in that it challenges the genuineness and seriousness of our Christianity," 439.

27. Von Oppen, *Der unerhörte Schrei*, 80.

28. Kelly, "Bonhoeffer and the Jews," 156–57. This was an effort to save a small number of Jews by assigning them to service as undercover agents working in Switzerland. The intention was to save them from the deportation of Jews from Berlin then in full swing. Their actual role was to inform the outside world of Nazi atrocities.

29. Von Oppen, *Der unerhörte Schrei*, 83; emphasis added.

30. Andreas Pangritz, "Dietrich Bonhoeffers Begründung der Beteiligung am Widerstand," *Evangelische Theologie* 55 Jg, Heft 6 (1996). See also Pangritz, "Sharing the Destiny of His People," in John de Gruchy, ed., *Bonhoeffer for a New Day* (Grand Rapids, 1997), 258–277.

31. *Ethics*, 90–91

32. Pangritz, "Sharing the Destiny of His People," 270–71.

33. Von Oppen, *Der unerhörte Schrei*, 85.

34. Ibid., 111–12.

35. Ibid., 113.

36. Von Oppen, *Der unerhörte Schrei*, 93.

37. *Ethics*, 114–115.

38. Ibid., 90–91.

39. Pangitz, "Sharing the Destiny of His People," 271.

40. Haynes, *The Bonhoeffer Legacy*, 142.

41. William Jay Peck, "From Cain to the Death Camps: An Essay on Bonhoeffer and Judaism," *Union Seminary Quarterly Review* 28, no. 2 (Winter, 1973): 158–76.

42. See Hans Küng and David Tracy, eds., *Paradigm Change in Theology: A Symposium for the Future* (New York, 1989); Hans Küng, *Theologie im Aufbruch* (Munich, 1987), 274–306, where Küng explores the question whether there can be only one true religion.

43. Pangritz, "Sharing the Destiny of His People," 271.

44. Haynes, *The Bonhoeffer Legacy*, 147–8. See Franklin H. Littell, *The Crucifixion of the Jews: the Failure of Christians to Understand the Jewish Experience* (Macon, Ga., 1986); Franklin H. Littell and Hubert G. Locke, eds., *The German Church Struggle and the Holocaust* (San Francisco, 1990); Paul van Buren, *A Theology of the Jewish-Christian Reality*, 3 vols. (San Francisco, 1988). There are, as well, a range of studies by non-German authors that investigate the theme of reconciliation and dialogue. See, for example, Marcus Braybrooke, *Time to Meet: Towards a Deeper Relationship between Jews and Christians* (London, 1990) and Darrell J. Fasching, *Narrative Theology after Auschwitz* (Minneapolis, 1992). In this context the prophetic work of the Anglican priest-scholar James Parkes, begun already in the 1920s at Oxford, needs to be cited. See the two recent studies by Colin Richmond and Tony Kushner, *Campaigning against Antisemitism* (London, 2005) and Haim Chertok and Irving Greenberg, *He Spoke as a Jew. The Life of the Reverend James Parkes* (London, 2006).

8

BONHOEFFER AS CRITIC OF HIS CLASS IN RETROSPECT

To recapitulate: It is recalled that by early 1934, at the latest, Bonhoeffer had identified the Führer as a menace—indeed, as the agent of the anti-Christ—lost confidence in his own class for submitting so spinelessly to the seducer (the *Verführer*, "misleader"), identified the Nazi Jewish policy as the key issue for the future of the church—indeed, as a *status confessionis*—and come to the conclusion that sooner or a later "a spoke will have to be jammed into the wheel" of the Nazi movement. The fact that the "German Christians" had declared unequivocal support for the Führer issued a challenge to traditional Lutherans to declare where they stood, and the result was the formation of the Confessing Church of which Bonhoeffer was a major personality.

Clearly, Bonhoeffer regretted the myopia of the majority of his colleagues in the church, whose famous Confession at Barmen really only addressed the Nazi violation of the autonomy the church and demonstratively failed to mention the Jewish question. Indeed, on this issue the majority of his coreligionists were still committed to a *theologia gloriae* according to which the *ecclesia* had totally displaced the synagogue in the history of salvation. The Jews, for their alleged disobedience, were compelled to suffer the consequences and henceforth must wander the earth in a state of dissolution, forced to endure persecution. In short, they had incurred the wrath of God, and their only salvation was to submit to baptism into the *ecclesia*. Bonhoeffer continued his struggle all through the period from 1933 onward, moving, as we have seen, from preaching and teaching against the Nazi regime in the form of lectures and publications as well as very prominent participation in the ecumenical movement, urging its members to unite more purposefully to agitate for world peace, until finally he moved into conspiratorial opposition and began actively to participate in a process that he hoped would lead to the overthrow of a criminal regime.

Meanwhile, Bonhoeffer felt compelled by circumstances in Germany to withdraw from direct involvement in the struggle to become pastor of two German Lutheran congregations in London, during which time he busied himself with, among other things, a ministry to German Jewish exiles in Britain. He also strengthened his links with the Church of England[1] through his friendship with Bishop Bell of Chichester, and acquainted himself with the various denominations in Britain, but most significantly with the religious communities in the Anglican Church. All during this time Bonhoeffer maintained close touch, either by telephone or by trips back to Germany, with the progress of the church struggle there.

The Council of Brethren of the Confessing Church in 1935 finally requested Bonhoeffer to return home to train students for the ministry. This was a productive period for Bonhoeffer, during which he composed a major work, *Nachfolge*. In it he developed, as has been seen, his ideas about "cheap grace," on which subject he had some very critical things to say. Indeed, one could say with justification that "cheap grace" was what the majority of the *Bildungsbürgertum* relied on so long as they considered themselves members of the church. Thus, in a real sense Bonhoeffer's attack on "cheap grace" was tantamount to a critique of his class.

The year 1939 was a crucial one for Bonhoeffer. In June, as we have seen, he embarked for the United States again but spent only a couple of weeks reflecting on how best to serve his church, and then he decided that he must return home to witness for the truth among his own people against the massive injustices of the Nazi regime. Bonhoeffer arrived back in Germany to become a clandestine opponent of the Hitler regime, joining a conspiracy that aimed, initially, to stage a coup d'état with a view to bringing Hitler to trial for his crimes against humanity. In the course of the very next year Bonheoffer began work on what he intended to be a major study of a Protestant ethic. This he did while being involved in missions outside Germany, ostensibly on behalf of the *Abwehr* but in reality in the service of the resistance and in aid of Jewish refugees. Through his contacts with the ecumenical movement in Switzerland he learned more about the Nazi Jewish policy in German occupied countries and gained a better idea of the nefarious objectives of this policy.

"After Ten Years"

By the end of 1942 Bonhoeffer had penned the aforementioned manuscript intended for the few friends in the conspiracy, entitled "After Ten Years," in which he reflected on the barbarity of the Nazi regime and, in particular, on what "men of conscience" had done to support it, or, alternatively, not done to protest against its crimes. Bonhoeffer was understandably disturbed by the fact that the Nazis had perpetrated unprecedented outrages against human rights that remained effectively unchecked and uncriticized, especially by his church. Similarly, the invasion of Poland, where likewise atrocities occurred on an unprecedented scale, had not aroused the conscience of the German educated class. Bonhoeffer's thoughts were expressed in this succinct essay in a very measured and cool manner, revealing his understanding of the problems confronted by the *Bildungsbürgertum*; but he is nevertheless rigorous in his judgement of the moral failure of a class that, in his view, should have behaved better under the circumstances.[2]

Clearly, Bonhoeffer was exercised by the spectacle of so many highly educated and honorable people submitting without apparent demur to the Hitler regime or entering into complete cooperation with it, ostensibly for the sake of security. It had to be asked, then, how was it possible for those people, having witnessed so many Nazi atrocities such as the pogrom of November 1938 or the unprovoked attack on Poland the very next year, to enter willingly into the service of a manifestly criminal regime? What was the state of their morality, their intellectual-spiritual integrity—in short, how did they reconcile their inaction with their conscience?

Here, in this reflection after a decade of Nazi misrule, Bonhoeffer was not interested in the mind-set of the convinced Nazis themselves, nor in the soulless opportunists characterized by Friedrich Meinecke as *homo faber*, but precisely in *homo sapiens* in their presumed highest manifestation—namely, the men of culture and conscience, the *Bildungsbürger* themselves, that class of Germans who were supposed to be inwardly led by an informed conscience.

Bearing in mind that Hitler had made no secret of the fact that he demanded the total submission of all Germans to his will as leader, it might have been expected that many thoughtful people would protest somehow. It is well known, of course, that some intellectuals of the calibre of Thomas Mann and the Roman Catholic priest Georg Moenius found that the only course of action in the situation was to emigrate to the United States or elsewhere to a country in which the rule of law prevailed.[3] To remain in Germany once having declared opposition would have led to arrest and, at the very least, an uncertain future in a concentration camp. Clearly, it is extremely difficult to survive in declared opposition to a regime of terror when every day there was the possibility of denunciation followed by a sudden visit by the secret police. Bonhoeffer was probably not very surprised when the vast majority of his countrymen conformed and submitted to the Nazi regime, for they would not have had the discernment and training to enable them to analyze it critically and adequately. Indeed, it was very difficult, even for the highly educated, to form a balanced judgement. Here is how Bonhoeffer tried to explain the submission of the *Bildungsbürgertum*:

> Then there is the man with a conscience, who fights single-handed against heavy odds in situations that call for a decision. But the scale of the conflicts in which he has to choose—with no advice or support except from his own conscience—tears him to pieces. Evil approaches him in so many respectable and seductive disguises that his conscience becomes nervous and vacillating, till at last he contents himself with a salved instead of a clear conscience, so that he lies to his own conscience in order to avoid despair; for a man whose only support is conscience is unable to grasp that a bad conscience may be stronger and more wholesome than a deluded one.[4]

This is how Bonhoeffer characterized the failure of his class: it resulted from a confused conscience. People were unable, under the peculiar circumstances of the times, to achieve absolute clarity about what was really happening. And here he identified the first factor as the Nazi regime's ability to justify its policies in terms of historical and social justice, giving the bewildering and deceptive impression that it represented, after all, in spite of evil deeds, a cause that was essentially good and in the best interests of the German people.[5] There were plenty of examples of prominent German intellectuals, including theologians, who welcomed the Nazi regime and justified its policies. The philosophers Martin Heidegger (1889–1976) and Carl Schmitt (1888–1985) and the theologian Emanuel Hirsch (1888–1972) were accomplices of the type of high-profile Germans who allowed themselves to be deceived by Hitler and even enthusiastically served the regime in their various academic and ecclesiastical positions. Bonhoeffer suggested that they faced a dilemma, and that meant that each of the choices with which they were confronted had to violate their conscience. They chose the lesser evil and persuaded themselves that having done so, having avoided the greater evil, their conscience was relatively clear. As Heinz Eduard Tödt succinctly put it, "That was the great temptation for those who stayed in their influential positions under the Hitler regime, collaborated with it against their conviction and placated their conscience by referring to their still good intentions. Objectively, however, they became accomplices to unimaginable atrocities to which they closed their eyes."[6]

The problem with this state of mind, as Bonhoeffer assessed it, was that these collaborators should at least remain honest and have a bad conscience instead of feigning blindness to events. And what Bonhoeffer observed here is perceptive, namely, that it was impossible for a man whose life was stabilized solely by his good conscience to achieve peace of mind. Such a man could not live without self-respect and had to be honorable at all costs. As a result, he was forced to play down or trivialize the evil reality in order to escape from the salutary pressure of a bad conscience that was urging him to abandon collaboration and become dangerously obstinate, that is, to go virtually into opposition by refusing to collaborate. As Bonhoeffer formulated it:

> Here and there people flee from public altercation into the sanctuary of private virtuousness. But anyone who does this must shut his mouth and his eyes to the injustice around him. Only at the cost of self-deception can he keep himself pure from the contamination arising from responsible action. In spite of all that he does, what he leaves undone will rob him of his peace of mind. He will either go to pieces because of this disquiet, or become the most hypocritical of Pharisees.[7]

Bonhoeffer then puts the crucial question, "Who stands fast?" and gives the hard but only answer: the one who was ready to sacrifice his principles, his conscience, his freedom, and indeed his virtue when he is called to responsible action in faith and in exclusive allegiance to God. That individual was the responsible man who sought to make his entire life an answer to the question and call of God. "But," inquires Bonhoeffer, "where are these people?"[8]

Clearly there had been a lamentable lack of civil courage among the *Bildungsbürgertum*, and here Bonhoeffer had no hesitation in employing the first-person plural *ourselves*. This deficit in civil courage was not just a question of personal cowardice. Germans, Bonhoeffer acknowledged, had had to learn the need for obedience and to develop the strength of character to comply with their conscience. Indeed, over centuries they had acquired the virtue of obedience to "the authorities" and thereby had learned to subordinate personal goals to higher national tasks.[9] Here is an obvious reference to the political culture engendered in the age of enlightened despotism, which was brought to its highest expression in the Prussia of Frederick II (r.1740–86).

This, of course, imparts a positive gloss to traditional Prusso-German subservience to the state. Indeed, as Bonhoeffer said, "We have looked upwards, not in servile fear, but in free trust, seeing in our tasks a call, and in our call a vocation."[10] Obedience was thus a great Prusso-German virtue, as Bonhoeffer affirmed, from Luther to the idealist philosophers, and here he must mean Hegel. The positive aspect of this was the subjugation of self-will through service to the community, and this was the great virtue of the *Bildungsbürgertum*. But, as Bonhoeffer concedes, these virtuous people misjudged the world; they simply did not realize that submissiveness and self-sacrifice could be exploited for evil ends.

Here we have a supreme example of Bonhoeffer's restraint in confronting his class with their political naivety. He goes on to observe that in misjudging the world, as they did, the continued belief in the virtue of submissiveness and self-sacrifice became questionable, and then all moral principles of the German were bound to totter.[11] It would appear then that generations of Lutheran-Hegelian conditioning rendered many Germans politically naïve. Their behavior oscillated between an irresponsible lack of scruple on the one hand and a self-tormenting punctiliousness on the other, which never led to action in critical opposition to the diabolical regime. And here Bonhoeffer made the perceptive observation that civil courage could develop only out of the free responsibility of free men. Learning this virtue had come too late. Free responsibility depended on a God who demanded responsible action in a bold venture of faith and who promised forgiveness and consolation to the man who became a sinner in that venture.[12]

Here the problem of the "unpolitical German," meaning precisely the *Bildungsbürger* that Fritz Stern identified independently, is summed up.[13] That man is, after all, only flesh and blood and therefore prone to all the mistakes and misjudgements that the "flesh is heir to." The trouble appears to have been that very few could develop the critical perception that Bonhoeffer had acquired by virtue of his own extremely sharp theologically informed intelligence and through his encounter with the outside world, as has been seen. These people struggled for moral integrity according to their lights but became mere supine witnesses to evil events perpetrated by a criminal regime, and thereby became accomplices in its crimes. Paradoxically, then, their inaction was tantamount to approval of atrocity. Nevertheless, these people continued to believe in their personal integrity and their honor, which was so important to them.[14]

When Bonhoeffer analyzed the situation of his own class in this way, he clearly perceived the tragedy that was unfolding in countless similarly situated families throughout the Reich. It was a tragedy of inevitable failure in the face of the evil power of the Nazi regime that had control over all the elements of society. And for Bonhoeffer personally, because he possessed the requisite critical faculty, there was only one course of action open to him: to enter into what Heinz Eduard Tödt called the "alien business" of conspiratorial resistance.[15] And in the light of everything he had perceived, Bonhoeffer had no real alternative.

In "After Ten Years" Bonhoeffer expatiated, as well, on human folly and stupidity (*Dummheit*) in a subsection that explains how intelligent people could act foolishly in the service of evil. He noted that if we are to comprehend this we must realize that folly is a moral rather than an intellectual defect, and he observed that there were people who were mentally agile but foolish, as well as people who were mentally slow but far from foolish. It was not a congenital defect but one acquired in particular situations in which people made fools of themselves, or, as he said, allowed others to make fools of them. And here Bonhoeffer concluded that folly was a sociological rather than a psychological problem, a condition brought about by a special form of historical circumstances, indeed a psychological by-product of particular external factors.[16] These were such things as the violent manifestation of political or religious power, which, as history had shown, resulted in the foolish, indeed, wicked and violent behavior of many people. Bonhoeffer did not give any historical examples here but the behavior of the wider German population in the face of the unprecedented display of brutal Nazi power in the form of the Brown Shirt legions and the secret police illustrated just how intimidated the majority of the population must have been. As Bonhoeffer phrased it, the power of some required the folly of others in order to succeed. In the face of the massive displays of power, so argued Bonhoeffer, individuals lost their capacity for independent judgment and practically gave up trying to make an objective assessment of the daunting new circumstances in which they found themselves.

Obviously, Bonhoeffer was speaking from experience when he wrote that the fact that the fool was often stubborn should not mislead us into believing that he was an independent or autonomous individual: "One feels in fact, when talking to him, that one is dealing not with the man himself, but with slogans, catchwords . . . which have taken hold of him. He is under a spell, he is blinded, his very nature is being misused and exploited."[17] And here Bonhoeffer has described the effect of the mesmerizing power of the diabolical spirit of Hitler on his generals, for example.

The late professor Karl Dietrich Erdmann (1910–90), once the doyen of the more conservative postwar German modern historians, independently identified the same phenomenon when he wrote that when very senior officers were in conference with the Führer—that is, in his immediate diabolical presence, as it were—they allowed themselves to be caught up in the euphoria of the grandiose projects that Hitler elaborated to them, and failed to use their intelligence and expertise to correct or contradict, or to point out possible flaws in the dictator's plans. There had been, of course, contests of will between Hitler and the generals on various occasions, but each time the generals deferred to the Führer, who had, in short, the diabolical power to make fools of these men who were all in reality far more highly trained in military matters than their supreme commander. Only after the conference, removed from Hitler's mesmerizing presence, in the clear light of day, did they begin to have reservations about the practical implementation and consequences of what Hitler had in mind; but, of course, they were too intimidated to contradict their Führer at the next opportunity. They were, in short, victims of their own foolishness, and even worse, greed.[18] And as Bonhoeffer noted, while people like the generals were under the hypnotic spell of their leader they were unaware that they were being made fools of, and thus they became passive instruments capable of perpetrating any evil required of them and at the same time were rendered incapable of recognizing that it was evil.

All this illustrates just how perceptive Bonhoeffer was. His final comment on folly, then, was that the only way these otherwise intelligent people could be saved from the consequences of their foolishness was for them to be liberated, first outwardly, and, once that happened, then the inward liberation could follow. Significantly, until that happened there was no chance of convincing the fool by rational argument.[19] What Bonhoeffer clearly recognized here was the requirement for the putatively "intelligent," but in reality stupid, supporters of Hitler to be forcibly detached, isolated and removed from their service to him, indeed separated from the person to whom the officer class in particular had been made to swear an oath of personal allegiance,[20] and that process would be called "liberation" (*Befreiung vom Nationalsozialismus*). Indeed, this is the terminology used by some historians to describe the defeat of the German army in 1945 and the occupation of Germany. They were "liberated" from the Führer's thrall. Once that happened then the inner emancipation of mind and soul could follow. As Bonhoeffer wrote, "The Bible's words that 'the fear of the Lord is the beginning of wisdom' (Psalm 111:10) tell us that a person's inward liberation to live a responsible life before God is the only real cure for folly."[21]

Heinz Eduard Tödt adduced another telling example of the stupidity of the highly intelligent and technically brilliant individual who offered himself in the service of Hitler. That was Hjalmar Schacht (1877–1970), president of the Reich Bank, who engineered economic policy from March 1933 just after Hitler's seizure of power, to further Nazi military ambitions. The Nazis themselves disposed over no party member with the requisite expertise in the field of economic policy, so the highly experienced Schacht placed himself at their disposal, believing that he could influence policy by virtue of his superior knowledge. However, once he had helped Hitler secure political power, it was the Führer's will to place the economy emphatically in the service of military production that overruled Schacht's own will.[22] After that, he and officials like him conscientiously fulfilled their master's directives, not appreciating that they were enabling Hitler to implement his criminal policies. Plainly, these men, trained in highly complex disciplines as they were, lacked perception for the political realities with which they were dealing.[23] They were in fact guilty of criminal stupidity in Bonhoeffer's judgement. Having "lost their heads and their bibles" most of the German elite also lost their sense of reality that came only through faith in God. They did not understand that obedience to the Creator was the only thing that enabled true virtues to take control of the individual will. Lamentably, however, "the fact could not be escaped that the German still lacked something fundamental: he could not see the need for free and responsible action."[24]

The Prison Experience

Bonhoeffer's concern for this issue became more intense once he had been arrested and imprisoned. It was during this time of incarceration that he began to reflect and write both theology and literature that included poetry, a novel, and short stories. In the latter, particularly, Bonhoeffer focused on the problem of the *Bildungsbürgertum* and the *Besitzbürgertum*, the landed and propertied classes as well as big business. There was something missing in their value system. Suffice it to say that everything Bonhoeffer wrote from prison, including the love letters,[25] had to do with the spiritual renewal of his class. This highly educated strata of German society needed to recognize their dereliction and do penance in order to recover their traditional role as the spiritual and intellectual leaders of the nation. Consequently, even the play, the novel, and the short story that have survived—the so-called *Tegel Fiction*—are strongly didactic. Each of these requires a brief investigation, but before proceeding, Bonhoeffer's ideal image of the lifestyle of the *Bildungsbürgertum* needs to be recalled.

Luther's Legacy

First, this phenomenon is a product of the Lutheran Reformation and the spirituality and culture that, as it were, organically grew out of it. When Luther translated the bible into German, he wrought a world-historical achievement of immeasurable significance. The word of God was placed into the hands of the ordinary people, at least those who could read their mother tongue, and so the bible became in time the platform for a revolutionary new piety. The Reformer had no time for *Winkelmesse*, the German name for private masses that had been commonly available to the faithful. He was more interested in emphasizing the corporate dimension, the spiritual health of the community at large. As well, Luther insisted that good works flowed from faith in the Word. And here the emphasis on the corporate dimension was expanded so that the individual fulfilled his or her Christian calling in doing whatever one did in this world for a living whatever it might be: everyone, from housewives to artisans, to public officials, to soldiers, princes and kings, all contributed to the "economy of God," and this was service to God, *Gottesdienst*. Through Luther, a seismic shift in how the faithful related to the Creator occurred. From now on the performance of "good works" had to be the consequence of faith in the Word. Indeed, this issue of faith is highly relevant here. In his "Preface to the Letter of Paul to the Romans," Luther observed:

> Faith is a work of God in us, which changes us and brings us to birth anew from God (cf. John 1). It kills the old Adam, makes us completely different people in heart, mind, senses, and all our powers, and brings the Holy Spirit with it. What a living, creative, active powerful thing is faith! It is impossible that faith ever stops doing good. Faith doesn't ask whether good works are to be done, but, before it is asked, it has done them. It is always active. Whoever doesn't do such works is without faith; he gropes and searches about him for faith and good works but doesn't know what faith and good works are. Even so, he chatters on with a great many words about faith and good works.[26]

Indeed, for Luther the whole of life was an expression of the divine love for creation. The role of the church in this new dispensation was to preach the Word. That included the celebration of the sacraments, the inculcation of inner piety, the sensitizing of the individual soul with the love of God, the arousal of a more profound sense of duty and service to society, and making the individual aware of his or her role in the hierarchy of service within the state. And the state, especially since Luther, was seen by Bonhoeffer as a divinely instituted "order of preservation."

This concept, "orders of preservation," was Bonhoeffer's counter to that of "orders of creation," which in the mind of some German Protestant theologians justified war as a necessary instrument in the realization of God's plan for humanity. Indeed, Bonhoeffer warned against applying the argument derived from the book of Genesis, chapter 1, verse 24, in the creation story, that God "saw that it was all very good" to specific things in the world. If one applied such thinking, *everything* in the world could be justified in principle as part of creation, including the fateful fragmentation of the nations, international rivalry, war, the class struggle, the exploitation of the weak by the strong, and ruthless economic competition. However, here Bonhoeffer made the crucial insight that all these things were the product of a *fallen* world in which creation and sin interpenetrated each other so that human beings could not distinguish one from the other. On the other hand, the "orders of preservation" from God derived their efficacy from the fact that Jesus Christ was the herald of a "new creation." The commandment of Christ was not modified by any "orders of creation."[27]

With this reorientation in the life of the Christian person that enabled Christian piety to be expressed in innumerable ways, beyond attendance at Mass, even by being busy at work, the more sensitive soul could seek spiritual nourishment in the new Lutheran hymnody that stressed the universal availability of God's saving grace through Calvary. As well, there developed then that unique German cultural phenomenon of Protestant church music of which J. S. Bach is the supreme example. Consequently, by the nineteenth century the ideal piety of the believing *Bildungsbürger* was characterized by service to the state, and thereby the community, simply by conscientious execution of one's duty, fortified by regular bible reading, the observance of Sunday worship, the Christian calendar (especially Christmas and Easter), and the regular Protestant holidays—whereby, as well, spiritual edification could be derived simply from attendance at a performance of one of Bach's oratorios or passions, whether in church or not. It all formed an organic cultural whole. Indeed, the entirety of life was meant to be saturated by the spirit of the gospel of Christ. In Lutheranism there occurred, over time, a mystical merging of the secular and spiritual realms. The old medieval catholic piety had been thus significantly augmented by Luther.

Indeed, one needs to be aware of a series of developments in Lutheran piety since Luther introduced the German Mass in 1525 and later, in 1529, the two catechisms. The Reformer stressed the need to sanctify the Sabbath by attendance at Mass, still using the ancient terminology (*Formula missae* and *deutsche Messe*). Corporate liturgical devotion was still of central importance. By the beginning of 1526, for example, a new order of service had appeared under the title *Deutsche Messe und Ordnung des Gottesdienstes*. And this obvious continuum with catholic tradition was augmented by the insistence that the pastor say the liturgy audibly, with the congregation also responding audibly. As well, the catholic doctrine of the real presence in the Eucharist was central Lutheran doctrine, say, in contrast to Zwinglian teaching.[28]

Dietrich Bonhoeffer stood on this spiritual foundation. He regretted that many of his class, indeed Germans of all classes, did not seek the spiritual riches offered by it. On the other hand, he could rejoice that it had been absorbed by many contemporaries who could not be described as openly religious. They evinced a caring attitude to fellow human beings, and, in doing so, were unconsciously Christian. In short, the practice of decency was attributable to the Christian foundations of society. The role now of Christians of all classes, but particularly of the upper middle class, because of their education and leading social status, was to set the example. The macabre success of Hitler in capturing the hearts and minds of many Germans of all classes was attributed by Bonhoeffer largely to the failure of his own class to sustain the values that they inherited. A more Christianly committed *Bildungsbürgtum* would have, at the very least, constituted a bulwark against the brutal deceptions of National Socialism.

The Tegel Fiction

The underlying concern of the texts of the Tegel Fiction is the failure of the *Bildungsbürgertum* to rise to the moral challenges posed by the blatant misrule of National Socialism. These short texts will now be investigated briefly. The first is the fragment entitled simply *Drama*.[29] It involves a civilian doctor whose wartime practice included treating wounded soldiers, among them his own 25-year-old son who has less than a year to live. *Drama* is essentially a meditation on dying with dignity, a subject that so obviously preoccupied the imprisoned Bonhoeffer considerably. "The last things" can be met only by individuals of faith. But faith, interestingly, is not the sole preserve of the Bildungsbürgertum although they enjoy every advantage to have it in abundance. Essentially, faith is a universal phenomenon that even the most socially disadvantaged can evince. Snobbery is not Christian. *Drama* is a statement on several layers, and is the most mystical of the fragments of Tegel Fiction. On the level of social criticism, however, Bonhoeffer attacks an ugly phenomenon, namely, the lack of compassion for the wounded veterans displayed in public by hooligan elements who insulted crippled soldiers on the street. This is a particularly poignant sign of cultural and moral decay that is clearly attributable to the evaporation of Christian values in society. This theme is taken up fiercely again by Bonhoeffer in the short story about the horribly disfigured Lance Corporal Berg, entitled *Story*. Here, Bonhoeffer graphically illustrated the contrast and conflict between decency and evil that characterized the Third Reich. The scene is a prison for deserters. One, in chains, is dragged in to the commandant's office. He is eighteen years old, has already been awarded an Iron Cross for bravery at the front, but is found disorientated and exhausted in the snow miles behind the lines, and confesses to desertion. The commandant, a senior NCO, abuses him mercilessly and he is ignominiously thrown into a cell to await almost certain execution.

In the meantime the commandant is portrayed in conversation with a junior NCO, his adjutant, who should by rights also be at the front but claims he has a heart condition and should remain at his desk job. It is interesting that he is able to supply the commandant regularly with black market butter, and so the story about his heart condition is not officially investigated or verified, so the malingerer is able to stay in his safe posting insulated from the terrors and deprivations of front-line service.

The commandant then receives a phone call from HQ to expect a new guard, retired from front duties because of wounds, and he is requested to treat this guard with special consideration. This is lance corporal Berg whose face has been literally burnt off and who has been patched up grotesquely. Berg duly arrives and settles down to duties. He is, unexpectedly, most solicitous of the welfare and treatment of the inmates, demanding better food for them than the swill they are usually served. He even recommends leniency in their treatment. Berg, is, in short, a decent man. Consequently, he is an embarrassment to the commandant on two counts. He had dutifully served at the front and suffered horrendous disfiguring wounds to prove it. Secondly, in spite of this, but perhaps because of it, he has compassion for the deserters who are being unjustly victimized by the system at the hands of duplicitous scoundrels. Berg's transference to duties in another location becomes a priority for the commandant. The petty bully and coward cannot bear the inner shame that the presence of the heroic and noble figure of Berg induces in him.

Clearly, in *Story*, Bonhoeffer was denouncing the system of which he himself is a victim. The Third Reich was the product of the catastrophic decline of Christian values. This is not how it should be, and in *Novel*, we are presented with an explanation for the triumph of evil. Significantly, the story begins with a corrosive critique of the church: The widow of the burgomaster of a small north German town, Frau Brake, leaves divine service one Sunday morning extremely depressed about the sermon. She is overtaken on her way home by an acquaintance, a woman of similar age, but one clearly not possessing the same intellectual or spiritual rigor as Frau Brake, who greets her and wants to talk about the sermon which had clearly impressed her very positively. She cannot recall the exact content but keeps saying how wonderfully the pastor had preached. Precisely that was the problem in Frau Brake's mind. The pastor had not preached the gospel, not said anything relevant, critical or challenging; he simply told the congregation what he thought they wanted to hear; in short it was an anti-sermon, but one had to be a perceptive Christian *Bildungsbürger* to recognize it as false gospel.

For Bonhoeffer, then, the widespread anti-intellectual, mindlessly nationalistic theological culture in Germany was an insidious evil, parallel in many ways to current manifestations of fundamentalism, not only in Christian countries. Pastors who were educated to read the signs of the times and give critical, intellectual leadership prostituted themselves, wittingly or unwittingly, in the service of the false god of nationalism. There had been, in short, a *trahison des clercs* that contributed to the susceptibility of Germans to the demonic charisma of Adolf Hitler. Attention to the genuine gospel and the original Reformation heritage would have immunized Christians against this. Unfortunately, the poor preaching had also alienated many otherwise well disposed people from the church and so they fell prey to the general nationalistic hysteria. The associated factor that Bonhoeffer identifies as betrayal was the failure of the *Bildungsbürgertum* generally to sustain values of decency in a way very similar to Friedrich Meinecke's analysis in his *The German Catastrophe* (1945).

This is graphically portrayed in the novel through an incident where the adult children of the Brake family decide to go on a Sunday afternoon picnic to a small lake in nearby woods. Into the midst of their bucolic idyll bursts a bad tempered young forester in a kind of uniform wearing inappropriately striking yellow boots. He abuses the young people for trespassing, threatening them with physical violence. At the height of his tirade the owner of the estate appears, a retired major, who upbraids the forester, a man of common background, who was obviously reveling in his power to intimidate the unintentional trespassers. In doing so, the major reveals himself to be a real gentleman who intervenes by lecturing the forester on good manners. One did not threaten or intimidate defenseless people who are only guilty of a simple mistake, and he demands that the forester apologize. That, however, the man steadfastly refuses to do, saying it would offend his sense of honor.

Bonhoeffer uses this incident essentially to make the point that those now in power have misunderstood what true authority is and how it should be exercised. This comes out in a speech by the major who spells it out in precisely these terms, but he blames his own class for setting a bad example. In short, the Nazis are an obscene caricature of what the major's class formerly was. Sadly, it was their own fault that things had degenerated to the extent they had. The novel then develops dramatically when the identity of the Brake children is finally revealed to the major. It transpires that the major who had left Germany after the Great War to farm in South Africa where he married an English woman, was a boyhood friend of the late Herr Brake, the father of the young trespassers. It is interesting that the major had recognized them from the first as being of his own class, and was anxious to make amends for the rough treatment they experienced at the hands of the forester, Herr Gelbstiefel, German for "Yellowboots." The major immediately adopts a very friendly attitude to them as though they were virtually close relatives, and explains how he became their father's boyhood friend when they were in the same class at school.

This is a penetrating insight into the mores of German boys' secondary schools prior to the First World War because it deals with a potentially bitter power struggle or clash of egos between the existing class leader, Brake, and a newcomer, the future major, for the kudos of being the most respected student both in the realm of the classroom and in athletics. What is remarkable for the Anglo-Saxon educated observer is the basic assumption on the part of all boys that there are permanent inequalities between and among the pupils based on family background, and this is accepted as quite normal. Instead of a situation in which the point of departure was that all boys were socially equal, and all had a degree of ability to contribute to team effort accordingly, in the German *Gymnasium* it was expected that one from better family background would naturally become spokesman of the class. He would clearly have to be superior, more mature, and brighter and also stronger physically. And so there was a competition between obvious candidates each one having a constituency among the other boys, the masses, so to speak.

This was subtly different from the Anglo-Saxon system in which prefects (class leaders) were nominated by the headmaster in consultation with his staff on the basis of leadership qualities, both on the sports field and in general classroom ability. Given this situation, then, one does not wish to claim that in all schools in Britain the upper class boys uniformly embrace egalitarian values and behave accordingly. Obviously, class consciousness is a factor of considerable significance. Nevertheless, given British political culture one may reckon with the permanent presence of a values system that prioritized fair play. Paradoxically, the German system was superficially more democratic but it was also more barbaric, encouraging a great deal of factionalism and attendant intrigue among class members. The major in Bonhoeffer's story recounts how, as a new boy, he arrived determined to come in at the top but realized that he would have to win the position away from the existing leader.

What Bonhoeffer makes clear is that it was expected of a son of the *Bildungsbürgertum* at that time, and particularly in that country-town situation, to demonstrate his ability to lead and set the example. This was a social obligation, a case of *noblesse oblige*, in German: *Adel verpflichtet*. A contest arose when the incumbent class spokesman also perceived himself in the same way, and this rivalry between the future burgomaster and the later army officer is described in some detail. There are two related outcomes: the rivals become firm friends and not only demonstrate the solidarity of their class but also the supremacy of noble values. Second, the preexistent factionalism is overcome. The toadies who thrived on intrigue are marginalized and put in their place. In this way the situation is resolved.

One is struck, though, by the contrast to the Anglo-Saxon secondary school culture. The German *Gymnasium* was meant also to be a microcosm of the "nation," certainly not dissimilar to the English public school system. In it were concentrated the educated elite who fostered their peculiar devotion to learning and cultivated ideas of superiority while, above all, acquiring the notion that in the fullness of time they would be leading the nation—whether it be in the army, the church, the public service, or in the university or *Gymnasium* teaching professions.

Where all this differed from Anglo-Saxon political culture in the same era is in the apparent total unawareness of an instituted class struggle. Boys in British or Australian secondary boarding schools knew that there was an organized working class that had already succeeded in claiming its place in the sun and had thrown up able national leaders to make that patently clear. Indeed, by the time of the First World War in the British Commonwealth there was a highly developed and successful political and industrial labor movement that had in various dominions successfully assumed office by being elected to government. The *Bildungsbürgertum* never really accepted that it would have to be one day the same in Germany, and there is strong evidence to suggest that Bonhoeffer came later to realize this.

In the concluding part of the novel, the Brake boys, after their visit to the major's estate, have the opportunity to reflect on what the major had told them and relate it all to Germany's current tragic circumstances. Their discussion is summed up in an incisive speech by one, Christoph Brake, clearly a mouthpiece for Bonhoeffer himself, speaking with his friend Ulrich, who is most likely modeled on Bonhoeffer's real-life friend Eberhard Bethge.

> And who is responsible for this whole calamity? . . . None other than the classes that set the tone, the so-called upper class, whom everybody sees as a model for success in life. And this upper class is for the most part already a bunch of rotten, obsequious lackeys; they combine bootlicking toward those above and brutality toward those below, lots of rhetoric on the outside and decay on the inside. And a few decent individuals and families who could play a significant role withdraw into themselves because they're repulsed by this vacuous, conceited society. . . . that is where the problem lies. We need a genuine upper class again; but where are we going to find one?

Bonhoeffer has used the form of drama, short story and novella as vehicles for strong social-political criticism. He was a true German patriot in the tradition of the *Bildungsbürgertum* who regretted immeasurably the inability of that class in the crisis to rise above it and lead the nation back to decency. But they had "lost their heads and their bibles."

Finally, *Tegel Fiction* shows that Bonhoeffer was scarcely a democrat in the Anglo-Saxon sense with its Whigish assumptions about equality and progress that left God out of the equation. Was Germany, therefore, a more Christian country? If so, there was a downside to the Lutheran legacy, namely, a susceptibility to authoritarian structures that became corrupted because they were operated by mere men, as Bonhoeffer recognized in his reflections "After Ten Years." It is relevant to observe here that the famous British historian Lord Acton (1834–1902), who was both a Roman Catholic and a Gladstonian liberal, had made acute observations along these lines in the context of Victorian England, and, interestingly, was of German ancestry on his mother's side and who had received a decisive part of his education in Munich, Bavaria. Germany, however, never produced a similar liberal leader or critic of the dominant political culture.[30] Perhaps Bonhoeffer was the closest Germany could get to producing a homegrown radical who reflected something of Actons's famous insights into the corrupting influence of power on individuals in high office.

State and Church

At this point, Bonhoeffer's despairing sentence from *Story* in *Tegel Fiction*, taken from the above quotation, "We need a genuine upper class again, but where are we going to find one?" requires comment.[31] Prior to his arrest and imprisonment, Bonhoeffer was devoting serious attention to this issue, and between April and December 1941 he had composed an essay, "State and Church," while he was engaged in drafting *Ethics*.[32] This is a key document in Bonhoeffer's intellectual-spiritual development, and it confirms him as a consciously Lutheran *Bildungsbürger* who is appalled at the moral decay of his class.

"State and Church" also reminds us that Bonhoeffer was very much a "reluctant revolutionary." He apparently had come to believe that the Nazi regime could succeed in Germany essentially because the Weimar Republic had opened the floodgates to a fateful political pluralism, the by-product of the false doctrine of the sovereignty of the people as enshrined in the Weimar Constitution. This radical departure from the doctrine of the sovereignty of God that was expressed in the divine-right monarchy allowed the formation of numerous political parties whose platforms appealed to the ignorant and uncultured, all competing in the Reichstag for power. It was an open invitation for the flourishing of unprincipled demagoguery. However, one must read "State and Church" with care; indeed with an eye on Bonhoeffer's discussion on the subject of "mandates" in *Ethics* to which attention will drawn below.

In "State and Church," Bonhoeffer quite unequivocally attributes the catastrophe to the democratic principle, the idea of popular sovereignty, very much in the way in which the Freiburg professor Gerhard Ritter in his several commentaries on this subject had done.[33] In a word, had the monarchical principle of divine right been preserved in 1919 that ensured a strong central executive authority, Germany would not have descended into chaos and become victim of the political thuggery that made it the devil's playground. It is little wonder that Lutheran people, by and large, despised the Republic.

The Freiburg Circle

In trying to unravel Bonhoeffer's vision for a solution to Germany's constitutional problems it will be instructive to draw attention to Bonhoeffer's link to the so-called Freiburg Circle led by the conservative pro-Prussian historian Gerhard Ritter (1888–1967).[34] The purpose of this subsection is twofold: first to illustrate the political values of the elite of the *Bildungsbürgertum*, and secondly to document how close Bonhoeffer was to this milieu.

Ever since *Reichskristallnacht*, the pogrom in November 1938, at the latest, Professor Gerhard Ritter and a number of high-profile coreligionists at the university of Freiburg had been meeting to discuss the fate of Germany under the blatantly criminal regime.[35] By the time that Bonhoeffer learned of the existence of the group it consisted of leading conservative intellectuals, including, at that time, Carl Goerdeler, mayor of Leipzig (1930–37) and former Reichkommissar (1934–35) for price control. The youngest member and survivor of the group was the theologian Helmut Thielicke (1908–86), from whose pen we have the text of the so-called Freiburg Memorandum, prepared in 1943 as Thielicke reports, at the behest of Dietrich Bonhoeffer.[36] According to Eberhard Bethge, Bonhoeffer actually met the Freiburg group at least twice—specifically, after the discussions with Bishop Bell in Sigtuna, Sweden (at the end of May, beginning of June 1942), and then again from 17 November 1942, when there were discussions lasting several days with members of the group including Carl Goederler, with the young Helmut Thielicke taking part.

Bonhoeffer had made notes previously for this meeting, probably already on 9 October, which list the questions that the planned memorandum would address, and named the personages who would be responsible for specific issues. It is significant that Ritter was designated to contribute reflections on the legacy of Luther. Ritter had already published a small book on the Reformer in 1925; and, of course, for him, as for Bonhoeffer, too, Luther was of crucial significance in the shaping of German political culture.[37] The subject of "Church and State" is also listed, though no name is bracketed with it, so it is highly likely the Bonhoeffer himself may have contributed material on it, as he had, as indicated, already formulated his ideas in that respect. These are to be found as a supplement to *Ethics*.[38]

Bonhoeffer clearly wanted to engage the expertise of these intellectuals to advance ideas about what the political scene of a postwar Germany should look like. The memorandum, though never presented to the occupying Powers, was indeed tabled at the 1948 meeting in Amsterdam of the World Council of Churches.[39] The document is valuable if only because it provides insight into the mind of the *Bildungsbürgertum* at that time. It has to be observed, however, that the *Freiburg Circle* around Gerhard Ritter was an elite group whose capacity for accurate social and political analysis was frankly crippled by their ivory-tower conservatism and isolation from the world of working-class politics.

Their proposed solution to the "German Problem" was formulated in apparent total unawareness of the aspirations of any other social groups in Germany, especially the labor movement and the Roman Catholic section that in many places comprised half the population, or the secular-minded liberal element. In short, the Freiburg Circle, the members of which called themselves by 1943 the "Bonhoeffer Circle," was distinctly chary of democratic movements and institutions. This position they shared with Bonhoeffer, who in his 1941 essay "State and Church" observed:

> No form of state is in itself an absolute guarantee for the proper discharge of government. Only concrete obedience to the divine commission justifies the form of state.... That form of state will be relatively the best in which it becomes evident that government is from above, from God, and in which the divine origin of government is most clearly apparent. A properly understood divine right of government, in its splendor and in its responsibility, is an essential constituent of the relatively best form of state.[40]

Bonhoeffer insisted that that form of state would be relatively the best that based its justification and power on the following three points: first, the strict maintenance of an outward justice; second, the preservation of the right of family and work, a right that has its foundations in the divine ordering of the world; and third, the proclamation of the gospel. So, the form of state is justified if it recommends itself to its subjects through its transparent dispensation of justice through just laws and action and truthful speech. And, he added, what is best for government is also best for the relationship between government and church.[41]

Clearly, the Freiburg professors had no difficulty in incorporating Bonhoeffer's ideas, which are reflected exactly in the section devoted to "Domestic Policy" which says:

> The call of God is directed to the conviction of those active in politics; the Word of God contains no political organizational program but is rather a wake-up call to the conscience on specific moral norms. It is our political task to indicate more closely this appeal to conscience and moral norms. We want to help build up a state committed to the principle of Christian morality; but as Lutheran Christians we recognize no Christian natural law that would provide us with ready directions. Therefore, we are not committed to any particular form of state. Rather we recognize expressly that each great epochal change requires new political organization, and that to meet the new challenge new forms of state will be required.[42]

What the memorandum then states is that the English constitutional model is completely inappropriate for Germany because that would result in the rise of a multiplicity of splinter parties, and thus cause a replication of the chaos of Weimar. Instead, what was needed was a government of "notables" who possessed the requisite knowledge of both history and theology to guide the damaged nation into the future—in short, a benign authoritarian state presided over by learned, just and God-fearing men.

In this way, both Bonhoeffer and his Freiburg colleagues sought to solve the "German Problem" on ultraconservative, indeed reactionary, lines that would have made Bismarck look almost like a nineteenth-century Whig. At least the Iron Chancellor accepted political parties and a Reichstag, though, of course, all these features had been a reluctant concession to the political movements that had begun to emerge prior to the 1848 revolution and which had refused to disappear in the period of reaction 1850–66. Now, however, the Freiburg intellectuals were prepared to jettison even these predemocratic institutions because, as they read history, the notion of the sovereignty of the people was a recipe for disaster. For them, and for Bonhoeffer, there was nothing sacrosanct about the doctrine of popular sovereignty. Indeed, sovereignty was the inalienable preserve of the Creator himself.

These convictions, however, had long been overtaken by history, even in Germany. The Western Allies already prior to 1945 had been actively cultivating the revival or reinstatement of the democratic parties of the Weimar era, while the Soviets were fostering the dictatorship of the proletariat in the East. The notion that the Western powers would have lent a sympathetic ear to the advocates of the Freiburg Memorandum is bizarre in the extreme. And it is interesting to note that the Basic Law, *das Grundgesetz* of 1949, was essentially a revival of the Weimar Constitution with specific safeguards against the emergence of both splinter and antidemocratic parties.[43]

However, as Heinz Eduard Tödt reports, there was some Protestant influence on the formulation of the Basic Law through the deliberations of the preliminary Parliamentary Council that was convened by the Allies from liberal notables and other surviving democrats. The most outstanding personality was Theodor Heuss, who had lent his support to Bonhoeffer already in 1933. Heuss became the first president of the Federal Republic, and he was a former student of the theologian and politician Friedrich Naumann.[44] Overall, the plans and proposals of the various resistance groups within Germany had little direct influence on the formulation of the constitution of the Federal Republic. An exception to this general rule, according to Tödt, would have been the economic ideas that derived from Walter Eucken's contribution from the Freiburg Circle.[45]

That the men of the "Bonhoeffer Circle" in Freiburg were the men of yesterday was painfully evident in yet another major provision: their formula for the solution of the Jewish Question. As an appendix to the 127-page memorandum is a section entitled "Proposals for a Solution to the Jewish Question in Germany," authored by professor Constantin von Dietze. This part of the text is proof-positive that Bonhoeffer never saw the final draft, and that the Freiburg scholars were totally unfamiliar with Bonhoeffer's revolutionary theology regarding the Jews. *Ethics* did not appear until 1948. How, then, did the Freiburg *Bildungsbürger* and humanists envision the problem?[46]

Their efforts to apply Christian principles to the continued presence of Jews in Germany reveal them as essentially anti-Judaisitic. The preamble to this section of the memorandum includes the statement: "For the sake of one's love for one's own people, the Christian must always consider whether close contact or even intermarriage with other races can have a damaging effect both for the body and the soul."[47]

It went on: "But the Christian must always be aware that the races and peoples, each with their various characteristics, were created by God and all, including our own race and nation, stand equally before God—namely as sinners—nevertheless at the same time called into

His grace. And if God in His wrath punishes a people, He does not give that right to any nation to lord it over others. Even less does He give any nation the right to persecute another, to oppress it or to exterminate it. God alone is the judge over the nations."[48]

The memorandum then argued that it was the task of Christianity to bring the gospel to all nations. This applied also to the Jewish people whose decisive guilt it was that they resisted to this day the revelation of God in Jesus Christ. And to accept Jews into the church merely for superficial reasons without the Christian faith having been awakened in their hearts would be a sin against the church. Where, however, there was faith, then baptism might be granted in the confidence that God's Holy Spirit made a "new creature" and helped thereby to overcome dangerous tendencies and peculiarities in the [Jewish] character. The Memorandum continued:

> The violence that one people does to another is always a sin against God. And those measures that a state under certain circumstances, has to take in order to combat the deleterious influence of a race on the national community have to be tempered by the obligation to exercise justice and responsibility which the state has toward all over whom it exercises power. Where this has not been respected the guilt must be confessed and expiated.[49]

Suffice it to observe here that Bonhoeffer would never have endorsed such views because they were based on the false, so-called *theologia gloriae*, that he emphatically repudiated and refuted in *Ethics*. This theology derives from the quite anti-scriptural assumption that the New Covenant of Christ abolished the Old Covenant of Moses, on which, of course, the church rested. The *theologia gloriae* is unequivocally anti-Jewish, and is the precursor of anti-Semitism in all its grotesque manifestations throughout history. And Bonhoeffer's great achievement was to have overcome that deep-seated mindset, and in its place establish the foundation for a partnership between church and synagogue.[50] Clearly, if Bonhoeffer had the opportunity to see the text he would have had no alternative but to veto it. History, however, decreed otherwise. So the historical value of this section of the Freiburg Memorandum lies arguably more in the fact that it provides an insight into the thinking of the *Bildungsbürgertum* on the Jewish question than it does on the issue of democratic institutions.[51]

It should be noted that since the 1871 constitution of Bismarck, Jews were completely emancipated, and that remained valid for the Republic from 1919–33. These enlightened provisions, however, did not mean that anti-Semitism was not rife in wide sections of the community. On the contrary, it was during the latter part of the nineteenth century, as we have seen, when rabid exterminatory anti-Semitism arose in Germany.[52] Significantly, when Hitler revoked all basic citizenship rights with his Aryan legislation in 1935, the Nuremberg Laws, there was no protest from the churches; only individual voices such as Bonhoeffer's and a few like-minded pastors were raised.

When, however, the Lutheran *Bildungsbürger* who formulated the *Freiburg Memorandum* learned of the policy of annihilation toward the Jews their Christian conscience recoiled as their reaction to *Kristallnacht* indicated. Consequently, it was recommended first, that insofar as was humanly possible, the crimes against the Jews had to be expiated, and, additionally, appropriate and just living conditions be ensured for the Jews. As rider to these generous-sounding guidelines, however, the Memorandum stated:

> The state relinquishes, after the abolition of the Nuremburg Laws, all exceptional legislation for Jews because the surviving number returning to Germany *will not be so great as to be regarded as a danger to the German national character* [emphasis added]. It would be the task of the administration to reintroduce Jews, who had emigrated, back into their former professions with the necessary tact in order not to arouse again anti-Semitic feelings.[53]

Clearly, the authors were still thinking in blatantly racist terms. Jewish characteristics were essentially alien and a danger for the German community. Next, the Memorandum recommended an international convention on the rights and duties of Jews to be binding on all states, including freedom of religion, freedom of education, and economic freedom. As well, an international Jewish statute should be enacted to include the following points:

1) "The Jews have in all countries where they reside the status of foreigners. They may not be treated worse than other foreigners. At least they have a right to run businesses, practice in the professions and enjoy freedom of education. This right can be enacted by an international court. A representation of the entire world Jewish community should form a supreme council located preferably in a neutral country with representative officials in all countries."
2) "Those persons are to be regarded as Jews who belong to the Jewish faith as well as those who formerly belonged to it and have not joined another religion. And if Jews convert to Christianity they still remain members of the Jewish community unless they are granted naturalisation by the country in which they live."

3) "Jews who can be naturalized are those who apply for it and can advance compelling reasons such as if they can indicate that by family tradition they have rendered special service to the nation where they live. Decisions on this to be made from case to case. Finally, naturalized Jews should not be subject to exceptional legislation."[54]

What needs to be observed is that the authors of the Memorandum clearly thought they were being particularly enlightened and Christian. Clearly, they never understood that they were still imprisoned in the categories of the old *theologia gloriae* that Bonhoeffer had so emphatically rejected. It can only be conjectured as to what would have happened had Bonhoeffer not been arrested and had the opportunity to continue to participate in the deliberations of his Freiburg coreligionists. He would have had to educate them in the fallacies of the *theologia gloriae* which they held to be written in stone.

As indicated, these good, highly educated Lutherans in 1943 could not advance a better plan. What they had produced with regard to the Jewish question was, theologically speaking, still very anti-Jewish and illiberal. It was only with great difficulty that they could apply the principle of Christian charity not to recommend the complete banning of the Jews from Germany for all time.

Such conservatism did not predominate in postwar German politics because a peace settlement could only be negotiated with the Western Allies that fulfilled the requirements of a modern, liberal parliamentary democracy that was based on the sovereignty of the people. Further, sufficient politicians of both social democratic and liberal persuasion would reemerge to ensure that all vestiges of anti-Semitism were eliminated from the statute books.

What can now be said about Bonhoeffer? The evidence is that he remained a *Bildungsbürger* with an unshakable Lutheran conviction that any constitutional arrangement for Germany should enshrine the sovereignty of almighty God. He firmly rejected an immediate embracing of Western-style parliamentary democracy. Rather, Bonhoeffer prioritized a solution that ensured that sovereignty derived from God, not exclusively from the people. In this respect, it can only be concluded that Bonhoeffer himself was part of the "German Problem," but only in part, because on 20 September 1941, he had written to his American colleague Paul Lehmann, reflecting on what should happen to Germany after the war, when he confidently predicted that the Americans would emerge victorious and come to exert the influence of a superpower in the world. At that time, Bonhoeffer's concern was what kind of constitution a postwar Germany should have. President Roosevelt had enunciated in his New Year address of 6 January 1941, his famous four freedoms, upon which the postwar world was to be founded: freedom of speech, of worship, freedom from want and from fear. And it is significant just how Bonhoeffer responded to this. He wrote:

> USA domination is indeed one of the best solutions to the present crisis. But what is to become of Europe? What, for instance, of Germany? Nothing would be worse than to impose upon her any anglosaxon [sic] form of government—*as much as I would like it.* [emphasis added] It simply would not work. The four liberties of your President seem to indicate something in this direction. As far as I know Germany, it will be just impossible, for instance, to restore complete freedom of speech, of press, of association. That sort of thing would throw Germany right into the same abyss. I think we must try to find a Germany in which justice, lawfulness, freedom of the churches is being restored. I hope there will [be] something like an authoritarian 'Rechtsstaat' as the Germans call it. I[t] will need a long process of education before the people as a whole will be in the position to enjoy all the liberties it used to have.[55]

This seems without doubt to preempt the conceptions expressed in the Freiburg Memorandum. And it was indeed written approximately one year prior to the latter's formulation. Obviously, Bonhoeffer, very much like the Freiburg conservatives around Gerhard Ritter, was far from confident that the broader German population could cope with Western style parliamentary democracy. The experience of the Weimar Republic seemed to confirm that, but as has been shown, Bonhoeffer had theological reservations concerning the revolutionary doctrine of popular sovereignty that supplanted the sovereignty of God. At first glance, this seems to locate him in a world of political ideas totally out of kilter with both the Western democracies and the old German Social Democratic Party that had for so many decades stood for a modern parliamentary democracy against Bismarck's conception of the *Rechtsstaat* and that of the wider *Bildungsbürgertum* subsequently.

This suggests that Bonhoeffer lived in a very rarefied atmosphere as far as the cut and thrust of domestic politics was concerned, certainly remote from the political aspirations of the working class, despite his early experience with the proletarian Berlin population in the suburb of Wedding. One can only conjecture as to the reasons for this. It is clear from the experience of prison life that Bonhoeffer was not impressed by the way in which many of his fellow inmates lost their self-control during air raids, and of course, the brutal behavior of guards and of SS people, men of crude and unrefined background, generally filled him with disgust. This is very evident from the image that Bonhoeffer projected in those writings discussed above from his *Fiction from*

Tegel Prison. What exercised his mind most was the lack of decency and character exhibited by the majority of individuals who could not be considered part of the *Bildungsbürgertum*—but crucially, as well, elements of this class, who, through lack of character, had succumbed to their baser instincts: greed, desire for comfort, and lust for power, no matter how petty. Above all, they had shown themselves to have betrayed all the higher attributes of *noblesse oblige* and thrown in their lot with the criminal Nazi state. Clearly, Bonhoeffer envisioned a postwar period of tutelage for the German people. This, however, has to be squared with his expressed preference, in the above letter to Paul Lehmann, for an "anglosaxon" (sic) form of government. What is to be made of this in view of the fact that *anglosaxon* meant "sovereignty of the people"?

The clue to comprehending this apparent contradiction in Bonhoeffer's mind, where he insisted on the sovereignty of God on the one hand and the acceptance—indeed, even endorsement—of popular sovereignty on the other, is provided by a passage in *Ethics* in the section entitled "The Concrete Commandment and the Divine Mandates." Bonhoeffer averred that "the commandment of God wishes to find man always in an earthly relation to authority, in a clearly defined order of superiority and inferiority."[56] This means that for Bonhoeffer, it would be legitimate for a people to elect a sovereign parliament out of which an executive authority would be formed, provided that this executive comprehended that its authority was "under God." In practice that would mean that those persons appointed to office in the government would necessarily perceive themselves as an authority under a superior, indeed, divine authority. As Bonhoeffer formulated it:

> [I]t must be emphasised that the divine mandate establishes not only superiority but also inferiority. Superiority and inferiority pertain to one another in an indissoluble relation of mutual limitation . . . superiority and inferiority here represent a relation not of concepts or of things but of persons; it is a relation between those persons who, whether they be superior or inferior, submit to the commission of God and to it alone. The master, too, has a Master, and this fact alone establishes his right to be master and authorizes and legitimates his relations to the servant. Master and servant owe to one another the honor which arises from any particular act of participation in the mandate of God.[57]

This makes patently clear that Bonhoeffer saw nothing irreconcilable between the concepts of the sovereignty of God on the one hand and popular sovereignty on the other; the concepts coexisted in a reciprocal relationship. Obviously, the essential element was that the "inferior" earthly authority of mere men as governors on earth was seen as ultimately deriving from the superior authority of almighty God.

In the German situation of the 1940s, as Bonhoeffer made clear in his above letter to Paul Lehmann, the implementation of "anglosaxon" type democracy would have to wait until the Germans had survived the "dumbing down" and brutalization that they had suffered under National Socialism. From many of his writings, it is clear that Bonhoeffer had great difficulty in forgiving, for example, the grotesque display of spinelessness and lack of character on the part of members of his own class. Consequently, it is not surprising that he had little confidence in their ability to fit into a political system that was based on a high degree of personal integrity, incorruptibility, and morality in order to make it work. It was, therefore, logical from Bonhoeffer's standpoint that at least a period of tutelage would be necessary for Germans to be able to be reintegrated into normal political life, if by "normal" is meant liberal, parliamentary democracy.

Notes

1. On Bonhoeffer's sojourn in England, see Keith Clements, *Bonhoeffer and Britain* (London, 2006).
2. See Hannes Heer, *Hitler war's: Die Befreiung der Deutschen von ihrer Vergangenheit* (Berlin, 2005), 125–59, for a perceptive analysis of "After Ten Years," in the chapter entitled "die Feigen und die Dummen," i.e., "the cowardly and the stupid."
3. Gregory Munro, *Hitler's Bavarian Antagonist: Georg Moenius and the Allgemeine Rundschau of Munich, 1929–1933* (Lewiston/Queenstown/Lampeter, 2006).
4. "Prologue: After Ten Years: a Reckoning Made at New Year 1943," in *Letters and Papers from Prison*, 4. See *Nach zehn Jahren*, DBW, VIII, 21–22.
5. Cf. Heinz Eduard Tödt, "Conscience in Bonhoeffer's Ethical Theory and Practice," in *Bonhoeffer's Ethics*, 50.
6. Ibid. 51
7. "After Ten Years," in *LPP*, 5
8. Ibid.
9. Ibid., in the subsection on "Civil Courage."
10. Ibid., 6.
11. Ibid.
12. Ibid.
13. See Stern, "The Political Consequences of the Un-political German."
14. Cf. Tödt, *Theologische Perspektiven nach Dietrich Bonhoeffer* (Gütersloh, 1993), 165.
15. Ibid.
16. "After Ten Years," 8. Hannes Heer, *Hitler War's*, 157. Heer comments that this section of "After Ten Years" is Bonhoeffer's most penetrating criticism of the failure of the German elite to overcome their self-torturing scruples and take meaningful action against a regime they knew to be criminal.

17. Ibid., 8. This kind of thing is a widespread human phenomenon. It is precisely this that one encounters in discussions with Christian fundamentalists—indeed, fundamentalists of all kinds. They are locked in a paradigm of slogans—indeed, walled up in a fortress with their "little flock"—and firmly reject dialogue with outsiders unless they, the outsiders, submit to and appropriate the fundamentalist set of slogans that will guarantee them fellowship in the "little flock."

18. Karl Dietrich Erdmann, *Die Zeit der Weltkriege* (Stuttgart, 1976), 341. For an up-to-date analysis of this question, see Norman J.W.Goda, "Black Marks:Hitler's Bribery of His Senior Officers" *Journal of Modern History* 72 (2000): 413–452. Here is portrayed how Hitler literally "bought" the loyalty of many of the most senior officers who had not joined the Nazi Party by rewarding them with large tax-free secret grants of money and/or by so-called *Dotationen*, that is the gift of landed estates.

19. "After Ten Years," 8.

20. It should be noted that immediately after the death of the Reich Chancellor Paul von Hindenburg (2 August 1934) Hitler declared himself to be both Führer and Reich Chancellor, and thereby assumed the supreme command over the armed forces. Hitler then took a step that had the most deleterious consequences for the Reich, namely, he required that all officers and men swear an oath of personal allegiance to him that repudiated the existing law governing the military oath of allegiance, passed, 1 December 1933. It was a fateful novelty in German military history that violated all previous constitutional arrangements. The oath now read: "I swear by God this sacred oath, that I will render to the leader of the German Reich and people, Adolf Hitler, the commander [from 20 July 1935, in the *Reichsgesetzblatt* 1935 I, 1035, "supreme commander"] of the forces, unconditional allegiance, and as a brave soldier am prepared at any time to lay down my life for this oath." See *DBW*, XV, 160, note 6.

21. Ibid., 8.

22. On Schacht's role in the economic crisis, see his autobiographical statement, *Account Settled (Abrechnung mit Hitler)* (London, 1949).

23. Another dramatic example of this kind of highly educated person who placed his skills at the disposal of Hitler was the man who became Hitler's architect and sometime minister for munitions production, Albert Speer (1905–81). See Gitta Sereny. *Albert Speer: His Battle with the Truth* (New York, 1995).

24. "After Ten Years," 6.

25. See, *Brautbriefe Zelle 92, Dietrich Bonhoeffer Maria von Wedemeyer, 1943–1945* (Munich, 1997).

26. Translation of *"Vorrede auff die Epistel S. Paul: an die Romer,"* in *Dr M. Luther: Die gantze Heilige schrift Deudsch 1545 aufs new zurericht,* ed. Hans Volz and Heinz Blanke (Munich, 1972), vol. 2, 2254–2268, by Bro. Andrew Thornton OSB. Located at <http://www.ccel.org/l/luther/romans/pref_romans.html> accessed 22 July 2008.

27. See the editors' postscript to Bonhoeffer's *Schöpfung und Fall* [Creation and Fall] *DBW*, III, 138–39. As well, see above the analysis of Bonhoeffer's address "A Theological Basis for the World Alliance?" from 26 July 1932, at Ciernohoské Kúpele, at the ecumenical youth peace conference there in chapter 4.

28. See Walter von Loewenich, *Martin Luther: Der Mann und das Werk* (Munich, 1982), 295–301 passim.

29. The source for the present discussion is the authorized English translation, entitled *Fiction from Tegel Prison*, which is vol. 7 of the projected complete English-language translation of the works of Dietrich Bonhoeffer being published by Fortress Press, Minneapolis. This volume appeared under the general editorship of Clifford Green in 1999.

30. On J.E.E. D Acton, see the biography by Roland Hill. *Lord Acton* (New Haven/London, 2000). His famous statement on the corrupting influence of power was made in a letter to Bishop Mandell Creighton in April 1887, relating to the latter's book on the history of the papacy. Acton wrote: "Historic responsibility has to make up for the want of legal responsibility. *Power tends to corrupt, and absolute power corrupts absolutely.* [Emphasis added.] Great men are almost always bad men, even when they exercise influence and not authority: still more when you superadd the tendency or the certainty of corruption by authority. There is no worse heresy than the office sanctifies the holder of it." Quoted after *Lord Acton on papal Power*, compiled by H.A. Mac Dougall (London, 1973), 230-231. For a perceptive commentary on Acton's significance, see Ulrich Noack, *Geschichtswissenschaft und Wahrheit. Nach den Schriften von John Dalberg-Acton, 1834-1902* (Frankfurt, 1947).

31. *Fiction from Tegel Prison*, ed. Clifford J. Green, vol. 7, *Dietrich Bonhoeffer Works* (Minneapolis, 2000), 103. The original German editors, Ilse Tödt and Renate Bethge, suggest here [footnote 29] that in 1941 (when Bonhoeffer was writing "State and Church") he had been reading Gerhard Ritter's *Machtstaat und Utopie* where, commenting on the rulers of the utopian state in Thomas More's *Utopia*, book 2, Ritter states: "They will not be isolated as a class for they will be distinguished from the masses as an elite of those of greatest intellectual gifts and moral maturity. They are Plato's ἀρίστοί [the best, cf. 'aristocrats'], a class of people of noble qualities where you find neither ambition nor passion." This work of Ritter's appeared in English in a revised form as *The German Problem*. See footnote 33. See also, John A. Moses, "Dietrich Bonhoeffer's Fiction from Tegel Prison, 1943–1945: His Reflections on the Dark Side of Cultural Protestantism in Nazi Germany," in *The Dark Side*, ed. C. Hartney and A. McGarrity (Sydney, 2004), 89–101.

32. Published as part of *Ethics* in the English-language edition cited above, note 11, 327–57.

33. Gerhard Ritter, *The German Problem Basic Questions of German Political Life, Past and Present*, trans. Sigurd Burckhardt (Columbus, 1965).

34. Ritter's views on resistance to the Nazis are summarized in his book *The German Resistance: Carl Goerdeler's Struggle against Tyranny* (London, 1958). See also, *Gerhard Ritter: Ein Politischer Historiker in seinen Briefen*, ed. Klaus Schwabe and Rolf Reichardt with Reinhard Hauf (Boppard am Rhein, 1984). The *Freiburg Memorandum* is reproduced at 629–74.

35. See Anthony Read and David Fisher, *Kristallnacht: The Unleashing of the Holocaust* (New York, 1990) for an extensive analysis of this event.

36. See *In der Stunde Null: die Denkschrift des Freiburger "Bonhoeffer Kreises": Politische Gemeinschaftsordnung. Ein Versuch zur Selbstbestimmung des christlichen Gewissens in den politischen Nöten unserer Zeit*, intro. Helmut Thielicke

(Tübingen, 1979), 27. Bonhoeffer is reported as having visited Freiburg, late summer 1942, on behalf of the Confessing Church, requesting the results of the work of the Freiburg Circle. The Confessing Church leadership had become aware that the Church of England hierarchy planned a conference of the World Council of Churches after the war and wished to resume fraternal relations with the churches of former enemy nations. For this purpose it was deemed advisable to have worked out in advance the principles upon which a permanent world peace could be established. It was, according to Bethge, used "as one of the preliminary works for the Amsterdam conference that founded the World Council of Churches in 1948, as it had successfully combined theological principles with practical details." See Bethge, *Bonhoeffer*, 682 [cf. 2000, 775–76].

37. See the English translation by John Riches, *Luther: His Life and Work* (New York and Evanston, 1963).
38. See Bethge, *Bonhoeffer*, 681–2 [cf. 2,000, 775–7], and *Ethics*, 327–48.
39. Bethge, *Bonhoeffer,* 682 [cf. 2000, 775–76]
40. *Ethics,* 347.
41. Ibid., 348.
42. *Freiburger Denkschrift*, 74.
43. For detailed information on Allied policy toward occupied Germany, see Rolf Steininger, *Deutsche Geschichte seit 1945: Darstellung und Dokumente in vier Bänden* [Vol. 1, 1945–1947 and Vol. 2, 1948–1955] (Frankfurt am Main, 1996).
44. Heinz Eduard Tödt, *Theologische Perspektiven nach Dietrich Bonhoeffer,* 138.
45. Ibid., 139.
46. According to the editors of Volume XVI *DBW,* 695, note 88, the section, "Proposals for a Solution to the Jewish Question in Germany," could not have been seen by Bonhoeffer. Hans Mommsen agrees in his *Alternatives to Hitler: German Resistance under the Third Reich* (Princeton, 2003). 267. Mommsen comments on von Dietze's ideas: "He favored the founding an international Jewish state, and he wanted to see the passing of a Jewish statute. This would automatically deprive Jews of German citizenship, but as compensation they would have their 'claim to economic activity and the opportunity for education guaranteed' under international law. It is extremely painful to read in the same document: 'the number of surviving Jews returning to Germany will not be so great as to be regarded as a threat to German national life.'" Mommsen added: "We can also be sure that the memorandum did not meet with the approval of Bonhoeffer, who commissioned the work in the first place."
47. *Freiburger Denkschrift,* 147
48. Ibid.
49. Ibid.
50. See Asta von Oppen, *Der unerhörte Schrei,* 87–121 passim. .
51. See *Freiburger Denkschrift,* 21–23, for Helmut Thielicke's comments on this section of the memorandum. Here the older (by thirty-six years) theologian observed how the authors of the memorandum were locked into the world view of their time: "Obwohl dieser Schluss der Denkschrift alles andere als erfreulich ist, so wird jeder Augen- und Leidenszeuge von damals, aber auch ein Nachgeborener, der über einigen historischen Sinn verfügt, doch

Eines zugeben müssen: Selbst dieses uns heute fadenscheinig vorkommende Program konnte einem unter dem damligen Druck fast als aufregend revolutionär erscheinen. (Die Gestapo jedenfalls hätte es zweifellos für ausreichend gehalten, um eine Anklage wegen Staats- und Parteifeindlichkeit darauf zu gründen.) Dass wir heute schärfere Augen für die Fesseln des Zeitgebundenen von damals haben, ist nicht unser Verdienst. Auch wir werden dem kritischen Blick der nach uns Kommenden ausgesetzt sein, und hoffentlich sind wir dann nicht der Gegenstand ihres Hohns."

52. Paul W. Massing, *Rehearsal for Destruction: A Study of Political Anti-Semitism in Imperial Germany* (New York, 1949).

53. *Freiburger Denkschrift*, 146–51.

54. Ibid.

55. Bonhoeffer to Lehmann, 20 August 1941 in *DBW*, XVII, 136–37; emphasis added. Cf. Green, *Bonhoeffer*, 346.

56. *Ethics*, 284–85.

57. Ibid., 285.

9

The Postwar Confrontation with the Nazi Past

With the final collapse of Nazi Germany, an overriding problem for the compromised German Protestant Church was to achieve reconciliation with the churches of the former enemy countries. It was a priority of the highest order for the Protestant leadership to be reintegrated into ecumenical fellowship. Consequently, anyone who had identified with the pro-Nazi "German Christian" movement needed to keep a low profile, but members of the Confessing Church felt that they had retained a modicum of honor and decency that allowed them to address their foreign counterparts without being totally paralyzed by shame and remorse. And as far as the international Christian community was concerned, there was certainly a willingness to welcome German Protestants back into fraternal dialogue; but it was expected that they should frankly declare regret for their generally supine attitude to the Nazi state and apparent acquiescence in its policies of genocide and brutal aggression. In short, the foreign churchmen expected an expression of guilt from the German brethren for their toleration of such inhumanity, if not complicity in silently condoning the numberless Nazi atrocities.

In the event, however, formal expressions of remorse, let alone of guilt, on behalf of German Protestants generally, had to be virtually dragged out of the German church leadership—although there had been a number of such declarations made by individual regional church leaders during the early postwar period.[1] Statements by the national church in which guilt or coresponsibility for the crimes committed against humanity by the Nazi regime church were painfully slow in coming. These occurred in a series of postwar statements that gradually became less and less reticent, especially with regard to the Jewish question. One can only speculate about how different the situation might have been had Bonhoeffer still been alive to state publicly the position he had so eloquently expressed in his *Ethics* manuscript. He would certainly have proved a most uncomfortable interlocutor for some personalities in the church leadership who, in the event, were more concerned with reproaching the allied occupation authorities for failing to alleviate the postwar hardships that the German civilian population was forced to endure.[2]

Here, by tracing the evolution of admissions of guilt for tolerating the Hitler regime and its genocidal policies, one gains a greater appreciation of the theological depth of Bonhoeffer's earlier perceptions of the problem. Further, since knowledge of his energetic pro-Jewish stance has been received, not least through the efforts of the International Dietrich Bonhoeffer Society but chiefly, of course, through the tireless output of Eberhard Bethge, the German church, and indeed, the world at large, now appreciate the pioneering achievements of the young German pastor and theologian. It is noted, of course, that this recognition was slow to come and that, initially, even among Bonhoeffer's coreligionists, he was regarded not as a martyr but rather—surprising as it may seem to Western Christians—as a traitor. For example, the Lutheran bishop of Bavaria, Hans Meiser, refused in 1953 to attend a remembrance service for Bonhoeffer in Flossenbürg because he judged Bonhoeffer in neo-Lutheran terms to have been essentially a political traitor and hardly a Christian martyr. Others shared this view.[3] Indeed, one could argue that the rate of acceptance among Germans of Bonhoeffer as a true Christian martyr has been a gauge of the rate of change in the political culture of postwar Germany and its intellectual-spiritual integration into the West.[4] The British, for example, as we have seen, were the first to hold a memorial service for Bonhoeffer, and now, since July 1998, his statue, alongside nine other twentieth-century martyrs, adorns the west façade of Westminster Abbey in London.

Bonhoeffer's prophetic vision and readiness, without fear or favor, to oppose the anti-Christian Nazi regime, first in word and then in deed, and to subject the history of Christianity with regard to the treatment of Jews to relentless criticism, led to his martyrdom. In retrospect, it must be acknowledged that he initiated a veritable revolution in the way the church in general relates to the state and in particular now assesses the role of the synagogue throughout history.[5]

The liberation of Germany from Nazi barbarism required the combined military resources of the Soviet Union, the British Empire, and the United States. The German people did not, as was vainly hoped in some quarters, rise up and overthrow their maniacal leader. Their hatred and fear of Communist Russia and the Western democracies were obviously far greater than any doubts they had about Hitler and his ruthless warlordism. Indeed, most people, in the light of the "doctrine of the two kingdoms," had had difficulty in comprehending that Hitler was not an "authority" ordained by God.[6]

Given this situation, Western Christian leaders felt that they had to be particularly circumspect in addressing their German counterparts. Consequently, from mid-1945, German Protestants had to confront rebuilding their church in a situation of unprecedented material and moral degradation and humiliation. Ecumenical contact was therefore essential. One had to seek reconciliation with the former enemy, most of whom had suffered extensively and acutely from unprecedented Nazi violations of international law, especially in terms of human rights abuse in occupied countries.

Considerably before the end of the war, a leading pastor of the Confessing Church, Hans Asmussen, was beginning to reflect on the need to build bridges to the Ecumenical movement, and in a letter to Willem Visser't Hooft of the World Council of Churches, Asmussen tried to stress the common link of all Christians, clearly with a view to heading off the inevitable reproaches that were expected to be made against the highly compromised German church once the war was over. Asmussen appealed, as follows: "Our relationship is not determined by the fact that one is right and the other wrong. We both stand together under the mercy of almighty God."[7] Clearly Asmussen was at pains to relativize the German guilt by stressing that all people, regardless of the political system in which they were forced to live, were guilty before God. It was therefore presumptuous of foreigners to reproach German fellow Christians for their abject failure to protest against the inhumanity of the Nazi regime. And as the devastation caused by the Allied bombing campaign and the privations suffered by the civilian population subsequently under the occupation regimes had brought home to the German people, they were indeed suffering severe retribution. They complained bitterly of allied brutality and duplicity. Under these circumstances, it was argued by German church leaders that British and American churchmen had no moral right to expect German confessions of guilt.

Interestingly, Visser't Hooft replied finally to Asmussen's appeal in May 1943 warning against the obvious tendency to generalize, privatize, and depoliticize the guilt issue. Indeed, there needed to be a precise recognition by the German churches of the nation's sin before God and man. Only then could there be genuine reconciliation between former enemies. Indeed, there could be no future encounter between churches except on the basis of historical reality where the crimes and injustices had to be acknowledged and not classified as political matters of no relevance to the church. Certainly, added Visser 't Hooft, the victor powers needed to be warned against self-righteousness on the one hand, and the vanquished against bitterness on the other.[8]

Consequently, well before the war ended, the German church leaders knew that an admission of guilt would be expected from them by their ecumenical counterparts. There could be no resumption of normal interchurch relationships without frank expressions of remorse and penitence from the Germans. These were the necessary prerequisites to reconciliation. Clearly, the Germans were aware of this, but they experienced considerable difficulty in openly and unreservedly confessing guilt. Again, Hans Asmussen appealed to the ecumenical brotherhood, this time in the person of the Archbishop of Canterbury, Geoffrey Fisher, already on 16 June 1945, admitting German guilt but at the same time pleading for the fellowship of the wider church and requesting help again to believe in the mercy of God. German Protestants did not want to be treated as though their guilt, great as it was, could not be forgiven.[9]

Private or Collective Guilt?

It has, however, to be noted that there were two concepts of guilt in the mind of the German Protestants. They made a distinction between private or personal guilt on the one hand, and collective guilt on the other, and this gave rise to intense and bitter division among several church leaders. The more conservative ones took refuge in the notion of religious guilt as being essentially a private issue between the individual fallen soul and God. Consequently, a collective admission of guilt by the church was really inadmissible because it assumed that God pronounced judgment on institutions as well as on individuals. In Lutheranism, this was not possible because church and state operated, as we have seen, above individuals as instruments of divine provenance that were distinct from the individual human beings who held office within them. This, indeed, is what the doctrine of the two kingdoms implied; but as Bonhoeffer had demonstrated in *Ethics*, this view could no longer be sustained.

Conservative German Protestants had not yet been able inwardly to digest this. Their old commitment to the Lutheran-Hegelian paradigm proved to be an insurmountable obstacle to reconciliation as required by the former enemies in the postwar world. In a profound sense, then, Protestant German religious-cultural formation was confronted with a challenge to effect a radical moral reassessment. Essentially, conservatives were being required to concede that the heritage they had held to be written in stone was not, after all a reflection of God's ordering of the world but rather a wish image of men, as Karl Barth, already in 1918, for example had tried, without much success, to make clear to them. In short, they needed to comprehend at last that the state was not an "order of creation" but simply an artifact of a *fallen* creation as Bonhoeffer had perceptively observed.

The task confronting these conservative Lutherans was how to come to terms with the fact that the doctrine of the two kingdoms was passé—indeed, far from being an adequate formula for the structuring of a just society in the postwar world. But this was the theological position that the conservative opponents of an open statement of guilt were trying to defend. Hence, their deep opposition to those who were ready to admit to the world not only the church's weakness in failing to protest, but its actual complicity in the genocidal policies and deeds of the Hitler regime. Consequently, after May 1945, the Protestant church leaders were torn between these two positions. The conservative element would only concede to "private" confession of guilt before God; the more liberal-minded wished frankly to make a public admission of guilt that acknowledged openly the flaws, indeed fallacies on which the old Lutheran-Hegelian paradigm was predicated. It was the latter position that the West European Protestant leaders were hoping to hear, but it was stifled from the beginning. Matthew Hockenos has very succinctly summed up the situation:

> Reformers [i.e., the liberal-minded] conceived of guilt more concretely as culpability for historical inaction. They maintained that the church and the Confessing Church as institutions were guilty of inaction when they failed to condemn anti-Semitism, the deification of Hitler, naked territorial aggression of the state, and systematic atrocities carried out against Jews, Slavs and Gypsies from eastern territories.[10]

The tension between the two positions prevailing among Protestant church leaders is reflected in their first post-war meeting in the town of Treysa, (Hesse) 27–31 August 1945, which was convened at the behest of Bishop Theophil Wurm of Württemburg to reconstitute the church in the new political situation. Essential to this position, as Jürgen Seidel has pointed out, was the issue of confession of guilt; confession and reparation were the necessary preconditions for forgiveness and reconciliation. If normal ecumenical relations were to be resumed this step, painful though it was, had to be taken.[11] And at Treysa two communiqués were formulated, one for the pastorate and another for the congregations of Germany. The first relied on the old Lutheran concept that "demonic forces" had been at work that had gained control of Germany and had driven the people to unspeakable atrocities. "Apocalyptic were the manifestations of total war," stated the communiqué; and it went on: "We confess our guilt and bow under the burden of its consequences."[12] Indeed, these were assessed as the terrible punishment meted out by God to Germany in the immediate postwar situation for the church's unfaithfulness.

What is of interest here is the apparent conviction that the drift away from God had begun prior to the Nazi take over. This is nothing less than a veiled allusion to the detested Weimar period, when there allegedly occurred a confusion of church and state power that led to the emergence of a managerial culture in the church. This presumably made the church susceptible to the illusion that National Socialism would bring about a new era in German history that would enable the church once again to flourish—in short, to be the embodiment of the spiritual realm. This was a fond hope that impaired the ability of the church leadership to see clearly the direction in which Germany was being led. That certainly was true.

Otherwise, the communiqué warned the pastors that a restoration of church-state relations as they had been prior to 1933 was not an option. Rather, it was necessary to focus firmly on God and on the 1934 Barmen Statement of the Confessing Church. Significantly, as in the latter case, no mention was made of the Jewish Question. The notable thing was that the derailment was attributed again to "demonic forces," not the failures of men who should have known better, as Bonhoeffer pointed out in "After Ten Years."[13] Still, even this amount of anguished breast-beating drew scathing criticism from the more conservative elements in the pastorate once they had read it. They were strenuously at pains to stress the "guilt" of others who were the former enemies of Nazi Germany. Against this, Karl Barth pointed out repeatedly that the "guilt" of others was irrelevant; Germans had to be clear that it was the course of their history, meaning that its antidemocratic and militaristic authoritarianism—in short, Prussianism—had led ultimately to the catastrophe of 1945.[14]

This was clearly an early expression of the negative *Sonderweg* thesis, which, of course, both conservative historians as well as like-minded theologians strenuously resisted. In the case of the Treysa communiqué to the congregations, it was indeed openly admitted that what Germans were suffering in 1945 was the consequence of their general unfaithfulness to God and failure to heed his word. As well, it was conceded that the pastorate had also failed to care adequately for their charges. This explained the desertion of the laity from the church. In short, the Nazi period was a time of desolation relieved only by the witness of a few faithful, some of whom had suffered martyrdom for their faith. As such, the communiqué to the congregations attempted to combine a conservative understanding of guilt and forgiveness with a frank recognition of collective culpability, as the following excerpt illustrates:

> Today we confess: Long before God spoke in anger, He sought us with His Word of love and we did not listen.... Long before the sham government of our land collapsed, justice had been thwarted. Long before men were murdered, human beings had become mere numbers and human life trivialized.[15]

Here is illustrated the difficulty of denying human complicity in Nazi criminality. But again the communiqué shied away from acknowledging the centuries of Christian anti-Judaism and instead highlighted the positive, but, in effect, quite ineffectual stance of the church by stating:

> When the church took its responsibility seriously, it reminded the population of God's commandments and minced no words when it condemned concentration camps, mistreatment and murder of Jews and the sick, and sought to protect youth from the seduction of National Socialist propaganda. But churchmen were pushed into the remote sanctuaries of the church as if in prison. Our people were separated from the church. The public was no longer allowed to hear its words; no one heard what it preached. Then came the wrath of God. God has taken from us that which men most desire to have.[16]

A more poignant admission of the abysmal lack of moral courage among German Lutherans can scarcely be imagined. Again we have confirmation of what Bonhoeffer had originally observed and deplored in "After Ten Years": "We have been silent witnesses of evil deeds. . . . experience has made us suspicious of others and kept us from being truthful and open; intolerable conflicts have worn us down and even made us cynical. Are we still of any use?"[17]

Indeed, it was the lingering, almost despairing, hope that the church in 1945 was not entirely beyond redemption that gained expression in the communiqué to the congregations. Personalities such as Martin Niemöller who had come under the strong influence of Karl Barth had been able to revise both their image of Prusso-German history since Luther as well as their understanding of church-state relations, wanted the church to be more open about confessing guilt. However, neither the communiqué to the pastors nor that to the congregations was endorsed by the church authorities. This did not, however, prevent leaks of the statements, but these simply unleashed bitter recriminations. Consequently, as Matthew Hockenos summed up: "How churchmen understood the legacy of the church struggle and how they explained the twelve year rein (sic) of Hitler was inexorably connected to the positions they took regarding the nature of confession, repentance-and-forgiveness."[18] It is interesting here to note that Hockenos perceptively adduces Bonhoeffer's concept of "cheap grace" as he formulated it in *The Cost of Discipleship* in 1936 to explain in part the attitude of the conservatives to their situation in 1945. He quotes Bonhoeffer stating: "The preaching of forgiveness must always go hand-in-hand with the preaching of repentance, the preaching of the gospel with the preaching of the law." The passage goes on, however, to state, "If the church refuses to face the stern reality of sin, it will gain no credence when it talks of forgiveness. Such a church walks unworthily of the gospel. It is an unholy church, squandering the precious treasure of the Lord's forgiveness."[19]

Neither of the Treysa statements persuaded foreign observers that the German church had fully acknowledged its implication in Nazi crimes against humanity. In short, the conditions had yet to be fulfilled that would allow the resumption of full ecumenical relations. Consequently, in the light of this, Visser 't Hooft, as general secretary of the World Council of Churches in Geneva, pleaded with his German colleagues to meet with him and other representatives of foreign churches in Stuttgart in the following October. His motivation was that one needed from the German church a clear expression of guilt in order to be able again to work with one another in a genuine ecumenical spirit. He asked the Germans: "Help us so that we can help."[20]

To the foreign ecumenists, all that seemed so very straightforward; and, of course, some Germans such as Niemöller were anxious to comply with a clear confession of guilt, one that would make up for the inadequate statements from Treysa. Certainly, from the standpoint of the former victims of Nazi aggression a frank admission from the German church of complicity would have cleared the air. And Visser't Hooft kept gently insisting that such a step was an essential prelude to the reconciliation of former enemies:

> This conversation will be very much easier if the Confessing Church of Germany would speak out openly—not only about the crimes of the Nazis, also particularly about the sins of omission of the German people, including the church. The Christians of other countries do not wish to appear as Pharisees. But they require that it be openly said that the German people and the church did not speak [against National Socialism] with sufficient clarity and with sufficient emphasis.[21]

Visser 't Hooft had made this clear to Martin Niemöller, who was requested to send invitations to the Stuttgart meeting. Obviously, Niemöller had no problem with what was expected at the meeting of the German delegation because, as has been shown, he had endorsed the views of Karl Barth. However, others were far less prepared to underwrite a virtual indictment of the course of German history. Consequently, when a statement was finally formulated it reflected the tensions between the Lutheran conservatives and the reforming liberals who were clearly more aligned with Bonhoeffer's position. The former felt as though they were being required to sign a "second Versailles," a virtual admission of sole German war guilt, whereas the latter perceived the Prussian conservative tradition as the ultimate cause of all

Germany's ills since the founding of the Bismarckian-Wilhelmine empire.[22] The result was a lukewarm collection of generalities, designed to placate the former enemies so that a resumption of ecumenical collaboration could proceed. Again, there was no mention of the Jewish question. The core statement read:

> With great anguish we state: through us endless suffering has been bought to many people and countries. What we have often borne witness to before our congregations, we now declare in the name of the whole Church. We have for many years struggled in the name of Jesus Christ against the spirit which found its terrible expression in the National Socialist regime of tyranny, but we accuse ourselves for not witnessing more courageously, for not praying more faithfully, for not believing more joyously, and for not loving more ardently.[23]

There is no doubt that the German church leaders of all persuasions were glad to have gotten over this hurdle, but it was a minimalist statement made for pragmatic reasons. Certainly, it avoided confrontation with the key issue of Lutheran-German political culture central to which was anti-Judaism. They were always going to shy away from any statement that could imply "ubiquitous complicity" (Hannah Arendt)[24] which is what Barth and Niemöller clearly believed was necessary and which, of course, had Bonhoefffer been alive, he would have insisted upon. What Germans had called *das Geschichtsbild* (the image of history), which the generation of Niemöller had imbibed at school and at university, remained an all powerful cultural-political-pedagogic artifact. That means, simply, that the Lutheran-Hegelian-Rankean schema of German history and the theology of the state and war that derived from it, remained potently efficacious, especially in the mind of the conservative Lutheran pastors and theologians.

Significantly, Karl Barth as a Swiss of strong social democratic persuasion, as we have seen, had never been affected by it; and so, consistent with the thesis of his commentary on *The Epistle to the Romans* (1918), he sustained his forthright judgment of his renowned German mentors for their blatant Prusso-German "statism." His post-1945 critique of his German colleagues was simply the continuity of the position he formulated some thirty years earlier. Martin Niemöller's stand at Treysa, and then at Stuttgart, against the conservatives and their reluctance to make a frank confession of guilt that would have fully satisfied the Western ecumenical colleagues derived clearly from his own experience of the Nazis and also very much from the influence exerted on him by his Swiss mentor. As Matthew Hockenos observed, by the spring of 1947 it was becoming clear to Niemöller and those of like mind that their willingness frankly to declare penitence as a prelude to reconciliation with Christians of other countries was far from popular and that they, with their particular agenda, were being elbowed aside.[25]

It was, of course, a time when the Cold War was intensifying and the postwar division of Germany into zones of occupation by the victor powers was being consolidated, chiefly because of the refusal of the Soviets to honor the Yalta and Potsdam agreements to treat the vanquished Germany as one economic unit and to hold all-German elections for a new national parliament in due course. Consequently, the division into zones of occupation solidified into the establishment of two rival German states. Interestingly, the Western zones occupied by the United States, Great Britain, and France coalesced into what became the Federal Republic, which perceived itself under the first chancellor, Konrad Adenauer, as the successor to the old German Reich. And under the conditions of the Cold War, it more and more developed a self-perception of being the true Germany as opposed to *die Zone* occupied by the Soviets. In short, the emerging Federal Republic under the conservative coalition led by Adenauer assured the continuation of a "Reich consciousness" and a corresponding prioritization of raison d'état that was reflected in the mentality of the Protestant church leadership. The threat posed by the Soviet Union to Western Europe generally and to West Germany in particular was seen as justification for stressing again national solidarity rather than the divisive issues of war guilt and the Holocaust.

It was against this background that the reformers around Niemöller and Hans-Joachim Iwand, a pastor also with strong personal associations with Bonhoeffer, encouraged again by Karl Barth, pressed in August 1947 for a much more frank statement of guilt to be formulated. Their efforts resulted in what is known as *das Darmstädter Wort*, or the "Darmstadt Statement." This document indicts most emphatically the old dominant Lutheran-Hegelian Rankean image of German history and the Prusso-German sense of mission that sprang from it. The initial draft was made by Pastor Iwand, who had been an intimate collaborator with Bonhoeffer in the "illegal" training of ordinands for the Confessing Church. It is, therefore, not surprising that the ideas in the Darmstadt Statement reflect strongly those expressed in the *Ethics* manuscript, which, of course, was not published until 1948. What is very obvious is the stark difference between the tentative Stuttgart statement and the comparatively forthright wording of Darmstadt. It is highly instructive to report on how Iwand developed his ideas. In 1949 he wrote to pastor Wilhelm Niemöller (1898–1983) as follows:

I gladly confess to you that since 1945 I have been investigating those events of the previous century that followed on the downfall of Napoleon in Europe, and I fear that we are in danger of falling back into the old ways of thinking which even at that time turned out to be dead ends.[26]

Clearly Iwand had encountered the fallacies of *Borussissmus* (i.e., the Hohenzollern legend or Prussianism) and had drawn his conclusions. Indeed, Iwand stood out as one German theologian who had taken pains to acquaint himself critically with the course of German history and its consequences, both for theology and for the church. This must be regarded as highly significant because, as we have seen, most German intellectuals, especially the theologians and historians, had appropriated the Lutheran-Hegelian-Prussian image of German history as paradigmatic. This, arguably, proved to be the major obstacle preventing Germans in the nineteenth and twentieth centuries from embracing a parliamentary democracy. Such a form of government, they were convinced, was culturally alien and therefore irrelevant to German cultural-political life.

Consequently, a theologian as perceptive as Hans-Joachim Iwand felt called, like Karl Barth and Martin Niemöller, to advance a rational explanation for what had overtaken Germany, especially since 1933. He was automatically driven to search out the historical roots of Prusso-Germany's antidemocratic, imperialistic, and racist political culture. So, his draft for the Darmstadt Statement was an indictment of the course of German history, indeed, a negative version of the *Sonderweg* thesis. And in this respect the Darmstadt Statement distinguishes itself radically from the Stuttgart Declaration of Guilt. The latter had been based on easily recognizable ideological assumptions that derived from Luther and Hegel. The former was based on a liberal, pragmatic, and critical reception of Prusso-German history, evincing a preparedness to see its evolution detached from the traditional Lutheran-Hegelian paradigm. In this regard, Iwand's comprehension of the problems of church-state relations in the Bismarckian-Wilhelmine Reich and after, parallels Bonhoeffer's assessment in the draft of a Confession of Guilt in the *Ethics* manuscript.

As Hartmut Ludwig reports, Iwand had, after 1945, not only reinvestigated Prusso-German history in the nineteenth century, he had, significantly, also engaged in discussion with the Social Democrat and former Prussian minister of culture, Adolf Grimme, before he drafted the text of the Darmstadt Statement.[27] Indeed, Iwand wanted to revise what Hartmut Ludwig called "the perverted national consciousness."[28]

In his draft proposals on how this should be done, Iwand identified three issues: first, the false path of nationalism; secondly, the false path of political-social conservatism, which was primarily concerned to maintain existing power relationships and thereby hindered all efforts at urgently required social reform (and here the church had placed itself in the service of those in power in exchange for the "mess of pottage" of keeping its status in society); and thirdly, the false path of hubris, namely, the moral overevaluation of its own, and the denigration of all other—especially foreign—ways of understanding the world.

Of course, all these false paths could in the future be changed for the better if, in the first instance, the Germans would mobilize their undoubted spiritual-intellectual resources and, instead of harboring resentments, collaborate with other nations for the common task of reconstruction. In the second instance, the Germans could contribute to reconstructing society to guarantee all classes their autonomy and freedom. And the third false path could be changed if the Germans would finally accept that they had transformed the free offer of God's grace to all humanity into the complacent belief that God had chosen them for a special destiny. This belief, clearly the consequence of the aforementioned Hegelianism and neo-Rankeanism, inevitably cast other nations into the role of enemy states; it caused Germans to see the world in terms of the just and the unjust, the good and the bad, "them and us."

In the immediate postwar period, Iwand was at pains to reeducate his fellow countrymen along these lines, and in doing so he had allotted to the church a special task. Indeed, he saw quite clearly that the forces that led to the catastrophe of National Socialism in 1933 were still latent after the collapse of 1945, and for these to be overcome the church had to liberate itself from involvement in the play of world forces and define a new path for Germany.[29]

In a word, what Iwand demanded was that the old established "historism" that overevaluated Prusso-German history needed to be discarded to enable Germany's rebirth for the good of the world at large. Not surprisingly, the same concerns also had gripped some German historians. It is important to note that the entire post-1945 period saw the historical profession in Germany engaged in precisely a parallel confrontation with the Lutheran-Hegelian-Prussian paradigm as the theologians.[30] It appeared that virtually all the German intellectual elite had become involved in a process called *Vergangenheitsbewältigung*, that is, "overcoming" or "coming to terms with" or "reassessing" the negative legacy of the past. And that meant, above all, to discard the baleful deterministic influence of historicism and to replace it with a more liberal, pluralistic understanding of Prusso-German history. This was essential for both a general renewal of broader intellectual life and the specifically Protestant theology that had been committed to the so-called union of throne and altar, an ultraconservative political stance, as well as a very anti-Judaistic theology and understanding of church history, as has been seen. There had to be, as it were, a lancing of the boil to eliminate the centuries of accumulated spiritual-intellectual poison.

And here it should be observed that the highly influential guild of German university history professors at their first postwar congress held in Munich 1949 had to confront the self-same issues. That congress has become famous, for it was the venue of a clash between the earlier-mentioned conservative Lutheran-Hegelian historian Gerhard Ritter from Freiburg and the liberal Hamburg historian Fritz Fischer. And it is interesting that both had been educated as pious Lutherans but each had reacted to the post-1945 situation in totally opposite ways. Ritter was adamant that the Lutheran-Hegelian-Rankean tradition of strong monarchical government was still best for Germany, even after Hitler, and he wanted to justify that in his address to the Munich congress. Indeed, he passionately argued that the reason Hitler was able to seize power in 1933 was that the old monarchical political culture had been supplanted in 1919 by the alien and chaotic parliamentary system of Weimar that enabled the rise of many undisciplined parties whose interminable bickering frustrated the formation of a strong government that could have vigorously addressed the serious economic and political problems that plagued post-1919 Germany. It was this virtually permanent political chaos that paved the way for the rise of the demagogic Hitler regime that advanced such draconic, inhumane, and ultimately insane solutions to the nation's problems.

Gerhard Ritter's assessment paralleled that of the conservative Lutherans—not surprisingly—whereas Fritz Fischer took the view that the basic cause of Germany's plight in 1945 was precisely the doctrinaire rejection of modern ideas about popular sovereignty and responsible parliamentary government that accompanied Prussia's rise to power and her success in unifying Germany with "blood and iron," as Bismarck actually did.[31] In the light of this it can be appreciated that educated people in Germany who reflected on the course of the nation's history could polarize along the line defended by Ritter on the one hand and that advanced by Fischer on the other, and this is still a feature of German intellectual life. But back in 1947 one did not have to be a university history professor to engage in such retrospection. As we have seen, theologians, especially, also made these reflections. They were challenged in a special way to come to terms with the violent German past, particularly as Lutheranism allocated to the uncontrolled "powers that be" such a key function in national life.

It is in this context that Iwand's Darmstadt Statement is to be understood. And, of course, it could not be expected to gain universal approval because most of the German bourgeoisie had been too deeply acculturated in the old paradigm to be able to discard it overnight. Iwand's formulation, edited, indeed watered down, by his peers, was certainly not as forthright as it could have been; but even in its final form it was clear enough: the course of Prusso-German history had been disastrous for Germany, Europe, and the world in general. This had to offend conservative church leaders such as Otto Dibelius, Theophil Wurm, Hanns Lilje (all bishops), and the already quoted Hans Asmussen. As well, theologians such as Helmut Thielicke and Walter Künneth were deeply affronted by it.[32] Despite this, however, and despite the failure of the official church to endorse it, the Darmstadt Statement has won its place in the history of the German church, just as Dietrich Bonhoeffer has. As well, it was nothing short of a milestone on the way to the normalization of relations with the ecumenical movement and the West in general. As Heinz Eduard Tödt observed, it was a most perceptive theological analysis of the German *Sonderweg*,[33] and, one could add, a penetrating critique.

As well, the Heidelberg church historian Gerhard Besier has made some incisive comments about the reception of the Darmstadt Statement.[34] He confirms the above observations regarding the conservative Lutheran reservations and expresses dismay about that, but he also documents very carefully how the East German church leadership welcomed and endorsed its sentiments as being most opportune for the rebuilding of the church under communism. It comes as no surprise that Darmstadt was positively received in East Germany under bishop Albrecht Schönherr, a former student of Bonhoeffer, at the 1970 Synod of the Federation of Evangelical Churches, as it served to focus the church people on a new role for Christians in their struggle to maintain their identity within the "second German dictatorship." Indeed, Schönherr stated, "It is against the background of such sentiment [as expressed in the Darmstadt Statement] that we see the commission for the church in the GDR."[35]

The Darmstadt Declaration

The first of its seven propositions accused the church of refusing to listen to the word of God, chiefly that of reconciliation with the world, and concedes that the church had incurred guilt, both in the past and in the present. The failure to follow loyally the Good Shepherd had led to false and evil ways in the pursuit of political goals and deeds. Here, of course, the continuity with the ideas of the Barmen Confession is clear, and that is attributable to the fact that none other than Karl Barth, who had been instrumental in formulating the Barmen statement, had prepared the decisive draft for Iwand for Darmstadt. And here it is significant that at Darmstadt in 1947, as at Barmen in 1934, no mention was made of the persecution of Jews.[36]

Back in 1934, Karl Barth had to accept that a mention of Nazi Jewish policy would not have been allowed since at that time most German theologians were still committed to the position, overthrown by Bonhoeffer, that the Jews had incurred the wrath of God and hence deserved what had happened to them. Obviously, neither Barth, Niemöller (by 1945 at the latest), or Iwand shared this view. So the question is why was the Holocaust, now in 1947, not specifically mentioned? One can only speculate here. Obviously, the majority of Protestant pastors in 1947 were still of the view that, in the history of salvation, the synagogue had been replaced by the church, as was assumed by the learned formulators of the Freiburg Memorandum. Given this situation at the time, it is probably not surprising that Iwand and his colleagues had to be content with the more general confession of guilt and failure. As will be seen, the journey to a position approaching that of Dietrich Bonhoeffer as spelled out in *Ethics* would take considerably longer. Indeed, when *Ethics* first appeared in 1948 it was far from being greeted with enthusiasm by most pastors.

The second concern addressed in Darmstadt focused on the long-entrenched Prusso-German tradition of glorifying political power that "placed the nation on the throne of God." This clearly repudiated all previous imperial or war theology that had captured the hearts and minds of most German theologians in the nineteenth and twentieth centuries. A decisive refutation of that tradition and mind-set by the church in 1947 was essential for spiritual renewal. The unavoidable conclusion to be drawn from the second paragraph was that the course of German history, especially since Bismarck had become minister-president of Prussia in 1862, had led inexorably to the chain of disasters that overtook Germany from 1914–18 and 1933–45.

Not unexpectedly, this paragraph drew angry criticism from those who were as yet unable to admit the continuity of essentially brutal un-Christian politics from Kaiser Reich to Third Reich. To believe now, in 1947, that God had not been with the German people after all was to plunge conservatives into a state of "cognitive dissonance." Similarly, the third paragraph addressed the issue of the church's alliance with the ancient conservative antidemocratic forces in German history. And when it said "we have denied the right to revolution but approved a lawless dictatorship," it really threw down the gauntlet to those who venerated the tradition of benevolent despotism. Its representatives had always felt threatened by the growth of democratic movements in Germany, as Bismarck's long career as chancellor illustrated. He had been incessantly at pains to mobilize all conservative forces precisely in order to frustrate the transition to modern parliamentary government.

What this shows is that Iwand and his associates saw very clearly that the church, in order to be relevant to the new age, had to throw off its theologically derived predisposition to kow-tow to the "powers that be" (*Obrigkeit*), and to discard the theology that the rulers were "ordained by God" (Romans 13). In short, the church had to assess the political order according to the degree it served human rights and the dignity of individuals and peoples. The implication was clear: the church must cease to be the handmaid of the state and instead speak out critically on all issues affecting human freedoms. Indeed, the fourth proposition reaffirms this by criticizing the espousal of a world view that demonized the other, meaning putatively rival nations. The notion that one political ideology was absolutely right and the other incorrigibly evil was a grave error.

The fifth proposition observed that the church had been wrong to blindly attack the economic materialism of Marxism, and instead should have accepted the challenge that Marxism posed—namely, to address social inequalities—and realized that the church was obliged by its very calling to be on the side of the poor and underprivileged, as the gospel unequivocally taught. The sixth proposition confirmed that in recognizing this, the church should forget about the old notion of Christianity being identified with what was understood by "Western culture" and focus instead on the diaconal role of the church in the world at large.

The seventh and final proposition of the Darmstadt Statement was an appeal to the faithful not to despair but to trust in Christ, to abandon all nostalgia for a putatively better past, and not to be consumed by speculation about another war. Instead, the faithful were encouraged to work for the rebuilding of a better German state that prioritized justice and welfare for the sake of peace within the nation itself and the reconciliation of the nations abroad.

The fact that the Darmstadt Statement was never officially endorsed by the official church leadership (*Amtskirche*) simply confirms that old nationalist values die hard. Only those Germans who had been sensitized through an encounter with the posthumous Bonhoeffer, and theologians who comprehended and appreciated his legacy, would be likely to embrace the revisionist and forward-looking values of the Darmstadt Statement. Those who cultivated a nostalgia for the old Prusso-German paradigm would (and will) always be allergic to the radical honesty of Darmstadt and resist taking it on board. The statement was very perceptive indeed, in that it implied that for Germans to have any stable and peaceful future in Europe they would have to abandon the dangerous concept of Germany being the heartland of Christendom.

The fact that these outdated notions are still cultivated in some circles in Germany, post reunification, has been attested to by the Dutch historian Jan Herman Brinks and others who have drawn attention to the revival of nostalgia for an unencumbered German past that involves relativizing the memory of the Holocaust.[37] Brinks cites the startling example of the speech that the notable German author Martin Walser made at the Frankfurt Book Fair in 1998, where he received the Peace Prize of the German Book Trade. In his acceptance speech in the Paulskirche, Walser argued in front of an audience of 1,200 guests that Auschwitz and the Nazi past, "our everlasting shame," as he put it, were being instrumentalized for "current purposes." He described Auschwitz as a "moral bludgeon" (*Moralkeule*) used to chastise the Germans and prevent them from becoming a normal people living in a normal society.

Brinks observed that while the speech received a standing ovation, the chairman of Germany's Central Jewish Council, the late Ignaz Bubis, stated that Walser's arguments were nothing less than "intellectual arson" (*geistige Brandstiftung*). In fact, the complaint that Auschwitz was used morally to blackmail the German people had been the battle cry of the German Right for many years.[38]

The overriding concern of those Germans like Martin Walser was to show that destructive racism was not an exclusively German phenomenon. In doing so, these people wished to "normalize" the course of German history in a way that the authors of the Darmstadt Statement would find today impossible to endorse. And what is central to our present argument is that the case of Martin Walser at the Frankfurt Book Fair is not at all an isolated one. As Brinks reports, these views are widely supported by Germany's cultural, economic, and political elites and conservative politicians.[39]

Obviously, in a pluralistic society like the Federal Republic of Germany it is impossible to legislate how people should think about the past and its legacy to the present. It is, therefore, instructive to trace how Protestants in Germany have coped with the central issue of how to relate to Jews since 1945. One needs to know how in fact the Holocaust has impacted on the consciousness of Christians. In a real sense Dietrich Bonhoeffer in *Ethics* provided the benchmark for the future of both theology and politics in his fatherland, but it took some time before Bonhoeffer's insights were internalized—and then, obviously, only by a section of society. Indeed, the overwhelming majority of Germans at the time (1933–45) acquiesced in the Nazi agenda. As Alexander and

Margarete Mitscherlich in their celebrated study on the question remarked:

> Though Adolf Hitler's function can certainly be understood on an individual level, he demanded nothing in which millions were not willing to follow him; not unlike Faust, he carried sadism and sentimentality, xenophobia and the deification of the ego-ideal as the master race, to extremes of barbarity. In terms of the psychic processes involved, what took place here was a breakthrough of innumerable gradations of aggressivity against objects that had been declared fair game. Such is the success of "conscience turned upside down": the Führer personifies a new conscience. Only his failure, not the old conscience, helps guilt feelings to break through.[40]

Here is another example of how perceptive Bonhoeffer had been in his essay "After Ten years." Most Germans, including the *Bildungsbürgertum*, had allowed themselves to be seduced by the evil that came in many guises. And while the Führer was successful, very few had the moral courage to protest. Only when Hitler failed did guilt feelings return. One had to be an autonomous *Bildungsbürger* with a conscience informed by the gospel to be able to resist the seduction of Hitler's undoubtedly persuasive powers, and such people were very few, as has been seen.

It was already clear to most German Protestant theologians, and not only to them, that they had a problem with the Holocaust, namely, how to account for their failure to protest against Nazi racial policy. And here we have a classic example of resistance to "paradigm change." If, for centuries, the church had been operating on the assumption that *Ecclesia* had superseded *Synagogia* in the history of salvation, then it was only to be expected that there would be a certain amount of resistance to revising that paradigm. This is apparent in the "Message Concerning the Jewish Question" issued by the Council of Brethren of the Evangelical Church at Darmstadt 8 April 1948. These men were largely Bonhoeffer's men, members of the Confessing Church, but they agonized at length over the issue of how, in the immediate post Holocaust era, they were to assess the massive atrocity perpetrated upon God's chosen people. There is no possible doubt that these men were genuinely at pains to find out what had led them into false paths, partly because they believed that it was God's judgment that Germany had been so severely defeated and was suffering unimaginable privations as a consequence of Nazi policy toward European Jewry.

What is interesting about the 1948 statement of the Council of Brethren is that the old "substitution theology" is still dominant in their thinking. The church is reproached only for not having shown the appropriate patience toward the Jews. It said that "Israel under the judgment is the ceaseless confirmation of the truth, the reality of God's Word, and God's constant warning to His church. The fate of the Jews is a silent sermon, reminding us that God will not allow Himself to be mocked. It is a warning to us, and an admonition to the Jews to be converted to him, who is their sole hope of salvation."[41]

In this regard, the 1948 statement evinced no progress in thinking from the Freiburg Memorandum. Indeed, how could it? The Jew was at best an erring brother, but it was added that it was not permissible for the church to regard the Jewish question as a racial or national problem and let that determine its attitude toward the Jews, collectively or individually. And here it needs to be recalled that this was Bonhoeffer's position back in his 1933 statement, "The Church and the Jewish Question." There he made clear that it was wrong for the state to maltreat any citizens on the grounds of race or religion. And as we have seen, Bonhoeffer read the signs of the times differently from the majority of his coreligionists. The church in 1948 was still in catch-up mode. It was conceded, though, that:

> It was a disastrous mistake when the church of our time adopted the secular attitude of mere humanity, emancipation and anti-Semitism towards the Jewish question. There was bound to be a bitter retribution for the fact that anti-Semitism rose and flourished not only among the people (who still seemed to be a Christian nation), and not only among the intelligentsia, and in government and military circles, but also among Christian leaders. And finally when this radical anti-Semitism, based on racial hatred, destroyed our nation and our church from within, and released all its brutal force from without, there existed no power to resist it—because the churches had forgotten what Israel really is, and no longer loved the Jews. Christian circles washed their hands of all responsibility, justifying themselves by saying there was a curse on the Jewish people. Christians no longer believed that the promises concerning the Jews still held good; they no longer preached it, nor showed it in their attitude towards the Jews. In this way, we Christians helped to bring about all the injustices and suffering upon the Jews in our country.[42]

Here indeed was a confession of guilt, more frank than anything previously, but still far short of Bonhoeffer's benchmark in *Ethics*. Essentially, still, Jews had to be converted and baptized in order to be saved; but this issue would not go away; German Protestant theologians continued to be exercised by the Jewish question in the light of the Holocaust. Indeed, by 1949 *Ethics* had been finally published. The very next year the Synod of the Evangelical Church in Germany, held in Berlin-Weissensee on 27 April 1950, produced a breakthrough "Statement on the Jewish Question." Clearly a definite learning process had taken place, for it was stated unequivocally that "We believe God's promise to be valid for his Chosen People even after the crucifixion of Jesus Christ."⁴³ As Matthew Hockenos has pointed out,

> The Berlin-Weissensee synod's rejection of supersessionism was unprecedented and momentous. Although church leaders never explicitly tied the church's anti-Judaism to the Holocaust, they rejected the central tenet of Christian anti-Judaism and brought about a sea change in German Protestant theology. The unanimous acceptance of the Berlin-Weissensee statement by the synod brought to an end the church's shameful silence on the "Jewish question."⁴⁴

It is, of course, acknowledged that the confirmation of a causal connection between the reception of Bonhoeffer's thought and the church's increasing readiness to engage with the "Jewish question" on a completely new basis would require an investigation of the formation of all the participating theologians. The fact is, however, that Bonhoeffer's findings were known to sufficient numbers of his surviving colleagues to make it impossible for them to ignore them in their deliberations. On the other hand, it was possible that the more repentant and liberal-minded theologians were able to arrive at the same conclusions as Bonhoeffer without necessarily having consulted *Ethics*, a fact that speaks for their newfound openness. Of course, it was a different matter for the vast majority of parish pastors and their congregations. "Reception" of different ways of thinking and new theological values is a process that is inevitably slow among Christian congregations of all denominations. There will always be resistance to abandoning beliefs that were once held to be written in stone, and to adopting new ones that contradict the old. In short, a "paradigm change" was being required, and people, having been conditioned for decades to thinking in certain patterns, obviously needed time to readjust to new information and methodologies.⁴⁵

The key issue in the mind of conservative Protestants was having to revise the former dominant attitude toward Jews, specifically, the requirement that they be baptized in order to be "saved." This was, of course, the essential justification for a mission to the Jews. How, indeed, could it be otherwise, given the command of the risen Jesus to the disciples in Matthew 28:19–20, "Go, therefore and make disciples of all nations, baptizing them in the name of the Father and of the Son and of the Holy Spirit"?⁴⁶ As we have seen, Bonhoeffer had long since developed a theological rationale that revised this command, certainly with regard to the Jews. So it was against considerable resistance that the Protestant church leadership persisted, reluctant to revise the centuries-old established anti-Judaistic theology. Change was slow to come.

Finally, sixteen years after the end of the war, German Protestants showed a readiness frankly to address the "Jewish question" at the tenth synod of the Evangelical Church held in Berlin in 1961. The intention to do so was announced at the ninth Protestant Church rally in Munich two years earlier when an Arab-Israeli evening session was held that attracted a surprisingly large audience, especially of young people. The theme was the relationship between Germans, Christians, and Jews, and a collection was taken up for funds to restore a synagogue that had been destroyed in the infamous pogrom of *Reichskristallnacht* in November 1938. People indicated that this was a subject of deep concern to many. Clearly, sufficient time had elapsed since the end of the war when the details of the Holocaust started to become public knowledge for at least Christian Germans openly to discuss what had happened and to display their "ability to mourn."[47] This moved the organizers of the Church Rally to set up a working group to investigate the relationship between Christians and Jews, and place this on the agenda of the tenth Church Rally scheduled for 20–22 July 1961, in Berlin. The committee responsible for this was called the Arbeitsgruppenleitung (AGL), and it was very worried whether the sessions planned would attract many participants. On the other hand, it was felt that not to go ahead with it in the light of the trial of former Obergruppenführer Adolf Eichmann, taking place in Jerusalem at that very time, would be inappropriate. One had to grasp the hot iron and not be seen to avoid confrontation with an issue that affected all living Germans. In addition, it was recognized that more and more Protestant Germans were becoming increasingly aware that traditional attitudes and behavior toward Jews were in dire need of theological revision.

Consequently, a group of German Protestants consisting of people who had either come to the aid of Jews during the period of Nazi persecution or who had subsequently begun to reflect on the correct relationship between Jews and Christians, was assembled. These, however, soon realized that for their deliberations to be meaningful they would have to include German Jews in the proceedings and listen to what they had to say. In short, there had to occur a dialogue of equal partners; a one-sided discussion among Christians, no matter how penitent they were for the crimes committed against the Jews, would not suffice. The voice of the other had to be heard and responded to. And so it happened: for the first time in the history of the Christian church since New Testament times, with the exception of the hostile disputations of the Middle Ages, a meeting of reconciliation between Jews and Christians took place. In an atmosphere of benign hospitality, a rabbi was invited to explain to Christians the self-perception of Judaism. Christians were enabled in a spirit of penitence to acknowledge their co-responsibility for the frightful sufferings of Jews throughout the centuries, and especially in the twentieth century, at the hands of Germans, who either actively prosecuted the Holocaust or passively allowed it to happen. It was nothing less than the epochal beginning of a long overdue learning process in which Christians and Jews are still engaged.

Indeed, the great concern of the organizers was just how the initiative that was grasped at that time in Berlin could be accelerated into the future. The central question, apart from the practical issue of compensation, was how should Christians, with their roots in the New Testament, understand the historical-theological commonality between church and synagogue alongside the undeniable differences? First and foremost, the discussions served to isolate the divisive issues, to understand how the church with its anti-Judaism through the centuries contributed to the rise of anti-Semitism, and how this could be overcome and a new, fully humane attitude toward Jews be established. In short, one had to focus on the question how God's Covenant with the Jews—the Old Covenant—could be reconciled with the New Covenant on which the Christian church stood. And here the breakthrough in the discussion came with the acceptance by the Christians that in contrast to what they previously believed about the Old Covenant having been superseded by the New Covenant, the Old could never have been dissolved. As we have seen, this is the insight already achieved in the early 1940s by Dietrich Bonhoeffer.

The conclusion of the deliberations in Berlin at that time was that the God of history had established a special relationship with the Jews that had significance for all humanity. Indeed, God had established an eternal Covenant with Israel that was not dissolved on Calvary but rather, as the prophets proclaimed, extended to the gentiles. The New Covenant grew out of the Old. But in reality there was only one Covenant that has not been dissolved, specifically, that in which God had united both Israel and the nations of the earth together. And this is not affected by the fact that Jews and Christians comprehend the Covenant differently.[48]

When these findings were made public, there was not by any means universal endorsement by German Protestants. In fact, there was an outcry in sections of the Protestant press that the above accords amounted to a sell-out of the entire history of the church.[49] Indeed, what the subsequent discussion among protestant Germans revealed was a gulf between those on the one hand who were obviously inwardly devastated by the Holocaust, acknowledged the church's co-responsibility, were sincerely penitent, and were eager to initiate a healing dialogue with Jews; while on the other hand there were still those who, while conceding that the Holocaust was a crime, were unable to overcome their belief in a theology of supersessionism, and consequently, as previously, still demanded that the only way for Christian-Jewish reconciliation was for Jews to accept baptism.

A key example of the latter position was the article by the high-profile, already mentioned (chapter 7), Lutheran church leader (Probst or Provost) Hans Asmussen in the church newspaper *Christ und Welt* of 13 August 1965, entitled "The Guilt of the Jews." Essentially, Asmussen, while acknowledging that human beings (he meant the Nazi regime) had no right to persecute the Jews (only God had the right to punish His erring children) and that, therefore, the Holocaust should not have happened, it was still necessary to convert the Jews. In short, Asmussen held firm to the belief that the Old Covenant had been indisputably superceded by the New, and that as a consequence, Jews had been abandoned by almighty God. There was no doubt whatsoever in Asmussen's mind that the Jews were guilty for the execution of Jesus. He stated:

> Of course, the guilt for Christ's death cannot be used to justify any acts of punishment against Israel. If that were the case it would be a serious injustice. That said, however, I have reservations concerning the arguments by Jews and their friends that it was solely or chiefly Christian teaching that caused the persecution of the Jews. Indeed, in all sobriety one has not only to speak of Christian hatred towards the Jews but also of Jewish hatred towards Christians as such. The fact that today the Jews are mostly liberalized can easily obscure this state of affairs. The hatred of Christians by Jews is already present in the "Acts of the Apostles." But since the victory of Christianity under the Emperor Constantine it became less evident. That is understandable. But it is still alive. Various reports from the Israel of today show that very clearly. One should not attempt to gloss over that.[50]

Not surprisingly, this statement by such a leading German Lutheran drew an energetic response both from the Jewish side as well as from fellow Lutherans who were coming to see the course of German history more and more, as it were, through the eyes of Dietrich Bonhoeffer. For these Lutherans, Asmussen's statement was a painful embarrassment indicating a virtual inability to learn from history. It was time to abandon the old theology of supersessionism and to replace it with one of compassion and freedom.[51] A Jewish writer, Michael Stone, took Asmussen severely to task by querying his capacity to understand history. For Stone, the crucifixion of Jesus had been the joint responsibility of a corrupt Jewish leadership in a country occupied by the Roman imperial power and had been carried out in order to nip a possible rebellion in the bud. So, asked Stone, how can today, two thousand years after the event, an entire nation be still held responsible?[52]

The decade of the 1960s in Germany, and indeed elsewhere such as in the Vatican, was a period when ancient attitudes toward the Jews were subjected to radical revision. For example, the "Catholic News Service" announced on 28 October 1965, the statement of the Second Vatican Council concerning non-Christian religions. This took the view that the guilt of the Jewish authorities for the crucifixion could not be burdened upon Jews today. In this way Rome, too, revised two thousand years of history.[53] And, as for Rome, so it continued to be for the German Lutherans, though, of course once the Vatican pronounces on an issue that statement becomes the official Roman position. No national conference of Roman Catholic bishops, for example, could overturn such a statement that would henceforth be binding on all the faithful in every land. For the Lutherans it is somewhat different. Their synods may debate issues and pronounce upon them, but whether they are binding in the Roman Catholic sense is another matter. One may, however, speak of consensus. In the meantime, individual theologians might give learned papers and publish their findings in a situation of open discourse. For example, the Lutheran professor Günther Harder published his theological insights into the consequences of the historic separation of the church from the synagogue in ten so-called theses. Reflecting on the stage of the Christian-Jewish dialogue up to that time (1964) he reported as follows:

1) It is both to be welcomed and wished for that responsible discussions take place between Jews and Christians.
2) Such discussions emerge out of a common sense of responsibility in questions of social and political life.
3) They presume there is a common basis for the religious life in and judgment of the world as well as a mutual recognition of the faith in the one true and living God.
4) They serve the improvement of knowledge of each other and the deepening of mutual recognition of the solidarity between Christians and Jews in a community of hope and service.
5) Those who conduct these discussions may be either individuals or institutes that exist for the deepening of understanding of Judaism.
6) These discussions do not signify any kind of dilution of religious positions and certainly no abandonment of the specifically Christian witness that within the framework of these discussions must, where ever necessary, be given.
7) These discussions do not presume that either side abandon their particular belief in that way of God's salvation to which they confess.
8) Indeed, as in primitive times the Christian church may not cease to praise the name of Christ and to offer baptism to Jews who sincerely seek it, and to seal it in Christ's name.

9) On the other hand Christians respect the standpoint of Jews who do not acknowledge Jesus as their Messiah, as a separate way of divine decision and do not attempt by means of special missionary enterprises and institutions to anticipate what God intends in His own good time.
10) In particular, Christians refrain from engaging in the frivolous proselytizing of new members, either among Jews or gentiles, using superficial means, without the winning of inner conviction.[54]

Here professor Harder had concisely summed up what might best be termed the progressive Lutheran position. It certainly contrasted dramatically with that of Probst Asmussen discussed above. And so it remained the task of future Protestant synods in Germany to arrive at a consensus on these lines. And by 1980 this happened. The Synod of the Evangelical Church of the Rhineland of that year issued a statement, "Towards the Renovation of the Relationship of Christians and Jews," that accomplished this and more.[55] The statement came as the result of high level interfaith deliberations between Christians and Jews on the issue whether there should be continued missionizing of the Jews or simply ongoing dialogue, as it were between equals, something that Bonhoeffer had foreshadowed.

The Rhineland Synod accepted without reservation a co-responsibility for the Holocaust and thereby made an unequivocal confession of guilt that was followed up by theological statements that emphasized the common roots of the church and the synagogue. Indeed, in contrast to previous theological assertions to the contrary, now the unbreakable connection of the New Testament with the Old Testament was affirmed. In fact, the old supersessionist theology was expressly declared to be false, and the conclusion was drawn that Christians and Jews had a joint task to witness and to proclaim the same creator God under whose blessing both Jews and Christians were meant to live and work for justice and peace in the world.[56] Hannah Holtschneider commented on this by observing that the Rhineland Synod succeeded in paving the way for other member churches of the EKD to formulate their own theological statements. Thereby, the Rhineland statement initiated an era of Jewish learning at church institutions in an effort to stress the need for Christian-Jewish conversations with a view to better mutual understanding.[57] Consequently, for the official church at least, the era of anti-Judaisim and anti-Semitism has been finally consigned to the dung heap of past errors, and a new era of Christian-Jewish relations has been ushered in. The question remaining is how wide and deep has been the reception of these momentous developments in the broader community? Certainly, the World Council of Churches, internationally, stands behind the resolutions of the Rhineland synod.[58]

Since Bonhoeffer arrived at his insights in the midst of war and the persecution of European Jewry a learning process has occurred, especially among Christian theologians, and this has spawned a vast literature that ensures that there can be no harking back to old attitudes and values. Christian theology has moved on, and Dietrich Bonhoeffer may be credited with having been arguably the first to identify what the issues were (in "After Ten Years," for example) that the German nation needed to address in order to become not only reintegrated, as far as the church was concerned, in the ecumenical movement, but also into the comity of liberal, democratic states. Seen in this light Bonhoeffer was at the very least a perceptive instigator of an epoch-making development in world history.[59]

Notes

1. Jürgen Seidel, "Der Umgang mit der Schuld nach dem Ende des 2. Weltkrieges im ökumenischen Kontext," seventh Berliner Staat-Kirche Kolloquium, 25–27 May 1998, Schriftenreihe des Instituts für vergleichende Staats-Kirche-Forschung, no. 7, 41, 48–49.

2. Ibid., 42.

3. Eberhard Bethge, *Bonhoeffer: Exile and Martyr* (London, 1975), 159–60. Bethge was appalled by those conservative Lutherans who refused to see Bonhoeffer's execution as a martyrdom of one who stood up for the truth of the gospel, but who only grudgingly concede that he may have been a "political" martyr. See also Craig J. Slane, *Bonhoeffer as Martyr* (Grand Rapids, 2004), 29–34.

4. For an excellent example of a positive German assessment of Bonhoeffer, see Renate Wind, *A Spoke in the Wheel: The Life of Dietrich Bonhoeffer* (London, 1991). This is a translation of *Dem Rad in die Speichen fallen* (Weinheim and Basel, 1990). Positive "Bonhoeffer reception" books continue to appear so that the German-reading public has ample opportunity to be informed as to his historical-theological significance. A more recent and excellent example is Christian Gremmels and Heinrich W. Grosse, *Dietrich Bonhoeffer: Der Weg in den Widerstand.* (Gütersloh, 1996).

5. Stephen R. Haynes, *The Bonhoeffer Legacy: Post-Holocaust Perspectives*, 31–45. Here the author challenges Eberhard Bethge's claim that Bonhoeffer in his *Ethics* manuscript achieved a breakthrough for a revised theology of Christian-Jewish relations after the Holocaust. See Bethge, "Dietrich Bonhoeffer and the Jews," 81, and also the discussion on this theme in chapter 7.

6. It is significant that the Lutheran Bishop of Berlin-Brandenburg Otto Dibelius had, in 1959, composed a reflection on what constituted lawful authority entitled *Obrigkeit* (Stuttgart, 1963) sparked by the capricious behavior of the GDR government, especially toward the church. Totalitarian states, either

fascist or communist, did not constitute "lawful authority" as understood by St Paul's Epistle to the Romans, chapter 13, i.e., they were not *Obrigkeit* and as such posed an existential problem for the church.

7. Cited after Jürgen Seidel, "Der Umgang mit Schuld," 39–40.
8. Ibid., 40.
9. Ibid., 41.
10. Matthew Hockenos, *A Church Divided: German Protestants confront the Nazi Past* (Bloomington and Indianapolis, 2004), 64.
11. Seidel, "Der Umgang mit der Schuld," 38.
12. Hockenos, *A Church Divided*, 181.
13. See chapter 8.
14. Barth did this in a series of lectures he held in his homeland of Switzerland in January-February 1945 entitled, "The Germans and Ourselves." See Hockenos, *A Church Divided*, 57
15. Cited in Hockenos, *A Church Divided*, 184.
16. Ibid., 185.
17. In *Letters and Papers from Prison*,16.
18. Hockenos, *A Church Divided*, 62.
19. Ibid., 72–73. See Bonhoeffer, *The Cost of Discipleship*, 259–60.
20. Seidel, "Der Umgang mit der Schuld," 44; cf. W.A. Visser 't Hooft, *Memoirs* (London, 1973), chapters 27 and 28.
21. Hockenos, *A Church Divided*, 77.
22. This is the view also of Johannes Willms, *Bismarck, Dämon der Deutschen: Anmerkungen zu einer Legende* (Berlin, 1997).
23. Hockenos, *A Church Divided*, 187. For a devastating critique of the Stuttgart Declaration of Guilt because of its mixture of truth, half-truth, and straight-out obfuscation, see Hans Prolingheuer, *Wir sind in die Irre gegangen* (Cologne, 1987), 92–105.
24. Hannah Arendt, *Eichmann in Jerusalem: A Report on the Banality of Evil* (New York: Penguin Books, 1964), 18.
25. Hockenos, *A Church Divided*, 121.
26. Hartmut Ludwig, "Entstehung, Wirkung und Aktualität des Darmstädter Wortes," in *In die Irre Gegangen? Das Darmstädter Wort in Geschichte und Gegenwart*, Schriftenreihe des Instituts für vergleichende Staat-Kirche-Forschung, no. 4 (1997), 10.
27. Ibid., 11. Note that Social Democrats had always been marginalized in the Bismarckian-Wilhelmine Empire as "die vaterlandslosen Gesellen," i.e., vagabonds without a fatherland. This is because they espoused a form of socialism, and in general republicanism, that set them at odds with the bourgeoisie and upper classes. They clearly did not endorse the glorification of the Hohenzollern dynasty that leading Prusso-German historians practiced at the time in German universities, and made no secret of the fact. The conservative classes thus feared and hated the German labor movement. See Carsten, *August Bebel*.
28. Ibid., 12. Cf. Prolingheuer, *Wir sind in die Irre gegangen*, 173–240. Here the author critically examines the history of the composition of the Darmstadt Statement and its reception in considerable detail.
29. Ibid., 13. For a full documentation on the background to and formulation of the Darmstadt Declaration, see Hartmut Ludwig, ed., "*Wir haben die*

christliche Freiheit verraten": Das Wort des Bruderrates der EKD zum politischen Weg unseres Volkes (1947). Eine Dokumentation. (Leipzig, 1997).

30. Most informative on this subject has been the pioneering work of Georg G. Iggers, *The German Conception of History* (Middletown, Conn., 1968). Since the appearance of this work, Professor Iggers has maintained a close scrutiny of developments in the German historical profession in numerous publications and must be regarded as the foremost authority on this aspect of modern German intellectual history.

31. See Fritz Fischer, "Der deutsche Protestantismus und die Politik im 19. Jahrhundert," *Historische Zeitschrift*, no. 171 (1951): 473–518 and Gerhard Ritter, "Deutsche Geschichtswissenschaft im 20. Jahrhundert," *Geschichte in Wissenschaft und Unterricht* 1 (1950): 129–37, for their contrary views.

32. Hockenos. *A Church Divided*, 115–17; 130–34. Hockenos examines very carefully the mentality of those leading conservative German theologians who essentially refused to concede any guilt or co-responsibility on their part for the catastrophe. These were the ones still imprisoned in the mind-set of Lutheran-Hegelian-Rankean historism.

33. Heinz Eduard Tödt, *Komplizen, Opfer und Gegner des Hitlerregimes: Zur inneren Geschichte von protestantischer Theologie und Kirche im "Dritten Reich"* (Gütersloh, 1997), 396.

34. Gerhard Besier, *Der SED-Staat und der Weg in die Anpassung* (Munich, 1993), 38–52.

35. Cf. Hans Prolingheuer. *Wir sind in die Irre gegangen*, 213–14.

36. Ludwig, "Entstehung, Wirkung und Aktualität des Darmstädter Wortes," 13–15.

37. A. Dirk Moses, "The Non-German German and the German German: Dilemmas of Identity after the Holocaust," *New German Critique*, no. 101 (Summer 2007): 45–94. This theme is examined in greater detail in A. Dirk Moses, *German Intellectuals and the Nazi Past*. (Cambridge/New York, 2007).

38. Jan Herman Brinks, "Germany's New Right," in *Nationalist Myths and Modern Media; Contested Identities in the Age of Globalization*, ed. Jan Herman Brinks, Stella Rock, and Edward Timms (London/New York, 2006), 134.

39. Ibid., 134–35. Here Brinks cites the case of the CDU politician Martin Hohmann, who in a speech on German Unity Day, 3 October 2003, argued that the Jews themselves could just as well be regarded as a "people of perpetrators" (Tätervolk) because in the first phase of the Russian Revolution in which many millions of people were massacred, Jews had been involved on the Bolshevik side. It is true that Hohmann was subsequently expelled from the party, but it became clear that a considerable number of Germans, both within and outside of the CDU, supported these so-called new right views.

40. The benchmark study on this problem is by Alexander and Margarete Mitcherlich, *The Inability to Mourn: Principles of Collective Behavior* (New York, 1975), 19.

41. Cited in from the English-language translation in Hockenos, *A Church Divided*, 196.

42. Ibid.

43. Ibid., 199.

44. Ibid., 170.

45. Siegfried Hermle, *Evangelische Kirche und Judentum: Stationen nach 1945* (Göttingen, 1990). See herein, the section, "Die 'Judenfrage' in kirchlichen Erklärungen," for the evolution of changed attitudes and theologies.

46. The force of this statement is revealed by quoting the surrounding verses that come right at the very end of Matthew's gospel, chapter 28, verses 18 to 20: "And Jesus came and said to them, 'All authority in heaven and on earth has been given to me. Go therefore and make disciples of all nations, baptizing them in the name of the Father and of the Son and of the Holy Spirit, teaching them to observe all that I have commanded you; and lo, I am with you always, to the close of the age'" (RSV).

47. Dietrich Goldschmidt and Hans-Joachim Kraus, ed., *Der ungekündigte Bund: Neue Begegnung von Juden und christlicher Gemeinde* (Stuttgart, 1962), 9.

48. Ibid., 14–15.

49. Ibid., 161–82. See also the commentary to the 1961 Kirchentag by Karl Kupisch, *Durch den Zaun der Geschichte* (Berlin, 1964), 371–406.

50. Helmut Gollwitzer and Eleonore Sterling, ed., *Das gespaltene Gottesvolk* (Stuttgart/Berlin, 1966), 204–205.

51. Ibid., 208.

52. Ibid., 121.

53. Ibid., 216–17.

54. Ibid., 283.

55. Karl Heinrich Rengstorf, "Begegnung statt Bekehrung: Welchen Sinn kann das jüdisch-christliche Gespräch für Christen haben?" in *Juden, Christen, Deutsche*, ed. Hans-Jürgen Schultz (Stuttgart, 1961) 265–69. For an authoritative overview of how the German churches (Roman as well as Protestant) post-1945 revised their attitudes to the Jewish question, see John S. Conway, "Changes in Christian-Jewish Relations since the Holocaust," in *Contemporary Responses to the Holocaust*, ed. Konrad Kwiet and Jürgen Matthias (Westport, Conn./ London, 2004), 61–85.

56. English text at: http:// www.coe.org/wcc/what/interreligious/cd32–04.html. "The people of Israel and the mission of the church: A study document of the Evangelical Church in the Rhineland." Cf. Hockenos, *A Church Divided*. 155.

57. K. Hannah Holtschneider, *German Protestants Remember the Holocaust: Theology and the Construction of Collective Memory* (Münster, 2000) 195.

58. Hockenos, *A Church Divided*. 155. The dialogue between church and synagogue continues as between two equally "covenanted" peoples of God.

59. A comprehensive bibliography of works on this subject would exceed the space available for this study, but see the following summary of Christian-Jewish relations since the end of the Second world War: *Church and Israel: A contribution from the Reformation Churches in Europe to the Relationship between Christians and Jew*, mandated by the Executive Committee of the Leuenberg Church Fellowship, edited by Helmut Schwier (Frankfurt/Main, 2001).

Epilogue

BONHOEFFER RECEPTION IN POSTWAR GERMANY

It has been already indicated that it took some considerable time after the end of the Second World War for Bonhoeffer's significance both as a theologian and an opponent of National Socialism to be recognized. Many pastors and theologians, not to mention church people generally, had difficulty in coming to a positive assessment of the young theologian's thought and action. Few were able to assess Bonhoeffer as a martyr for the gospel or, indeed, as a heroic political reformer. Indeed, the West German legal system took decades, as we have seen, to clear Bonhoeffer's name of the charge of treason precisely because he had conspired to overthrow the putatively legal government of Nazi Germany.

All this hesitation on the part of those Germans who were still unable to throw off deeply entrenched habits of mind was and remains a matter of some puzzlement to Anglo-Saxons who have been educated in a political culture that admires those who have had the courage to stand up against all forms of tyranny. The differences between the two ways of thinking about this has been documented by the fact that 1) a memorial service relatively soon after his execution was held in London (27 July 1945, in Holy Trinity Church, Kingsway); 2) the date of the execution, 9 April, is listed in the Anglican Church calendar as a feast day for a martyr; and 3) Bonhoeffer's statue along with nine other twentieth-century martyrs of various nationalities and Christian confessions currently adorns the façade of Westminster Abbey in London. What this makes clear is that Lutheran-Prussian culture had bequeathed to Germans a set of political values that was largely inflexible when it came to resistance against or criticism of state authority. The Anglo-Saxon Whig tradition has always stood in stark contrast to the "divine right of kings" or princely absolutism as was held so long in Prusso-Germany.

German political culture post-1945 did eventually change quite dramatically under two irresistible foreign influences: the Anglo-Saxon parliamentary tradition in the Western part of the country, and the inflexible political ideology of Marxism-Leninism (or *real existierender Sozialismus*, as it was called) in the former East Germany. In each part of the former Reich with "rival social systems," as they were once described, Bonhoeffer's legacy was appreciated quite differently for reasons that will be made clear by surveying what happened in the parliamentary, pluralistic Federal Republic on the one hand and in the communist dictatorship, the German Democratic Republic (GDR), on the other.

Bonhoeffer Reception in West Germany

As indicated, the acceptance of Bonhoeffer's legacy in West Germany encountered difficulties from the beginning because of the deeply entrenched neo-Lutheran conservatism of many church leaders and of the legal profession. Clearly, Bonhoeffer was far too revolutionary a figure because his theology, as it developed, overthrew centuries of endemic anti-Judaism and simultaneously also challenged the accepted understanding of the sacrosanct status and function of the head of state as an authority answerable only to God for his decisions. The monarch functioned autonomously in a separate sphere or discrete realm, beholden to no human agency. As Bonhoeffer eloquently phrased it, there were not two spheres, a sacred and a secular, where the secular authority exerted power in the world uncontrolled by any moral law; there was only one sphere in which everything was subject to the sovereignty of God. Bonhoeffer had, in short, disposed of a centuries-old doctrine that had justified princely absolutism and had reached its most grotesque form under the dictatorship of Adolf Hitler.

In spite of this, however, many West Germans were still unwilling to abandon the old Lutheran-Hegelian way of thinking about state authority; nor were they willing to confront the past to gain an objective perspective on what had brought about the "German Catastrophe." Neither were the earlier-mentioned apologetic introspections of scholars such as Friedrich Meinecke and Gerhard Ritter sufficient to ignite the necessary moral courage among the educated bourgeoisie even to begin asking questions about the real reasons for the disaster that had overtaken Germany. People were psychologically averse to engaging in any degree of harrowing soul-searching, as the resentment encountered by the Stuttgart Declaration of Guilt attested when it was made public. At that time, church offices received unprecedented quantities of protest mail from indignant church people who, in their own view, were victims rather than collaborators with a criminal regime. Similarly, the Darmstadt Statement elicited deep resentment from high-profile churchmen who undoubtedly perceived themselves as *Bildungsbürger* of the superior rank. They were particularly incensed by "Darmstadt" precisely because of its indictment of the course of Prusso-German history. A graphic example of this came out of the mouth of the then Lutheran bishop of Lower Saxony, Hanns Lilje, at the 1965 synod of that church in Hannover. Lilje observed that the normal German male was inhibited from speaking of three things, these being the fate of the Jews, the failed assassination attempt on Hitler's life, on 20 July 1944, and the unconditional capitulation in 1945.[1]

The fact is that the immediate postwar situation in Germany was so traumatic for the defeated and humiliated nation that objective analysis was simply demanding too much for most people, living as they were for many years in cities smothered in mountains of rubble caused by the unprecedented ferocity of Allied bombing raids. The first priority under those conditions was existential security. Indeed, the earlier discussion regarding the resentment expressed by leading churchmen at the prospect of having to acknowledge the guilt or co-responsibility of the churches for Nazi atrocities confirms the "inability to mourn." This explains to some extent why Bonhoeffer's *Ethics* at its initial publication in 1948 failed to gain enthusiastic attention. Indeed, the "reluctant revolutionary" remained largely unknown until the publication in 1951 of the first edition of *Widerstand und Ergebung* by Eberhard Bethge.

Ulrich Kabitz claims that the appearance of this collection of fragments of Bonhoeffer's writing from Tegel prison, loyally assembled by his closest friend, had an "epochal effect"—presumably upon educated church people who found various sections, letters, and poems, spiritually edifying because they articulated what many must have felt at the time but were too intimidated to express.[2] Then, in the early 1950s, the first Bonhoeffer conferences took place—(Bethel, 1954; Berlin-Weissensee, 1955; and Weissensee again in 1959). The kind of lively discussions unfolding at that time were documented in the journal *Die mündige Welt*.[3]

At the same time, however, this positive evaluation of Bonhoeffer was still passionately opposed in conservative Lutherans in the West, who could not bring themselves to approve of his participation in the resistance movement. Apart from the aforementioned bishop Meiser's refusal in January 1952 to participate in the ceremony at the Flossenbürg parish church to install a memorial plaque to commemorate Bonhoeffer's execution, the Erlangen professor Walter Künneth also aligned himself with the incorrigible critics.[4]

Clearly, we have here to do with how the deeply entrenched values and attitudes of many people made them resist contemplating change. But the world political climate was inevitably going to exert its influence on the Germans of the Adenauer era. It was a time when the then prominent German political scientist Waldemar Besson at the University of

Erlangen, with acerbic realism, pointed out that the Federal Republic was really forced to "dance at three weddings simultaneously" (*auf drei Hochzeiten gleichzeitig tanzen*). By that he meant that the Adenauer government had to take account, firstly, of the pressure being exerted from Moscow with regard to formulating policy in the East; secondly, the pressure from Washington, meaning the obligation to conform to and endorse U.S. Cold War policy, which involved the much contested issue of military rearmament; and, thirdly, the pressure from Brussels, which was the headquarters of the European Economic Union to which the Federal Republic was irrevocably committed.[5] These were the dominant constraints of the time: West German security concerns within a Europe confronting the seemingly permanent menace of Soviet expansion, the domestic priority of industrial-economic reconstruction, and, finally, the need for reconciliation with former enemies, particularly France.

Chancellor Konrad Adenauer, aided especially by his skilled economics minister and later Chancellor, Ludwig Erhardt, and others, piloted the Federal Republic to remarkable economic success by prioritizing these three goals. Thereby, a definitely and irreversibly Western-orientated new German state began to emerge in which the political culture had crystallized in a modern parliamentary mold, notwithstanding the conservative characteristics of Adenauer's party, the Christian Democratic Union. The failure of the right-wing NPD (National Democratic Party) to achieve any meaningful electoral resonance served only to confirm that most Germans saw no future in espousing long-since-discredited racist and nationalist politics. And with regard to the Evangelical Christians, the Adenauer era saw an unprecedented realignment of political loyalties. No longer were Protestants uniformly conservative; many found their way to democratic socialism. There were a number of reasons for this. Adenauer's well-known loyalty to the Church of Rome and his scathing views about leading Social Democrats such as Willy Brandt alienated not a few in the electorate. Added to this came the opposition to Germany's rearmament in the wake of the Korean war and also to the building of atomic power stations and nuclear armament generally, not least within the Evangelical population. Citizens had begun to experience what life was like in a modern parliamentary democracy—indeed, a pluralist society in which the right to peaceful protest was a given—and church leaders and lay representatives became actively involved in it.

In this new social-political climate, church people had become more receptive than ever to the discussion of alternative views, and this gained expression in the theological faculties of universities and in the regular Evangelical Church Rallies (*Evangelische Kirchentage*). As well, and perhaps less encouraging from a liberal point of view, was the development of a fundamentalist Protestantism, the so-called *evangelikalische Bekenntnisbewegung*, that tried to claim credibility by appealing to the legacy of Dietrich Bonhoeffer. The Swiss professor of theology Georg Huntemann, reacting to this development in 1989, described how Bonhoeffer was opposed in principle to all forms of religious pietism, stating that "already before his time in prison, Bonhoeffer rejected the psycho-sanctimonious pietistic cult of the soul, the psychological dissection involved in the inwardness of experiential religiosity. . . . Bonhoeffer was an enemy of the psychologization of Christianity—in this regard, also, he was, with his dynamic processual thought, an archenemy of any and all human attempts to fix or determine the encounter between Christ and the Christian."[6] There were others, too, who invoked Bonhoeffer for their cause. For example, Hans Schmidt, an *Assistent* of the high-profile Hamburg professor Helmut Thielicke, advanced Bonhoeffer as a crown witness for conservative right-wing politics precisely in accordance with his mentor's well-known views.[7]

These are examples of individuals and groups in an open society all apparently trying to seize upon an icon to rally support for their particular cause. The figure of Bonhoeffer sparked the imagination of somewhat disparate forces, something that still happens.[8] On the other hand, contemporary historians such as Hermann Graml and Hans Mommsen, who were personally aligned more with social democracy, identified Bonhoeffer as belonging to the national conservative right since he was associated with the resistance group around Carl Goerdeler, Hans Oster, and Hans von Dohnanyi. It is perfectly understandable, in the light of what we have learned about Bonhoeffer's political perceptions, that secular historians of social democratic persuasion would tend to categorize Bonhoeffer as a "national conservative." But, as we have come to appreciate, that would be too facile a judgment because it fails to take account of the peculiar circumstances and world of ideas in which people like Bonhoeffer lived and thought.[9]

In this period of the 1960s, a small book appeared from the hand of the bishop of Woolwich, England, and professor of theology, John Robinson, entitled *Honest to God*. It was published in German with an introduction by Eberhard Bethge under the title of *Gott ist anders*, or "God is different." In it Robinson surveyed the thought of the German theologians Bultmann, Tillich and chiefly Bonhoeffer, claiming that they had something of relevance to say to people of today who had lost faith in the traditional view of God. Karl Barth was singularly unimpressed by the English bishop, but at least it showed that outsiders were taking Bonhoeffer seriously. Bethge had this to say: "It is Robinson's great merit that in the debate that has been unleashed by those men

[Bultmann, Tillich, and Bonhoeffer] the new "word" and the new form of the church and its message has been brought into the foreground before the entire world at a time when our [i.e., Bethge's] efforts threatened to go unnoticed."[10] At least bishop Robinson stimulated discussion about Christianity in the broader community, whatever his theological shortcomings might have been. And he thereby heightened the international profile of Dietrich Bonhoeffer.

Bethge had already edited *Letters and Papers from Prison* and *Ethics* and was in the process of completing his monumental biography (1967) of Bonhoeffer, thereby placing him in the public eye in a manner perhaps unequalled in the history of biographical writing. The English translation followed in 1970, thus providing a welcome addition to the aforementioned texts from 1951. Certainly, an eager readership for Bonhoeffer literature was waiting in the Anglo-Saxon world. Indeed, out of the obscure and somewhat abstruse theologian a figure of towering international significance had been revealed. And in Germany even the Roman Church had begun to take cognizance of Bonhoeffer, as Ernst Feil's positive analysis of Bonhoeffer's theology illustrated. As well, the meticulous research work of the late Danish Bonhoeffer scholar Jørgen Glenthøj contributed to the progressing internationalization of Bonhoeffer studies. Bethge had also begun his edition of the then collected writings in six volumes, 1965–74, entitled *Gesammelte Schriften* that guaranteed that Bonhoeffer would become the object of serious international research.

This process went hand in hand with the politicization of Bonhoeffer. His legacy was enlisted to justify and encourage political resistance movements in countries suffering under the yoke of dictatorships both of the left and the right—in, for example, the Czechoslovakia of the Prague Spring of 1968 as well as in South Africa and South America in the manifestation of liberation theology.[11] In this connection, the influence of Bonhoeffer in the German Democratic Republic has to be flagged and will be investigated separately below. West German theologians and other writers continued to find inspiration in Bonhoeffer's life and work, as discussion and events during the Stuttgart Church Rally of 1969 were to show. Bonhoeffer was being discovered as a beacon for political activism. And in this context the appearance in 1990 of Renate Wind's book *Dem Rad in die Speichen fallen* was yet another indication of how Bonhoeffer was beginning to seize the imagination of a younger generation of Germans. Wind had been among the student demonstrators at the 1969 Stuttgart Rally. There was an undeniable reciprocal relationship (*Wechselwirkung*) between the social-political changes in West German political culture and those being experienced in the church.

A further sign that Bonhoeffer's legacy was being enthusiastically embraced not only within the two German states but also by foreign neighbors was the first international Bonhoeffer Congress at Bethel near Bielefeld in 1954. Here delegates from Poland, Holland, the United States, and the GDR, represented by the pro-communist professor Hanfried Müller and the former Bonhoeffer student and anti-communist bishop Albrecht Schönherr, all contributed. So, in Bethel was planted the seed of the idea of instituting the International Bonhoeffer Society that is today so active in promoting Bonhoeffer's theology in many countries, both within and outside Europe through the organizing of regular conferences.

By the 1970s, the interest in Bonhoeffer had advanced to such a degree that the circle around Eberhard Bethge and Heinz-Eduard Tödt launched the ambitious project that resulted in the publication of the *Dietrich Bonhoeffer Werke* in seventeen volumes. In addition, numerous dissertations were researched and published, many inspired not least by Professor Tödt. And now the availability of the complete works has resulted in wide-ranging individual studies from authors around the world, whereby English-language and translations into other European languages are steadily taking place.

There is no doubt that the career of Dietrich Bonhoeffer has contributed immeasurably to the changed character of German Protestantism. After 1945 the westernized Bonn constitution irrevocably dissolved the former bond between church and state, and this enforced a radical reorientation of attitudes on the part of conservative Protestants. As well, the conditions of the Cold War and the flourishing of ecumenism, with the raised awareness of the situation of people in third world countries, impinged strongly on the Christian churches in Germany. They were bound to make radical readjustments. And in these circumstances, the life and witness of a figure like Dietrich Bonhoeffer proved to be a lodestar. His theology that cast aside the role of the state in the history of salvation, his consequent reassessment of the diaconal role of the church in the world, the "church for others," and his theology of reconciliation with the synagogue, all propelled the church into new, and, for many, unexpected highways that remain, it needs to be recognized, problematic paths for some German Protestants. Certainly, though, the Bonhoeffer legacy has undoubtedly borne rich fruit in many places. And most interesting in this respect has been the Bonhoeffer legacy for the church in the former East Germany, to which we now turn.

Bonhoeffer Reception in the German Democratic Republic

With the hindsight of almost two decades since the collapse of the Berlin Wall, it is now possible to evaluate with greater clarity the deep-seated significance of Bonhoeffer's legacy in the "second German dictatorship." Indeed, it is difficult not to assess Bonhoeffer as a major source of inspiration for the survival and witness of the church under what were extremely trying conditions in which the communist state was using all means possible, short of declaring the church an illegal organization, to eliminate or at least marginalize its influence in the community. It was for the history of the church in that situation a matter of crucial importance that key personalities in the leadership had been students of Bonhoeffer, such as the bishop of Brandenburg-Berlin, Albrecht Schönherr. He proved to be a most doughty stalwart of the gospel against all the efforts of the regime to reduce the church to an insignificant "little flock." That it resolutely refused to allow that to happen has a great deal to do with legacy of Dietrich Bonhoeffer, as shall be seen.

For many Protestants in East Germany, the liberation in 1945 from the barbarism of National Socialism and the imposition of "socialism," Stalinist style, by the occupying Soviets was initially welcomed as the dawning of a new era in church-state relations.[12] However, these optimistic hopes were soon to be dashed. With the realization that "real (or actually) existing socialism" was the antithesis of an open society, indeed an even more pervasive and intrusive form of dictatorship than Nazism, if that can be imagined, the churches were thrown back into struggle mode. It inevitably became clear that the Soviets and their puppet East German regime, led by the veteran Stalinist Walter Ulbricht and his party faithful, were bent on the marginalization of all parties and groups that resisted submission to the "scientific truth" of Marxism-Leninism with its "claim to total truth" (*totaler Warheitsanspruch*).

Not unexpectedly, church leaders were challenged by the ambitions of the new totalitarian system with which the church was now confronted. The bishop Otto Dibelius of Berlin- Brandenburg (1945–66) reacted by producing an energetic statement entitled *Obrigkeit* (the Powers-that-Be), first published privately in 1959 and then in 1963 for the West German public. In it he rigorously examined St. Paul's Epistle to the Romans, especially the famous chapter 13 that establishes that all authority derives from God: "Let every soul be subject unto the higher powers. For there is no Power but of God; the powers that be are ordained of God," as it says in the more familiar King James version. Dibelius analyzed from a traditional Lutheran point of view what this meant throughout history for the relationship between ruler and subjects. His conclusion was that an authority did not have to be Christian to demand the obedience and loyalty of Christian subjects. He saw "order" in society as a divinely ordained condition to enable human life to flourish. Obviously, when St. Paul was writing, the "Power" was the pagan Roman emperor, but it was still divinely ordained. His authority was transmitted by a bureaucracy that administered a legal system under which all subjects received justice and were treated equitably and not capriciously. In short, there was a universally binding and transparent legal system that allowed all law-abiding citizens to prosper. In the case of the two totalitarian states through which Dibelius had lived, National Socialism and Communism, there was no such legal system. What stood for law issued from the capricious will of the dictator. There could be, therefore, no real justice for all, no impartiality, because the will of the dictator was subject to no guiding principles other than what might seem good or bad to the custodian of supreme power at a given time. And under both the Nazis and the Communists, all "subjects" were at the mercy of capricious and totally "unprincipled" men. Dibelius observed that "in all totalitarian states it is a common principle that the state has the right to extinguish the life of anyone who resists, or to destroy their personality, if there are no political or economic reasons to the contrary."[13]

In order to enforce the dictator's or the party's will, concentration camps were established in which brainwashing and summary executions took place as normal procedure. This was completely unacceptable for Christians for whom, as Dibelius argued, there were two groups of states. On the one hand there were those in which moral principles prevailed over the interests of naked power, where there was law recognized by both ruler and ruled that was somehow metaphysically underpinned (*irgendwie metapysich verankert ist*). It could be an absolute monarchy or a democracy and, according to Dibelius, this is what Paul had in mind when he wrote his Epistle to the Romans. On the other hand there were totalitarian systems directed by individuals or parties who determined what was good or bad for increasing their power, and in doing so recognized no boundaries whatsoever. The individual subject could be pursued right into his intimate sphere at any time or place. He had no rights at all. And this was certainly not the kind of state that St. Paul was writing about in his famous Epistle. Consequently, the church could not recognize such dictatorships as "authorities" in that sense. There then arose the problem as to what extent the individual Christian should dare to disobey such a state, or, in short, to resist the authorities. Here, however, St. Paul offered no solutions.[14] For advice here, Dibelius turned to Luther. His answer was that the church of Jesus Christ does not offer open resistance to those in power. Nor does the church call people to resist. In short, churches do not foment political opposition. Indeed, those in power could sleep soundly as they need not fear revolution being instigated by the churches.[15]

That said, however, the totalitarian state, by definition one in which the ruling dictator or party set the public agenda, had no claim on the conscience of the Christian. He or she may disobey such a dictatorship but, of course, would have to endure the consequences. In fact, how a Christian behaves in such a situation is left to the individual to judge. As we shall see below, the church in the GDR dictatorship had to live by these principles.

When the GDR devised its constitution in 1949, provision was made for "freedom of conscience"—but that was only window-dressing. Marxism-Leninism, as the only "valid" ideology, interpreted this as freedom for the liberating "truth" of that particular system. And in accordance with that the party (the Sozialistische Einheitspartei: SED) claimed an indisputable right to determine what people should believe about everything affecting the life of the community. Indeed, the party exercised a *totaler Wahrheitsanspruch*, which meant in effect that what was true was what the party decreed.

Initially, in the early postwar phase when the Protestant churches in the GDR which were still, until 1969, officially part of the all-German Protestant Church (EKD), there occurred the aforementioned series of meetings of theologians and church leaders concerned with the legacy of Bonhoeffer held in first in the West at Bethel 1954, and then in the East at Weissensee 1955 and 1959.[16] Here, though, the fact that the church was now confronted with survival in a hostile totalitarian state had its curious impact on the reception of Bonhoeffer's ideas. Under the influence of Professor Hanfried Müller of the Humboldt University's theological faculty, a group of pastors was formed, called the Weissensee Circle, with the object of making Bonhoeffer's theology compatible with Marxism-Leninism. We shall investigate the effect of this below.

By this time, the course of the Cold War had begun to have serious consequences for the unity of the German church. After the erection of the Berlin wall in 1961, the churches in the GDR experienced increasing frustration in their efforts to maintain contact with their Western brothers and sisters. Indeed, the church was vilified by the communist leadership in the GDR as the "NATO-church," and, as a consequence of enforced separation the territorial churches in the East, had eventually (in 1969) to form a federation of their own, isolated from fellow Protestants in the West. The BEK, *der Bund der Evangelischen Kirchen*, came about in order to ensure the survival of Christianity as far as it was possible in that hostile environment.[17]

All the churches of the various countries that were subjugated by the Soviets after 1945 experienced similar oppression. Each has a separate survival story to tell and each in their own way played a central role in the final implosion of the Soviet bloc. Poland experienced its Solidarity movement, and the church in Hungary also contributed to the final undermining of the communist regime. Not surprisingly, with hindsight, it proved impossible for the rulers of these countries successfully to eradicate the churches, although great efforts were made in each case to do so. In terms of communist ideology they should have all withered away, but Christianity, mysteriously, in the view of the communist party ideologues, persisted. Each developed survival strategies peculiar to their specific culture, and in Eastern Germany, the dominant religious culture was Protestant. And here our concern is to identify the ways in which Bonhoeffer's legacy was instrumentalized to sustain witness to the gospel. Clearly, the regime of "real existing communism" came to pose a unique and not so subtle threat to the church in contrast to the parliamentary democracy of the Federal Republic in the West where the church flourished, at least materially, due largely to the resumption of the church tax which was automatically deducted from the income of citizens who elected to remain members of their church. So the churches in the West were always assured of a sustaining income. In the East, however, all such privileges were gradually withdrawn.

Indeed, the church in the GDR became for the regime a central political issue precisely because the communist ideologues were obsessed with demonstrating that Marxism-Leninism (ML) was the only "truth." For Christians this was a challenge that had sooner or later to be confronted. Consequently, the church became per force the locus of political dissent. In it ever more disaffected groups coalesced that, in the end, could not be silenced.

How, indeed, could this happen? After the initial period of more or less benign collaboration between church and state, the SED determined to assert itself, and in March 1954 it set up a Task Force for Church Questions in order to establish its "claim to total truth." Consequently, the church was confronted with the decision whether to submit to the policy of ultimate "ghettoization" or to try to become proactive in the proclamation of the gospel. And already in 1949 bishop Dibelius had identified the problem by observing that, "At the present time we are oppressed more than anything else by the concern that the form of state which is emerging around us evinces so many of the characteristics which in the period of National Socialism, for the sake of God, merited our resistance."[18]

Dibelius' statement then unleashed a debate within the Protestant church on the question whether the state of RES should be regarded as a genuine *Obrigkeit* in the sense of St. Paul's Epistle to the Romans, chapter 13. Even the Swiss theologian, Karl Barth, offered his advice on how to serve God in a socialist country.[19] However, it was a typically Lutheran issue that was fought out between those on the one hand who regarded the GDR as a genuine *Obrigkeit* and those on the other who, like bishop Dibelius, following Saint Augustine in his *Civitas Dei*, designated all states in which there was no real rule of law as bands of robbers. They told lies if it served the regime, and further broke promises in the interests of the state. Such behavior became the norm, indeed the rule or principle of so-called "socialist morality."[20]

It was within the framework of this confrontation that Bonhoeffer's legacy as a celebrated opponent of fascism became intensely politicized. There arose the above-mentioned group of regime-friendly theologians and pastors who sought to apply a selection of Bonhoeffer's writings to legitimize Marxism-Leninism. This was Professor Hanfried Müller's Weissensee circle. These became, remarkably, apologists for the GDR as a state where the promise of the gospel was certainly going to be realized. Their objective, they believed, could be accomplished by parading Bonhoeffer posthumously as an apologist for the state of "real existing socialism."

In the GDR, most of the conspirators of the 20th July 1944 attempt against Hitler were dismissed as bourgeois opponents of fascism because, clearly, they could not have been inspired to overthrow the Nazi regime on behalf of the working class. Precisely why it became legitimate to remember Bonhoeffer, whose bourgeois origins could not have been more apparent, is only explainable within the framework of Marxist-Leninist casuistry, and a prime example of this is the communist writer Gerhard Winter, who on the occasion of Bonhoeffer's 75th birthday (4 February 1981) spelled out why such a bourgeois and Christian as Bonhoeffer was worthy of remembrance in a society that was destined to become entirely atheistic.

One may reasonably suspect that this preoccupation with Bonhoeffer was rooted in the fear that his legacy could become the focus of active opposition to the new dictatorship. It would therefore be prudent to head off such a possibility, and this would account for the fact that a communist apologist such as Winter would, on the one hand, dignify Bonhoeffer's memory, while on the other hand emphasize the inadequacy of his motivation for resistance because it was, after all, only "Christian" and hence not "scientific," and as such only of limited efficacy. But at least Bonhoeffer sacrificed his life in a struggle against a system in which human rights were being trampled under foot, and to that extent his motivation had much in common with communist resistance.

Clearly, Winter and other SED strategists had acquired some familiarity with Bonhoeffer's published writings such as *The Cost of Discipleship* and *Letters and Papers from Prison* and had gleaned ideas about peace and social justice that coincided sufficiently with communist propaganda so that a dialogue of common purpose with the church could, at least superficially, reasonably be pursued. The objectives of world peace and international social justice enabled, it was argued, both state and church to work together in good conscience.

While Gerhard Winter's efforts were directed at convincing the Christian laity in the GDR that collaboration with the SED-state was thoroughly legitimate and desirable, Professor Hanfried Müller and his Weissensee circle sought to win over the pastorate by interpreting Bonhoeffer's theology to show that, upon rigorous examination, it was perfectly compatible with the objectives of RES. In a word, the essence of the gospel was consistent with the social-political aims of the SED regime. Bonhoeffer's career presented itself in this new situation as most opportune. His church struggle had been a clear repudiation of the disastrous nationalist element in German Protestantism that had led in linear progression from Luther to Hitler. To the communists this was a feature of Bonhoeffer's thought that could be exploited to an advantage because it served to reinforce their doctrine of class struggle. In short, the Weissensee circle advocated that the cause of the gospel would be best served by the church abandoning its traditional role in society and ought instead function to support the secular Marxist-Leninist state in the realization of its goals since these were effectively identical with the essence of the gospel. Hanfried Müller advanced his version of Bonhoeffer's concept of "religionless Christianity" in his study *Von der Kirche zur Welt* already in 1961 purporting to show how the bourgeois opponent of Hitler, Dietrich Bonhoeffer, had advanced under the influence of the great social changes of the times that had resulted in the decisive defeat of fascism at Stalingrad, to being a vigorous antifascist. This experience, so argued Hanfried Müller, could be mediated to the church in order to encourage support for the "progressive movements" of the postwar era. Bonhoeffer had accelerated this possibility since he stood out from his contemporaries in that he had (allegedly) acknowledged the existence of recognizable laws in nature and history. This made him open to the ideology of Marxism-Leninism.

Indeed, the communist era spawned many such adventurous ideas in individual historians and theologians who were bent on ingratiating themselves with the regime. And today we look back over these efforts by presumably highly intelligent scholars and wonder how it was at all possible. The simplest explanation is that it was probably due to a combination of naïve sincerity and varying degrees of opportunism. At any rate, a selection of Bonhoeffer's works was deemed fit by the GDR literary censorship board to be published, and this included the proceedings of the Fourth International Bonhoeffer Conference at Hirschluch outside Berlin, 12–17 June 1984.[21] Clearly, the regime was persuaded that by allowing this, the Protestant population could be encouraged to accept its brand of socialism.

It was in this context that a further publication of *Bonhoeffer Studien* was allowed to appear in 1986.[22] The volume encompassed seventeen contributions from theologians, including those who opposed communism in principle as well as the regime-friendly Hanfried Müller. And in the GDR this was a curious thing, because it was tantamount to a concession by the regime that the church was able to resist the state's "claim to total truth." In a real sense, the regime was forced to resort to this tactic—obviously in the expectation that a hitherto obstinate section of society would come to accept party authority. This was, however, a vain hope given the strength of Christian conviction of many of the pastors and theologians. These, through their unshakable commitment, demonstrated that there was such a thing as ideological pluralism, which, of course, was not supposed to exist in RES. The state was powerless to legislate what occurred in the world of ideas of many of its subjects despite the best efforts of the Ministry of State Security to enforce ideological conformity. And it is of significance that the legacy of Dietrich Bonhoeffer played an undeniable role in what may be termed intellectual-ideological resistance. This is why the vagaries of GDR church policy merit close attention in any explanation of the ultimate failure of the regime to win the hearts and minds of the people.

Bonhoeffer as Theologian of the "Church in Socialism"

When tracing the history of the implosion of socialism in the GDR, its internal collapse, one cannot dismiss the Protestant churches as having long played a definite oppositional role. Of course, this opposition was never uniform or consistent throughout the four decades of communist rule. There was, however, an irreducible remnant of implacable Protestants who were undoubtedly inspired by the legacy of Dietrich Bonhoeffer. In any case, many parishes with members of unshakable faith continued to reflect on what it meant to be the church in a hostile, atheistic state. This became evident when leading personalities stood up at synods and made unequivocal appeals to the history of the Confessing Church during the Third Reich in which, as we have seen, Bonhoeffer had played such a significant part.[23]

In 1977 the federation of churches in the GDR actually established a committee designed to coordinate the activities of the various groups scattered throughout the country dedicated to Bonhoeffer studies.[24] The thought behind this development was that as far as the church was concerned, it had to fight for the truth of the gospel against a state that itself was trying to impose virtually an alternative form of religion. Marxism-Leninism claimed to be a system of thought whose advocates were convinced that it would assuredly bring real salvation, here and now, in this world.²⁵ Consequently, the situation in the GDR was quite different from the Federal Republic. In the communist East the state had issued an existential challenge to the church. It had, in response, to use all means at its disposal to counter the efforts by the regime to undermine its witness to the gospel. And precisely here the legacy of Bonhoeffer became an arsenal of ideas in the ongoing struggle. Consequently, in a real sense the Bonhoeffer-inspired pastors and their congregations, alongside the various dissident groups that they fostered, mounted an irremovable obstruction to the state in the execution of its mission, and this obstruction became increasingly more determined the more the legacy of Bonhoeffer was appropriated.

The peculiar situation of the church in the GDR is summed up in the ambiguous title that it acquired, namely, *Kirche im Sozialismus*. This designation derived from an admonition to the church from the secretary of state for church affairs, Hans Seigewasser, after the revised GDR constitution of 1968 was allegedly approved by 94.49 percent of the population.²⁶ At that time, Seigewasser warned that the conclusion to be drawn by clergy was that they could do justice to the spiritual commission of the "church in socialism" only if they abstained from denigrating socialism and its humanistic policies, especially foreign policy.²⁷

As it emerged, the church in the GDR adopted this designation largely under the leadership of Albrecht Schönherr, who made the point at the BEK Synod in Erfurt in 1971 that the church defined its position *in* the society of the GDR as neither beside nor against it. This was at once intended to express loyalty to the state and the intention of the church to preserve its autonomy. The state, however, expected that the church now abandon any attempt to assert itself in public life, to become literally a "niche church" (*Nichenkirche*), marginalized and without social or political relevance. This, however, it could not accept. The state's repeated abuses of human rights, including discrimination against children of church families as well as Christian students, compelled church leaders to take a stand. And in this respect the "freedom speech" address of the Erfurt prior (*Domprobst*), Heino Falcke, at the 1972 Synod of the BEK in Dresden under the title "Christ Liberates, therefore Church for Others," was a milestone. Falcke stoutly proclaimed that the church was not going to assume the supine role that the SED had assigned to it. Indeed, what Falcke said was virtually a public demand for freedom and social emancipation for which he had clearly drawn heavily on Bonhoeffer's *Ethics*.²⁸ To designate the church as the place of "critical loyalty" toward the state as Falcke did was a calculated act of defiance toward the dictatorship of RES, stressing that it required the critical input of Christians, not their quiescent submission. In this way the church in the GDR served notice on the state that it was quite determined to assume and maintain the role of political-ideological opposition against the "leading *Weltanschauung* of the working class."[29]

Not all Protestants in the GDR were, however, in agreement with this stance that derived from the Bonhoeffer legacy. It was, nevertheless, a position from which there was no turning back. A proactive element had been aroused that belatedly, it seemed, had revived the position adopted by bishop Dibelius in the decade 1949 to 1959. The difference was, however, that Dibelius had characterized the GDR state virtually as one of "liars and robbers" with whom any dealings would be disastrous, whereas the "church in socialism" accorded to the state a degree of legitimacy but reserved the right to criticize that state as one prone to exceed its competences and to violate human rights in the process. Vocal elements in the church believed it was right to insist on being the quasi-legal opposition. In this regard, Wolf Krötke has summed up four points where the challenge of RES to the church had to be confronted by employing categories derived from Dietrich Bonhoeffer:

1) The state of RES with its claim to absolute power in all spheres of life and society came to be assessed as an opportunity for the church to abandon its own claim to power and social privileges and finally to rely completely on God through Jesus Christ to rule.
2) Historical and dialectical materialism, as the official ideology, was accepted as a militant declaration of "coming of age of the world" and could thereby be interpreted as "hopeful Godlessness." It was "hopeful" because, fundamentally, it rested on the concept of building a more just society. And precisely because of that, Christians were called to collaborate as autonomous individuals. Indeed, this was not a privilege but a duty imposed by Christ by virtue of his propitiatory sacrifice on the cross.
3) The church was not a haven of retreat from society but the "church for others." It lived in solidarity with "the others," who, as the religionless, were pledged to build up socialism. In this sense, as Albrecht Schönherr formulated it, the church was not a church *beside*, not *against*, but *in* socialism.
4) The church should witness in this society without fear for its own existence by concentrating on its crucified Lord who is and continues to be the ruler of the world.[30]

This appeal to Bonhoeffer's ideas enabled the church to see in its oppressed situation the opportunity and promise to be the church, purified and unencumbered. What indeed appeared to be designed to enslave the church was in reality liberating and empowering it. It was, however, not an encouragement to those who adhered to an extreme form of the doctrine of the two kingdoms to withdraw into hibernation; on the contrary, the obligation to collaborate with the religionless in the construction of a more just society required a proactive response from Christians. And this response made itself most publicly apparent on the 30 April 1989, at the Dresden Synod, where a twelve-point manifesto (see Appendix IV) was proclaimed that addressed itself to all the problem areas in both the domestic and foreign affairs of the GDR.[31]

Erhart Neubert has designated that manifesto as the Magna Carta of all dissident groups because it provided the justification and the practical goals for what became the totally unexpected "Protestant Revolution." Its publication and reception was arguably the key event in spurring on the burgeoning "conciliar process" that was taking place in many centers all over the GDR at the time that formed a visible and vocal opposition to the SED dictatorship.[32] So there was an undeniable line of continuity between the witness of the persecuted Bonhoeffer in the Third Reich and the opposition movement in the GDR. Indeed, Erhart Neubert, as the preeminent champion of the idea of a "Protestant Revolution" among those pastors actively involved in dissent activities, identified the elements of opposition as having been both directly and indirectly influenced by Protestant thought. That means even that even the originally Marxist-oriented dissidents in the GDR drew upon the example of those Protestant critics who were becoming increasingly vocal ever since 1972 and soon after in the period 1973 to 1975, when the SED participated in the international conferences held in Helsinki to promote peace, justice, and the preservation of creation.[33]

These dissidents from within the ranks of the church as well as disaffected Marxists were the intellectual-spiritual precursors (*Vordenker*) of the revolution of 1989/90 in whose formation Bonhoeffer's legacy had played such a central role. And because of their activities they were able, by 1989, to bring the disparate elements of opposition in the land increasingly into alignment. These constituted the internal opposition in the GDR that surprisingly, in the face of the regime's strenuous efforts at marginalization, not only survived but were able to reproduce themselves. And this applies particularly to the dissident element among the pastorate in the eight provincial churches of the BEK, where, it has to be appreciated, a number of disparate, indeed rival, theological traditions coexisted particularly with regard to attitudes toward the state.

First, there were residual conservative elements that, as Edelbert Richter has pointed out, cultivated a radical form of the doctrine of the two kingdoms.[34] Their preferred mode of behavior was virtual hibernation in order to preserve the purity of the gospel as they understood it. Another group of conservatives were quite prepared to regard the SED state as a legitimate *Obrigkeit*. They were not persuaded to abandon this position even in the light of the best efforts of bishop Otto Dibelius to convince them that the regime was certainly not a true *Obrigkeit*.[35] Others, obviously conscious of the legacy of the Confessing Church, were ready to take advice given to them by Karl Barth in 1958, to regard the SED state as worthy of support and so try to function as a kind of loyal opposition.[36]

Next, as we have seen, the Weissensee circle around Hanfried Müller tried to instrumentalize Bonhoeffer's theology to implement what would have been the most extreme expression of the doctrine of the two kingdoms, in effect to promote the actual absorption of the church into the state, a situation tantamount to the total abandonment of the spiritual role of the church in society. This position was justified in the conviction that Marxism-Leninism would accomplish for the population the emancipatory promises of the gospel of Christ. Finally, there were those heirs of the Confessing Church for whom Bonheoffer was the preeminent prophet of emancipation. And it was these who came to prevail in the *Kirche im Sozialismus*, which proved to be, in the words of Wolf Krötke, the representative for a better form of state: "It was, from today's standpoint, when we consider the end of socialism, by no means a coincidence that the church at that time had come to fulfill a kind of representative function for a better body politic (*Staatswesen*)."[37]

Certainly, the stance adopted by the church, always insisting, against the express wishes of the state, that Christians had a right and duty to collaborate in the realization of freedom, withstood and discredited the regime's ideological terrorism. It was the church that was prepared, following Bonhoeffer's notion of collaboration with the religionless, to accept the state, but its ideologically ossified custodians were totally incapable of comprehending such a gracious offer.

Conclusion

There is no doubt that Bonhoeffer's lifework has captured the imagination of a considerable number of Christians of most traditions throughout the world. The explanation for this can only be that his particular theology, especially that of the church in the world, being there for others, being most effective when it is impoverished and apparently helpless, speaks above all to people in situations of existential crisis. This, of course, was particularly and even dramatically the case for those Germans who had the misfortune after the conclusion of the Second World

War in 1945 to have been liberated by the Soviet Union and endured, as a consequence, over forty years the benefits of being forced to live under the yoke of "real existing communism." In Appendix IV, we have documentary evidence of how Bonhoeffer's legacy enabled the churches in the GDR to cope with the "second German dictatorship" by providing tools of biblically based criticism of the absurd and cruel anomalies of that system that masqueraded so arrogantly as being the sole custodian of "truth." Finally, as indicated, with the inevitable spread of literature on Bonhoeffer throughout the world, his legacy became inspirational for many societies enduring the oppression of parties who justify their right to power on totalitarian, ultimately inhumane, often racist, ideologies, and maintain control through the daily violation of human rights. Bonhoeffer is indisputably a prophet for our times.

Notes

1. Ulrich Kabitz, "Bonhoeffers Wirkungsgeschichte in Westdeutschland," *Bonhoeffer Rundbrief*, no. 82 (March 2007): 19. In what follows I have followed the pattern of Kabitz's succinct survey. The precise source for Lilje's observation was a speech he made at 17th *Landessynode der Landeskirche Hannovers*, 10. *Sitzung* am 3. November 1965 [Archiv der LK Hannovers, Signatur AIII 3043 A]. I am indebted to Professor Dr. Heinrich W. Grosse for this confirmation.

2. For a systematic account of how Bonhoeffer's witness had been made public by his friend, Eberhard Bethge, see John de Gruchy, *Daring, Trusting Spirit: Bonhoeffer's Friend Eberhard Bethge* (Minneapolis, 2005), chapters 9 and 10.

3. See, *Die Mündige Welt II* (Munich, 1956), foreword.

4. Kabitz, "Bonhoeffers Wirkungsgeschichte," 19.

5. Personal recollection of the author, who was for the three years (1963–65) a doctoral student of the late Waldemar Besson.

6. Georg Huntemann, *The Other Bonhoeffer: An Evangelical Reassessment of Dietrich Bonhoeffer*, trans. Todd Huizinga (Grand Rapids, 1993). In chapter 9, "The Religious Perversion of Christianity," Huntemann shows Bonhoeffer to be scathing: "This type of personal, individualistic, salvation-egotistic interaction with God was repulsive to Bonhoeffer. In his opinion, this type of religion was a means to the end of generating medicine for spiritual suffering and power to fulfill egoistic wishes," 100–101.

7. Hans Schmidt. *Verheissung und Schrecken der Freihei* (Stuttgart/Berlin, 1964).

8. See Clifford Green's comment on this with regard to George W. Bush's policy toward Saddam Hussein's dictatorship in Iraq and the justification for it advanced by University of Chicago professor Jean Bethke Elshtain by appealing to Bonhoeffer's saying regarding the "jamming [of] a spoke in the wheel." Green rightly comments that this is a blatant misuse of Bonhoeffer's ideas. See his "Pacifism and Tyrannicide: Bonhoeffer's Christian Peace Ethics," *Studies in Christian Peace Ethics* 18, no. 3 (2005): 31, and "Bonhoeffer-

Forschung in der englischensprachigen Welt heute," *Bonhoeffer Rundbrief*, no. 82 (March 2007): 41.

9. Hermann Graml, Hans Mommsen et al., *The German Resistance to Hitler* (London, 1970). See in particular Mommsen's section entitled "Social Views and Constitutional Plans of the Resistance," 55–148.

10. Eberhard Bethge's Introduction to *Gott ist anders* (Honest to God) by John A. T. Robinson, (Munich, 1963). 17.

11. The writings of the South Americans Guttierrez and Santa Ana on so-called liberation theology that appealed to Bonhoefffer were registered with some surprise in Germany, according to Ulrich Kabitz, "Bonhoeffers Wirkungsgeschichte," 22.

12. This topic is covered in some detail in my chapter "Bonhoeffer's Reception in East Germany," in *Bonhoeffer for a New Day*, ed. John W. de Gruchy (Grand Rapids, MI, 1992), 278–97.

13. Otto Dibelius, *Obrigkeit* (Stuttgart, 1963), 92.

14. Ibid., 95–96.

15. Ibid., 105–06.

16. The proceedings of these meetings are recorded in *Die Mündige Welt*. The first meeting was dedicated expressly to the memory of Dietrich Bonhoeffer.

17. For a concise analytical overview of SED church policy, see Joachim Heise, "Kirchenpolitik von SED und Staat zwischen ideologischem Dogma, praktischer Toleranz und politischen Misstrauen," in Horst Dähn, *Die Rolle der Kirche in der DDR*. München, 1993. 73–91. As well, see Hans-Gerhard Koch, *Staat und Kirche in der DDR* (Stuttgart, 1975), 139–52.

18. *Die mündige Welt*, 279–80.

19. Karl Barth, *How to Serve God in a Socialist Land* (New York, 1959).

20. Robert Stupperich. *Otto Dibelius. Ein evangelsicher Bischof im Umbruch der Zeiten* (Göttingen, 1989), 545–47 and Hartmut Fritz, *Otto Dibelius: Ein Kirchenmann in der Zeit zwischen Monarchie und Demokratie* (Göttingen, 1998), 500. Dibelius, in his critique of the GDR because of the caprice of the rulers, cited Saint Augustine of Hippo's *Civitas Dei:* "Where there is no law, what else are those states than bands of robbers?" It was so bad in the GDR that not even the party officials kept the laws that they themselves had promulgated.

21. See Martin Kuske Hrsg. *Weltliches Christentum. Dietrich Bonhoeffers Vision nimmt Gestalt an* (Berlin, 1984).

22. Albrecht Schönherr and Wolf Krötke, eds., *Bonhoeffer Studien: Beiträge zur Theologie und Wirkungsgeschichte Dietrich Bonhoeffer* (Berlin 1986).

23. Albrecht Schönherr, "Die Bedeutung Dietrich Bonhoeffers für das Christentum in der DDR," in *Glauben Lernen in einer Kirche für andere*," ed. Ernst Feil (Gütersloh, 1993) 42.

24. See note 19.

25. Wolf Krötke, "Die Kirche und die friedliche Revolution in der DDR," *Zeitschrift für Theologie und Kirche* 87 (1990): 539.

26. Cf. Hermann Weber, *Die DDR 1945–1986* (Munich, 1988) 235.

27. Zum Gebrauch des Begriffes "Kirche im Sozialismus" in *Information und Texte der Theologischen Studienabteilung beim BEK*, no. 15 (March 1988): 2.

28. Erhart Neubert, "'Obwohl der scheinbar tiefe Frieden . . . ': Zur Genese der systemimmanenten protestantisch geprägten Opposition in

der DDR—1972–1978," in *Rückblicke auf die DDR*, ed. Gisela Hellwig, *Edition Deutschland Archiv* (Cologne, 1995), 48.

29. See *SED und Kirche: Eine Dokumentation ihrer Beziehungen*, vol. 2 (1968–89), ed. Frédéric Hartwig and Horst Dohle (Neukirchen-Vluyn, 1995), 211–12.

30. Wolf Krötke. "Dietrich Bonhoeffer als Theologe der DDR," 302–303. For a thorough examination of the career of Lutheran Professor Wolf Krötke as a doughty opponent of the totalitarianism of the GDR, see Philip G. Ziegler, *Doing Theology When God Is Forgotten: The Theological Achievement of Wolf Krötke* (New York, 2007).

31. For the text of this manifesto see, *Ökumenische Versammlung für Gerechtigkeit, Frieden und Bewahrung der Schöpfung*, Dresden, 1989. Kirchenamt der Evangelischen Kirche in Deutschland (Hanover, 1991), 23–108.

32. Erhart Neubert, *Eine Protestantische Revolution* (Osnabrück, 1990) 14–17.

33. See Appendix 4.

34. Edelbert Richter. "Die Zweideutigkeit der lutherischen Tradition," *Deutschland Archiv* 4, no. 26 (1993): 407–17.

35. Otto Dibelius. *Obrigkeit* (Stuttgart, 1963).

36. Karl Barth and Johannes Hamel, *How to Serve God in a Marxist Land* (New York, 1959).

37. Krötke, "Dietrich Bonhoeffer als Theologe der DDR," 308.

Appendix I

The Barmen Declaration of Faith

(Confessing Church, May 1934)

[The following translation of the six Barmen theses is a conflation of Arthur Cochrane's translation in *The Church's Confession* and Douglas S. Bax's translation in Eberhard Jüngel, *Christ, Justice and Peace*. Bax's translation first appeared in the *Journal of Theology for Southern Africa* 47 (June 1984). I am indebted to Dr. Matthew Hockenos of Skidmore College, Saratoga Springs, New York, for allowing me to use his version of this document here. Each of the six theses has three parts: a quote from the scriptures, an interpretation of the quote by the authors of the declaration, and a rejection of false doctrine by the declaration's authors].

1. "I am the Way and the Truth and the Life; no one comes to the Father except through me" (John 14:6). "Truly, truly, I say to you, he who does not enter the sheepfold through the door but climbs in somewhere else, he is a thief and a robber.... I am the Door; if anyone enters through me, he will be saved" (John 10:1, 9).

Jesus Christ, as he attested to us in Holy Scripture, is the one Word of God which we have to hear, and which we have to trust and obey in life and in death.

We reject the false doctrine that the church could and should recognize as a source of its proclamation, beyond and besides this one Word of God, yet other events, powers, historic figures, and truths as God's revelation.

2. "Jesus Christ has been made wisdom and righteousness and sanctification and redemption for us by God" (1 Cor. 1, 30).

As Jesus Christ is God's assurance of the forgiveness of all our sins, so, and with equal seriousness, he is also God's mighty claim [*Anspruch*] upon our whole life. Through him befalls us a joyful deliverance from the godless fetters of this world for a free, grateful service to his creatures.

We reject the false doctrine, as though there were areas of our life in which we would not belong to Jesus Christ, but to other lords—areas in which we would not need justification and sanctification through him.

3. "Rather, speaking the truth in love, we are to grow up in every way into him who is the head, into Christ, from whom the whole body [is] joined and knit together" (Eph. 4:15–16).

The Christian Church is the congregation of the brethren in which Jesus Christ acts presently as the Lord in Word and sacrament through the Holy Spirit. As the church of pardoned sinners, it has to testify in the midst of a sinful world, with its faith as with its obedience, with its message as with its order, that it is solely his property, and that it lives and wants to live solely from his comfort and his direction in the expectation of his appearance.

We reject the false doctrine, as though the church were permitted to abandon the form of its message and order to its own pleasure or to changes in prevailing ideological and political convictions.

4. "You know that the rulers of the Gentiles lord it over them, and their great men exercise authority over them. It shall not be so among you; but whoever would be great among you must be your servant" (Matt. 20:25–26).

The various offices in the church do not establish a dominion of some over the others; on the contrary, they are for the exercise of the ministry entrusted to and enjoined upon the whole congregation.

We reject the false doctrine, as though the church, apart from this ministry, could and were permitted to give to itself, or allow to be given to it, special leaders vested with ruling powers.

5. "Fear God. Honor the emperor" (I Peter 2:17).

Scripture tells us that, in the as yet unredeemed world in which the church also exists, the state has by divine appointment the task of providing for justice and peace. [It fulfills this task] by means of the threat and exercise of force, according to the measure of human judgment and human ability. The church acknowledges the benefit of this divine appointment in gratitude and reverence before him. It calls to mind the Kingdom of God, God's commandment and righteousness, and thereby the responsibility both of rulers and ruled. It trusts and obeys the power of the Word by which God upholds all things.

We reject the false doctrine, as though the state, over and beyond its special commission, should and could become the single and totalitarian order of human life, thus fulfilling the church's vocation as well.

We reject the false doctrine, as though the church, over and beyond its special commission, should and could appropriate the characteristics, the tasks, and the dignity of the state, thus itself becoming an organ of the state.

6. "Lo, I am with you always, to the close of the age" (Matt. 28:20). "The word of God is not fettered" (II Tim. 2:9).

The church's commission, upon which its freedom is founded, consists in delivering the message of the free grace of God to all people in Christ's stead, and therefore in the ministry of his own Word and work through sermon and sacrament.

We reject the false doctrine, as though the church in human arrogance could place the Word and work of the Lord in the service of any arbitrarily chosen desires, purposes, and plans.

Appendix II

The Stuttgart Declaration of Guilt

Council of the Protestant Church of Germany

(St. Mark's Church, Stuttgart, 19 October 1945)
[*Translation by the author*]

After the collapse of the National Socialist regime and the totally devastated situation at the end of the war, a new beginning was made at Treysa in Hesse in August 1945 through the decision to establish a union of the Protestant Church in Germany. The Stuttgart Declaration of Guilt of October 1945 made further steps toward this goal possible. It has sought to express unresolved problems of the immediate past and to open the way to entry into the fellowship of the worldwide ecumenical movement. The Council of the Protestant Church in Germany welcomes representatives of the Ecumenical Council of Churches in Stuttgart 18–19 October 1949.

We are all the more grateful for this visit, as we not only find ourselves with our people in a great community of suffering but also in a solidarity of guilt.

In great pain we affirm: Through us infinite suffering was inflicted on many peoples and countries. What we often testified to in our parishes we now express in the name of the whole church: For many years we fought in the name of Jesus Christ against the spirit that found its frightful expression in the National Socialist regime of violence, but we reproach ourselves for not having stood up for the faith more courageously, for not having prayed more ardently, for not having believed more joyously and not having loved more ardently.

Now a new beginning is to be made in our churches. Based on the sacred scriptures with utter earnestness before the Lord of the church our people begin to purify themselves from influences alien to the faith and to regroup. We hope before the God of mercy and grace that He will use our churches as His instruments and empower them to proclaim

His word and to enable them to be obedient to His will among ourselves and within our entire people.

The fact that we, in this new beginning, find ourselves in warm ecumenical fellowship fills us with the deepest joy.

We hope to God that through the common service of the churches the spirit of violence and revenge which today threatens to rise up again will be brought under control throughout the world and that the spirit of peace and love comes to predominate in which alone humanity in its anguish can find healing.

Thus we pray at a time when the entire world cries out for a new beginning, "Veni creator spiritus!"

   Signed:

   D. Wurm
   (Bishop of Wüttemburg)

   Asmussen
   (President of the Chancellory of the EKD)

   H. Meiser
   (Bishop of Bavaria)

   Held
   (Pastor in Essen, later Präses of the Rhenish Church)

   Dr. Lilje
   (Secretary General of the Lutheran World Convention and later Bishop of Hanover)

   Hahn
   (Pastor, later Professor of Theology)

   Lic. Niesel
   (Pastor and Professor of Theology)

   Smend D. Dr.
   (Professor of Theology)

   Dr. G. Heinemann
   (Attorney at Law, later President of the Federal Republic)

   Dibelius
   (Bishop of Berlin-Brandenburg)

   Martin Niemöller
   (Pastor, later President of the Church in Hesse-Nassau)

Appendix III

A Statement by the Council of Brethren of the EKD Concerning the Political Course of our People

(The Darmstadt Statement, August 1947)

[Source: Matthew Hockenos, *A Church Divided: German Protestants Confront the Nazi Past* (Bloomington, 2004), 193–94. Published here with the author's kind permission].

1. We have been given the message of the reconciliation of the world with God in Christ. We must listen to this Word, accept it, act upon it and fulfil it. We are not listening to this Word, nor accepting it, nor acting upon it, nor fulfilling it, unless we are absolved from our common guilt, from our fathers' guilt as well as our own, and unless we follow the call of Jesus Christ, the Good Shepherd, leading us out of all the false and evil ways into which we, as Germans, have strayed in our political aims and actions.

2. We went astray when we began to dream about a special German mission, as if the German character could heal the sickness of the world. In so doing we prepared the way for the unrestricted exercise of political power, and set our own nation on the throne of God. It was disastrous to lay the foundations of our state at home solely on a strong government, and abroad solely on military force. In so doing we have acted contrary to our vocation, which is to cooperate with other nations in our common tasks, and to use the gifts given to us for the benefit of all nations.

3. We went astray when we began to set up a "Christian Front" against certain new developments which had become necessary in social life. The alliance of the Church with the forces which clung to everything old and conventional has revenged itself heavily upon us. We have betrayed the Christian freedom which enables us and commands us to change the forms of life, when such a change is necessary for men

to live together. We have denied the right of revolution; but we have condoned and approved the development of absolute dictatorship.

4. We went astray when we thought we ought to create a political front of good against evil, light against darkness, justice against injustice, and to resort to political methods. In so doing we distorted God's free grace to all by forming a political, social and philosophical front, and left the world to justify itself.

5. We went astray when we failed to see, that the economic materialism of Marxist teaching ought to have reminded the Church of its task and its promise for the life and fellowship of men. We have failed to take up the cause of the poor and unprivileged as a Christian cause, in accordance with the message of God's Kingdom.

6. In recognizing and confessing this, we know that we are absolved as followers of Christ, and that we are now free to undertake new and better service to the glory of God and the welfare of mankind. It is not the phrase "Christianity and Western Culture" that the German people, and particularly we Christians, need today. What we need is a return to God and to the service of our neighbour, through the power of the death and resurrection of Jesus Christ.

7. We have born witness, and today we do so once again: "Through Jesus Christ we experience a joyous liberation from the ungodly fetters of this world for free and grateful service to all whom he has created." We therefore pray constantly: Do not let yourselves be overcome by despair, for Christ is the Lord. Say good-bye to the indifference of unbelief; do not be led astray by dreams of a better past or by speculations about another war; but in freedom and all soberness realize the responsibility which rests upon us all to rebuild a better form of government in Germany, that shall work for justice and for the welfare, peace and reconciliation of the nations.

 APPENDIX IV

ECUMENICAL ASSEMBLY

MORE JUSTICE IN THE GDR—OUR TASK AND OUR EXPECTATIONS

[In April 1989, in Dresden, the third and final session of the Ecumenical Assembly of Churches and Christians in the GDR on Justice, Peace, and the Preservation of Creation took place. The following text sums up its results. A close reading will show that the Lutheran contributors, who were in the majority in collaboration with the Roman Catholics and others, derived much of their ability to analyze the situation in the "second German dictatorship" from Dietrich Bonhoeffer's experience of the Third Reich. The church has to be actively engaged in society being "the church for others."]

[The following translation was prepared by the author. Source: Gerhard Rein, ed., *Die Opposition in der DDR* (Berlin, 1989), 205–13.]

1. Justification and Identifying the Tasks

During the course of our common path toward justice, peace, and the preservation of creation numerous texts, experiences, questions, and expectations with regard to the social situation in our country have been tabled. We cannot and certainly do not wish to avoid these questions. Indeed, we pose them because we consider them to be in the best interests of our society. In doing so we are guided in the commitment and freedom of our faith by the following biblical insights:

1.1. According to the will of almighty God every person being created in His image is called to live in dignity. Therein is grounded the essential equality of all without the diminution of the individuality and uniqueness of each person. In this we acknowledge the duty to respect and protect the rights of others and to stand up for those deprived of rights, the oppressed and the weak. Where we describe instances of suffering in our country we are attempting to follow the way of Jesus who took up the cause of people in their need.

1.2. According to the biblical understanding, justice is a gift and promise of God which awaits our response in behavior that promotes the common good. Consequently, our responsibility extends beyond concerns for the situation of the individual in order to include all of society. In the pursuit of our efforts for justice we should ensure that communal life in our country takes account of all human beings in their multifaceted reality. "For us the criterion for true justice is solidarity with the weakest member of our society."

"More justice in the GDR" today means also to take into account quite decisively the question of survival in the process of shaping of our social development. And the responsibility for the necessary decisions cannot be burdened on just a few. Preferably, we need organs of social cooperation which require and enable the participation and co-responsibility of many. So, when we identify certain needs and expectations we wish to make our contribution to the process of necessary social renewal.

1.3. Jesus has promised us in his proclamation of the kingdom of God the perfection of justice. Indeed, God's justice provides the yardstick and perspective for our action. Measured against that, human justice can only be provisional. Equally, our own efforts for justice are often ambiguous and subject to failure and the perversion of the best intentions. As Christians and churches we, too, have to ask ourselves, in our parishes and churches, to what extent, in sharing responsibility and in cooperation with others, we have achieved justice. Whenever we formulate tasks for Christians, parishes and churches we do so in the knowledge that we will be judged against that which we ourselves are prepared to do. We believe that almighty God will perfect our efforts for justice when His kingdom arrives. In the meantime we have the trust that the spirit of God is working among us everywhere where human beings honestly strive for justice.

As Christians we are called "to seek the welfare of the city" (Jeremiah 29:7). Of course, we are not called to do so because we believe ourselves to be better than others or know everything better. Important questions are disputed among us and always need further discussion. Nevertheless, we want to try, with our knowledge and insights, with our gifts, strengths, and in awareness of our limitations, to serve the common good and to assume our tasks responsibly. For this reason we are in favor of an encompassing dialogue within our society in which problems can be openly identified in order that decisions can be reached and the necessary steps taken together.

2. Practical Knowledge and Problems

The GDR is one of the countries in which the satisfaction of the basic material needs of all is guaranteed. On the other hand, there are many people living in our country with disappointed expectations. Of course, not all reasons for such disappointment are specific to the GDR. The rapid economic and social transformation which the scientific-technical revolution has brought about challenges the capacity of many people to orientate themselves adequately. Often the realities of everyday life appear impenetrable to many and this situation gives rise to a "drop out" mentality and causes some people to withdraw into their niches. The GDR shares this phenomenon with many other countries.

However, there are problems which in addition aggravate community life. For example, in both training and the work place great value is placed on so-called "community work." But many feel oppressed by it. They take it up for various reasons but often because they feel obliged to demonstrate their loyalty to the state through these activities and membership in organizations in the conviction that thereby advancement, recognition, and privileges depend on these things to a higher degree than from their normal professional function. Indeed, already at school students experience the pressure to join the "young pioneer" organization and the FDJ as well as to participate in the youth dedication and pre-military training. These are the components of an encompassing ideological indoctrination. The outcomes are often conformism and opportunism.

The claim of the state and party leadership to know in both political and economic questions what is necessary and good for the individual and society as a whole causes the citizen to perceive him or herself as a mere object of regulations, as watched over, so that he or she cannot sufficiently develop independent, critical and creative work. Thereby the solution of existing social, ecological and economic problems in our country is hindered and at the same time the perception of worldwide problems in which we are inextricably enmeshed is distorted. The tension that consequently arises between governors and the governed prejudices not only domestic peace but as well the peace within the broader European family.

Why, then, are so few prepared to assume responsibility for the common good? Many do not want to become involved either out of indolence or fear of too close contact with the authorities. Others take the view that it is not worth while; it only results in disadvantages. And this attitude comes from every day experiences. These are:

- Whenever citizens meet together to pursue common interests outside the state-sponsored social organizations they quickly come under suspicion of being engaged in activities hostile to the state.
- Whoever proposes something not exactly approved by the authorities often encounters a public servant whose chief priority is to implement party guidelines and seldom one who is prepared to assess an issue on its merits and to make rational decisions within his area of competence.
- Whoever behaves in an unexpected way that attracts the attention of the authorities will inevitably experience disadvantages in quite different areas of his life. Such occurrences cause people to be very discouraged and embittered.

In the GDR there is a deficit in honesty and truthfulness. Since the citizen is expected to say what one wants to hear he has become accustomed to say something quite different from what he really thinks and to act in ways that do not correspond to his convictions.

Many in our country perceive their particular circumstances or problems to be inadequately provided for such as for example, alcoholics, cripples, homosexuals, and released prisoners. They therefore regard themselves as having been pushed to the edge of society and to be unjustly treated. The opportunities for them to speak up or to coalesce in self-help organizations are limited.

Youth are socially and politically encouraged. However, if they come to the attention of the authorities by virtue of particular ways of thinking, speaking and dressing they are often considered a disturbance in the community and even treated as criminals. Clearly the bureaucracy and many in the community find it difficult to grasp that the behavior of these youths is really drawing attention to existing problems in our society.

Women in the GDR enjoy equality before the law. However, in the existing system, designed, of course, by men, they cannot adequately develop themselves and exert sufficient influence in their sphere. They are prevented by the onerous responsibilities of both their jobs and family and by dependence upon outmoded traditions from recognizing their own value and realizing it.

Many take refuge from the burden of their jobs and social obligations by withdrawing into the private sphere. But even here there are tensions and problems. As in other industrial countries prosperity and professional success are the standards for happiness and fulfilment. However, this one-sided orientation towards an egoistic lifestyle is an essential cause for the crisis of the family, which is evident, among other things, in the high divorce rate. Many children grow up without their father. In this situation it is difficult to do justice to the children. Indeed, for the sake attaining desired or necessary professional goals, the task of raising children is left to state-run agencies (crèches, kindergartens, daycare centers) without considering the consequences for the children. The child's need for love is often inadequately met. And in many cases this leads to later behavioral problems such a diminished capacity to bond and aggression. Consequently, the communicative and creative capacities of future generations are being impaired.

As well, the relationships to grandparents, friends and others which are so important for the stability of the family diminish. The possibility for old and sick people to be cared for within the family is narrowly limited and as well the preparedness to do so is just not there. Indeed, the placement of old people in homes is considered by many to be the normal course of events instead of a last resort. Understaffed and overcrowded old people's and nursing homes result in undignified conditions. And the encounter with suffering and dying people is being almost completely eliminated from social experiences.

3. Demands and Expectations

We are called to "seek the welfare of the city," i.e. the common good. In this regard the declaration of human rights of the United Nations is helpful and is to a large extent replicated in our constitution. And to a high degree the human rights of social content are realized; others however need to be more effectively implemented in the law of our country and in social practice. And we wish to encourage this with the following reflections.

3.1. In order for us to find our right place in our society and to be able to contribute to its formation we need to come to agreement about the present situation, assess what should be retained and how the future might appear. So, in order that our society might be able to hold its own in the wider world and develop, and as well, so that we know what we hold in common, we urgently need the necessary information and an uninhibited and honest exchange of opinions in areas of common concern to take place in public meetings as well as in the media. We can find practical ways for our society to go forward beyond the present grievances and the conflict between contrary standpoints that have to be publicly ventilated.

3.2. We need an atmosphere which encourages participation in public affairs. At present this is inhibited by secret surveillance and the still inadequate protection of information. More legal safe guards would enhance the situation. The criminal code and the associated regulations should be formulated in such a way that the interpretative possibilities are clear and kept as narrow as possible. The legal review of administrative decisions made possible since 1 July 1989, is an advance on the previous situation. However, the legal review of administrative decisions ought to be extended to cover more regulations than previously envisioned. As well, substantive factors should be included in the review process. A court whose task would be to examine the constitutionality of laws and the observance of constitutional principles would serve the further improvement of the legal system.

3.3. In order that responsibility in our society can be pertinently implemented we need agencies with clearly delineated competences at the various levels of the state as well as a clear separation of the areas of competences between state and party. In this way it can be avoided that the state is wholly and solely made responsible for all difficulties that arise. As well, concrete accountability can be requested and given. The duty of ministries to explain the grounds for their decisions to the citizens affected and to do so in writing on request would be a good beginning. The maintenance of secrecy should be limited to cases where it is absolutely unavoidable.

3.4. Only elections in which the capacity for judgment of the citizen is really tested can give the elected candidate a viable mandate. Indeed the franchise should be reformed in such a way that the constituents can exert an effective influence on the nomination of candidates and exercise their vote in secret from among a number of candidates.

3.5. Our society needs an education and training system in which people can develop to become ready and able to assume responsible conduct and mature collaboration on community projects. It should encourage creativity and achievement instead of demanding just standard performance. It should enable people to form judgments themselves instead of merely taking over those of the party. It should afford sufficient space for teachers to work freely and self-reliantly and for the individual development of students. In the education and training system there must be equal chances for all quite apart from ideological conviction and membership in state organizations or of the type and duration of military service.

3.6. We need the free development of art and culture. In spite of relaxations they are still being hindered by political supervision and the obligation to seek state approval.

3.7. Our society needs responsible citizens who know their rights and duties and who can discharge their tasks and perceive their possibilities responsibly, who think, and say what they think without grumbling and who do not stand aside and wait until all obstacles have been removed for them. And to do this they need the unhindered possibility of free assembly, to be able to form independent associations in order together to be able to reflect and to act.

3.8. Our society needs responsible citizens who within the borders of the GDR perceive their homeland. The expectations already described also have this goal. Unfortunately, the new travel regulations have not brought a relaxation in this situation which make it difficult for many citizens to perceive the GDR as their true homeland. The efforts to realize more of the steps in the CSCE resolutions may not be relaxed.

3.9. In our society those individuals who do not conform to the general expectations and who are different, or want to be, need more understanding and tolerance. Of course they, too, have to reflect to what extent they are demanding too much of others if they want a chance to be understood.

As well, those who feel disturbed or provoked by individuals who are different ought to examine whether the limits of what is endurable have been exceeded or whether here greater tolerance promotes understanding. However, official "measures" against these people, be it in the family, school, work place, the public, or in the church, are only then justified if those who are different offend human dignity or whether their presence creates unreasonable disadvantages for others. Even minorities need public space in which to ventilate their problems.

3.10. In our society people who cannot cope on their own need qualified helpers who can identify with their special circumstances, provide help so they can help themselves to integrate into society. For this purpose comprehensive information is a prerequisite, for example on alcohol abuse, criminality problems in prisons and after the release of prisoners, violence in the family and suicide.

3.11. Our society needs more than previously the active cooperation of women. They should be more strongly and responsibly involved in all spheres of the state, the economy and society. They should, however, be enabled to pioneer new ways of independent development and be given the possibility of doing so. And for this reason it is necessary to revise the traditional roles in the family and in the work place, consciously change them in order to achieve more partnership between men and women in the structuring of social life and in their responsibility for the household and family.

3.12. While acknowledging the social political provisions in the GDR for marriage and family life we still need an in-depth discussion on how the significance of the family and parental responsibility can be consciously strengthened because the shelter of the family is irreplaceable for the healthy growth and development of children. It should be made possible that one or other parent during the first three years of the child's life can, finances and other restriction on the household permitting, remain at home and that more jobs for part time workers are thereby created. Families who want to have an invalid relative at home should be supported with additional living space and assistance.

4. Tasks for Christians, Parishes and Churches

We Christians and churches live and function in this society. It therefore depends on us how justice is dispensed in it.

4.1. Tasks of the Christians

Each one of us experiences how he or she thinks more about themselves and acts selfishly, seeks his or her own advantage and misuses whatever power over which one might dispose.

In the light of the promises of the kingdom of God we are required to examine our communal life in both church and society and identify wherever unjust, inhumane and antisocial structures and behavior exist. And so, in order to be able to judge situations correctly, we should be as fully informed as possible with the relevant data. Indeed, Christians are encouraged within their personal and social sphere to become proactive in establishing more just circumstances and to be prepared to accept sacrifices and disadvantages for themselves. We have to respect and allow for the rights of others, in particular those who cannot speak for themselves, the anxious, those pushed to edge of society and strangers. We should strive to adjust our individual interests to those of the common good. Of course conflicts are unavoidable in interpersonal relationships and are part of the social reality. We should recognize and identify these as well as attempt peacefully to mediate them.

4.2. Tasks of the Parishes

We experience in our parishes how even we Christians wear ourselves out in conflicts and fail one another and deny hospitality to strangers among us. But in the light of the promises of the kingdom of God the parishes can be the place of reconciliation where love, compassion, tolerance and justice are lived out in exemplary fashion. For this reason parishes should be so reorganized as to enable the strengthening of individuals, the release of the energy of renewal in persons, practice fraternal behavior and question existing power structures. Parishes should become the advocates for people who have lost courage and hope, feel themselves robbed of their rights and stripped of their human dignity. Parishes should become advocates for all those who stand up for justice, peace, and the preservation of creation. Particularly today parishes should reflect again on their old traditions, to be open to the persecuted and to show hospitality to strangers.

4.3. Tasks of the Churches

We recognize that the churches as institutions throughout history and the present have often not lived up to their high moral standards. Consequently, in the light of the promise of the kingdom of God the churches need constantly critically to examine their behavior both internally and toward the world. Decision-making and development processes should be transparent so that many parishioners can participate in these processes. Free information and open discussion on matters of common concern should be a matter of course. The number of women in leading positions stands often in crass contrast to the reality of parish life where women are frequently in the majority. They should be therefore more intensively involved. As well the churches should encourage dialogue in the community and attempt to expand it. They should stand up publicly for the preservation of human rights be prepared to accept disadvantages in doing so. And for this all who bear responsibility in the church will have to pay heed to the fact that they do not appear only as representatives of the interests of the church but also credibly stand up for the welfare and good of all.

5. Open and Disputed Questions

In the attempt to understand and describe the historical background and present circumstances of our country we were not able in important points to achieve a common position.

We are all prepared to participate in dialogue within our society but do not always have a common language in which to express our concerns. And beyond that we differ on the question to what extent we agree with the actual methods and goals of socialism.

We recognize in common the social security and the guarantee of the basic material needs in the GDR as steps toward more justice but we are divided in the evaluation of the many problems associated with it. For this reason we seek open discussion on this issue among ourselves and in society generally.

5.1. What are the defining elements and values of a socialist society?

What economic structures will most rapidly realize these?

What contribution can a socialist society and economic system make to the questions of the survival of humanity?

5.2. In what do the necessary functions of the state consist for the achievement of the best possible just society? How do we arrive at a redefinition of the relationships within state and society?

5.3. What is our position on the historical development of our country?

With what can we identify ourselves?

Where do questions have to be raised?

What information and facts are missing?

5.4. What does it mean to be a German in the GDR?

How do we work through our identity problems?

How can the nationality question within the European peace process be clarified?

5.5. How can we find a basic theological orientation for our political responsibility in society and for the dialogue between Christians and Marxists?

Bibliography

Arendt, Hannah. *Eichmann in Jerusalem: A Report on the Banality of Evil.* New York, 1964.
———. *The Origins of Totalitarianism.* New York, 1966.
Arnett, Ronald C. *Dialogic Confession: Bonhoeffer's Rhetoric of Responsibility.* Carbondale, Ill., 2005.
Bailie, Gil. *Violence Unveiled: Humanity at the Crossroads.* NewYork, 1965.
Bankier, David, ed. *Probing the Depths of Antisemitism: German Society and the Persecution of the Jews, 1933–1941.* New York/Oxford, 2000.
Barnes, Kenneth. "Dietrich Bonhoeffer and Hitler's Persecution of the Jews," In *Betrayal: German Churches and the Holocaust,* ed. Robert P. Eriksen and Susanne Heschel, Minneapolis, 1999.
Barnett, Victoria J. "Dietrich Bonhoeffer's Relevance for Post-Holocaust Christian Theology," *Studies in Christian-Jewish Relations* 2, no. 1 (2007): 53–67.
Barth, Karl. *The Epistle to the Romans* (translated from the sixth edition by Edwyn C. Hoskyns). Oxford, 1968.
———. *How to Serve God in a Socialist Land.* New York, 1959.
———. *The German Church Conflict.* London, 1965.
Baumann, Zygmunt. *Modernity and the Holocaust.* Cambridge, 1991.
Baybrooke, Marcus. *Time to Meet: Towards a Deeper Relationship between Jews and Christians.* London. 1990.
Bekennende Kirche: Martin Niemöller zum 60. Geburtstag. Munich, 1952.
Bell, George K. *Christianity and World Order.* London, 1940.
Beller, Steven. *Vienna and the Jews 1867–1938: A Cultural History.* Cambridge, 1989.
Berg, Nicolas. *Der Holocaust und die westdeutschen Historiker: Erforschung und Erinnerung.* Göttingen, 2003.
Bergen, Doris L. *The Twisted Cross – The German Christian Movement.* Chapel Hill, N.C./London, 1996.
Berghahn, Volker, R. *Der Tirpitzplan: Genesis und Verfall einer innerpolitischen Krisenstrategie unter Wilhelm II.* Düsseldorf, 1971.
———. *Germany and the Approach of War in 1914.* 2^d ed. London, 1993.
Besier, Gerhard. *Der SED-Staat und die Kirche: Der Weg in die Anpassung.* Munich, 1993.

———, ed. *Zwischen "nationaler" Revolution und militärischer Aggression: Transformationen in Kirche und Gesellschaft während der konsolidierten NS-Gewaltherrschaft (1934–1939)*. Munich, 2001.

———. *Die Kirchen und das Dritte Reich: Spaltungen und Abwehrkämpfe 1934–1937*. Munich, 2001.

Bethge, Eberhard. *Dietrich Bonhoeffer – Theologian, Christian, Contemporary*. London, 1970.

———. *Dietrich Bonhoeffer –Theologian, Christian, Man for His Times. A Biography*, revised and edited by Victoria J. Barnett. Minneapolis, 2000.

———. *Bonhoeffer: Exile and Martyr*, edited and with an essay by John W. de Gruchy. London, 1975.

———. "Dietrich Bonhoeffer und die Juden" in Heinz Kremer, *Die Juden und Martin Luther – Martin Luther und die Juden*. Vluyn, 1988.

Beyerchen, Allan. *Scientists under Hitler: Politics and the Physics Community in the Third Reich*. New Haven, 1977.

Blackbourn, David and Geoff Eley. *The Peculiarities of German History: Bourgeois Society and Politics in Nineteenth-Century Germany*. Oxford, 1984.

Böhme, Klaus. *Aufrufe und Reden deutscher Professoren im ersten Weltkrieg*. Stuttgart, 1975.

Bonhoeffer, Dietrich. *Ethics*. New York/London, 1995. [Touchstone edition, translated by Neville Horton Smith from the German *Ethik*, Chr. Kaiser Verlag Munich, 1949].

———. *Dietrich Bonhoeffer Werke* in Siebzehn Bänden, ed. Eberhard Bethge, Ernst Feil, Christian Gremmels, Wolfgang Huber, Hans Pfeifer, Albrecht Schönherr, Heinz Eduard, Tödt, Ilse Tödt, *et al*. Munich, 1986–1999.

———. *Zettelnotizen für eine "Ethik,"* ed. Ilse Tödt. Munich, 1993.

———. and Maria von Wedemeyer. *Brautbriefe Zelle 92 1943–1945*. München, 1997.

Bonhoeffer Rundbrief: Mitteilungen der internationalen Bonhoeffer-Gesellschaft. Sektion Bundesrepublik Deutschland. Düsseldorf. Internet: http://www.bonhoeffer-gesellschaft.de.

Bonhoeffer-Studien: Beiträge zur Theologie und Wirkungsgeschichte Dietrich Bonhoeffers (Im Auftrag des Bonhoeffer-Komitees beim Bund der Evangelischen Kirchen in der DDR), ed. Albrecht Schönherr und Wolf Krötke. Berlin, 1985.

Boyens, Arnim, et al. *Kirchen in der Nachkriegszeit*. Göttingen, 1979.

Brakelmann, Günter, Martin Greschat, and Werner Jochmann. *Protestantismus und Politik: Werk und Wirkung Adolf Stöckers*. Hamburg, 1982.

Brändle, Rainer. *Am wilden Zeitenpass: Motive und Themen im Werk des deutschjüdischen Dichters Ernst Lissauer*. Frankfurt/Main, 2002.

Brendel, Steffen. *Volksgemeinschaft oder Volksstaat: "Die Ideen von 1914" und die Neuordnung Deutschlands im ersten Weltkrieg*. Berlin, 2003.

Brinks, Jan Herman. "Germany's New Right," in *Nationalist Myths and Modern Media, Contested Identities in the Age of Globalization*, ed. Jan Herman Brinks, Stella Rock, and Edward Timms. London/New York, 2006.

"Luther and the German State" *The Heythrop Journal* 39 no. 1 (1998):1-17.
Browning, Christopher. *Nazi Policy, Jewish Workers, German Killers*. Cambridge, 2000.
Bruendel, Steffen.*Volksgemeinschaft oder Volksstaat*: "*Die Ideen von 1914*" *und die Neuordnung Deutschlands im ersten Weltkrieg*. Berlin, 2003.
Carsten, Francis L. *August Bebel und die Organisation der Massen*. Berlin, 1991.
Carter, Guy Christopher. "Confession at Bethel, August 1933—Enduring Witness: The Formation, Revision, and Significance of the First Full Theological Confession." Doctoral Dissertation, Marquette University, Milwaukee, Wisconsin, April 1987.
Cecil, Lamar. *Albert Ballin: Big Business and Politics in Imperial Germany*. Princeton, 1967.
Chandler, Andrew. *Brethren in Adversity: Bishop Bell, the Church of England and the Crisis in German Protestantism, 1933–1939*. Rochester, N.Y., 1997.
———. "A Question of Fundamental Principles: The Church of England and the Jews of Germany 1933-1937" *Leo Baeck Institute Year Book* (1993): 221–61.
———. "Lambeth Palace, The Church of England and the Jews of Germany and Austria in 1938" *Leo Baeck Institute Year Book* (1995).
———. "The Death of Dietrich Bonhoeffer," *Journal of Ecclesiastical History* 45 no.3 (1994): 448–59.
———. *The Moral Imperative: New Essays on the Ethics of Resistance in National Socialist Germany, 1933–1945*. London, 1998.
Chertok, Haim. *He also spoke as a Jew. The Life of the Reverend James Parkes*. London/Portland, 2006.
Chickering, Roger. *Imperial Germany and a World without War: The Peace Movement in German Society, 1892–1914*. Princeton, 1975.
Clark, Christopher M. *The Politics of Conversion: Missionary Protestantism and the Jews in Prusssia, 1728–1941*. Oxford, 1995.
Clements, Keith. *Bonhoeffer and Britain*. Peterborough, 2006.
Conway, John S. *The Nazi Persecution of the Churches 1933–1945*. London, 1968.
———. "Protestant Missions to the Jews 1810–1980: Ecclesiastical Imperialism or Theological Aberration," *Holocaust and Genocide Studies* 1 (1986): 127–46.
———. "Between Pacifism and Patriotism-a Protestant Dilemma: The Case of Friedrich Siegmund-Schultze," in *Germans against Hitler*, ed. Francis R. Nicosia and Lawrence D. Stokes. New York, 1990, 87–113.
———. "Coming to Terms with the Past," *German History* 16, no. 3 (1998): 377–96.
———. "Changes in Christian-Jewish Relations Since the Holocaust," in *Contemporary Responses to the Holocaust*, ed. Konrad Kwiet and Jürgen Matthäus. Westport, Conn./London, 2004, 61–85.
———. "Bonhoeffer's Last Writings from Prison," *Crux* 42, no. 3 (2006): 2–10.
Dähn, Horst and Joachim Heise. *Luther in der DDR*. Berlin, 1996.
de Gruchy, John W., ed. *The Cambridge Companion to Dietrich Bonhoeffer*. Cambridge, 1999.

———. *Daring, Trusting Spirit: Bonhoeffer's Friend Eberhard Bethge*. Minneapolis, 2005.

Denzler, Georg. *Widerstand ist nicht das richtige Wort: Katholische Priester, Bischöfe und Theologen im Dritten Reich*. Zurich, 2003.

Deuerlein, Ernst. "Hitlers Eintritt in die Politik und in die Reichswehr," *Vierteljahrshefte für Zeitgeschichte* 7 (1959): 177–227.

Dibelius, Otto. *Obrigkeit*. Stuttgart/Berlin, 1963.

Dietrich Bonhoeffer Jahrbuch, 2003 and *Jahrbuch 2*, 2005/2006. Gütersloh, 2003 and 2005.

Die Mündige Welt. vols I–IV, München 1955, 1956, 1960, 1963.

Dokumentation 1/97: Erfahrungen aus zwei Diktaturen in Deutschland und unsere politische Verantwortung im demokratischen Rechststaat heute, Referate und Gesprächsrunden einer Fachtagung der Bundeszentrale für politische Bildung vom 14. bis 17 November 1996 in Berlin.

Duchrow, Ulrich. "The Confessing Church and the Ecumenical Movement," *Ecumenical Review* 33, no. 3 (1981): 212–31.

Dumas, André. *Dietrich Bonhoeffer – Theologian of Reality*. New York, 1968.

Ebert, Theodor. "Traditionen christlichen Ungehorsams,"*Gewaltfreie Aktion:Vierteljahreshefte für Frieden und Gerechtigkeit*" 55/56, 15 Jg 1.und 2. Quartal (1983):1-11.

Eckardt, A. Roy. "Can There be a Jewish-Christian Relationship?" *Journal of the American Academy of Religion* 33 (1965): 122-30.

Eley, Geoff, ed. *The "Goldhagen Effect": History, Memory Nazism—Facing the German Past*. Ann Arbor, 2000.

———. *A Crooked Line: From Cultural History to the History of Society*. Ann Arbor, 2005.

Elias, Norbert. *Studien über die Deutschen*. Frankfurt am Main, 1990.

Endrass, Elke. *Bonhoeffer und seine Richter: Ein Prozess und sein Nachspiel*. Stuttgart, 2006.

Erdmann, Karl-Dietrich. *Die Zeit der Weltkriege*. vol. 4. *Handbuch der deutschen Geschichte*. Stuttgart, 1976.

Eriksen, Robert P. and Susannah Heschel, eds. *Betrayal: German Churches and the Holocaust*. Minneapolis, 1999.

Evangelsisches Kirchenlexikon – Internationale theologische Enzyklopädie, 4 vols, ed. Erwin Fahlbusch, et al. Göttingen, 1996.

Evans, Richard. *Lying about Hitler: History, Holocaust, and the David Irving Trial*. New York, 2002.

———. *The Third Reich in Power, 1933–1939*. New York, 2005.

Fabricius, D. Cajus. *Positive Christianity in the Third Reich*. Dresden, 1937.

Fackenheim, Emil L. "The Nazi Holocaust as a Persisting Trauma for the Non-Jewish Mind," *Journal of the History of Ideas* 36, no. 2 (1975): 369–76.

Fasching, Darrell J. *Narrative Theology after Auschwitz*. Minneapolis, 1992.

Feil, Ernst Hrsg. *Glauben lernen in einer Kirche für andere: Der Beitrag Dietrich Bonhoeffers zum Christsein in der Deutschen Demokratischen Republik*. Gütersloh, 1993.

Feldmann, Christian. *"Wir hätten schreien müssen": Das Leben des Dietrich Bonhoeffer*. Freiburg, Basel, Wien, 2006.

Fischer, Fritz. "Der deutsche Protestantismus und die Politik im 19. Jahrhundert," *Historische Zeitschrift*, no. 171 (1951): 473–518.

Fischer, Hans Gerhard. *Evangelische Kirche und Demokratie nach 1945: Ein Beitrag zum Problem der politischen Theologie*. Lübeck/Hamburg, 1970.

Fleischner, Eva. *Judaism in Christian Theology since 1945: Christianity and Israel Considered in Terms of Mission*. Metuchen, N.J., 1975.

Friedländer, Saul. *Nazi Germany and the Jews: the Years of Persecution, 1933–1939*. vol. I. New York, 1997.

Frick, Peter. ed. *Bonhoeffer's Intellectual Formation: Theology and Philosophy in His Thought*. Tübingen, 2008.

Fritz, Hartmut, *Otto Dibelius: Ein Kirchenmann in der Zeit zwischen Monarchie und Demokratie*. Göttingen, 1998.

Fröhlich, Michael. *Von Konfrontation zur Koexistenz. Die deutsch-englische Kolonialbeziehungen in Afrika zwischen 1884 und 1914*. Bochum, 1990.

Funkenstein, Amos. *Perceptions of Jewish History*. Berkeley/Los Angeles/Oxford, 1993.

Gailus, Manfred. *Protestantismus und Nationalsozialismus: Studien zur nationalsozialistischen Durchdringung des protestantistischen Sozialmilieus in Berlin*. Köln/Weimar, 2002.

Gall, Lothar. *Bismarck – The White Revolutionary*. 2 vols. London, 1986.

Gerlach, Wolfgang. *And the Witnesses Were Silent: The Confessing Church and the Persecution of the Jews*, trans. Victoria Barnett. Lincoln, Neb./London, 2000.

Giese, Bernhard. *Intellectuals and the Nation in a German Axial Age*. Cambridge, 1998.

Girard, René. *Things Hidden since the Foundation of the World*. Stanford, 1978.

———. *Violence and the Sacred*. Baltimore, 1979.

Glenthøj Jørgen, *Dokumente zur Bonhoeffer-Forschung*. Munich, 1969.

———. *Zu Dietrich Bonhoeffers Eintritt in die ökumenische Arbeit*. Frederica, 1974.

Goda, Norman J. W. "Black Marks: Hitler's Bribery of His Senior Officers," *Journal of Modern History* 72 no. 2 (2000):413-52.

Goeckel, Robert F. *The Lutheran Church and the East German State: Political Conflict and Change under Ulbricht and Honecker*. Ithaca/London, 1990.

Goethe, Johann Wolfgang von. *Gesammelte Werke*. Weimar, 1887–1919.

Goldhagen, Daniel J. *Hitler's Willing Executioners: Ordinary Germans and the Holocaust*. London, 1996.

———. *A Moral Reckoning: The Role of the Catholic Church in the Holocaust and its Unfulfilled Duty of Repair*. London, 2002.

Goldschmidt, Dietrich and Hans-Joachim Kraus, eds. *Der ungekündigte Bund. Neue Begegnung von Juden und christlichen Gemeinden*. Stuttgart, 1963.
Gollwitzer, Helmut and Ursula Bohn. *Das gespaltene Gottesvolk*. Stuttgart/Berlin,1966.
Grab, Walter. *Der deutsche Weg der Judenemanzipation, 1789–1938*. Munich/Zürich, 1991.
———. "The German Way of Jewish Emancipation," *Australian Journal of Politics and History* 30, no. 2 (1984): 224–34.
Graml, Hermann. *Antisemtism in the Third Reich*, Oxford, 1992.
Graml, Hermann and Hans Mommsen, et al. *The German Resistance to Hitler*. London, 1970.
Gramley, Hedda. *Propheten des deutschen Nationalismus: Theologen, Historiker und Nationalökonomen (1848–1880)*. Frankfurt/Main, 2001.
Green, Clifford. *Dietrich Bonhoeffer: A Theology of Sociality*. Grand Rapids, Mich., 1999.
———. "Pacifism and Tyrannicide: Bonhoeffer's Christian Peace Ethic," *Studies in Christian Ethics* 18, no. 3 (2005): 31–47.
———. "Bonhoeffer-Forschung in der englischensprachigen Welt heute," *Bonhoeffer Rundbrief*, no. 82 (March 2007): 33–42.
Gremmels, Christian and Heinrich W. Grosse. *Dietrich Bonhoeffer: Der Weg in den Widerstand*. Gütersloh, 2004.
Günther, Niklas and Sönke Zanke, eds. *Abrahams Enkel: Juden, Christen, Muslime und die Schoa*. Stuttgart, 2006.
Hamerow, Theodore S. *On the Road to the Wolf's Lair: German Resistance to Hitler*. Cambridge, Mass./London, 1997.
Hammer, Karl. *Deutsche Kriegstheologie 1870–1918*. Frankfurt/Main, 1971.
Hanspeter, Michael and Michael A. Signer, eds. *Coming Together for the Sake of God: Contributions to Jewish-Christian Dialogue from Post Holocaust Germany*. Collegeville, Pa. 2007.
Hauwerwas, Stanley. *Performing the Faith: Bonhoeffer and the Practice of Nonviolence*. Grand Rapids, Mich., 2004.
Haynes, Stephen R. *Prospects for post-Holocaust Theology*. Atlanta, Ga., 1991.
———. *The Bonhoeffer-Phenomenon: Portrait of a Protestant Saint*. Minneapolis, 2004.
———. *The Bonhoeffer Legacy: Post-Holocaust Perspectives*. Minneapolis, 2006.
———. "Bonhoeffer, the Jewish People and Post-Holocaust Theology: Eight Perspectives—Eight Theses," *Studies in Christian-Jewish Relations* 2, no. 1 (2007): 36–52.
Heer, Hannes. *Hitler war's: Die Befreiung der Deutschen von ihrer Vergangenheit*. Berlin, 2005.
Heimbucher, Martin. *Christus Friede Welt Frieden: Dietrich Bonhoeffers kirchlicher und politischer Kampf gegen den Krieg Hitlers*. Gütersloh, 1997.
Henley, Grant. *Cultural Confessionalism: Literary Resistance and the Bekennende Kirche*. Oxford/Bern/Berlin, 2007.

Herbert, Karl. *Der Kirchenkampf – Historie oder bleibendes Erbe?* Frankfurt/Main, 1985.

Herbert, Ulrich, ed. *National Socialist Extermination Policies: Contemporary German Perspectives and Controversies.* New York, 2000.

Hermle, Siegfried. *Evangelische Kirche und Judentum – Stationen nach 1945.* Göttingen, 1990.

Heschel, Susannah, "Nazifying Christian Theology: Walter Grundmann and the Institute for the Study and Eradication of Jewish Influence on German Church Life," *Church History* (December 1994): 587–605.

Hewitson, Mark. *Germany and the Causes of the First World War.* Oxford/New York, 2004.

Hilberg, Raul. *The Destruction of the European Jews.* Chicago, 1962.

Hitler, Adolf. *Mein Kampf.* London, 1939.

Hockenos, D. Matthew. *A Church Divided: German Protestants and the Nazi Past.* Bloomington, Ind., 2004.

———. "The Church Struggle and the Confessing Church: An Introduction to Bonhoeffer's Context," *Studies in Christian-Jewish Relations* 2, no. 1 (2007): 1–20.

Hoffmann, Christhard, et al., eds. *Exclusionary Violence: Anti-Semitic Riots in Modern German History.* Ann Arbor, 2002.

Hoffmann, Peter. *History of the German Resistance 1933–1945.* London, 1977.

Holtschneider K. Hannah. *German Protestants Remember the Holocaust: Theology and the Construction of Collective Memory.* Münster, 2001.

Hoover, Arlie J. *The Gospel of Nationalism: German Patriotic Preaching from Napoleon to Versailles.* Wiesbaden/Stuttgart, 1986.

Horst, Max, ed. *Moltke: Leben und Werk in Selbstzeugnissen: Briefe, Schriften, Reden.* Birsfeld bei Basel, no date.

Howard, Thomas Albert. *Protestant Theology and the Making of the Modern German University.* Oxford, 2006.

Huber, Wolfgang. "Ein ökumensiches Konzil des Friedens – Hoffnungen und Hemmnisse," In *Ökumenische Existenz Heute,* ed. W. Huber, D. Ritschl, and T. Sundmeier. Munich 1986.

———. "Die jüdisch-christliche Tradition," in EKD Kolloquium, "Die kulturelle Werte Europas," in der Europäischen Akademie Otzenhausen, 29 March 2004 (5 August 2007).

Hübinger, Gangolf. *Kulturprotestantismus und Politk: zum Verhältnis von Liberalsmus und Protestantismus im wilhelminischen Deutschland.* Tübingen, 1994.

Huntemann, Georg, *The Other Bonhoeffer: An Evangelical Reassessment of Dietrich Bonhoeffer,* trans. Todd Huizinga. Grand Rapids, Mich., 1993.

Hutchison, William R. and Hartmut Lehmann, eds. *Many Are Chosen: Divine Election and Western Nationalism.* Minneapolis, 1994.

Iggers, Georg G. *The German Conception of History.* Middletown, Conn. 1968.

———. and Konrad von Moltke, eds. *The Theory and Practice of History.* Indianapolis/New York, 1973.

Jäckel, Eberhard. *Hitler's World View*. Cambridge, Mass., 1981.
Janz, Oliver. *Bürger besonderer Art: Evangelische Pfarrer in Preussen 1850–1914*. Berlin, 1994.
Jenkins, Julian. *German Pacifism Confronts German Nationalism—The Ecumenical Movement and the Cause of Peace in Germany, 1914–1933*. Lewiston, Queenstown, Lampeter, 2002.
Jones, Larry Eugene. *German Liberalism and the Dissolution of the Weimar Party System*. Chapel Hill, N.C., 1988.
Kabitz, Ulrich. "Bonhoeffers Wirkungsgeschichte in Westdeutschland," *Bonhoeffer Rundbrief*, no. 82 (March 2007): 17–26.
Kaiser, Jochen-Christoph and Martin Greschat, eds. *Der Holocaust und die Protestanten: Analyse einer Verstrickung*. Frankfurt/Main, 1988.
Kantorwicz, Hermann. *The Spirit of British Policy and the Myth of the Encirclement*. London, 1931.
Kershaw, Ian. *Hitler 1889–1936*, vol. 1, *Hubris*. London, 1998; vol. 2 *Hitler 1936–45: Nemesis*. London, 2000.
Kelly, Geffrey and F. Burton Nelson, eds. *A Testament to Freedom. The Essential Writings of Dietrich Bonhoeffer*. San Francisco, 1995.
Kiesewetter, Hubert. *Von Hitler zu Hegel, eine Analyse der Hegelschen Machtstaatsideologie und der politischen Wirkungsgeschichte des Rechtshegelianismus*. Hamburg, 1974.
Koch, Hans-Gerhard. *Staat und Kirche in der DDR: Zur Entwicklung ihrer Beziehungen 1945–1974*. Stuttgart, 1975.
Koebner, Thomas, et al., eds. *Deutschland nach Hitler: Zukunfstpläne im Exil und aus der Besatzungszeit 1939–1949*. Opladen, 1987.
Krieger, Leonard. *The German Idea of Freedom: History of a Political Tradition*. Chicago/London, 1957.
Kroetke, Wolf. "Karl Barths und Dietrich Bonhoeffers Bedeutung für die Theologie in der DDR," *Kirchliche Zeitgeschichte* 7, no. 2 (1994): 279–99.
———. "'Nur das ganze Wort ist mutig': Oekumene als Ernstfall theologischer Existenz. Das Beispiel Dietrich Bonhoeffers," *Bonhoeffer Jahrbuch* (2004/5): 125–45.
Kruck, Alfred. *Geschichte des Alldeutschen Verbandes, 1890–1939*. Wiesbaden, 1954.
Krüsche, Günter. "The Church between Accommodation and Refusal: the Significance of the Lutheran Doctrine of the 'Two Kingdoms' for the Churches of the German Democratic Republic," *Religion, State and Society* 22, no. 3 (1994): 323–32.
Kupisch, Karl. *Quellen zr Geschichte des deutschen Protestantismus (1871–1945)*. Göttingen, 1960.
———. *Durch den Zaun der Geschichte : Beobachtungen und Erkenntnisse*. Berlin, 1964.

Kuske, Martin. *The Old Testament as the Book of Christ: An Appraisal of Bonhoeffer's Interpretation.* Philadelphia, Pa, 1976.

Kwiet, Konrad and Jürgen Matthäus, eds. *Contemporary Responses to the Holocaust.* Westport, Conn, 2004.

Langmuir, Gavin. *History, Religion and Antisemitism.* Berkeley, 1990.

Leibholz-Bonhoeffer, Sabine. *Vergangen erlebt überwunden: Schicksale der Familie Bonhoeffer.* Gütersloh, 1995.

Lepenies, Wolf. *The Seduction of Culture in German History.* Princeton/Oxford, 2006.

Lessing, Eckhard. "Die theologischen Anfänge," in *Verkündigung und Forschung* 46, no. 2 (2001).

Librett, Jeffrey S. *The Rhetoric of Cultural Dialogue: Jews and Germans from Moses Mendelsohn to Richard Wagner.* Palo Alto, 2000.

Lilje, Hanns. *Valley of the Shadow*, translated with an introduction by Olive Wyon. London, 1950.

Lilla, Mark. *The Stillborn God: Religion, Politics, and the Modern West.* New York, 2007.

Lindemann, Albert, S. *The Jew Accused: Three anti-Semitic Affairs—Dreyfuss, Beilis, Frank, 1894–1915.* Cambridge, 1991.

Lindsay, Mark. *Covenanted Solidarity: The Theological Basis of Karl Barth's Opposition to Nazi anti-Semitism and the Holocaust.* New York/Bern, 2001.

———. "'The Righteous among the Nations': Bonhoeffer, Yad Vashem and the Church," *Toronto Journal of Theology* 22, no. 1 (2006): 23–38.

Littell, Franklin and Hubert G. Locke, eds. *The German Church Struggle and the Holocaust.* Detroit, 1974.

Loewenich, Walter von. *Martin Luther: Der Mann und das Werk.* Munich, 1982.

Lohr, Christian. "Dietrich Bonhoeffer – Wirkungen und Wahrnehmungen in der DDR," *Bonhoeffer Rundbrief*, no. 82 (March 2007): 2–16.

Ludwig, Hartmut. "Entstehung, Wirkung und Aktualität des Darmstädter Wortes," in *In die Irre gegangen? Das Darmstädter Wort in Geschichte und Gegenwart*, no. 4 Schriftenreihe des Instituts für vergleichende Staat-Kirche-Forschung. 1997, 9–25.

———. ed. *"Wir haben die Christliche Freiheit verraten": Das Wort des Bruderrates der EKD zum politischen Weg unseres Volkes (1947) Eine Dokumentation.* Leipzig, 1997.

McGrath, Alister. *J.I. Packer – A Biography.* Grand Rapids, Mich. 1997.

———. *Justitia Dei: A History of the Christian Doctrine of Justification.* 2nd ed., Cambridge, 1998.

Machiavelli, Nicolo. *The Prince* (Penguin Classics edition). London, 1999.

Mack, Michael. *German Idealism and the Jew – The inner Anti-Semitism of Philosophy and German-Jewish Responses.* Chicago and London, 2003.

Marsh, Charles. *Reclaiming Dietrich Bonhoeffer.* Oxford, 1994.

Massing, Paul W. *Rehearsal for Destruction: A Study of Anti-Semitism in Imperial Germany*. New York, 1949.
Meinecke, Friedrich. *Machiavellism: The Doctrine of Reason of State and its Place in Modern History*. London, 1924.
———. *Cosmopolitanism and the National State*. Princeton, 1970.
———. *Historism: The Rise of a New Historical Outlook*. London, 1972.
Meier, Kurt, *Kreuz und Hackenkreuz*. Munich, 1992.
Meiser, Hans, *Verantwortung für die Kirche: stenographische Berichte und Mitschriften von Landesbischof Hans Meiser, 1881–1956*. Göttingen, 1985.
Mengus, Raymond. "Dietrich Bonhoeffer and the Decision to Resist," *Journal of Modern History* 64 Supplement (1992):134–46.
Mennel, Stephen and John Goudsblom, eds. *Bildung: Norbert Elias on Civilization, Power and Knowledge: Selected Writings*. Chicago, 1998.
Metz, Johann-Baptist, "Christians and Jews after Auschwitz," in *Bitburg and Beyond: Encounters in American and Jewish History*, ed. Ilya Lekov (New York, 1987), 509–19.
Meyer, Michael, ed. *German-Jewish History in Modern Times*. 4 vols. New York, 1996–98.
Mick, Günther. *Die Paulskirche:Streiten für die Einigkeit und Recht und Freiheit*. Darmstadt, 1997.
Milfull, John, ed. *Why Germany? National Socialist Anti-Semitism and the European Context*. Providence/Oxford, 1993.
Missala, Heinrich. *"Gott mit uns". Die deutsche katholische Kriegspredigt 1914–1918*. Munich, 1968.
Mommsen, Hans. *Alternatives to Hitler: German Resistance under the Third Reich*. Princeton/Oxford, 2003.
Mommsen Wolfgang J. *Max Weber and German Politics, 1890–1920*. Chicago/London, 1984.
———, ed. *Kultur und Krieg: die Rolle der Intellektuellen, Künstler und Schriftsteller im ersten Weltkrieg*. Munich, 1996.
Moses, A. Dirk. *German Intellectuals and the Nazi Past*. Cambridge/New York, 2007.
Moses, John A. *The Politics of Illusion: The Fischer Controversy in German Historiography*. London/New York, 1975.
———. *Trade Unionism in Germany from Bismarck to Hitler*. 2 vols. London/New York, 1982.
———. "The Effect of the Stab-in-the-Back-Legend (*Dolchstosslegende*) on German Historical Awareness," *Teaching History* 16, no. 2 (July 1982): 1–17.
———. "The Collapse of the GDR in 1989/90: A Protestant Revolution?" *European Studies Journal* 10, no. 1–2 (1993): 147–60.
———. and Gregory Munro. "Rewriting East German History: the Role of the Churches in the Collapse of the German Democratic Republic" in *Rewriting the German Past*, ed. Reinhard Alter and Peter Monteath. Atlantic Highlands, N.J., 1997. 222–52.

———. "Dietrich Bonhoeffer as Conspirator against the Hitler Regime: The Motivation of a Protestant Revolutionary," *War and Society* 17, no. 1 (1999): 25–40.

———. "Dietrich Bonhoeffer's Prioritization of Church Unity (Oekumene)," *Journal of Religious History* 24, no. 2 (June 2000): 196–212.

———. "Bonhoeffer's Reception in East Germany," in *Bonhoeffer for a New Day: Theology in Transition*, ed. John W. de Gruchy. Grand Rapids, Mich., 1997, 278–97.

———. "Dietrich Bonhoeffer und die ökumenische Bewegung in den dreissiger Jahren," *Schriftenreihe des Instituts für Staat-Kirche – Forschung*, no. 7, Berlin, 1998, 15–25.

———. "Bonhoeffer's Germany: the Political Context," in *The Cambridge Companion to Dietrich Bonhoeffer*, ed. John W. de Gruchy, Cambridge, 1999, 3–21.

———. "The Mobilisation of the Intellectuals 1914–1915 and the Continuity of German Historical Consciousness," *Australian Journal of Politics and History* 48, no. 3, (September 2002): 336–52.

Mosse, Werner. *Jews in the German Economy*. Oxford, 1987.

———. and Arnold Pauker, eds. *Juden im wilhelminsischen Deutschland 1890–1914*. Tübingen, 1976.

Müller, Christine-Ruth. *Dietrich Bonhoeffers Kampf gegen die nationalistische Verfolgung und Vernichtung der Juden*. Munich, 1990.

Müller, Hanfried. *Von der Kirche zur Welt: Ein Beitrag zu der Beziehung des Wortes Gottes auf die societas in Dietrich Bonhoeffers theologicher Entwicklung*. Hamburg-Bergstedt, 1961.

———. "Dietrich Bonhoeffer – Christuszeuge in der Bekennenden Kirche für die mündige Welt," in *Bonhoeffer-Studien*, ed. Albrecht Schönherr und Wolf Krötke. Berlin Ost, 1985.

Munro, Gregory. *Hitler's Bavarian Antagonist: Georg Moenius and the Allgemeine Rundschau of Munich, 1929–1933*. Lewiston, Queenstown, Lampeter, 2006.

Neubert, Ehrhart. *Geschichte der Opposition in der DDR 1949–1989*. Bonn, 1997.

Neumann, Peter H. A., ed. *"Religionloses Christentum" und "nicht-religiöse" Interpretation bei Dietrich Bonhoeffer*. Darmstadt, 1990.

Nicholls, William. *Systematic and Philosophical Theology: The Pelican Guide to Modern Theology*. vol.1, Harmondsworth, 1969.

Nickson, Ann L. *Bonhoeffer on Freedom – Courageously Grasping Reality*. Aldershot, 2002.

Nipperdey, Thomas. *Deutsche Geschichte 1864–1918*. Munich, 1993.

Noack, Ulrich. *Geschichtswissenschaft und Wahrheit: Nach den Schriften von John Dalberg-Acton 1834–1902*. Frankfurt, 1947.

Oberman, Heiko. *The Roots of Anti-Semitism in the Age of the Renaissance and Reformation*. Philadelphia, 1984.

———. *Luther: Man between God and the Devil*. New Haven, 1989.

Ökumenische Versammlung für Gerechtigkeit, Frieden und Bewahrung der Schöpfung:Dresden, Magdeburg, Dresden. EKD Texte, herausgegeben vom Kirchenamt der Evangelischen Kirche in Deutschland. Hannover, 1991.

Oppen, Asta von. Der unerhörte Schrei–Dietrich Bonhoeffer und die Judenfrage im dritten Reich. Hannover, 1996.

Pagels, Elaine. Beyond Belief: The Secret Gospel of Thomas. New York, 2004.

Pangritz, Andreas. Karl Barth in der Theologie Dietrich Bonhoeffers – eine notwendige Klarstellung. Berlin, 1989.

———. "Dietrich Bonhoeffers Begründung der Beteiligung am Widerstand," Evangelische Theologie 55, no. 6 (1996): 491–519.

———. Sharing the Destiny of His People," in Bonhoeffer for a New Day," ed. John de Gruchy. Grand Rapids, Mich., 1997, 258–77.

Parkes, James. Judaism and Christianity. Chicago, 1948.

———. The Foundations of Judaism and Christianity. London, 1960.

———. Prelude to Dialogue. London, 1969.

———. Israel, the Jews and the Gentile World, 3^d ed. Marblehead, Mass. 2005.

Paton, William. The Church and the New Order. London, 1941.

Peck, William Jay. "From Cain to the Death Camps: An Essay on Bonhoeffer and Judaism," Union Seminary Quarterly Review 28, no. 2 (Winter 1973): 158–76.

Petzold, Joachim. Die Dolchstosslegende. Berlin-Ost, 1963.

Plant, Stephen. Bonhoeffer. London/New York, 2004.

Pois, Robert. National Socialism and the Religion of Nature. London/Sydney, 1986.

Powers, Thomas. Heisenberg's War – the Secret History of the German Bomb. London, 1993.

Preradovich, Nikolaus von and Josef Stingl, "Gott segne den Führer": Die Kirchen im dritten Reich – eine Dokumentation von Bekenntnissen und Selbstzeugnissen. Leoni am Starnberger See, 1986.

Pressel, B.W. Die Kriegspredigt 1914–1918 in der evangelischen Kirche Deutschlands. Göttingen, 1967.

Prolingheuer, Hans. Wir sind in die Irre gegangen. Die Schuld der Kirche unter dem Hakenkreuz. Cologne, 1987.

Pulzer, Peter. The Rise of Political anti-Semitism in Germany and Austria. Cambridge, Mass., 1988.

Raina, Peter. Bishop George Bell:The Greatest Churchman – A Portrait in Letters. London, 2006.

Rasmussen, Larry. Dietrich Bonhoeffer: Reality and Resistance. Louisville, 2005.

Read, Anthony and David Fisher. Kristallnacht. The Unleashing of the Holocaust. New York, 1989.

Rein, Gerhard, ed. Die Opposition in der DDR : Entwürfe für einen anderen Sozialismus. Berlin, 1989.

Renneberg, Monika and Mark Walker, eds. Science, Technology and National Socialism. Cambridge, 1994.

Richmond, Colin. *Campaigning against Antisemitism*. London/Portland, 2005.
Ringer, Fritz. " *'Bildung'*: The Social and Ideological Context of the German Historical Tradition," *History of European Ideas* 10, no. 2 (1989): 193–202.
Ritter, Gerhard. "Gegenwärtige Lage und Zukunftsaufgaben deutscher Geschichtswissenschaft," *Historische Zeitschrift*. No. 170 (1950): 1–22.
———. "Deutsche Geschichtswissenschft im 19. Jahrhundert," *Geschichte in Wissenschaft und Unterricht* 1 (1950): 129–37.
———. *The German Resistance: Carl Goerdeler's Struggle against Tyranny*. London, 1958.
———. "Geschichtsunterricht oder 'Gemeinschaftskunde'," *Geschichte in Wissenschaft und Unterricht* 13 (1962): 281–94.
———. *The German Problem: Basic Questions of German Political Life, Past and Present*, trans. Sigurd Burkhardt. Columbus, Ohio, 1965.
———. *Sword and Scepter*, vol. I. Coral Gables, Fla., 1972.
Robertson, Edwin, ed. *Dietrich Bonhoeffer – No Rusty Swords – Letters Lectures and Notes from the Collected Works*. London, 1965.
———. *The Shame and the Sacrifice: the Life and Teaching of Dietrich Bonhoeffer*. London/Sydney, 1987.
———. *Bonhoeffer's Heritage*. London, 1989.
———. *Unshakeable Friend: George Bell and the German Churches*. London, 1995.
Robinson, J.A.T. *Gott ist anders*. mit einer Einführung von Eberhard Bethge. Munich, 1964.
Röhm, Eberhard and Jörg Thierfelder. *Juden – Christen – Deutsche*. 2 vols. Stuttgart, 1992.
Roman Catholic/Lutheran Joint Commission on the Augsburg Confession, signed at Augsburg, 23 February 1980. *Lutheran World Information* (December, 1980).
Roseman, Mark. *The Wannsee Conference and the Final Solution: A Reconsideration*. New York, 2002.
Rosenbaum, Stanley R. "Dietrich Bonhoeffer: A Jewish View," *Journal of Ecumenical Studies* 18 (Spring 1981): 301–07.
Rubenstein, Richard L. "Religion and the Goldhagen Thesis," in *Religion in a Secular Society:Essays in Honor of Harvey Cox*. ed. Arvind Sharma. Harrisburg, Pa, 2007.
Rupp, Gordon. *'I seek my brethren': Bishop George Bell and the German Churches*. London, 1975.
Rürup, Reinhard. *Emanzipation und Antisemitismus*. Göttingen, 1975.
Sander, Hartmut, ed. Veröffentlichungen des Evangelischen Zentralarchivs, vol. II. *Friedrich Siegmund-Schultze 1855-1969*, ed. Christa Stache. Berlin 1985.
Scharffenroth, Ernst-Albert. "Der Einsatz von George Bell und Gerhard Leibholz für eine konstruktive Deutschlandpolitik Grossbritanniens 1941–1943," in *Die Aufgabe der Kirche in Kriegszeiten*. Göttingen, 1988, 94–115.
Schiefel, Werner. *Bernhard Dernburg 1865–1937: Kolonialpolitiker und Bankier im wilhelminischen Deutschland*. Zürich, no date.

Schild, Maurice. "Sasse and Bonhoeffer: Churchmen on the Brink," *Lutheran Theological Journal* 29 (1995): 3–6.

———. "Dietrich Bonhoeffer and the Burden of Discipleship in Contemporary Australia," *Lutheran Theological Journal* 39, nos. 2 and 3 (2005): 169–80.

Schleunes, Karl. *The Twisted Road to Auschwitz: Nazi Policy Towards German Jews, 1933–1939*. Urbana, Ill., 1990.

Schlingelsiepen, Ferdinand. "De mortuis nihil nisi bene oder wie arrogant war Dietrich Bonhoeffer," *Deutsches Pfarrblatt* 1 (2002).

———. *Dietrich Bonhoeffer, 1906–1945: eine Biographie*. Munich, 2006.

Schmidt, Hans. *Verheissung und Schreken der Freiheit*. Stuttgart/Berlin, 1964.

Schmidt, Kurt Dietrich, ed. *Die Bekenntnisse und grundsätzlichen Äusserungen zur Kirchenfrage des Jahres 1933*. Göttingen, 1934.

———. *Die Bekenntnisse und grundsätzlichen Äusserungen zur Kirchenfragen des Jahres 1934*. Göttingen, 1935.

Schnabel, Franz. *Deutsche Geschichte im 19. Jahrhundert*, 4 vols. Freiburg, 1959.

Scholder, Klaus. *The Churches and the Third Reich*. 2 vols. London 1988.

Schönherr, Albrecht, *"Aber die Zeit war nicht verloren": Erinnerungen eines Altbischofs*. Berlin, 1993.

Schoeps, Julius and Michael Ley, eds. *Der Nationalsozialismus als politische Religion*. Bodenheim bei Mainz, 1997.

Schultz Hans-Jürgen, ed. *Juden, Christen, Deutsche*. Stuttgart, 1961.

Schwabe, Klaus, Rolf Reichardt, Reinhard Hauf, ed. *Gerhard Ritter: Ein politischer Historiker in seinen Briefen*. Boppard am Rhein, 1984.

Schwier, Helmut, ed. *Church and Israel: A Contribution from the Reformation Churches in Europe to the Relationship between Christians and Jews*. Frankfurt/Main, 2001.

Seeberg, Reinhold. *Geschichte, Krieg und Seele: Reden und Aufsätze aus den Tagen des Weltkrieges*. Leipzig, 1916.

Seidel, Jürgen, "Der Umgang mit der Schuld nach dem Ende des 2. Weltkrieges im ökumenischem Kontext. 7. Berliner Staat-Kirche Kolloquium (May 25–27, 1998). *Schriftenreihe des Instituts für vergleichende Staats-Kirche-Forschung*, vol. 7. 37–50.

Seim, Jürgen, "Israel und die Juden im Leben und Werk Hans Joachim Iwand," in *Die Juden und Martin Luther – Martin Luther und die Juden*. Neukirchen-Vluyn, 1985, 249–88.

Shriver Jr., Donald W. *An Ethic for Enemies: Forgiveness in Politics*. Oxford, 1995.

Siegele-Wenschkewitz. *Nationalsozialismus und Kirchen: Religionspolitik von Partei und Staat bis 1935*. Düsseldorf, 1974.

——— and Carsten Nicolaisen, eds. *Theologische Fakultäten im Nationalsozialisozialismus*. Göttingen, 1993.

———, ed. *Christlicher Antijudaismus: Theologische und kirchliche Programme Deutscher Christen*. Frankfurt/Main, 1994.

Siegmund-Schultze. *Die Überwindung des Hasses*. Zürich, 1946.

Slane, Craig. *Bonhoeffer as Martyr: Social Responsibility and Modern Christian Commitment*. Grand Rapids, Mich., 2004.

———. "Martyrdom and a 'World come of Age'," *Crux* 42, no. 3 Fall (2006): 11–21.

Smith, Helmut Walser. *German Nationalism and Religious Conflict: Culture, Ideology, Politics, 1870–1914*. Princeton, 1995.

Smith, Robert O. "Reclaiming Bonhoeffer After Auschwitz," *Dialogue: A Journal of Theology* 43, no. 3 (Fall 2004): 205–20.

Smith, Ronald Gregor, ed. *World Come of Age: A Symposium on Dietrich Bonhoeffer*. London, 1967.

Smith, Woodruff D. *The Ideological Origins of Nazi Imperialism*. New York/Oxford, 1986.

Smith-von Osten, Annemarie. *Von Treysa 1945 bis Eisenach 1948: zur Geschichte der Grundordnung der Evangelischen Kirche*. Göttingen, 1980.

Sontheimer, Kurt. *Antidemokratisches Denken in der Weimarer Republik: die politischen Ideen des deutschen Nationalismus*. Munich, 1962.

Sorkin, David. *The Transformation of German Jewry, 1780–1840*. New York/Oxford, 1987.

Spong, John Shelby and Jack Daniel Spiro. *Dialogue: In Search of Jewish-Christian Understanding*. Haworth, N.J., 1999.

———. *The Sins of Scripture*. San Francisco, 2005.

Srbik, Heinrich Ritter von. *Geist und Geschichte, vom deutschen Humanismus bis zur Gegenwart*. Munich, 2 vols., 1950.

Stackelberg, Roderick. *Hitler's Germany: Origins, Interpretations and Legacies*. London, 2001.

Steininger, Rolf. *Deutsche Geschichte seit 1945: Darstellung und Dokumente in vier Bänden*. Frankfurt/Main 1996.

Stern, Fritz. *Gold and Iron: Bismarck, Bleichröder, and the Building of the German Empire*. New York, 1977.

———. *Dreams and Delusions*: *The Drama of German History*. London, 1987.

Stone, Dan, ed. *The Historiography of the Holocaust*. London, 2004.

Strauss, Herbert, A. and Norbert Kampe, eds. *Antisemitismus – von der Judenfeindschaf zum Holocaust*. Frankfurt/Main, 1984.

Tal, Uriel. *Christians and Jews in Germany: Religion, Politics and Ideology in the Second Reich, 1970–1914*. Ithaca/London, 1975.

Thadden, Rudolf von, "Dietrich Bonhoeffer und der deutsche Nachkriegsprotestantismus," in *Kirchen in der Nachkriegszeit*, ed. Arnim Boyen, et al. Göttingen, 1979. 125–38.

Thielicke, Helmut, ed. *In der Stunde Null: die Denkschrift des Freiburger 'Bonhoeffer Kreises': Politische Gemeinschaftsordnung. Ein Versuch zur Selbstbestimmung des christlichen Gewissens in den politischen Nöten*. Tübingen, 1979.

't Hooft, Visser. *Memoirs*. London, 1973.

Tödt, Heinz-Eduard. *Theologische Perspektiven nach Dietrich Bonhoeffer*. Gütersloh, 1993.

———. *Komplizen, Opfer und Gegner des Hitler Regimes: Zur "inneren" Geschichte von protestantischer Theologie und Kirche im "Dritten Reich."* Gütersloh, 1997.

———. *Authentic Faith: Bonhoeffer's Theological Ethics in Context*, trans. David Stassen and Ilse Tödt. Grand Rapids, Mich./Cambridge, U.K. 2007.

Tödt, Ilse, ed. *Dietrich Bonhoeffers Hegel Seminar 1933. Nach Aufzeichnungen von Ferenc Lehel.* Gütersloh, 1988.

———. "Paradoxical Obedience: Dietrich Bonhoeffer's Theological Ethics, 1933–1943," *Lutheran Theological Journal* 35, no.1 (May 2001): 3–16.

Travers, Martin. *Thomas Mann.* London, 1992.

Troeltsch, Ernst, *The Social Teaching of the Christian Churches*, 2 vols. Louisville, 1992. [reprint of the 1931 edition in translation of *Die Soziallehren der christlichen Kirchen und Gruppen*, 1912].

Vorlink, Peter, ed. *Bonhoeffer in a World Come of Age.* Philadelphia, Pa, 1976.

Ungern-Sternberg, Jürgen von und Wolfgang von Ungern-Sternberg. *Der Aufruf 'An die Kulturwelt!'* Stuttgart, 1996.

Urbach, Karina, "Between Saviour and Villain: 100 years of Bismarck Biographies," *The Historical Journal* 41, no. 4 (1998): 1141–60.

Wehler, Hans-Ulrich. *Deutsche Gesellschaftsgeschichte. Vol. 3. Von der "deutschen Doppelrevolution" bis zum Beginn des Ersten Weltkriegs 1849–19.* Munich, 1995.

———. "Deutsches Bildungsbürgertum in vergleichender Perspektive – Elemente eines 'Sonderwegs'?" in *Bildungsbürgertum im 19. Jahrhundert*, Part IV, ed. Jürgen Kocka. Stuttgart, 1989. 215–37.

Weindling, Paul. *Health, Race and German Politics between National Unification and Nazism, 1870–1945.* Cambridge, 1989.

Weisenborn, Günther, ed. *Der lautlose Aufstand: Bericht über die Wiederstandsbewegung des deutschen Volkes 1933–1935.* Hamburg, 1962.

Weyer, Adam. *Kirche im Arbeiterviertel.* Gütersloh, 1971.

Wheeler-Bennett. *The Nemesis of Power. The German Army in Politics 1918–1945.* London, 1961.

Wiener, Philip P., ed. *Dictionary of the History of Ideas: Studies of Selected Pivotal Ideas.* 4 vols. New York, 1968.

Williams, James G. *The Bible, Violence, and the Sacred: Liberation from the Myth of Sacred Violence.* New York, 1992.

Williamson, George S. "A Religious *Sonderweg*? Reflections on the Sacred and the Secular in the Historiography of Modern Germany." *Church History* 75, no. 1 (2006): 139–56.

Willis, Robert E. "Bonhoeffer and Barth on Jewish Suffering: Reflections on the Relationship between Theology and Moral Sensibility," *Journal of Ecumenical Studies* 24, no. 4 (1987): 598–615.

Willms, Johannes, *Nationalismus ohne Nation: deutsche Geschichte von 1789 bis 1914.* Düsseldorf, 1983.

———. *Bismarck :Dämon der Deutschen: Anmerkungen einer Legende.* Berlin, 1997.

Wind, Renate. *Dem Rad in die Speichen fallen: Die Lebensgeschichte des Dietrich Bonhoeffer.* Weinheim and Basel, 1999.
Wistrich, Robert. *Hitler and the Holocaust.* London, 2001.
Wright, J.R.C. *"Above Parties": The Political Attitudes of the German Protestant Church Leadership 1918–1933.* Oxford, 1974.
Wüstenberg, Ralf K. "Dietrich Bonhoeffer on Theology and Philosophy," *Anvil* 12, no. 1 (1995): 45–56.
———. "Der Einwand des Offenbarungspositivismus – Was hat Bonhoeffer an Barth eigentlich kritisiert?" – Forschungsbericht – *Theologische Literaturzeitung* 121, no. 10 (1996): 998–1004.
———. *A Theology of Life: Dietrich Bonhoeffer's Religionless Christianity*, trans. Doug Stott. Grand Rapids, Mich./Cambridge, UK, 1998.
Young, Josiah Ulysses. *No Difference in the Fare: Dietrich Bonhoeffer and the Problem of Racism.* Grand Rapids, Mich. 1998.
Zerner, Ruth. "Dietrich Bonhoeffer's American Experiences: People, Letters and Papers from Union Seminary," *Union Seminary Quarterly Review* 31, no. 4 (1976): 261–82.
———. "Dietrich Bonhoeffer and the Jews: Thoughts and Action, 1933–1945," *Jewish Social Studies* 37, nos. 3-4 (1975): 235–50.
———. "Dietrich Bonhoeffer's Views on the State and History," in *A Bonhoeffer Legacy – Essays in Understanding*, ed. A. J. Klassen, Grand Rapids, Mich., 1981. 131–60.
Ziegler, Philip G. *Doing Theology when God is Forgotten: The Theological Achievement of Wolf Krötke.* New York, 2007.
Zimmermann, Jens. "Suffering with the World: The Continuing Relevance of Dietrich Bonhoeffer's Theology," *Crux* 42, no. 3 (2006): 37–54.
Zimmermann, Moshe. *Die deutschen Juden 1914–1945.* Munich, 1997.
Zimmermann, Wolf-Dieter, *Wir nannten ihn Bruder Bonhoeffer.* Berlin, 1995.

Index

ABC (Australian Broadcasting Corporation), xvii, xxi
Abraham, 46
Abwehr (Military Counter Intelligence), xx, 140, 160–162, 174
Abyssinian Baptist Church, New York, 80
Act and Being, see Akt und Sein
Acton, Lord (John Emerich Edward Dalberg-Acton, *Baron Acton*), 189, 201n.30
Acts of the Apostles, 31, 46, 226
Adenauer, Konrad, 213, 235–236
Africa, 17, 186, 238
"After Ten Years" ("Nach zehn Jahren"), 141, 143, 147n.31, 147n.38, 174, 178, 189, 199n.2, 199n.16, 209, 210, 221, 229
Akt und Sein (*Act and Being*), 75–76, 100n.9, 155
"All Under One Christ" ("Alle unter einem Christus"), 36
Allgemeine Evangelische Lutherische Kirchenzeitung, 84
Alsace, 47
Althaus, Paul, 79, 84, 102 n.34
Amritsar Massacre (Jallianwala Bagh Massacre, April 13, 1919), 92
Anglican Church, *see* Church of England
Anglican theological colleges, 136
Anglo-Saxon theology, xix, 78, 82, 85, 88, 89
Antichrist, xviii, 6, 15, 77, 108, 109, 123, 125, 126, 126n.1, 133, 138, 140, 146n.29, 173

Anti-Judaism, xix, xx, 46–47, 52, 53–56, 63, 68n.9, 110, 115, 148, 149, 150, 152, 154, 156, 162, 164, 166, 168, 193, 194, 196, 210, 212, 216, 223, 225, 228, 234
Anti-Semitism, xii, xvii, xix, 1, 46–49, 51–52, 55–56, 58, 61–63, 65, 67, 68n.9, 68n.14, 71n.50, 72n.55, 72n.61, 104, 116, 126n.4, 129n.34, 148–149, 154, 156–157, 194–196, 208, 222, 225, 228
An Appeal to the Civilized World (*Aufruf an die Kulturwelt*), 32
Arendt, Hannah, 145n.7, 212, 230n.24, 273
Arierparagraph, see Aryan Paragraph
Armistice Day, 80, 101n.28, 101n.30
Aryan, 48, 66, 120, 125, 130, 195, *see also* Non-Aryan
Aryan Paragraph, 65, 107, 115, 117–119, 122, 150, 152–154, 156, 171n.14
Asmussen, Hans, 157, 206, 207, 217, 226, 228, 260
Aufruf an die Kulturwelt, see An Appeal to the Civilized World
Augustine of Hippo, *Saint*, 53, 243, 252n.20
Auschwitz, 57, 66, 220
Australian Broadcasting Corporation, *see* ABC
Austria, 14, 19, 20, 21, 26n.37, 26n.38, 28, 57, 67, 71n.43, 121, 148

Bach, Johann Sebastian, 183
Ballin, Albert, 50, 62, 72n.58

Barcelona, 40–42, 45n.42, 75, 90
Barmen Confession (Barmen Declaration), 120–123, 133, 152, 173, 209, 217–218, 255–257
Barth, Karl, xix, 10, 30, 32–33, 35, 37–38, 39, 45n.32, 74–75, 79, 82–83, 88–89, 120, 149, 151–152, 207, 209–214, 217–218, 230n.14, 237, 243, 250
Basler Nachrichten, 157
Bavarian People's Party (*Bayerische Volkspartei*), 64
BEK, *see* Bund der Evangelischen Kirchen
Bekennende Kirche, see Confessing Church
Belgium, 15, 32, 33
Bell, George Kennedy Allen, *bishop of Chichester*, 122–123, 125, 174, 190
Berlin, 20, 27, 30, 49–50, 55, 57, 75, 78, 98, 101n.32, 104, 117–120, 138–139, 154, 162, 172n.28, 223, 224, 225, 229n.6, 240, 245
Berlin-Charlottenburg, 99
Berlin-Dahlem, 120, 133, 154
Berlin-Grunewald, 30
Berlin Olympics, 66
Berlin-Steglitz, 156, 158–159
Berlin Technical University, 89, 102n.35
Berlin, University, 17, 24n.14, 27, 30, 33, 36, 39, 44n.24, 71n.47, 71n.51, 133
Berlin wall, 239, 242
Berlin-Wedding, 97–99, 197
Berlin-Weissensee, 222–223, 235, 242, 244, 245, 250
Besier, Gerhard, 217
Besson, Waldemar, 235, 251n.5
Bethel, 235, 238, 239, 242
Bethel Confession, 114–116, 118, 122, 128n.28, 129n.30, 150–151, 170n.9

Bethge, Eberhard, ix, 13, 33, 35–38, 75, 79, 97, 99, 100n.6, 100n.8, 110, 112–113, 115–116, 132, 136, 146n.29, 155, 188, 190, 202n.36, 205, 229n.3, 229n.5, 235, 237–239, 251n.2
Biesenthal, 98
Bildung, 59, 60, 61, 71n.45, 148
Bildungsbürger, Bildungsbürgertum, xix, xx, 1, 10–11, 13–14, 22, 24n.18, 30–31, 51, 56, 58–59, 61–63, 67, 70n.30, 71n.43, 80–81, 88, 98–99, 130, 134–135, 141–143, 145, 148–149, 160, 169, 174–178, 181, 183–191, 193–198, 221, 234
Bismarck, Otto von, xix, xx, 8, 11, 15–21, 25n.29, 26n.37, 28, 30, 48, 62, 72n.55, 72n.58, 149, 160, 192, 194, 197, 212, 214, 216, 218, 230n.27
Blackbourn, David, 1
Bleichroder, Gerson, 62, 72n.55
blood and soil, *see* Blut und Boden
Bluntschli, Johann Kaspar, 28
Blut und Boden (Blood and soil), 103, 106, 132, 137
Bodelschwingh, Friedrich von, 153
Bonhoeffer, Dietrich, xi, xvii, xviii, 2, 3, 13, 22, 30, 39, 43n.1, 44n.24, 45n.30, 45n.41, 76, 77, 82, 84, 86, 88, 90–100, 101n.27, 101n.28, 102n.35, 103–104, 118, 120–123, 125, 127n.1, 130, 132–136, 138–139, 141–143, 145, 146n.12, 146n.29, 150, 152, 171n.15, 173–180, 182–184, 199n.16, 200n.27, 201n.36, 204, 205, 207, 209–214, 217, 218–221, 229, 229n.3, 229n.4, 233–235, 237–240, 242–251, 251n.2, 251n.6, 251n.8, 252n.16, 263
  America, experiences in, xviii, 42, 77–81, 83, 88–89, 134
  Anglo-Saxon theology, xix, 78, 82, 85, 89, 126
  Barcelona, experience in, 40–42, 75

education, xix, 14, 27, 34
England, experience in, 122–123,
  133, 136, 154–155, 173, 174, 199n.1
Jewish question, xviii, xx, 46, 63,
  67, 106–118, 122, 127n.6, 148–169,
  170n.9, 171n.26, 173, 193–196,
  202n.46, 205, 210, 218, 220–223,
  225–226, 228–229, 229n.5, 234
political values, xix, xx, 11, 34,
  74–77, 85, 87, 89–93, 95–97, 99,
  103–107, 111–114, 118, 121, 124,
  126n.1, 127n.7, 128n.19, 128n.25,
  128n.30, 132–134, 137–138, 140–
  142, 144–145, 160, 168, 189–194,
  196–199, 205, 207, 209, 234, 237
relationship with Adolf Deissmann,
  14, 31, 36, 75
relationship with Adolf von Harnack, 10, 14, 30–31, 33, 36, 42, 75
relationship with Eberhard Bethge,
  33, 75, 100n.6, 100n.8
relationship with Elisabeth Zinn, 134
relationship with Erwin Sutz, xviii,
  79, 89, 98, 102n.50, 130, 145n.3
relationship with Frank Fisher,
  xviii, 79
relationship with Franz Hildebrandt, 152, 157
relationship with Friedrich
  Siegmund-Schulze, 99
relationship with George Bell, 122,
  123, 125, 174
relationship with Gerhard Leibholz, 155
relationship with Gerhard Ritter, 10
relationship with Hans-Christoph
  von Hase, 38
relationship with Hans von
  Dohnanyi, 138, 140, 160, 237
relationship with Helmut Rössler,
  83, 101n.31
relationship with Jean Lasserre,
  xviii, 79, 81, 89, 134

relationship with Karl Barth, xix,
  30, 33, 37, 38, 74, 79, 82, 83
relationship with Karl Holl, 14, 36
relationship with Leonard Hodgson, 108, 125, 129n.53
relationship with Paul Lehmann,
  81, 138, 196, 198, 199
relationship with Reinhold Nie-
  buhr, 139
relationship with Reinhold See-
  berg, 14, 33, 36, 37, 39
Roman experience, 35, 36
Tegel experience, 76, 181, 184–189,
  197, 235
Westminster Abbey, 205, 233
Bonhoeffer, Karl, 30
Bonhoeffer, Karl Friedrich, 31, 134
Bonhoeffer, Klaus, 31, 35, 160
Bonhoeffer, Paula (née von Hase),
  30, 90
Bonhoeffer, Sabine, 30, 136, 155
Bonhoeffer, Walter, 31, 40, 42
Born, Max, 131
Born, Stephan, 55
Brandt, Willy, 236
Braun, Wernher Magnus Maximilian
  von, 130
Brinks, Jan Herman, 220, 238n.39
Brüdergemeinde, see Moravians
Brüderrat, see Council of Brethren
Bubis, Ignaz, 220
Bullock, Alan Louis Charles, 65
Bultmann, Rudolf, 75, 237
Bund der Evangelischen Kirchen, 242
bureaucracy, 7, 9, 16, 22, 58, 62, 140,
  241, 266

Caiaphas, 4
Calvary; Golgotha, 96, 116, 151, 164,
  166–167, 169, 183, 225
Cambridge, England, 63, 82, 83
Canaris, Wilhelm Franz, *Admiral*,
  138, 140, 141, 160

CDU, Christian Democratic Union, 231n.39, 236
Chamberlain, Houston Stewart, 57
Charité Hospital, Berlin, 30
Charlemagne, 53
Charlottenburg, *see* Berlin-Charlottenburg
Chełmno nad Nerem, Poland, 57
Christ und Welt, 226
Christian Democratic Union, *see* CDU
Christlichsoziale Partei, 61
"Church for others", 39, 239, 247, 248, 263
Church of England, 8, 23n.13, 174, 202n.36, 233
Church Struggle, xi-xii, xix-xx, 35, 104, 106
Class (Claß), Heinrich, 17
Clausewitz, Carl Philipp Gottlieb von, 29
Codex Justinianus, 53
"Cognitive dissonance", 5, 218
Communist Party, KPD, 34, 64, 90
Concordat, *see* Konkordat
Confessing Church, *Bekennende Kirche*, xviii, xx, 78, 108, 114–115, 120–121, 123, 125, 133–134, 139, 149, 152, 154–158, 164, 173–174, 202, 204, 206, 208–209, 211, 213, 221, 246, 250
Cost of Discipleship (*Nachfolge*), 134–136, 139, 174, 210, 244
Council of Brethren (*Brüderrat*) of the Church of the Old Prussian Union, 155
Council of Brethren (*Brüderrat*) of the Confessing Church, 129, 174
Council of Brethren (*Brüderrat*) of the Evangelical Church, 221
Council of Rome, 1215 (Fourth Lateran Council), 53
Cromwell, Oliver, xviii, 7

Crusades, 4, 53–54
Czechoslovakia, 11, 84, 238

Dahlem, *see* Berlin-Dahlem
Darfur, 3
Darmstadt Statement (*Das Darmstädter Wort*), 213–214, 216–220, 230n.28, 230n.29, 234, 261
Deissmann, Gustav Adolf, 14, 31, 43n.14, 75
Denmark, 14, 26n.38, 28, 88
Depression (Great Depression), 80, 89, 90
Deutsche Arbeiterpartei, *see* German Workers' Party
Deutsche Christen, *see* "German Christians"
Deutsche Demokratische Republik (*DDR*), *see* German Democratic Republic (GDR)
Deutsche Volkspartei, *see* German People's Party
Deutschnationale Volkspartei, *see* German National People's Party
Dernburg, Bernhard, 62
Dibelius, (Friedrich Karl) Otto, bishop, 217, 229n.6, 240, 241, 243, 248, 250, 252n.20
Dietze, (Friedrich Karl Nicolaus) Constantin von, 193, 202n.46
"Divine mandates", 198
"Divine right of kings", 7, 15, 189, 190, 233
Dohnanyi, Hans von, 138, 140, 160, 162, 237
Dresden, 247, 249, 263
Dreyfus Affair, 48, 69n.14
Droysen, Johann Gustav, 21, 26n.37

Ecumenical movement, xx, 36, 81–86, 88–89, 96, 98, 122–123, 125–126, 133, 160, 162, 173, 174. 206, 217, 229, 259

Eichmann, (Karl) Adolf, 57, 224
Einstein, Albert, 131
Eley, Geoff, 1
Emergency Decree (*Notverordnung*), 64
Enabling Law (*Ermächtigunsgesetz*), 64
Epistle to the Galatians, *see* Galatians, Epistle to the
Erdmann, Karl Dietrich, 179
Erfurt, 247
Erhard, Ludwig, 236
Ermächtigungsgesetz, *see* Enabling Law
Ethics, xx, 102n.41, 110, 114, 126n.1, 143, 161, 163–169, 189–191, 193–194, 198, 204, 207, 213–214, 218, 220, 222, 223, 229n.5, 235, 238, 247
"Ethics of responsibility", xx, 141
Eucken, Walter, 193
Evangelische Kirchentage, 236

Faith and Order, 123, 125
Falcke, Heino, 247
Fanø, 88, 123, 125
Feil, Ernst, 238
Fichte, Johann Gottlieb, 19, 27
Finkenwalde, 79, 99, 133, 134, 136, 138, 155
Fischer, Fritz, 43n.4, 216
Fisher, Frank, xviii, 79
Fisher, Geoffrey Francis, *archbishop of Canterbury*, 207
Fleischner, Eva, 109, 110
Flossenbürg, 205, 235
Flottenpolitik, 17
"Folkish" (*völkisch*), 48, 61, 82, 84, 102n.35, 103
France, xviii, 14, 19–20, 26n.38, 27–28, 33, 48, 58, 149, 162, 213, 236
Führerprinzip, *see* Leadership principle

Galatians, Epistle to the, 80
Gandhi, (Mohandas Karamchand), *mahatma*, 91–92, 97
GDR, *see* German Democratic Republic (GDR)
Gemeinsames Leben, *see Life Together*
Genesis, Book of, 10, 182
Geneva, 162, 211
"German Christians" (*Deutsche Christen*), xix, xx, 78, 106–108, 115–122, 127n.11, 130, 133, 150–153, 173, 204
German Confederation, 21
German Democratic Republic (GDR), 39, 43n.1, 217, 229n.6, 234, 238–239, 242–249, 251, 252n.20, 253n.30, 263–266, 269, 271–272
German Dualism, 19–21
German National People's Party (*Deutschnationale Volkspartei, DNVP*), 64, 74
German paradigm, xix, 14, 18, 22, 219
German People's Party (*Deutsche Volkspartei, DVP*), 31
German question, xix, 19, 20, 21, 26n.37
German Workers' Party (*Deutsche Arbeiterpartei, DAP*), 63
Germany, xi, xvii–xviii, xx–xxi, 1–3, 5, 7–8, 10–11, 13–19, 21–22, 26n.37, 27–29, 31–35, 40–41, 46–52, 54–56, 58–59, 61–63, 65–66, 68n.14, 70n.30, 71n.43, 79, 81, 84–86, 89, 96, 100, 104–105, 108, 113, 116–119, 122–123, 130–131, 133, 137, 139–140, 142, 148–149, 152, 154–155, 158–163, 173–175, 180, 186, 188–193, 195–197, 204–205, 208–209, 212–218, 220–221, 226, 228, 233–236, 238–239, 262
Gleichschaltung, 64, 131
Glenthøj, Jørgen, 98, 238
Goebbels, (Paul) Joseph, 66

Goerdeler, Carl Friedrich, 190, 237
Goethe, Johann Wolfgang von, 19
Göttingen, 30, 136
Goldhagen, Daniel Jonah, 47, 68n.9
Golgotha, *see* Calvary
Gospel, xx, 4–7, 22, 23n.9, 28, 38, 46, 67n.3, 78–81, 83, 85–89, 97, 101n.27, 104, 106–107, 116–117, 123, 132–134, 151, 183, 185–186, 192, 194, 210–211, 219, 221, 229n.3, 232n.46, 233, 240, 243–247, 249, 250
"*Gott mit uns*", 15
"*Gott strafe England*", 15, 25n.24, 32
Grab, Walter, 48, 148–149
Graml, Hermann, 237
Great Depression, *see* Depression (Great Depression)
Green, Clifford J., xi, 251n.8
Greiser, Arthur, *Gauleiter*, 57
Grimme, Adolf, 214
Grosse, Heinrich W., 251n.1
"*Grundfragen einer christlichen Ethik*", 40
Grunewald, *see* Berlin-Grunewald
Grynszpan, Herschel Feibel, 66
Guilt (theological), 88, 124, 143–145, 163–164, 168, 170, 194, 204–213, 217–218, 222, 226–228, 231n.32, 235, 259, 261
Guilt (war), 40, 81, 85, 211, 213
Gynmasium, humanistisches, 13, 187, 188

Haber, Fritz, 62
Hamburg, 47, 50, 83, 216, 237
Harder, Günther, 227–228
Harnack, Adolf von, 10, 14, 30–33, 36–37, 42, 45n.32, 75
Hase, Hans-Christoph von, 38
Hase, Paula von, *see* Bonhoeffer, Paula
Haynes, Stephen R., 128n.19, 165–166, 168–170, 170n.9

Heckel, Theodor, 122–123
Hegel, Georg Wilhelm Friedrich, xviii, xix, 8–16, 21, 24n.4, 24n.17, 24n.18, 24n.20, 27–28, 34, 36–38, 42, 43n.5, 44n.25, 61, 64, 71n.50, 75, 83, 89–91, 93, 97, 177–178, 207–208, 212–216, 231n.32, 234
Heidegger, Martin, 75, 131, 176
Heilsgeschichte, see History of Salvation
Heimbucher, Martin, 86
Heine, Heinrich (Johann Christian Heinrich), 1, 54, 69n.18, 71n.50
Heisenberg, Werner Karl, 130
Helsinki, 249
Herder, Johann Gottfried von, 19, 60–61, 71n.49
Herrnhut, 80
Heuss, Theodor, 104, 193
Heydrich, Reinhard, 57
Hilberg, Raul, 67
Hildebrandt, Franz, 152, 157
Himmler, Heinrich Luitpold, 57
Hirsch, Emanuel, 79, 84, 102n.34, 176
History of Salvation (*Heilsgeschichte*), 22, 37, 74–75, 79, 89, 113, 165, 168, 173, 218, 221, 239
Hitler, Adolf, xviii–xix, 10, 12, 29, 34–35, 42, 48, 51, 52, 57, 63–66, 69n.20, 72n.61, 73n.69, 74, 77–78, 96–97, 103–106, 108, 114, 117–119, 121, 124, 126, 126n.2, 128n.25, 130–132, 136, 138–144, 146n.8, 146n.29, 149, 157, 162, 166, 168–169, 174–176, 179–180, 184, 186, 195, 200n.18, 200n.20, 200n.23, 205, 208, 210, 216, 221, 234–235, 244, 245
Hockenos, Matthew D., 208, 210, 212, 222, 231n.32, 255
Hodgson, Leonard, 108, 125, 129n.53
Hohmann, Martin, 231n.39
Holl, Karl, 14, 36
Holtschneider, K. Hannah, 228

Holy Roman Empire, 6, 7, 19, 21
Holy Trinity Church, Kingsway, London, 233
Holy war, 3–4, 15
homo faber, 75
homo sapiens, 75
Hoogstraten, Hans Dirk van, 140
Horn, Käthe, 80
Humanistisches Gymnasium, see Gymnasium, humanistisches
Huntemann, Georg Hermann, 237, 251n.6

"Ideas of 1789", 20
India, xviii, 3, 18, 91, 92, 93, 97
Institutional violence, 4
International Dietrich Bonhoeffer Society, 2, 13, 205, 239
Israel, 46, 53, 151, 157, 158, 161, 165, 221, 222, 225, 226
Israelites, 3, 110, 112, 115, 116, 161, 169, 171n.26
Iwand, Hans Joachim, xxi, 13, 127n.5, 213–219

Jallianwala Bagh Massacre, *see* Amritsar Massacre
Jesus of Nazareth, 4, 23n.6, 31, 46–47, 78, 80, 94, 96–97, 104, 109, 111–112, 119–120, 125, 134–138, 143, 149, 151–152, 154–155, 158–159, 161–169, 183, 194, 212, 222–223, 226, 228, 232n.46, 241, 248, 255–256, 259, 261, 262, 264
Jochmann, Werner, 56, 70n.35
John Chrysostom, 53
John Maurice (Johann Moritz), *prince of Nassau-Siegen*, 54
Judenmission (Mission to the Jews), 108, 115, 151, 165, 223, 228
Junker, 9, 17
Justinian I, *emperor*, 53
Just war, 15

Kabitz, Ulrich, 235, 251n.1
Kairos, 31, 155
Kant, Immanuel, 12, 71n.50
Kiel, 26n.37
Kirche im Sozialismus, 247, 250
Kittel, Gerhard, 79
Königsberg, 12
Konkordat, 117
Korean War, 236
KPD, *see* Communist Party
Krause, Reinhold, 119
Krötke, Wolf, xi, 248, 250, 253n.30
Kultur, xix, 11, 15, 18–19, 32–33, 60, 63, 148
Kulturprotestanten, 89
Küng, Hans, 167, 172n.42
Künneth, Walter, 113, 217, 235

Lagarde, Paul Anton de, 62
Landsberg, 63, 126n.2
Lassalle, Ferdinand, 55
Lasserre, Jean, xviii, 79, 81, 89
Lasson, Georg, 11
Lateran Council, 4th (1215), *see* Council of Rome, 1215
Leadership principle, 103, 117, 123, 132
League of Nations, 11
Lebensraum, 42, 91, 96
Lehmann, Paul Louis, 81, 138, 196, 198, 199
Leibholz, Gerhard, 136, 155
Leibholz, Sabine, *see* Bonhoeffer, Sabine
Levi, 3
Life Together, 136, 137
Lilje, Hanns (Johannes Ernst Richard), 217, 235, 251n.1
London, 111, 118, 121–122, 133, 154–155, 171n.15, 173, 205, 233
Luke, *Saint, Evangelist*, 46
Luther, Martin, xvii, xix, 2, 5–6, 8, 23n.9, 27–28, 36–37, 43n.2, 52, 54, 62, 109–110, 119, 121, 131, 133,

135–136, 144, 149–150, 153–154, 177, 181–183, 191, 210, 214, 241, 245

Machiavelli, Niccolò, 5, 10, 23n.8
Machiavellism, 4
Machtstaat (Power State), 10, 12, 28, 75, 104
Manifestos, War, 32, 33
Mann, Heinrich (Luiz Heinrich), 30
Mann, Thomas (Paul Thomas), 63, 175
Marr, Wilhelm, 47, 56, 68n.8
Marx, Karl Heinrich, 53, 55, 90
Meinecke, Friedrich, 18, 24n.16, 60, 71n.48, 71n.51, 175, 186, 234
Mein Kampf, 51, 63, 69n.15, 126n.2, 146n.8
Meiser, Hans Oswald, *bishop*, 205, 235
Mendelssohn, Moses, 71n.50
Middle East, 3
Military Counter Intelligence, *see* Abwehr
Milton, John, xviii
Mission to the Jews, *see Judenmission*
Mitscherlich, Alexander and Mitscherlich, Margarete, 220, 231
Moenius, Georg, 175
Moltke, Helmuth (Karl Bernhard), *the elder*, 28
Mommsen, Hans, 202n.46, 237
Moravians, 80
Moses, *the Lawgiver*, 3, 4, 149, 19
Moslems, 53
Mosse, *publisher*, 50
Müller, Adam Heinrich, *von Nitterdorf*, 24n.16
Müller, Hanfried, 44n.24, 239, 242, 244–246, 250
Müller, Ludwig, *Reichsbischof*, 118, 153

Nachfolge, see Cost of Discipleship
"*Nach zehn Jahren*", *see* "After Ten Years"

Napoleon I, Napoleon Bonaparte, *emperor*, 14, 19, 27, 54, 214
National community, *see Volksgemainschaft*
Nationalsozialistische Deutsche Arbeiterpartei, see Nazi Party
Nazi, Nazis, Nazism, xvii-xx, 1, 11, 16, 35, 46, 48-49, 52, 56-57, 62-67, 68n.9, 71n.51, 72n.61, 73n.70, 74, 82, 88-89, 96-97, 99-100, 103-104, 106-113, 115, 117-123, 125, 127n.6, 128n.25, 130-133, 137-142, 144, 147n.31, 148-151, 154-156, 159-160, 162, 166, 168, 172n.28, 173-176, 178-180, 186, 189, 198, 201n.34, 204-206, 208-212, 218, 220-221, 224, 226, 233, 235, 240, 241, 244
Nazi Party (NSDAP; *Nationalsozialistische Deutsche Arbeiterpartei*), xviii, 52, 95, 141, 200n.18
"Negro question (problem)", 79, 89
Neubert, Erhart, 249
New Guinea, 17
New Testament, 31, 36, 41, 46-47, 119, 132, 134, 165, 224, 225, 228
Niebuhr, Reinhold (Karl Paul Reinhold), 139
Niemöller, Martin (Friedrich Gustav Emil Martin), xxi, 118, 136, 151, 153-155, 210-214, 218
Niemöller, Wilhelm, 213
Nietzsche, Friedrich [Wilhelm], 94
Night of broken glass, *see Kristallnacht*
Nipperdey, Thomas, 49-51, 69n.19
Non-Aryan, 65, 103, 107, 118, 136, 156, 164, *see also* Aryan
Notbischof (Emergency bishop), 6, 28
Notverordnung, see Emergency decree
NSDAP, *see* Nazi Party
Nuremberg Laws (*Nürnberger Gesetze*), 65, 156-157, 195

Oath of Allegiance to Hitler, 140, 141, 144, 180, 200n.20
Oath of Loyalty to the *Führer*, 121
Obrigkeit (Powers that be; State authorities), xx, 23n.9, 28, 77, 166, 168, 219, 230n.6, 240, 243, 250
Old Testament, 3, 4, 32, 94, 115, 119, 134, 150-151, 165, 171n.26, 228
Olympics, see Berlin Olympics
Ordnungstheologie (Theology of Orders of Creation), 35, 40, 78
"Organic State", 16, 24n.16
Oster, Hans, *colonel*, 140, 237

Pan German League (*Alldeutscher Verband*), 17
Pangritz, Andreas, 128n.25, 161, 165, 169
Paris Commune, 17
Pastors' Emergency League (*Pfarrernotbund*), 118, 153
Paul, *Saint*, xx, 6, 23n.9, 36, 45n.41, 77, 80, 115, 119, 132, 150, 230n.6, 240-241, 243
Peace Prize of the German Book Trade, 220
"Penal substitutionary atonement", 4, 23n.6, 23n.7
Pfarrernotbund, see Pastors' Emergency League
Plato, 201n.31
Potsdam agreement, 213
Power State, *see Machtstaat*
Powers that be, *see Obrigkeit*
"Protestant revolution", 27, 43n.1, 249
Prussian school of historians (history), 21, 43, 131
Prussian solution, xix, 20, 21, 26n.37, 31
Prusso-German history, xix, 2, 3, 20, 166, 210, 214-215, 217, 235

Rathenau, Walther, 50

Realpolitik, xix, 26n.37, 97
Reformation, xvii, 2-3, 5-7, 14, 23n.13, 27, 54, 78, 85, 119, 153, 181, 186
Reichskristallnacht, see Kristallnacht
Reichstag, 16, 64, 82, 97, 190, 192
Revelation, Book of, 46
Revolution, American, xvii, xviii
English, xvii, xviii, 7
French, xvii, xviii, 20, 54
Protestant, see Protestant revolution
Rhineland Synod, 228, 229
Ringer, Fritz K., 58, 59, 60, 71n.50
Ritter, Gerhard Albert, 10, 24n.18, 190-191, 197, 201n.31, 201n.34, 216, 234
Robinson, John Arthur Thomas, *bishop of Woolwich*, 237, 238
Roman Catholic Church, 15, 36, 117, 232n.55, 236, 238
Roman empire, 5, 46
Roman Empire, Holy, see Holy Roman Empire
Roman occupation, 4, 226
Romans XIII (Paul's Epistle to the Romans), xx, 6, 77, 132, 219, 230n.6, 240, 243
Rome, 35-36, 117, 227
Roosevelt, Franklin Delano, 196
Rössler, Helmut, 83, 101n.31
Rothe, Richard, 23n.14
Rürup, Reinhard, 55
Russia, 48, 205

SA, *see Sturmabteilung*
Sanctorum Communio, 36, 38, 42, 76, 86, 155
"Sacred violence", 3, 68n.13
Sasse, Hermann Otto Erich, xviii, 118, 150-151, 170n.6
Schacht, Hjalmar Horace Greeley, 180, 200n.22
Schleiermacher, Friedrich Daniel Ernst, 10, 19

Schmidt, Hans, 237
Schmitt, Carl, 176
Schönherr, Albrecht, *bishop*, 217, 239-240, 247, 248
Schöpfungstheologie, see Ordnungstheologie
Schutzstaffel, see SS
Schwarze Reichswehr, 34
SED, *see Sozialistische Einheitspartei*
Seeberg, Reinhold, 14, 33, 36, 37, 38, 39
Seidel, Jürgen, 208
Seigewasser, Hans, 247
Sendungsbewusstsein (Sense of mission), 29
"Sermon on the Mount", 4, 79, 85, 97, 134, 135
Siegmund-Schultze, Friedrich, 83, 99, 101n.32, 102n.54
Simmel, Georg, 51, 60, 71n.47
Social democracy, 8, 17, 29, 33, 51-52, 55, 62, 99, 103, 196, 212, 237
"Social imperialism", 18
Socialist Unity Party, *see Sozialistische Einheitspartei*
Sonderweg, 1, 209, 214, 217
Sonnemann, Leopold, 50
South African War, 18
Sozialistische Einheitspartei (SED), 242
Spong, John Shelby, bishop, 47
Sportpalast (Sport Palace), 119
SS, 57, 141, 197
"Stab-in-the-back" ("*Dolchstoßlegende*"), 34-35, 44n.23, 51-52, 69n.23
Staemmler, Wolfgang, 139
Stalingrad, 245
State authorities, *see Obrigkeit*
Status confessionis, 108, 150, 153-154, 171n.14, 173
Steglitz, see Berlin-Steglitz
Stoecker, Adolf, 61, 62, 72n.54, 157
Stone, Michael, 226
Stresemann, Gustav, 31

Sturmabteilung (SA), 64, 66
Stuttgart Declaration of Guilt, 214, 230n.23, 234, 259
Supercessionist idea, 164
Sutz, Erwin, xviii, 79, 89, 98, 130
Synagogue, 4, 46, 53-54, 66, 109, 113, 115, 155, 158, 164-168, 171n.17, 173, 194, 205, 218, 224-225, 227-228, 232n.58, 239

Tal, Uriel, 62, 70n.35
Technical University of Berlin, see Berlin Technical University
"Tegel fiction", 181, 184, 189
"Tegel theology", 39
Theologia gloriae, 47, 173, 194, 196
Theological guilt, see Guilt (theological)
Theology of Orders of Creation, *see Ordnungstheologie*
Thielicke, Helmut, 190, 202n.51, 217, 237
Third Reich, xvii, xviii, xx, 2, 10, 29, 42, 46, 48, 67, 69n.14, 89, 110, 111, 126n.1, 127n.4, 128n.19, 130-133, 140, 144, 150, 166, 167, 171n.26, 184-185, 218, 246, 249, 263
Throne and altar, 74, 215
Tillich, Paul Johannes, 237
Timothy, First Epistle to, 23n.9
Tirpitz, Alfred von, 18
Tödt, Heinz-Eduard, 176, 178, 180, 193, 217, 239
Tönnies, Ferdinand, 38
Tories, 7
Treitschke, Heinrich Gotthard von, 17, 56, 62
Treysa, 208-209, 211-212, 259
Tribal spirit, *see Volksgeist*
Troeltsch, Ernst, 38
Tübingen, University, 34-35
Tyrannicide, xviii, xx, 141, 144

Ullstein, publishers, 50
Unemployment, 84, 89-90, 97, 99
Unitas Fratrum, see Moravians
United States of America (USA), 2, 77, 83, 103, 138, 160, 174-175, 197, 205, 213, 239
University of Berlin, see Berlin, University
University of Tübingen, see Tübingen, University
Urban II, *Pope*, 4
USA, *see* United States of America

Vatican, 117, 226, 227
Vicar of Christ, 5
Visser 't Hooft, Willem Adolph, 206, 211
Völkisch, see "Folkish"
Volksgeist (Tribal spirit), 19, 61
Volksgemeinschaft (National community), 103, 132, 137

Walser, Martin, 220
War, xviii, 4, 10, 12, 14, 27-29, 41, 43n.2, 87, 89, 92-93, 95-96, 114, 123-124, 182, 262
Warburg, 50
War, First World, see World War I
Warrior God, 4, 10, 14, 27
War, Second World, see World War II
"War theology" (*Kriegstheologie*), 25n.24, 33-35, 42, 212, 218
War guilt, *see* Guilt (war)
Washington (DC), 236
Washington, George, xviii
Weber, Max (Maximilian Carl Emil), 3, 29, 38
Wedding, *see* Berlin-Wedding
Wehrmacht, 29, 138
Weimar Constitution, xx, 149, 189, 193
Weimar Republic, 11, 16, 34, 52, 63-64, 69n.14, 74, 105, 189, 192-193, 197, 209, 216

Weissensee, see Berlin-Weissensee
Weltbund, see World Alliance
Westminster Abbey, 205, 233
Westphalia, Peace of, 27
Whigs, 7
Wilhelm I, *Kaiser*, 21
Wilhelm II, *Kaiser*, 11, 33
Wind, Renate, 238
Winter, Gerhard, 244
"Witness people", 165, 168-170
Wittenberg, 27, 118, 153
World Alliance (*Weltbund*), 82-83, 85-89, 101n.32, 121, 122, 123
World Council of Churches, 162, 191, 202n.36, 206, 211, 229
World War I, 11, 15, 25, 31-34, 40-41, 51-52, 62-63, 65, 81, 84-85, 87, 93, 97, 101n.28, 134, 148
World War II, 12, 22, 28, 56, 79, 138-139, 144, 196, 233, 250, 259
Wurm, Theophil, *bishop*, 208, 217

Yalta, 213
Yugoslavia, 3

Zarathustra (Nietzsche), 94
Zimmermann, Wolf-Dieter, 99
Zingst, 155
Zinn, Elisabeth, 134
Zion parish, Berlin-Wedding, 98-99
Zyklon B gas, 66

www.ingramcontent.com/pod-product-compliance
Lightning Source LLC
Chambersburg PA
CBHW072144100526
44589CB00015B/2090